GREEK LYRIC

V

LCL 144

GREEK LYRIC
V

THE NEW SCHOOL OF POETRY
AND
ANONYMOUS SONGS AND HYMNS

EDITED AND TRANSLATED BY

DAVID A. CAMPBELL

HARVARD UNIVERSITY PRESS
CAMBRIDGE, MASSACHUSETTS
LONDON, ENGLAND
1993

Library of Congress Cataloging-in-Publication Data

Greek lyric.
(The Loeb classical library)
Text in Greek with translation into English.
Includes indexes. Bibliography.
Contents: v. 1. Sappho, Alcaeus — v. 2. Anacreon,
Anacreontea — v. 3. Stesichorus, Ibycus, Simonides,
and others — v. 4. Bacchylides, Corinna, and others.
v. 5. The new school of poetry and anonymous songs and hymns.
1. Greek poetry—Translations into English.
2. Greek poetry.   I. Campbell, David A.   II. Series.
PA3622.C3   1982   884'.01'08   82–178982
ISBN 0–674–99559–7 (v. 5)

Typeset by Chiron, Inc, Cambridge, Massachusetts.
Printed in Great Britain by St Edmundsbury Press Ltd,
Bury St Edmunds, Suffolk, on acid-free paper.
Bound by Hunter & Foulis Ltd, Edinburgh, Scotland.

CONTENTS

CONTENTS

CONTENTS

Cynthia

ἀρχὰ καὶ τέρμα

PREFACE

This final volume includes the fragments, mainly dithyrambic, of the 'New School' of poets who composed in the late fifth and early fourth centuries, together with folk songs, drinking songs (scolia) and other anonymous pieces.

I wish to record my gratitude for a research grant awarded by the Social Sciences and Humanities Research Council of Canada. I should like also to thank Michael Chase, John Fitch, Michael Haslam and John Oleson for their help, the Librarian and staff of the McPherson Library, University of Victoria, for obtaining rare books and periodicals, Philippa Goold for performing her editorial work with great care and unfailing cheerfulness, Gary Bisbee for endless patience in setting a difficult text, and once again A. Nancy Nasser for typing the manuscript.

David A. Campbell

University of Victoria
July 1992

INTRODUCTION

THE 'NEW SCHOOL' OF POETRY

'I DO not sing the ancient songs, for my new ones are better.... Let the ancient Muse depart!' Timotheus' declaration of independence (fr. 796) is our clearest statement of the programme of the 'new poets' whose lyrics held the field from the mid-fifth to the mid-fourth century. It finds its parallels in Comedy: Strepsiades in the *Clouds* (423 B.C.) wanted his son to sing Simonides' song about the shearing of the Ram (fr. 507), but his son refused and called Simonides a bad poet; old-style education, commended by the Just Argument, prescribed songs like 'Pallas, sacker of cities, the grim' (see Lamprocles 735 = Stesichorus 274) or 'A far-travelling shout of the lyre' (adesp. 948) rather than the contemporary 'twists' favoured by Phrynis and the like (Phrynis test. 2). The comic poets made the new composers the butt of many jokes; in particular, Pherecrates in his *Cheiron* provided an amusing list of offenders against Music (fr. 155 K.-A.: see the testimonia of the various poets): he names four, perhaps five, of them in a sequence which purports to represent both chronological order and an

1

increase in viciousness: Melanippides, Cinesias, Phrynis, Timotheus, worst of them all, and perhaps Philoxenus (see Timotheus test. 1 n. 4). The jokes are based on the musical innovations of the poets: the increased number of notes on the cithara, due either to a greater number of strings, twelve on the instruments of Melanippides and Timotheus, or in the case of Phrynis to the use of a device for the rapid altering of pitch; the associated *kampai*, 'twists' or 'bends', modulations from one *harmonia* to another, ascribed to Cinesias, Phrynis and Timotheus (or Philoxenus); and the 'ant-runs' of Timotheus, which were probably his wandering melodies.

The poets also altered the triadic structure of the dithyramb, for which see Bacchylides 15–17, 19, by introducing *anabolai*, long solo-songs, in place of passages with strophic responsion: see Melanippides test. 4, Cinesias test. 2 n. 6. This was perhaps intended to add greater realism and variety; Bacchylides himself had composed his *Theseus* (18) in which Aegeus answered a chorus or chorus-leader, but his poem is in four strophes of identical metre. The Cyclops of Philoxenus wore a costume and sang a solo to the cithara (frr. 819, 820), although the dithyramb was traditionally a choral song accompanied by the pipes; see D. F. Sutton, 'Dithyramb as Δρᾶμα', *Quaderni Urbinati di Cultura Classica* 13 (1983) 37 ff.

Our most extensive example of the new poetry

comes not from a dithyramb but from a nome of Timotheus, *The Persians*. Although the nome differed completely from the dithyramb in its performance, being sung by a soloist to his cithara accompaniment, its language was no different. Many of the new poets composed both nomes and dithyrambs—Melanippides, Phrynis, Timotheus and Philoxenus—and it is not always possible to ascribe a given fragment to one genre or the other. The poets' diction was florid. They relished the compound words which were a feature of earlier choral poetry: a drowning Persian can address the sea as 'gadfly-crazed ancient-hate, unfaithful darling of the dash-racing wind' (Timotheus 791.79 ff.), or the Cyclops his beloved Galatea as 'fair-faced, golden-tressed, Grace-voiced offshoot of the Loves' (Philox. 821). Novelties abound: 'the emerald-haired sea' (791.31), 'mantic, frantic, Bacchic, fanatic' Artemis (778 (b)), 'the flashing-winged breath' of Athena (Telestes 805 (c). 2). Periphrasis is in vogue: wine and water are 'the blood of the Bacchic god' and 'the fresh-flowing tears of the Nymphs' (Tim. 780. 4 f.), oars are 'firwood arms' or 'the sailing device of the noisy pine' or 'the ship's mountain feet' (791. 5 f., 12 f., 90 f.). The aim was to excite and astonish.

Only occasionally do we have firm facts about the lives of the poets. It will be noted that with the exception of Cinesias they were not born in Athens. Melanippides of Melos was the forerunner, according to Pherecrates. His dates are in dispute: the

3

Suda lists two poets of the same name, grandfather and grandson, each the son of Criton and each a dithyrambic poet, and such duplication is suspect although not impossible. If we grant him a long life, we can accept almost all of the testimony: born in 520/516 (test. 1), he won his first dithyrambic victory in Athens in 494/3 (test. 2); he spent some time at the court of Perdiccas of Macedonia, who ruled from *c.* 450 to *c.* 413 (test. 1), and he is called a contemporary of Thucydides, who was born *c.* 460 (test. 3); but he will scarcely have bought Philoxenus at some time after 424 (Philox. test. 1). Plutarch implies that Perdiccas' successor Archelaus was also his patron, but perhaps he confused the two rulers. Melanippides was famous for his dithyrambs, and his musical innovations, the *anabolai* or arias (test. 4) and the ornate pipe-music (test. 6), must have been associated with them; but Pherecrates shows that he developed the twelve-stringed cithara also (test. 6), and his lament for the Python (see test. 5 with n. 2) may have been a nome. His poetic language is traditional enough; Xenophon reports that one of Socrates' contemporaries had warm praise for the dithyrambs (test. 7), and Plutarch likewise mentions him in exalted company (test. 9).

Cinesias was well known in Athens from at least 414 (Aristophanes, *Birds*: test. 2) till 392 (*Eccles.*: test. 4 n. 1). Like his father (test. 11 n. 2), he was a target of the comic poets, not only for the words and music of his dithyrambs but for his physical appearance: he was tall and skinny, walked with a limp and seemed to be at death's door. Pherecrates included him in his catalogue of the debauchers of Music, Aristophanes mocked him in at least four plays (*Birds, Frogs, Eccles., Gerytades*: Cinesias, the distraught husband in *Lysistrata*, owes his presence there to his name, which suggests sexual activity), Plato made fun of his appearance (test. 8), and Strattis devoted a whole comedy to him. He took part in political life: he was said to have abolished the system of *choregiai* about the end of the Peloponnesian War (test. 5), and he brought forward a motion in the *boule* in 393 (test. 10 n. 1). His impiety is alleged by Aristophanes (test. 4) and by the orator Lysias (test. 7). Pherecrates makes fun of his 'exharmonic twists' and the shapelessness of his music (test. 1), and Aristophanes mocks his *anabolai*, 'arias' (test. 2). The parody in *Birds* fastens on his compound epithets and his lack of substance— he is associated with air, clouds, wind, flight and feathers. Plato reports the view of Socrates and Callicles that he thought only of pleasing his audience, not of improving them (test. 11).

Phrynis of Mytilene was famous for his new-style nomes and won the prize for cithara-singing in Athens in 446/5 (test. 2). His instrument had more strings than the traditional seven (testt. 1 n. 5, 5, 6), and he used a device, the *strobilos*, to effect modulation from one *harmonia* to another (test. 1): both Aristophanes (test. 2) and Pherecrates (test. 1) allude to his 'twists' (cf. test. 4).

We are better informed about Timotheus of Miletus than about the other new musicians. He was the foremost among them, the most distinguished or the most outrageous according to one's viewpoint, and it is fortunate that a papyrus find provided 240 lines of his nome, *The Persians* (fr. 791), most of them clearly legible. The *Parian Marble* says that he was 90 when he died at a date between 366/5 and 357/6, and if the *Suda* is correct in linking him with Philip II of Macedon (test. 2), the date will be 359 or later, and he will have been born soon after 450. He exulted in a victory (in cithara-singing, presumably) over his older contemporary Phrynis (fr. 820); but Aristotle put the victory in perspective when he said that without Phrynis there would have been no Timotheus (Phrynis test. 3). Euripides gave him encouragement and composed the prelude to *The Persians* (test. 6) with which he won a victory, perhaps between 412 and 408 (see S. E. Bassett, *Classical Philology* 26 (1931) 153 ff.). Like his predecessors he used a cithara with extra strings, ten, eleven or twelve (fr. 791. 230, testt. 1, 2, 7), and Pherecrates may have mocked his 'twists' (test. 1 n. 4: cf. test. 10) as well as his 'ant-runs'. His earliest nomes were said to have been composed in hexameters (test. 9); *The Persians* had a hexameter prelude, the work of Euripides (fr. 788), but the main body of the poem is in a variety of metres, mostly free iambics but with aeolic sequences (see Page's analysis in *P.M.G.* and M. L. West, *Zeitschrift für Papyrologie und Epigraphik* 45 (1982) 1 ff.); Dionysius of Halicarnassus and Hephaestion noted the license of his versification (testt. 10, 11). In addition to nomes he composed eighteen dithyrambs (test. 2), and he may have made innovations in the pipe-music which accompanied them (test. 12). His popularity endured: his dithyramb *Elpenor* was performed in Athens in 319 (fr. 779), *The Persians* at Nemea in 207 (fr. 788), and other nomes in Arcadia and elsewhere in the second century B.C. (testt. 13, 14).

Philoxenus of Cythera is the last important figure in the group. He was born in 435/4 and died in 380/79 (test. 2). He is said to have been a slave and to have had Melanippides as his second owner (test. 1). He spent time in Syracuse, where he had an uneasy relationship with the tyrant Dionysius (testt. 3, 4), and he died in Ephesus (test. 1). He was famous for his dithyrambs and for his experimental composition (test. 5, frr. 819, 820, 826, Timotheus test. 10). Like his predecessors he indulged in *kampai*, 'twists' or modulations (test. 12, Timotheus test. 1 nn. 4, 5); yet Philodemus saw his style as Pindaric (test. 7). Unusually for a dithyrambic poet he won high praise from a comic poet, Antiphanes, soon after his death (test. 12).

We have dates for three other dithyrambic poets: Telestes of Selinus won the Athenian contest in 402/1, Polyidus of Selymbria at a date between

399/8 and 380/79, and Stesichorus II of Himera in 370/69 or 369/68.

SCOLIA

Athenaeus (test. 3) preserves twenty-five examples of 'the well-known Attic scolia' (884–908) together with the song of the Cretan Hybrias (909) which 'some authorities call a scolion' and Aristotle's poem for Hermeias (842), which is alleged to be a unique kind of scolion. He presents the Attic scolia anonymously, but in his prefatory remarks he speaks of their antiquity and refers also to the praise won by Alcaeus, Anacreon and Praxilla for their scolia. Other authorities ascribe 890 to Simonides among others; 891 is part of a poem by Alcaeus; the Harmodius song (see 893) is attributed to an unknown Callistratus; 897 is variously ascribed to Alcaeus, Sappho and Praxilla, and 903 is also ascribed to Praxilla. Scolia are known from other sources: Athenaeus in a different context says that Pythermus of Teos, who may have belonged to the sixth century B.C., composed scolia (910); the scholiast on *Lysistrata* refers to Pindar's scolia (912), the scholiast on *Wasps* to scolia by Simonides and Stesichorus (test. 1).

The Attic scolia are all short pieces, two or four lines long. The first seven, the four Harmodius poems and the Leipsydrion lament (907: cf. 911) show the same metrical pattern, four brief lines of

aeolic rhythm; most of the remainder are couplets of
longer aeolic lines, six of them in greater asclepiads:
one tune would have fitted each group.

The most reliable ancient authority for the scolia
is Dicaearchus, a pupil of Aristotle. He speaks of
three kinds of song sung after dinner (test. 2): the
first sung by everyone, the second sung by individu-
als in sequence, the third performed by the most
skilled guests, οἱ συνετώτατοι. The first is likely to
have been the paean, sung while libations were
poured. The second will have been the simple stan-
zas exemplified by the Attic scolia: they are likely to
have been accompanied by the piper (see *Wasps*,
test. 1), and the singers held myrtle twigs (not
lyres). The third and most demanding kind will
have been the more complex songs of Stesichorus,
Simonides and the others, performed by skilled
singers to their own lyre accompaniment. Aris-
totle's poem for Hermeias and the poems of Pindar
and Bacchylides which were later classed as
encomia are good examples: Pindar fr. 124 and Bac-
chylides fr. 20B in particular are clearly intended to
give pleasure to fellow-drinkers.

The origin of the term *scolion* was disputed by
ancient authorities. The word means 'crooked' (as
in 892) and was explained by Dicaearchus as refer-
ring to the haphazard course of his third type of
song as it passed round the room from one expert to
another. Whether he was correct or not, the term
came to be applied—exclusively in the end—to the

simpler songs of his second group, brought together in the collection used by Aristotle in his *Constitution of Athens* (906, 907) and by Athenaeus.

SELECT BIBLIOGRAPHY

Barker, A. (ed.), *Greek Musical Writings*. Vol. i: *The Musician and His Art*, Cambridge 1984

Bassett, S. E., 'The Place and Date of the First Performance of the Persians of Timotheus', *Classical Philology* 26 (1931) 153–165

Bergk, T., *Poetae Lyrici Graeci*[4], 3 vols., Leipzig 1882

Bowra, C. M., *Greek Lyric Poetry from Alcman to Simonides*[2], Oxford 1961 (= *G.L.P.*)

Brussich, G. F., 'Su alcuni frammenti adespoti dei *Poetae Melici Graeci* del Page', *Quaderni Urbinati di Cultura Classica* 22 (1976) 131–146

Cambridge History of Classical Literature, vol. 1: *Greek Literature*, ed. P. E. Easterling and B. M. W. Knox, Cambridge 1985

Campbell, D. A., *Greek Lyric Poetry: A Selection of Early Greek Lyric, Elegiac and Iambic Poetry*, London 1967 (repr. Bristol 1982); *The Golden Lyre: The Themes of the Greek Lyric Poets*, London 1983

Diehl, E., *Anthologia Lyrica Graeca*, vol. ii[2], Leipzig 1942

Edmonds, J. M., *Lyra Graeca*, vol. iii, London 1927

Gerber, D. E., 'A Survey of Publications on Greek Lyric Poetry since 1952', *The Classical World* 61 (1967–68) 265–79, 317–30, 378–85; 'Studies in Greek Lyric Poetry: 1967–1975', *C.W.* 70 (1976–77) 65–157; 'Studies in Greek Lyric Poetry: 1975–1985', *C.W.* 81 (1987–88) 73–144

11

BIBLIOGRAPHY

Grande, C. del, *Ditirambografi: Testimonianze e frammenti*, Naples 1946

Harvey, A. E., 'The Classification of Greek Lyric Poetry', *Classical Quarterly* 49 (1955) 157–175

Janssen, T. H., *Timotheus, Persae: A Commentary*, Amsterdam 1984

Lloyd-Jones, H. and Parsons, P., *Supplementum Hellenisticum*, Berlin and New York 1983 (= *Suppl. Hell.*)

Maas, P., *Epidaurische Hymnen*, Königsberger Gelehrte Gesellschaft G. Kl. IX 5, Halle 1933

Page, D. L., *Poetae Melici Graeci*, Oxford 1962 (= *P.M.G.*); *Lyrica Graeca Selecta*, Oxford 1968 (= *L.G.S.*); *Supplementum Lyricis Graecis*, Oxford 1974 (= *S.L.G.*); *Epigrammata Selecta*, Oxford 1975; *Further Greek Epigrams*, Cambridge 1981 (= *F.G.E.*)

Pickard-Cambridge, A. W., *Dithyramb, Tragedy and Comedy*[2] (revised by T. B. L. Webster), Oxford 1962

Powell, J. U., *Collectanea Alexandrina*, Oxford 1925 (= *Coll. Alex.*)

Reitzenstein, R., *Epigramm und Skolion*, Giessen 1893 (repr. Hildesheim 1970)

Sutton, D. F., 'Dithyramb as Δρᾶμα: Philoxenus of Cythera's *Cyclops or Galatea*', *Q.U.C.C.* 42 (1983) 37–43; *Dithyrambographi Graeci*, Hildesheim 1989

Valk, M. van der, 'On the Composition of the Attic Skolia', *Hermes* 102 (1974) 1–20

West, M. L., *Iambi et Elegi Graeci ante Alexandrum Cantati*, 2 vols., Oxford 1971 (= *I.E.G.*); *Greek Metre*, Oxford 1982; 'Metrical Analyses: Timotheos and others', *Zeitschrift für Papyrologie und Epigraphik* 45 (1982) 1–9

Wilamowitz-Moellendorf, U. von, *Timotheos, Die Perser*, Leipzig 1903

GREEK LYRIC

THE NEW SCHOOL OF POETRY
AND
ANONYMOUS SONGS AND HYMNS

MELANIPPIDES

TESTIMONIA VITAE ATQUE ARTIS

1 *Sud.* (iii 350 Adler)

(a) M 455: Μελανιππίδης, Κρίτωνος, γεγονὼς κατὰ τὴν ξε' Ὀλυμπιάδα, Μήλιος. ἔγραψε δὲ διθυράμβων βιβλία πλεῖστα καὶ ποιήματα ἐπικὰ καὶ ἐπιγράμματα καὶ ἐλέγους καὶ ἄλλα πλεῖστα.

(b) M 454: Μελανιππίδης, θυγατριδοῦς τοῦ πρεσβυτέρου, παῖς δὲ Κρίτωνος, λυρικοῦ καὶ αὐτοῦ· ὃς ἐν τῇ τῶν διθυράμβων μελοποιΐᾳ ἐκαινοτόμησε πλεῖστα καὶ διατρίψας παρὰ Περδίκκᾳ τῷ βασιλεῖ ἐκεῖ τὸν βίον κατέστρεψεν. ἔγραψε καὶ αὐτὸς ᾄσματα λυρικὰ καὶ διθυράμβους.

2 *Marm. Par.* Ep. 47 (p. 15 Jacoby)

ἀφ' οὗ Με[λαν]ιππίδ[ης] Μ[ήλιος ἐνίκησ]εν Ἀθήνησιν ἔτη ΗΗΔΔΔΙ, ἄρχοντος Ἀθήνησι Πυθοκρίτου.

---

[1] See also Diagoras test. 1   [2] I.e. 494/3 B.C., 231 years before 263/2: see T. J. Cadoux, *J.H.S.* 68 (1948) 116. The date squares with the date of birth of the elder Mel. (test. 1a).

14

MELANIPPIDES

LIFE AND WORK[1]

1 *Suda*

(a) Melanippides, son of Criton, born[2] in the 65th Olympiad (520–516 B.C.); from Melos. Wrote many books of dithyrambs as well as epic poems, epigrams, elegies[3] and much else.

(b) Melanippides, grandson of the elder Melanippides, son of Criton who was himself a lyric poet. In the music for his dithyrambs he made many innovations. Lived at the court of king Perdiccas[4] and died there. He too wrote lyric poetry and dithyrambs.[5]

---

[1] See also Philoxenus test. 1.   [2] 'Born' rather than 'flourished'.   [3] There is no trace of the epics and elegies; for the epigrams see test. 8.   [4] King of Macedonia c. 450–c. 413 B.C.
[5] E. Rohde, *Rh. Mus.* 33 (1878) 213 f. argued that there was only one Melanippides, active c. 480–c. 436, but that is not certain. Mel. is mentioned in a papyrus fr. (P. Graec. Vindob. 19996a: 929 *P.M.G.*) along with fellow dithyrambic poets Telestes and Philoxenus.

CHRONOLOGY[1]

2 *Parian Marble*

From the time when Melanippides of Melos won the victory in Athens 231 years[2]; Pythocritus was archon at Athens.

15

3 Marcellin. *Vit. Thuc.* 29 (O.C.T. Thuc. i)

συνεχρόνισε δ᾽, ὥς φησι Πραξιφάνης ἐν τῷ περὶ ἱστορίας (fr. 18 Wehrli), Πλάτωνι τῷ κωμικῷ, Ἀγάθωνι τραγικῷ, Νικηράτῳ ἐποποιῷ καὶ Χοιρίλῳ καὶ Μελανιππίδῃ.

4 Arist. *Rhet.* 3. 9. 1409b (p. 197 Römer)

ὁμοίως δὲ καὶ αἱ περίοδοι αἱ μακραὶ οὖσαι λόγος γίνεται καὶ ἀναβολῇ ὅμοιον, ὥστε γίνεται ὃ ἔσκωψεν Δημόκριτος ὁ Χῖος εἰς Μελανιππίδην ποιήσαντα ἀντὶ τῶν ἀντιστρόφων ἀναβολάς·

οἵ τ᾽ αὐτῷ κακὰ τεύχει ἀνὴρ ἄλλῳ κακὰ τεύχων,
ἡ δὲ μακρὰ ἀναβολὴ τῷ ποιήσαντι κακίστη.

5 [Plut.] *Mus.* 15. 1136c (p. 118 Lasserre, vi 3. 13 Ziegler)

Ὄλυμπον γὰρ πρῶτον Ἀριστόξενος ἐν τῷ πρώτῳ περὶ μουσικῆς (fr. 80 Wehrli) ἐπὶ τῷ Πυθωνί φησιν ἐπικήδειον αὐλῆσαι Λυδιστί. εἰσὶν δ᾽ οἳ Μελανιππίδην τούτου τοῦ μέλους ἄρξαι φασίν.

---

[1] The serpent of Delphi, killed by Apollo. [2] The Lydian mode? Or the lament for the Python?

3 Marcellinus, *Life of Thucydides*

According to Praxiphanes[1] in his work *On History* Thucydides[2] was a contemporary of the comic poet Plato, the tragedian Agathon, the epic poet Niceratus and Choerilus and Melanippides.

[1] Peripatetic writer, *c.* 305–250 B.C.   [2] Born 460–455 B.C., died *c.* 400.

MUSICAL INNOVATIONS

4 Aristotle, *Rhetoric*

Similarly, a long period turns into a speech in itself, like an aria,[1] and the result is what Demetrius of Chios[2] spoke of in his jibe at Melanippides who composed arias instead of antistrophes: 'a man does evil to himself who does evil to another, and the long aria is the greatest evil to its composer.'

[1] 'Anabolē', originally a prelude, instrumental or vocal, is used here of a long aria: i.e., in his dithyrambs Mel. abandoned the structure of strophe and answering antistrophe and introduced long solos instead; see also Arist. *Problems* 19. 15.   [2] A contemporary musician, himself mocked for innovation by Aristophanes fr. 930 K.-A.

5 'Plutarch', *On Music*

For Aristoxenus *On Music* Book 1 says that Olympus was the first to use the Lydian mode, when he played on his pipes a lament for the Python.[1] Some say it was Melanippides who originated this song.[2]

17

GREEK LYRIC

6 [Plut.] *Mus.* 30. 1141c–e (p. 124s. Lasserre, vi 3. 24s. Ziegler)

ὁμοίως δὲ καὶ Μελανιππίδης ὁ μελοποιὸς ἐπιγενό-
μενος οὐκ ἐνέμεινε τῇ προϋπαρχούσῃ μουσικῇ, ἀλλ᾽
οὐδὲ Φιλόξενος οὐδὲ Τιμόθεος· ... ἀλλὰ γὰρ καὶ <ἡ
add. Ziegler> αὐλητικὴ ἀφ᾽ ἁπλουστέρας εἰς ποικιλω-
τέραν μεταβέβηκε μουσικήν· τὸ γὰρ παλαιόν, ἕως
εἰς Μελανιππίδην τὸν τῶν διθυράμβων ποιητήν,
συμβεβήκει τοὺς αὐλητὰς παρὰ τῶν ποιητῶν λαμ-
βάνειν τοὺς μισθούς, πρωταγωνιστούσης δηλονότι τῆς
ποιήσεως, τῶν δ᾽ αὐλητῶν ὑπηρετούντων τοῖς διδα-
σκάλοις. ὕστερον δὲ καὶ τοῦτο διεφθάρη, ὡς καὶ Φερε-
κράτη τὸν κωμικὸν εἰσαγαγεῖν τὴν Μουσικὴν ἐν γυναι-
κείῳ σχήματι, ὅλην κατηκισμένην τὸ σῶμα· ποιεῖ δὲ
τὴν Δικαιοσύνην διαπυνθανομένην τὴν αἰτίαν τῆς
λώβης καὶ τὴν Ποίησιν λέγουσαν (fr. 155 K.-A.)

λέξω μὲν οὐκ ἄκουσα· σοί τε γὰρ κλυεῖν
ἐμοί τε λέξαι θυμὸς ἡδονὴν ἔχει.
ἐμοὶ γὰρ ἦρξε τῶν κακῶν Μελανιππίδης,
ἐν τοῖσι πρῶτος ὃς λαβὼν ἀνῆκέ με
5 χαλερωτέραν τ᾽ ἐποίησε χορδαῖς δώδεκα.
ἀλλ᾽ οὖν ὅμως οὗτος μὲν ἦν ἀποχρῶν ἀνὴρ
ἔμοιγε –⏑–⏑ πρὸς τὰ νῦν κακά.
Κινησίας δέ ...

18

6 'Plutarch', *On Music*

Similarly Lasus' successor, the lyric poet Melanippides, broke with the earlier music, as did Philoxenus and Timotheus ...; pipe-music too changed from a simpler to a more ornate style: previously, down to the time of Melanippides the dithyrambic poet, pipers had been paid by the poets, obviously because poetry played the leading role and the pipers were the servants of their instructors[1]; but later this practice too was abolished, so that the comic poet Pherecrates[2] brought Music on to the stage dressed as a woman and physically a total wreck; in his play Justice asks her how she came to be so maltreated, and Poetry (i.e. Music) replies: 'I am happy to speak, for you will take pleasure in hearing and I in telling. It was Melanippides who began my troubles: he was the first of them: he took me and pulled me down and left me looser with his twelve strings. But *he* was all right compared with my present troubles: Cinesias on the other hand ...[3]

[1] Cf. Pratinas 708. 7.   [2] Older contemporary of Aristophanes; the play was the *Cheiron*.   [3] Continued at Cinesias test. 1.

7 Xen. *Mem.* 1. 4. 3 (p. 31 Hude)

ἐπὶ μὲν τοίνυν ἐπῶν ποιήσει Ὅμηρον ἔγωγε
μάλιστα τεθαύμακα, ἐπὶ δὲ διθυράμβῳ Μελανιππίδην,
ἐπὶ δὲ τραγῳδίᾳ Σοφοκλέα, ἐπὶ δὲ ἀνδριαντοποιίᾳ
Πολύκλειτον, ἐπὶ δὲ ζωγραφίᾳ Ζεῦξιν.

8 *Anth. Pal.* 4. 1. 7 = Meleager i 7 Gow-Page

νάρκισσόν τε τορῶν Μελανιππίδου ἔγκυον ὕμνων

Reiske: χορῶν cod.

9 Plut., *Non posse suav.* 13 (vi 2. 145 Pohlenz)

οὐδὲ γὰρ Ἱέρων γ᾿ ἂν οὐδ᾿ Ἄτταλος οὐδ᾿ Ἀρχέ-
λαος ἐπείσθησαν Εὐριπίδην καὶ Σιμωνίδην καὶ Μελα-
νιππίδην καὶ Κράτητας καὶ Διοδότους ἀναστήσαντες
ἐκ τῶν συμποσίων κατακλῖναι . . .

THE VERDICT OF ANTIQUITY

7 Xenophon, *Memoirs*

For my part[1] I admire most Homer in epic poetry, Melanippides in the dithyramb, Sophocles in tragedy, Polycleitus in sculpture, Zeuxis in painting.

[1] Aristodemus is speaking to Socrates.

8 *Palatine Anthology*: Meleager, *The Garland*[1]

... and the narcissus, pregnant with the clear hymns of Melanippides.

[1] Introductory poem to M.'s collection of epigrams in which he compares each poet's work to a flower or plant. Our *Anthology* contains no poems ascribed to Melanippides. Since he shares a couplet here with Simonides, he may be the elder Mel. (if there were two).

9 Plutarch, *That Epicurus actually makes a pleasant life impossible*

For not even Hiero[1] nor Attalus[2] nor Archelaus[3] could have been persuaded to remove Euripides and Simonides and Melanippides and the likes of Crates and Diodotus from their banquets and replace them at their tables by . . .[4]

[1] Tyrant of Syracuse, patron of Simonides. [2] King Attalus II of Pergamum, patron of the scholar Crates of Mallos and presumably of the unidentified Diodotus. [3] King of Macedon, host of Euripides and successor of Perdiccas, Mel.'s host. [4] Various barbarians and buffoons are listed.

MELANIPPIDES

FRAGMENTA

ΔΑΝΑΪΔΕΣ

757 Athen. 14. 651f (iii 441s. Kaibel)

Μελανιππίδης δ' ὁ Μήλιος ἐν ταῖς Δαναῖσιν φοίνικας τὸν καρπὸν οὕτως ὀνομάζει τὸν λόγον ποιούμενος περὶ αὐτῶν τῶν Δαναΐδων (Dobree: αὐτῶν τῶν γὰρ ἀΐδων cod.)·

οὐ γὰρ ἀνθρώπων φόρευν μομφὰν ὄνειδος,
οὐδὲ τὰν ὀργὰν γυναικείαν ἔχον,
ἀλλ' ἐν ἁρμάτεσσι διφρού-
χοις ἐγυμνάζοντ' ἀν' εὐ-
ήλι' ἄλσεα πολλάκις
θήραις φρένα τερπόμεναι,
5   <αἱ δ'> ἱερόδακρυν λίβανον εὐώ-
δεις τε φοίνικας κασίαν τε ματεῦσαι
τέρενα Σύρια σπέρματα

1 Lloyd-Jones: μορφὰν cod.   West: ἐνεῖδος cod.   2 West: τὰν
αὐτὰν cod., τὰν ἀλκὰν Lloyd-Jones   3 Emperius: ασδεα cod.
Page: πολλάκι cod.   4 Porson: θῆρες cod.   5 suppl. Page
Emperius: -δακρυ, πατεῦσαι cod.   6 Fiorillo: συρίας τέρματα cod.

22

MELANIPPIDES

FRAGMENTS

THE DANAIDS

757 Athenaeus, *Scholars at Dinner*

Melanippides of Melos in his *Danaids* calls the fruit of the palm *phoinikes* ('dates') in his passage about the Danaids themselves:

for they did not bear the censure of mankind as a reproach,[1] nor did they have a woman's temperament[2]: in seated chariots they exercised in the sunny glades, often delighting their hearts in hunting, or again seeking out frankincense with its sacred tears and fragrant dates and the smooth Syrian grains of cassia.

[1] Text uncertain.   [2] Or 'valour'? Text uncertain.

GREEK LYRIC

ΜΑΡΣΥΑΣ

758 Athen. 14. 616ef (iii 360 Kaibel)

περὶ μὲν γὰρ αὐλῶν ὁ μέν τις ἔφη τὸν Μελανιππίδην καλῶς ἐν
τῷ Μαρσύᾳ διασύροντα τὴν αὐλητικὴν εἰρηκέναι περὶ τῆς 'Αθηνᾶς·

> ἁ μὲν 'Αθάνα
> τὥργαν' ἔρριψέν θ' ἱερᾶς ἀπὸ χειρὸς
> εἶπέ τ'· ἔρρετ' αἴσχεα, σώματι λύμα·
> ὔμμε δ' ἐγὼ κακότατι δίδωμι.

1s. Bergk: ἀθάνατα ὄργανα cod. A, ἀθάνα ὄργανα E   2 ἔρριψέ τε
A, ἔρριψεν E   3 σωματόλυμα ci. Meineke   4 Wilamowitz:
ἐμὲ δ' ἐγὼ codd., ἐμὲ δ' ἐγὼ <οὐ> ci. Maas

ΠΕΡΣΕΦΟΝΗ

759 Stob. 1. 49 (περὶ ψυχῆς) 50 (i 418 Wachsmuth)

Πορφυρίου ἐκ τῶν περὶ Στυγός·
. . . 'Αχέροντα μὲν διὰ τὰ ἄχη, ὡς καὶ Μελανιππίδης ἐν Περσε-
φόνῃ·

> καλεῖται δ' <εἴνεκ'> ἐν κόλποισι γαίας
> ἄχε' εἰσιν προχέων 'Αχέρων.

1 suppl. Bergk   2 Bergk: ἀχεοῖσι cod. F, ἀχαιοῖσιν P

760 Athen. 10. 429bc (ii 433 Kaibel)

οἱ δὲ ἀγνοοῦντες τὴν τοῦ οἴνου δύναμιν τὸν Διόνυσον φάσκουσιν
μανιῶν εἶναι αἴτιον τοῖς ἀνθρώποις, βλασφημοῦντες οὐ μετρίως·
ὅθεν ὁ Μελανιππίδης ἔφη·

MELANIPPIDES

MARSYAS

758 Athenaeus, *Scholars at Dinner*

On the subject of pipes one guest noted that Melanippides in his splendid ridicule of pipe-playing in the *Marsyas* said of Athena,

Athena flung the instruments from her holy hand and said, 'Away with you, you shameful objects, outrage to the body![1] I consign you to ruination.'[2]

[1] Since the pipes distorted the player's cheeks. See J. Boardman, *J.H.S.* 76 (1956) 18 ff.   [2] Text uncertain; perhaps 'I do not consign myself to ruination.' The passage continues at Telestes 805.

PERSEPHONE

759 Stobaeus, *Anthology*

From Porphyry, *On the Styx*

... They named the Acheron for its pains (*achē*): cf. Melanippides in his *Persephone*:

And it is called Acheron since within the bosom of the earth it goes forward pouring forth pains.[1]

[1] Continued at Licymnius 770.

760 Athenaeus, *Scholars at Dinner*

Those who are ignorant of the true power of wine allege that Dionysus is the cause of fits of madness in mankind, but this is extreme slander. It was ignorance that made Melanippides say,

πάντες δ᾽ ἀπεστύγεον ὕδωρ
τὸ πρὶν ἐόντες ἀίδριες οἴνου·
τάχα δὴ τάχα τοὶ μὲν οὖν ἀπωλλύοντο,
τοὶ δὲ παράπληκτον χέον ὀμφάν.

3 Kaibel: ἀπωλαυοντο cod. A

761 Athen. 2. 35a (i 81 Kaibel)

τὸν οἶνον ὁ Κολοφώνιος Νίκανδρος ὠνομάσθαι φησὶν ἀπὸ Οἰνέως (fr. 86 Schneider = Gow-Scholfield), φησὶ δὲ καὶ Μελανιππίδης ὁ Μήλιος (Μιλήσιος codd.)·

ἐπώνυμον δέσποτ᾽ οἶνον Οἰνέως

δὸς δέσποτ᾽ Hartung

762 Clem. Alex. *Strom.* 5. 14. 112 (ii 402 Stählin)

ὁ μελοποιὸς δὲ Μελανιππίδης ᾄδων φησίν·

κλῦθί μοι ὦ πάτερ, θαῦμα βροτῶν,
τᾶς ἀειζώου ψυχᾶς μεδέων.

cf. Euseb. *Praep. Evang.* 13. 680 (κλῦθι — μεδέων ψυχᾶς)

763 Plut. *Amator.* 15 (iv 360 Hubert)

γλυκὺ γὰρ θέρος ἀνδρὸς ὑποσπείρων πραπίδων πόθῳ

κατὰ τὸν Μελανιππίδην τὰ ἥδιστα μίγνυσι τοῖς καλλίστοις (sc. Ἔρως).

πόθῳ cod. E, πόθον B: πραπίδεσσι πόθων ci. Bergk

764 Philodem. *De Piet.* (p. 23 Gomperz: v. A. Henrichs, *Cron. ercol.* 5 (1975) 18s.)

Μελανιπ[πί]δης δὲ Δήμητρ[α καὶ] Μητέρα θεῶν φ[η]σιν μίαν ὑπάρχ[ειν].

26

And they all[1] began to loathe water, having no previous knowledge of wine; soon, very soon, some were dying, others were uttering frenzied cries.

[1] The Centaurs? Cf. Pind. fr. 166.

761 Athenaeus, *Scholars at Dinner*

Nicander[1] of Colophon says that wine (*oinos*) gets its name from Oeneus, as does Melanippides of Melos:

(give me?) wine, master,[2] named from Oeneus.

[1] Didactic poet, 2nd c. B.C.   [2] Text uncertain.

762 Clement of Alexandria, *Miscellanies*

The lyric poet Melanippides says in a song,

Hear me, father, marvel to mortals, ruler of the ever-living soul.

763 Plutarch, *Dialogue on Love*

For in sowing a sweet harvest in the desire of a man's heart,

as Melanippides puts it, he (sc. Eros) mingles what is most pleasant with what is finest.

764 Philodemus, *On Piety*

Melanippides says that Demeter and the Mother of the gods are one and the same.[1]

[1] Continued at Telestes 809.

765 Schol. T Hom. *Il.* 13. 350 (iii 466 Erbse)

ἐντεῦθεν δὲ Μελανιππίδης κύουσαν ἀπὸ Διὸς Θέτιν ἐκδοθῆναι Πηλεῖ διὰ τὰ ῥηθέντα ὑπὸ Προμηθέως ἤτοι Θέμιδος (Bergk: Θέμιδι cod.).

766 Schol. T Hom. *Il.* 18. 570c (iv 556 Erbse)

ἡ δὲ περὶ τὸν Λίνον ἱστορία καὶ παρὰ Φιλοχόρῳ ἐν τῇ ιθ' (*F.Gr.H.* 328 F207) καὶ παρὰ Μελανιππίδῃ.

MELANIPPIDES

765 Scholiast on Homer, *Iliad* ('Zeus was doing honour to Thetis')

That is why Melanippides says that Thetis was pregnant by Zeus when she was given in marriage to Peleus because of the remarks of Prometheus or Themis.

766 Scholiast on Homer, *Iliad* ('he sang the Linus song')

The story of Linus is in Philochorus Book 19 and in Melanippides.

PRONOMUS

767 Paus. 9. 12. 5–6 (iii 23 Rocha-Pereira)

ἀνδριάς τέ ἐστι Προνόμου ἀνδρὸς αὐλήσαντος ἐπαγωγότατα ἐς τοὺς πολλούς.... καί οἱ καὶ ᾆσμα πεποιημένον ἐστὶ [[ἐς]] προσόδιον ἐς Δῆλον τοῖς ἐπ᾽ Εὐρίπῳ Χαλκιδεῦσι.

PRONOMUS

767 Pausanias, *Description of Greece*

There is also[1] a statue of Pronomus, a man whose pipe-playing enchanted the crowds.[2] ... There is even a song composed by him, a processional hymn to Delos for the Chalcidians on the Euripus.[3]

[1] In Thebes, the home of Pronomus. [2] For his pipe-playing see in addition to this passage Athen. 14. 631e, *Plan. Anth.* 28 = *F.G.E.* anon. xxiii, for his compositions for pipes Paus. 4. 27. 7, for his beard Ar. *Eccl.* 98 (produced 392 B.C.); he taught pipe-playing to Alcibiades *c.* 435 B.C. (Athen. 4. 184d). For his son Oeniades see *P.M.G.* 840. [3] I.e. the people of Chalcis in Euboea.

LICYMNIUS

TESTIMONIA VITAE ATQUE ARTIS

1 Arist. *Rhet.* 3. 12. 1413b (p. 211s. Römer)

βαστάζονται δὲ οἱ ἀναγνωστικοί, οἷον Χαιρήμων (ἀκριβὴς γὰρ ὥσπερ λογογράφος) καὶ Λικύμνιος τῶν διθυραμβοποιῶν.

2 Pl. *Phdr.* 267b

τὰ δὲ Πώλου πῶς φράσωμεν αὖ μουσεῖα λόγων — ὡς διπλασιολογίαν καὶ γνωμολογίαν καὶ εἰκονολογίαν — ὀνομάτων τε Λικυμνιείων (Ast: Λικυμνίων codd.) ἃ ἐκείνῳ ἐδωρήσατο πρὸς ποίησιν εὐεπείας;

Schol. ad loc.

ὁ Λικύμνιος δὲ Πώλου διδάσκαλος, ὃς διῄρει τὰ ὀνόματα εἰς κύρια, σύνθετα, ἀδελφά, ἐπίθετα καὶ εἰς ἄλλα τινά.

LICYMNIUS[1]

LIFE AND WORK

1 Aristotle, *Rhetoric*

The popular poets are those who can be read,[2] for example, Chaeremon,[3] who is as precise as if he were a speech-writer, and Licymnius among dithyrambic poets.

[1] From Chios: see 768, 771, 772.   [2] I.e., who do not rely on the performance of their work by actor or chorus.   [3] Tragic poet, mid-4th c. B.C.

2 Plato, *Phaedrus*

And what about Polus and his Muses' treasury of speech — his diplasiology and gnomology and iconology — and of the Licymnian terminology which he presented to him to effect a fine diction?

Scholiast on the passage

Licymnius was Polus' teacher[1]; he divided nouns into proper, compound, cognate, epithet and so on.

[1] C. 420 B.C. Dionysius of Halicarnassus says L. and Polus were pupils of Gorgias (*Lys.* 3; cf. *Thuc.* 24). For L.'s writing on rhetoric see Arist. *Rhet.* 3. 2. 1405b, 3. 13. 1414b with schol., and fr. 773.

LICYMNIUS

FRAGMENTA

768 Athen. 13. 603d (iii 331 Kaibel)

Λικύμνιος (Reinesius: Ἀλκύμνιος cod. A) δ᾽ ὁ Χῖος ἐν Διθυράμβοις Ἀργύννου φησὶν ἐρώμενον Ὑμέναιον (Musurus: ὑμαινεον A) γενέσθαι.

Ἀργύννου: Διονύσου Wilamowitz

768A Philodem. *de piet.*: P. Herc. 243 VI 12–18: v. A. Henrichs, *Z.P.E.* 57 (1984) 53ss.

φησὶν δὲ καὶ [Κλε]ιὼ τὴν Μοῦσα[ν ἀνδρὸ]ς ἐρασθῆναι [Λι]κύ[μ]νιος, οἱ δὲ καὶ [τὸ]ν Ὑ[μ]ένα[ιο]ν υἱὸν α]ὑτῆς [εἶν]αι νο[μίζουσι]ν.

769 Sext. Emp. *adv. math.* xi 49 (ii 386s. Mutschmann)

Σιμωνίδης μὲν γὰρ ὁ μελοποιός φησι (fr. 604)· Λικύμνιος δὲ προειπὼν ταῦτα·

> λιπαρόμματε μᾶτερ ὑψίστα θρόνων
> σεμνῶν Ἀπόλλωνος βασίλεια ποθεινὰ
> πραΰγελως Ὑγίεια

†ποῖον ὑψηλὸν† ἐπιφέρει· <᾽Ἀρίφρων δέ φησι> (fr. 813. 3, 4, 10).

1 Wilamowitz: ὑψίστων codd.   3 Schneidewin: ὑγεία codd.
post 3 obelos add. Page, suppl. Maas

34

LICYMNIUS

FRAGMENTS

768 Athenaeus, *Scholars at Dinner*

Licymnius of Chios in his Dithyrambs says that
Hymenaeus was the beloved boy of Argynnus.[1]

[1] But Athen. has just said that Argynnus was the boy with whom
Agamemnon fell in love. Wilamowitz read 'Dionysus' for
'Argynnus' here.

768A Philodemus, *On Piety*

Moreover Clio the Muse fell in love with a man, accord-
ing to Licymnius, and some think Hymenaeus is her son.[1]

[1] For Hymenaeus see also Telestes 808, Philoxenus 828.

769 Sextus Empiricus, *Against the ethicists* (on health)

Simonides the lyric poet says (fr. 604); Licymnius, hav-
ing spoken this prelude,

Bright-eyed mother, highest queen of Apollo's
august throne, desirable, gently-laughing Health,

goes on to add . . . ; (Ariphron says . . .)[1]

[1] The text of the second quotation is corrupt or missing; the words
which follow are from Ariphron 813.

770 Stob. 1. 49 (περὶ ψυχῆς) 50 (i 418 Wachsmuth)

Πορφυρίου ἐκ τῶν περὶ Στυγός·
. . . Ἀχέροντα μὲν διὰ τὰ ἄχη, ὡς καὶ Μελανιππίδης (fr. 759)·
ἐπεὶ καὶ Λικύμνιός φησι·

(a) μυρίαις παγαῖς δακρύων ἀχέων τε βρύει,

καὶ πάλιν

(b) Ἀχέρων ἄχεα πορθμεύει βροτοῖσιν.

(a) Grotius: πάσαις codd.   <Ἀχέρων> ἀχέων ci. Grotius

771 Athen. 13. 564cd (iii 244 Kaibel)

Λικύμνιος δ' ὁ Χῖος τὸν Ὕπνον φήσας ἐρᾶν τοῦ Ἐνδυμίωνος
οὐδὲ καθεύδοντος αὐτοῦ κατακαλύπτει τοὺς ὀφθαλμούς, ἀλλὰ ἀνα-
πεπταμένων τῶν βλεφάρων κοιμίζει τὸν ἐρώμενον ὅπως διὰ
παντὸς ἀπολαύῃ τῆς τοῦ θεωρεῖν ἡδονῆς. λέγει δ' οὕτως·

Ὕπνος δὲ χαίρων
ὀμμάτων αὐγαῖς, ἀναπεπταμένοις
ὄσσοις ἐκοίμιζεν κόρον.

3 Fiorillo: κοῦρον codd.

772 Parthen. ἐρωτ. παθ. 22 (Myth. Gr. ii 38 Sakolowski)

περὶ Νανίδος. ἡ ἱστορία παρὰ Λικυμνίῳ τῷ Χίῳ μελοποιῷ καὶ
Ἑρμησιάνακτι (fr. 6 Powell). ἔφασαν δέ τινες καὶ τὴν Σαρδίων
ἀκρόπολιν ὑπὸ Κύρου τοῦ Περσῶν βασιλέως ἁλῶναι προδούσης τῆς
Κροίσου θυγατρὸς Νανίδος. ἐπειδὴ γὰρ ἐπολιόρκει Σάρδεις Κῦρος
καὶ οὐδὲν αὐτῷ εἰς ἅλωσιν τῆς πόλεως προῦβανεν, ἐν πολλῷ τε
δέει ἦν μὴ ἀθροισθὲν τὸ συμμαχικὸν αὐτῆς τῷ Κροίσῳ διαλύσειεν
αὐτῷ τὴν στρατιάν, τότε τὴν παρθένον ταύτην εἶχε λόγος περὶ
προδοσίας συνθεμένην τῷ Κύρῳ, εἰ κατὰ νόμους Περσῶν ἕξει

770 Stobaeus, *Anthology*

From Porphyry, *On the Styx*

... They named the Acheron for its pains (*achē*): cf. Melanippides (fr. 759). Licymnius also says of it,

(a) in ten thousand streams it gushes with tears and pains;

and again

(b) the Acheron carries pains for mortals.

771 Athenaeus, *Scholars at Dinner* (on the loved one's eyes)

Licymnius of Chios says that Sleep loves Endymion and does not close the eyes of his beloved boy even while he is asleep, but lulls him to rest with eyes wide open so that he may without interruption enjoy the pleasure of gazing at them. His words are:

And Sleep, rejoicing in the rays of his eyes, would lull the boy to rest with eyes wide open.

772 Parthenius, *Love-stories*

The story of Nanis, told by the lyric poet Licymnius of Chios and by Hermesianax

Some have said that the acropolis of Sardis was captured by Cyrus, king of the Persians, as the result of the treachery of Nanis, daughter of Croesus. Cyrus was besieging the city and failing completely to capture it, and he was terrified that its allies might rally to Croesus and destroy his army; at this point, so the story went, the girl Nanis reached an agreement with Cyrus that she would betray the city to him if he took her as his wife in accordance with the laws of the Persians, and with the help of

γυναῖκα αὐτήν, κατὰ τὴν ἄκραν μηδενὸς φυλάσσοντος δι᾽ ὀχυρό-
τητα τοῦ χωρίου εἰσδέχεσθαι τοὺς πολεμίους, συνεργῶν αὐτῇ καὶ
ἄλλων τινῶν γενομένων· τὸν μέντοι Κῦρον μὴ ἐμπεδῶσαι αὐτῇ
τὴν ὑπόσχεσιν.

773 Dion. Hal. *Demosth.* 26 (i 185s. Usener-Rader-
macher)

φησὶ γάρ· δεῖ δὴ τοιούτου τινὸς λόγου, ὅστις τοὺς μὲν τετελευ-
τηκότας ἱκανῶς ἐπαινέσει, τοῖς δὲ ζῶσιν εὐμενῶς παραινέσει (Pl.
Menex. 236e). οὐκοῦν ἐπίρρημα ἐπιρρήματι ἀντιπαράκειται καὶ
ῥήματι ῥῆμα, τὸ μὲν ἱκανῶς τῷ εὐμενῶς, τῷ δ᾽ ἐπαινέσει τὸ παραι-
νέσει, καὶ ταῦτα πάρισα; οὐ Λικύμνιοι ταῦτ᾽ εἰσὶν οὐδ᾽ Ἀγάθωνες
οἱ λέγοντες ὕβριν ἢ <Κύ>πριν, †μισθῷ ποθὲν ἢ μόχθον πατρίδων,†
ἀλλ᾽ ὁ δαιμόνιος ἑρμηνεῦσαι Πλάτων.

<Κύ>πριν suppl. M. Schmidt   μ. πραπίδων ci. idem

some accomplices she let the enemy in at the summit of the acropolis, where no one was on guard because of the natural strength of the position. Cyrus, however, refused to keep the promise he had made to her.

773 Dionysius of Halicarnassus, *Demosthenes*

Plato says (*Menex.* 236e), 'We require such a speech as will adequately praise the dead and gently exhort the living.' Does not the adverb 'adequately' balance the adverb 'gently', the verb 'praise' balance the verb 'exhort', and are not the phrases of equal length? Yet this is not a Licymnius or an Agathon, the sort who talks of 'hybris or Cypris[1] . . .', but Plato, the divine stylist.

[1] Following words corrupt. It is not clear what belongs to L. and whether it is poetry or prose; see Agathon F31 Snell.

CINESIAS

TESTIMONIA VITAE ATQUE ARTIS

1 Pherecrates fr. 155 Kassel-Austin = [Plut.] *Mus.* 30.
1141ef

    Κινησίας δέ <μ'> ὁ κατάρατος Ἀττικός,
    ἐξαρμονίους καμπὰς ποιῶν ἐν ταῖς στροφαῖς
10 ἀπολώλεχ' οὕτως ὥστε τῆς ποιήσεως
    τῶν διθυράμβων, καθάπερ ἐν ταῖς ἀσπίσιν,
    ἀριστέρ' αὐτοῦ φαίνεται τὰ δεξιά.
    ἀλλ' οὖν ἀνεκτὸς οὗτος ἦν ὅμως ἐμοί.
    Φρῦνις δ' . . .

---

[1] Continued from Melanippides test. 6. The speaker is Music.
[2] Modulations from one *harmonia* to another: cf. Ar. *Clouds* 333,
'the song-twisters of the circular choruses', where the scholiast
says the dithyrambic poets Cinesias, Philoxenus and Cleomenes
are meant; also 969 ff. = Phrynis test. 2. See A. Barker, *Greek
Musical Writings* i 237 n. 200. The 'twists' and 'turns' (*strophai*) fit
Music's account of her sexual misadventures.

2 Ar. *Av.* 1372ss.

Κ. ἀναπέτομαι δὴ πρὸς Ὄλυμπον πτερύγεσσι κού-
      φαις·
    πέτομαι δ' ὁδὸν ἄλλοτ' ἐπ' ἄλλαν μελέων —
Π. τουτὶ τὸ πρᾶγμα φορτίου δεῖται πτερῶν.   1375
Κ. — ἀφόβῳ φρενὶ σώματί τε νέαν ἐφέπων.

CINESIAS

LIFE AND WORK

THE COMIC POETS

1 Pherecrates, *Cheiron*[1]

Cinesias on the other hand, that damned Athenian, has so damaged me with the exharmonic twists[2] he makes within his strophes that just as in shields[3] you can't tell his right from his left when he composes his dithyrambs.[4] But *he* was bearable all the same: Phrynis on the other hand . . .[5]

[3] With their reflecting surfaces.   [4] 'You might as well play [his music] backwards' (Barker, loc. cit.). E. K. Borthwick, *Hermes* 96 (1968) 63 ff. relates the shields and 'right' and 'left' to C.'s Pyrrhic dance (see test. 3).   [5] Continued at Phrynis test. 1.

2 Aristophanes, *Birds* (414 B.C.) (Cinesias turns up in Cloudcuckooland and speaks with Peisetaerus)

C. See, I fly up on light wings to Olympus,[1] I fly now to this path of song, now to that —

P. Here's something that needs a load of feathers.

C. — with fearless heart and body following a new path.

[1] Anacreon 378. 1.

41

Π. ἀσπαζόμεσθα φιλύρινον Κινησίαν.
  τί δεῦρο πόδα σὺ κυλλὸν ἀνὰ κύκλον κυκλεῖς;

Κ. ὄρνις γενέσθαι βούλομαι λιγύφθογγος ἀηδών.   1380

Π. παῦσαι μελῳδῶν, ἀλλ' ὅ τι λέγεις εἰπέ μοι.

Κ. ὑπὸ σοῦ πτερωθεὶς βούλομαι μετάρσιος
  ἀναπτόμενος ἐκ τῶν νεφελῶν καινὰς λαβεῖν
  ἀεροδονήτους καὶ νιφοβόλους ἀναβολάς.   1385

Π. ἐκ τῶν νεφελῶν γὰρ ἄν τις ἀναβολὰς λάβοι;

Κ. κρέμαται μὲν οὖν ἐντεῦθεν ἡμῶν ἡ τέχνη.
  τῶν διθυράμβων γὰρ τὰ λαμπρὰ γίγνεται
  ἀέρια καὶ σκοτεινὰ καὶ κυαναυγέα
  καὶ πτεροδόνητα· σὺ δὲ κλυὼν εἴσει τάχα.   1390

Π. οὐ δῆτ' ἔγωγε.   Κ. νὴ τὸν Ἡρακλέα σύ γε·
  ἅπαντα γὰρ δίειμί σοι τὸν ἀέρα.
  εἴδωλα πετηνῶν
    αἰθεροδρόμων
    οἰωνῶν ταναοδείρων —   Π. ὠόπ.

Κ. — τὰν ἀναδρομὰν ἀλάμενος   1395
  ἅμ' ἀνέμων πνοαῖσι βαίην —

Π. νὴ τὸν Δί' ἢ 'γώ σου καταπαύσω τὰς πνοάς.

Κ. τοτὲ μὲν νοτίαν στείχων πρὸς ὁδόν,
  τοτὲ δ' αὖ βορέᾳ σῶμα πελάζων,
  ἀλίμενον αἰθέρος αὔλακα τέμνων —   1400
  χαρίεντά γ', ὦ πρεσβῦτ', ἐσοφίσω καὶ σοφά.

Π. οὐ γὰρ σὺ χαίρεις πτεροδόνητος γενόμενος;

1377 ἐπέων v. l. ap. schol.   1395 tent. Sommerstein: τὸν
ἀλάδρομον, ἀλα- codd.

---

2 As light as lime-wood (schol.), but see also test. 7, L. B. Lawler,
T.A.P.A. 81 (1950) 78 ff.   3 The dithyrambic chorus danced
in a circle.   4 With ref. to C.'s halting gait (test. 8) and

CINESIAS

P. We greet Cinesias, the lime-wood man.[2] Why do you circle here in circles[3] your crippled foot?[4]

C. I want to turn into a bird—[*sings*] a clear-voiced nightingale.

P. Stop singing lyrics and tell me what you mean.

C. I want to be feathered by you and fly aloft to get from the clouds[5] new arias,[6] air-driven, snow-clad.

P. A man can get arias from the clouds?

C. Yes, our craft depends on them: the brilliant dithyrambs are airy and murky and dark-gleaming and feather-driven. You'll soon know when you hear them.

P. Oh no, I shan't.

C. By Heracles, you will: I'll traverse the whole air for you. You images of winged sky-racing long-necked birds, —

P. Whoa there!

C. — bounding on my upward path may I go with the breath of the winds —

P. By Zeus, I'll stop your breath.

C. — now going to the path of the south, now drawing near to the north wind, cleaving the harbourless furrow of the sky—that was a pretty trick you played, old man, a clever trick.[7]

P. Why, don't you enjoy being feather-driven?

---

halting metre.   [5] Cf. *Clouds* 332 ff.   [6] *Anabolai*: see Melanippides test. 4 n. 1 and cf. *Peace* 827–31.   [7] P. has stuck feathers on him.

K. ταυτὶ πεποίηκας τὸν κυκλιοδιδάσκαλον,
   ὃς ταῖσι φυλαῖς περιμάχητός εἰμ᾽ ἀεί;
Π. βούλει διδάσκειν καὶ παρ᾽ ἡμῖν οὖν μένων   1405
   Λεωτροφίδῃ χορὸν πετομένων ὀρνέων,
   Κρεκοπίδα φυλήν; K. καταγελᾷς μου, δῆλος εἶ.
   ἀλλ᾽ οὖν ἔγωγ᾽ οὐ παύσομαι, τοῦτ᾽ ἴσθ᾽ ὅτι,
   πρὶν ἂν πτερωθεὶς διαδράμω τὸν ἀέρα.

1407 Kock: Κεκροπιδα codd.

Schol. ad loc. (p. 250ss. White)

(1379) ὁ δὲ Ἀριστοτέλης ἐν ταῖς Διδασκαλίαις (fr. 629 Rose) δύο φησὶ γεγονέναι.

(1385) παίζει δὲ πρὸς τὰ ἐπίθετα τῶν διθυραμβοποιῶν καὶ πρὸς τὸ κοῦφον αὐτῶν.

(1392) πλείστη γὰρ αὐτῶν ἡ λέξις τοιαύτη, ὁ δὲ νοῦς ἐλάχιστος, ὡς ἡ παροιμία· καὶ διθυράμβων νοῦν ἔχεις ἐλάττονα.

3 Ar. Ran. 152s.

   νὴ τοὺς θεοὺς ἐχρῆν γε πρὸς τούτοισι κεἰ
   τὴν πυρρίχην τις ἔμαθε τὴν Κινησίου.

---

[1] The frustrated husband in *Lysistrata* 845 ff. is called 'Cinesias of the deme Paeonidae' solely because the names suggest sexual intercourse (κινεῖν, παίειν).   [2] A war-dance; see Lawler (test. 2. n. 2), Borthwick (test. 1 n. 4).

44

CINESIAS

C. This is what you've done to me, the circular-chorus trainer that the tribes are always fighting to get[8]?

P. Do you want to stay here with us, then, and train Leotrophides[9] a chorus of flying birds, Corn-crake tribe[10]?

C. You're making fun of me, that's clear. But I shan't stop, let me tell you, till I have been feathered and race through the air. [*exit*]

[8] For the dithyrambic contests in which tribes competed.
[9] As choregus; general in 409/8 B.C.   [10] Crecopis (*krex* = corn-crake), a pun on Cercopis, the Athenian tribe.

Scholiast on the passage

(1379) Aristotle in his *Dramatic Catalogues* says there were two poets named Cinesias.[1]

(1385) He is making fun of the epithets of the dithyrambic poets and their lack of substance.

(1392) Most of their diction is like this, but they make little sense. As the proverb puts it, 'You have less sense than dithyrambs.'

[1] Very improbable: see *R.E.* s.v. Kinesias.

3 Aristophanes, *Frogs*[1] (405 B.C.) (Dionysus completes Heracles' list of the criminals in Hades)

By the gods, you should have added anyone who learned that Pyrrhic dance[2] of Cinesias.

Schol. ad loc. (*Sud.* Π 3225) (p. 279 Dübner)

Κινησίας διθυραμβοποιός· ὃς ἐποίησε πυρρίχην. . . .
ὁ Κινησίας ἐπραγματεύσατο κατὰ τῶν κωμικῶν ὡς
εἶεν ἀχορήγητοι. ἦν δὲ καὶ τὸ σῶμα ὀκνηρὸς καὶ κατε-
σκελετευκώς. . . . ἦν δὲ Θηβαῖος, μελοποιὸς κάκιστος,
ὃς ἐν τοῖς χοροῖς ἐχρῆτο πολλῇ κινήσει.

4 Ar. *Ran.* 366

ἢ κατατιλᾷ τῶν Ἑκατείων κυκλίοισι χοροῖσιν ὑπᾴδων

Schol. ad loc. (p. 286 Dübner)

τοῦτο δὲ εἰς Κινησίαν τὸν διθυραμβοποιόν.

5 Ar. *Ran.* 404ss.

σὺ γὰρ κατεσχίσω μὲν ἐπὶ γέλωτι
κἀπ᾽ εὐτελείᾳ τόδε τὸ σανδαλίσκον
καὶ τὸ ῥάκος,
κἀξηῦρες ὥστ᾽ ἀζημίους
παίζειν τε καὶ χορεύειν.

CINESIAS

Scholiast on the passage

Cinesias was a dithyrambic poet; he composed a Pyrrhic dance.... He took measures against the comic poets to deprive them of their *chorēgoi*.[1] His body was shaky (lit. 'timid, shrinking') and reduced to skin and bones. He was a Theban,[2] the worst lyric poet, who introduced much movement (*kinēsis*) in his choral dances.

[1] See scholiast on *Frogs* 404 below. [2] An error.

4 Aristophanes, *Frogs* (the chorus-leader lists people who are unwelcome in the Mystic ceremonies)

... or anyone who shits on Hecate's shrines[1] while singing the tune for the dithyrambic choruses.

[1] Cf. *Eccl.* 330; for C.'s impiety see test. 7.

Scholiast on passage

This is directed at Cinesias, the dithyrambic poet.

5 Aristophanes, *Frogs* (the chorus address the god Iacchus)

For it was you[1] who tore this poor sandal and this ragged coat of mine with an eye on laughter and economy, and found a way for us to sport and dance without paying.

[1] As representing the festival of Dionysus. Presumably less was being spent on dressing the choruses.

Schol. ad loc. (p. 287 Dübner)

ἔοικε δὲ παρεμφαίνειν ὅτι λιτῶς ἤδη ἐχορηγεῖτο τοῖς ποιηταῖς. ἐπὶ γοῦν τοῦ Καλλίου τούτου φησὶν Ἀριστοτέλης (fr. 630 Rose) σύνδυο ἔδοξε χορηγεῖν τὰ Διονύσια τοῖς τραγῳδοῖς καὶ κωμῳδοῖς· ὥστε ἴσως ἦν τις καὶ περὶ τὸν Ληναϊκὸν ἀγῶνα συστολή. χρόνῳ δ' ὕστερον οὐ πολλῷ τινι καὶ καθάπαξ περιεῖλε Κινησίας τὰς χορηγίας· ἐξ οὗ καὶ Στράττις ἐν τῷ εἰς αὐτὸν δράματι ἔφη (fr. 16 K.-A.)·

σκηνὴ μὲν < > τοῦ χοροκτόνου Κινησίου

6 Ar. Ran. 1437

[εἴ τις πτερώσας Κλεόκριτον Κινησίᾳ]

Schol. ad loc. (p. 312 Dübner)

ὡς λεπτὸς σφόδρα ὢν κωμῳδεῖται καὶ ὡς ξένος καὶ ὡς κόλαξ.

7 Athen. 12. 551a–552b (iii 215ss. Kaibel)

καὶ Ἀριστοφάνης δ' ἐν Γηρυτάδῃ λεπτοὺς τούσδε καταλέγει, οὓς καὶ πρέσβεις ὑπὸ τῶν ποιητῶν φησιν

CINESIAS

He seems to suggest that the poets' plays were now being staged on the cheap by the *chorēgoi*.[1] At any rate Aristotle says that a decree was passed in the archonship of this Callias (406/5 B.C.) that the tragedies and comedies be staged by joint *chorēgoi* at the Dionysia, so perhaps there was a similar cutback for the Lenaean festival. Soon afterwards Cinesias abolished the *chorēgiai* once for all[2]: that is why Strattis says in his play about him, 'The setting (is the house?) of Cinesias the chorus-killer.'[3]

[1] Wealthy citizens who undertook the expenses of staging plays as a service to the city. [2] Cf. test. 3 (schol.), but see A. W. Pickard-Cambridge, *The Dramatic Festivals of Athens*[2] 87 n. 2. [3] From the prologue of Strattis' comedy *Cinesias*.

6 Aristophanes, *Frogs* (a fantastic suggestion for saving the city)

If someone, having feathered Cleocritus with Cinesias[1] . . .

[1] For C.'s feathers cf. test. 2.

Scholiast on the passage

Cinesias is mocked as being excessively thin and as a foreigner[1] and a flatterer.

[1] Erroneous as well as gratuitous?

7 Athenaeus, *Scholars at Dinner* (on thin people)

Aristophanes too in his *Gerytades* lists the following thin men, saying that they are sent to Hades by

49

εἰς Ἅιδου πέμπεσθαι πρὸς τοὺς ἐκεῖ ποιητὰς λέγων
οὑτωσί (fr. 156 K.-A.)·

A. καὶ τίς νεκρῶν κευθμῶνα καὶ σκότου πύλας
   ἔτλη κατελθεῖν; B. ἕνα τιν' ἀφ' ἑκάστης
      τέχνης
   εἱλόμεθα κοινῇ γενομένης ἐκκλησίας,
   οὓς ᾖσμεν ὄντας ᾁδοφοίτας καὶ θαμὰ
5 ἐκεῖσε φιλοχωροῦντας. A. εἰσὶ γάρ τινες
   ἄνδρες παρ' ὑμῖν ᾁδοφοῖται; B. νὴ Δία
   μάλιστά γ'. A. ὥσπερ Θρᾳκοφοῖται; B. πάντ'
      ἔχεις.
A. καὶ τίνες ἂν εἶεν; B. πρῶτα μὲν Σαννυρίων
   ἀπὸ τῶν τρυγῳδῶν, ἀπὸ δὲ τῶν τραγικῶν χορῶν
10 Μέλητος, ἀπὸ δὲ τῶν κυκλίων Κινησίας.

. . . ἦν δ' ὄντως λεπτότατος καὶ μακρότατος ὁ Κινη-
σίας, εἰς ὃν καὶ ὅλον δρᾶμα γέγραφεν Στράττις (v. fr.
775 inf.). . . . ἄλλοι δ' αὐτόν, ὡς καὶ Ἀριστοφάνης,
πολλάκις εἰρήκασι φιλύρινον Κινησίαν (v. Ar. Av.
1377) διὰ τὸ φιλύρας λαμβάνοντα σανίδα συμπεριζών-
νυσθαι, ἵνα μὴ κάμπτηται διά τε τὸ μῆκος καὶ τὴν
ἰσχνότητα.
   ὅτι δὲ ἦν ὁ Κινησίας νοσώδης καὶ δεινὸς τἄλλα
Λυσίας ὁ ῥήτωρ ἐν τῷ ὑπὲρ Φανίου παρανόμων ἐπι-
γραφομένῳ λόγῳ εἴρηκεν, φάσκων αὐτὸν ἀφέμενον τῆς

the poets as ambassadors to the poets down there. His words are:

A. Who dared to descend to the hiding-place of corpses and the gates of darkness?

B. We held a general assembly and chose one representative from each art, men whom we knew to be Hades-visitors and frequent travellers there.

A. What, you have Hades-visitors among you?

B. Oh yes, indeed.

A. Like Thrace-visitors?

B. Now you've got it.

A. And who might they be?

B. First there is Sannyrion from the comic poets, then Meletus from the tragic choruses, and Cinesias from the circular.

... Cinesias really was very thin and very tall. Strattis wrote a whole play about him (see fr. 775 below). Others, Aristophanes among them, often called him 'Cinesias the lime-wood man'[1] because he would take a board of lime-wood and strap it to his waist so that he would not bend by reason of his height and leanness.

Cinesias was a sick man and a strange figure altogether, as we are told by the orator Lysias[2] in the speech entitled *In Defence of Phanias, accused of proposing an unconstitutional measure*: Lysias alleges that Cinesias gave up his poetic craft to

[1] See test. 2 with n. 2.   [2] See also test. 9.

τέχνης συκοφαντεῖν καὶ ἀπὸ τούτου πλουτεῖν. ὅτι δὲ ὁ
ποιητής ἐστι καὶ οὐχ ἕτερος, σαφῶς αὐτὸς ὢν σημαίνε-
ται ἐκ τοῦ καὶ ἐπὶ ἀθεότητι κωμῳδούμενον ἐμφανίζεσθαι
καὶ διὰ τοῦ λόγου τοιοῦτον δείκνυσθαι. λέγει δ' οὕτως
ὁ ῥήτωρ (fr. 53 Thalheim)· 'θαυμάζω δὲ εἰ μὴ βαρέως
φέρετε ὅτι Κινησίας ἐστὶν ὁ τοῖς νόμοις βοηθός, ὃν
ὑμεῖς πάντες ἐπίστασθε ἀσεβέστατον ἁπάντων καὶ
παρανομώτατον ἀνθρώπων γεγονέναι. οὐχ οὗτός ἐστιν
ὁ τοιαῦτα περὶ θεοὺς ἐξαμαρτάνων ἃ τοῖς μὲν ἄλλοις
αἰσχρόν ἐστι καὶ λέγειν, τῶν κωμῳδοδιδασκάλων <δ'>
ἀκούετε καθ' ἕκαστον ἐνιαυτόν; οὐ μετὰ τούτου ποτὲ
Ἀπολλοφάνης καὶ Μυσταλίδης καὶ Λυσίθεος συνει-
στιῶντο, μίαν ἡμέραν ταξάμενοι τῶν ἀποφράδων, ἀντὶ
δὲ νουμηνιαστῶν κακοδαιμονιστὰς σφίσιν αὐτοῖς τοὔ-
νομα θέμενοι, πρέπον μὲν ταῖς αὐτῶν τύχαις· οὐ μὴν
ὡς τοῦτο διαπραξόμενοι τὴν διάνοιαν ἔσχον ἀλλ' ὡς
καταγελῶντες τῶν θεῶν καὶ τῶν νόμων τῶν ὑμετέ-
ρων. ἐκείνων μὲν οὖν ἕκαστος ἀπώλετο ὥσπερ εἰκὸς
τοὺς τοιούτους. τοῦτον δὲ τὸν ὑπὸ πλείστων γιγνω-
σκόμενον οἱ θεοὶ οὕτως διέθεσαν ὥστε τοὺς ἐχθροὺς
βούλεσθαι αὐτὸν ζῆν μᾶλλον ἢ τεθνάναι παράδειγμα
τοῖς ἄλλοις, ἵν' εἰδῶσιν ὅτι τοῖς λίαν ὑβριστικῶς πρὸς
τὰ θεῖα διακειμένοις οὐκ εἰς τοὺς παῖδας ἀποτίθενται
τὰς τιμωρίας ἀλλ' αὐτοὺς κακῶς ἀπολλύουσι, μείζους
καὶ χαλεπωτέρας καὶ τὰς συμφορὰς καὶ τὰς νόσους ἢ

---

[3] See test. 4   [4] Aristotle, *Eud. Eth.* 1233b mentions the Fel-
lowship of the Good Spirit, abstainers who drank only the toast 'to
the Good Spirit (*Daimon*)'.

become an informer and made his fortune as a result. That this is the poet and not another Cinesias is clear from the fact that the comic poets mock him as an atheist[3] and that Lysias' speech paints the same picture. The orator's words are as follows: 'I am amazed that you do not find it outrageous that Cinesias is the upholder of the laws, since you all know that there is no one more impious, more lawless, in the whole world. Is this not the man who commits against the gods crimes of such enormity that most people regard it as disgraceful even to mention them, although you hear about them from the comic poets year in, year out? Is this not the man with whom Apollophanes and Mystalides and Lysitheus used to dine at one time, arranging their feast for one of the forbidden days and calling themselves not the New-mooners but the Fellowship of the Evil Spirit[4] — a title that fitted their fortunes; not that they thought it up in the belief that they would bring this about: rather they were mocking the gods and your laws. Now each of them died as you would expect such men to die; but Cinesias here, the best known of them, was reduced to such a plight by the gods that his enemies prefer to have him not dead but alive, an example to teach others that in the case of those who display extreme insolence towards divinity the gods do not postpone the punishment for their children to suffer but destroy the culprits miserably, sending greater and harsher misfortunes and diseases to them than to

53

τοῖς ἄλλοις ἀνθρώποις προσβάλλοντες. τὸ μὲν γὰρ
ἀποθανεῖν ἢ καμεῖν νομίμως κοινὸν ἡμῖν ἅπασίν ἐστι,
τὸ δ᾽ οὕτως ἔχοντα τοσοῦτον χρόνον διατελεῖν καὶ καθ᾽
ἑκάστην ἡμέραν ἀποθνῄσκοντα μὴ δύνασθαι τελευτῆ-
σαι τὸν βίον τούτοις μόνοις προσήκει τοῖς τὰ τοιαῦτα
ἅπερ οὗτος ἐξημαρτηκόσιν.᾽ περὶ μὲν οὖν Κινησίου
ταῦτα ὁ ῥήτωρ εἴρηκεν.

8 Gal. in Hipp. *aphor.* (18. 1. 149 Kühn)

ἐμπύους . . . οὓς ὅτι συνήθως ἔκαιον οἱ παλαιοὶ
μαθεῖν ἔστι καὶ ἐξ ὧν εἴρηκε Πλάτων ὁ κωμικὸς ἐπὶ
Κινησίου κατὰ τήνδε τὴν ῥῆσιν (fr. 200 K.-A.)·

> μετὰ ταῦτα δὲ
> παῖς Οἰάγρου ᾽κ Πλευρίτιδος Κινησίας
> σκελετός, ἄπυγος, καλάμινα σκέλη φορῶν,
> φθόης προφήτης, ἐσχάρας κεκαυμένος
> 5 πλείστας ὑπ᾽ Εὐρυφῶντος ἐν τῷ σώματι

2 Kock: Εὐαγόρου ὁ παῖς ἐκ πλ. K. codd.: ὁ Διαγόρου παῖς ἦλθεν οὐκ Πλ.
Kaibel   3 Meineke: ἄπνος codd.: διάπνος Jouanna

9 Lys. 21. 20 (p. 244 Thalheim)

καὶ ὧν Κινησίας οὕτω διακείμενος πλείους στρα-
τείας ἐστράτευται, οὗτοι περὶ τῶν τῆς πόλεως ἀγανα-
κτοῦσι.

the rest of mankind. To die or to be ill in a normal way is the common lot of us all; but to continue for so long in such a condition and to die every day without being able to end one's life is appropriate only for those who have committed such crimes as he has.' This, then, is what the orator said about Cinesias.[5]

[5] See also Harpocration, *Suda* s.v. Kinesias.

8 Galen, *On the aphorisms of Hippocrates*

That the ancients regularly cauterised people with suppurating wounds can be learned from what Plato the comic poet says about Cinesias in this speech: 'next, the son of Oeagrus[1] by Pleurisy, Cinesias, skin and bone, no buttocks, legs like reeds, spokesman of consumption,[2] scabs burned all over his body by Euryphon.'[3]

[1] Text uncertain: 'the son of Oeagrus' was Orpheus; perhaps 'the son of Diagoras' as being an atheist.　　[2] Cf. fr. 775.
[3] Famous physician from Cnidos.

OTHER CONTEMPORARY MATERIAL[1]

9 Lysias, *Defence against a charge of taking bribes*

Why, Cinesias — and we know what he is like — has served on more campaigns than they[2] have, yet they are the ones who wax indignant over the city's fortunes.

[1] See also Timotheus 778(b).　　[2] The accusers.

10 *I.G.* II² 3028

]ατος Φαληρεὺς ἐχ[ορήγε . . .], Κινησίας ἐδίδ[ασκε].

11 Pl. *Gorg.* 501e–502a

ΣΩ. τί δὲ ἡ τῶν χορῶν διδασκαλία καὶ ἡ τῶν διθυράμ-
βων ποίησις; οὐ τοιαύτη τίς σοι καταφαίνεται; ἢ ἡγῇ
τι φροντίζειν Κινησίαν τὸν Μέλητος ὅπως ἐρεῖ τι τοι-
οῦτον ὅθεν ἂν οἱ ἀκούοντες βελτίους γίγνοιντο, ἢ ὅτι
μέλλει χαριεῖσθαι τῷ ὄχλῳ τῶν θεατῶν;
ΚΑΛ. δῆλον δὴ τοῦτό γε, ὦ Σώκρατες, Κινησίου γε
πέρι.
ΣΩ. τί δὲ ὁ πατὴρ αὐτοῦ Μέλης; ἢ πρὸς τὸ βέλτιστον
βλέπων ἐδόκει σοι κιθαρῳδεῖν; ἢ ἐκεῖνος μὲν οὐδὲ πρὸς
τὸ ἥδιστον; ἠνία γὰρ ᾄδων τοὺς θεατάς.

---

[1] I.e. they aim only to give pleasure.   [2] Cf. Pherecrates fr. 6
K.-A. (from the *Savages*, produced in 420 B.C.): 'Who was the worst
cithara-singer?' 'Meles, son of Peisias.' Aristides concedes that he
enjoyed Plato's satire of Cinesias and Meles (3.627 Behr: cf. 3.614).
See also Plutarch, *Quaest. Conviv.* 7. 8. 3.

10 Athenian inscription

... of Phalerum was the *chorēgos* ..., Cinesias
trained the chorus.[1]

[1] He would also have composed the work, presumably a dithyramb,
which won the competition. Another marble slab (*I.G.* II² 18)
records that in 393 B.C. C. moved in the Council that compliment be
paid to Dionysius I, tyrant of Syracuse, and his brothers and
brother-in-law; see M. N. Tod, *Greek Historical Inscriptions* vol. II
no. 108.

LATER MATERIAL

11 Plato, *Gorgias*

Socrates. What about the training of choruses and
the composition of dithyrambs? Don't you think it is
the same with them[1]? Or do you imagine that
Cinesias, the son of Meles, has any thought of say-
ing something that will make his audience better
men, or only of what is likely to gratify the crowd of
spectators?
Callicles. Clearly the latter, Socrates, in the case of
Cinesias.
Socrates. What about his father, Meles? Did you
think that when he sang to the cithara his motives
were the best? Or did he not even aim at giving the
greatest pleasure? His singing used to distress the
spectators.[2]

12 Plut. *de glor. Athen.* 5. 348b (2. 2. 129 Nachstädt)

ἐπικῆς μὲν οὖν ποιήσεως ἡ πόλις οὐκ ἔσχηκεν ἔνδοξον δημιουργὸν οὐδὲ μελικῆς· ὁ γὰρ Κινησίας ἀργαλέος ἔοικε ποιητὴς γεγονέναι διθυράμβων· καὶ αὐτὸς μὲν ἄγονος καὶ ἀκλεὴς γέγονε, σκωπτόμενος δὲ καὶ χλευαζόμενος ὑπὸ τῶν κωμῳδιοποιῶν οὐκ εὐτυχοῦς δόξης μετέσχηκε.

13 Apostol. 15. 89 (ii 652 Leutsch-Schneidewin)

τὰ Κινησίου δρᾷ· ἐπὶ τῶν μαλακῶν· τοιοῦτος γὰρ ὁ Κινησίας ἦν.

12 Plutarch, *On the fame of the Athenians*

Certainly Athens had no famous writer of epic or of lyric poetry; for Cinesias seems to have been a painfully bad dithyrambic poet: he lacked both descendants and distinction, but because he was jeered and mocked by the comic poets he won his share of an unfortunate fame.

13 Apostolius, *Proverbs*

'He does what Cinesias does': used of effeminates, since that is what Cinesias was.[1]

[1] So scholiast on Ar. *Eccl.* 330, but Ar.'s text gives no ground for the assertion.

CINESIAS

FRAGMENTA

774 Philodem. *De Piet.* (p. 52 Gomperz: v. A. Henrichs, *Cronache ercolanesi* 5 (1975) 8s.)

Ἀσκληπιὸ[ν δὲ Ζ]εὺς ἐκεραύνωσ[εν, ὡς μ]ὲν ὁ τὰ Ναυπα[κτι]ακὰ συνγράψας (fr. 3B Davies) [κὰ]ν Ἀσκληπιῶ[ι Τελ]έστης καὶ Κεινη[σίας] ὁ μελοποιός, ὅ[τι τὸ]ν Ἱππόλυτον [παρα]κληθεὶς ὑπ' Ἀρ[τέμι]δος ἀνέστ[η]σε[ν, ὡς δ'] ἐν Ἐριφύληι Σ[τησίχορ]ος ὅτι Καπ[ανέα καὶ Λυ]κοῦρ[γον . . .

775 Athen. 12. 551d (iii 216 Kaibel)

ἦν δ' ὄντως λεπτότατος καὶ μακρότατος ὁ Κινησίας, εἰς ὃν καὶ ὅλον δρᾶμα γέγραφεν Στράττις, Φθιώτην Ἀχιλλέα αὐτὸν καλῶν διὰ τὸ ἐν τῇ αὐτοῦ ποιήσει συνεχῶς τὸ

Φθιῶτα

λέγειν. παίζων οὖν εἰς τὴν ἰδέαν αὐτοῦ ἔφη· Φθιῶτ' Ἀχιλλεῦ (fr. 17 K.-A.).

776 Erotian. (p. 75 (Nachmanson)

ῥαιβοειδέστατον· καμπυλώτατον. ῥαιβὸν γὰρ καὶ γαῦσον τὸ στρεβλὸν λέγεται. . . . †πλασίων† ἐπὶ τοῦ κατά τι μὲν κοίλου, κατά τι δὲ καμπύλου, ὡς Κινησίας τάσσει τὴν λέξιν.

CINESIAS

774 Philodemus, *On Piety*

Zeus killed Asclepius with his thunderbolt, according to the author of the *Naupactica* and Telestes in his *Asclepius* (fr. 807) and Cinesias the lyric poet, because he raised Hippolytus from the dead at Artemis' request; according to Stesichorus in his *Eriphyle* (fr. 194), it was because he raised Capaneus and Lycurgus . . .

775 Athenaeus, *Scholars at Dinner*[1]

Cinesias really was very thin and very tall. Strattis wrote a whole play about him,[2] calling him 'Phthian Achilles' since he often used the vocative form

Phthian

in his poetry. So Strattis in mockery of his physical appearance[3] addressed him as 'Phthian Achilles'.

[1] See test. 7.   [2] See test. 5 (schol.).   [3] With a pun on *phthisis*, 'consumption'.

776 Erotian, *Glossary to Hippocrates*

ῥαιβοειδέστατον ('very crooked-looking'): very bent, for what is twisted can be called ῥαιβός or γαῦσος (by Hippocrates); . . . of what is partly hollow, partly bent, as Cinesias uses the word.[1]

[1] Text corrupt: presumably C. used the word ῥαιβός.

61

PHRYNIS

TESTIMONIA VITAE ATQUE ARTIS

1 Pherecrates fr. 155. 14ss. Kassel-Austin = [Plut.] *Mus.*
30. 1141f

 Φρῦνις δ᾽ ἴδιον στρόβιλον ἐμβαλών τινα
15 κάμπτων με καὶ στρέφων ὅλην διέφθορεν,
 ἐν πέντε χορδαῖς δώδεχ᾽ ἁρμονίας ἔχων.
 ἀλλ᾽ οὖν ἔμοιγε χοῦτος ἦν ἀποχρῶν ἀνήρ·
 εἰ γάρ τι κἀξήμαρτεν, αὖτις ἀνέλαβεν.
 ὁ δὲ Τιμόθεος . . .

16 π. χ. a² A² Barb.: πενταχόρδαις vel -χορδαῖς vel -χόρδοις cett.
ἑπτὰ χ. Burette, ἐννέα χ. Ulrici

2 Ar. *Nub.* 969ss.

 εἰ δέ τις αὐτῶν βωμολοχεύσαιτ᾽ ἢ κάμψειέν τινα
  καμπὴν
 οἵας οἱ νῦν, τὰς κατὰ Φρῦνιν ταύτας τὰς δυσκολο-
  κάμπτους,
 ἐπετρίβετο τυπτόμενος πολλὰς ὡς τὰς Μούσας
  ἀφανίζων.

PHRYNIS

LIFE AND WORK[1]

1 Pherecrates, *Cheiron*[2]

Phrynis on the other hand thrust in a peg of his own[3] and by twisting me and turning me[4] made a complete wreck of me, with a dozen tunings on five strings.[5] But *he* was all right with me, for if he did make a mistake, he corrected it again. Timotheus on the other hand . . .[6]

[1] See also Timotheus 802.   [2] Continued from Cinesias test. 1: Music is complaining of her sexual mauling. For the *double entendre* see E. K. Borthwick, *Hermes* 96 (1968) 67 ff.   [3] A device for the rapid raising or lowering of pitch? The noun can mean 'pine-cone' or 'whirlwind'.   [4] See Cinesias test. 1 n. 2.   [5] Text uncertain: perhaps 'in his pentachords' (two conjunct pentachords on nine strings) or 'on seven strings' or 'on nine strings' (see test. 5).   [6] Concluded at Timotheus test. 1.

2 Aristophanes, *Clouds*

And if any of the boys fooled around or performed the kind of twist[1] they perform nowadays, one of those real twisters, Phrynis-fashion, he would get a thorough hammering for doing away with the Muses.

[1] See Cinesias test. 1 n. 2.

GREEK LYRIC

Schol. ad loc. (p. 187s. Holwerda)

971a. α   ὁ Φρῦνις κιθαρῳδὸς Μιτυληναῖος. οὗτος
δὲ δοκεῖ πρῶτος παρ' Ἀθηναίοις κιθαρῳδικῇ νικῆσαι
Παναθήναια ἐπὶ Καλλιμάχου (M. H. E. Meyer: Καλ-
λίου codd.) ἄρχοντος. ἦν δὲ Ἀριστοκλείτου μαθητής.
ὁ δὲ Ἀριστόκλειτος τὸ γένος ἦν ἀπὸ Τερπάνδρου,
ἤκμασε δὲ ἐν τῇ Ἑλλάδι κατὰ τὰ Μηδικά. παρα-
λαβὼν δὲ τὸν Φρῦνιν αὐλῳδοῦντα κιθαρίζειν ἐδίδαξεν.
ὁ δὲ Ἴστρος (F.Gr.H. 334. 56) Ἱέρωνος αὐτόν φησι
μάγειρον ὄντα σὺν ἄλλοις δοθῆναι τῷ Ἀριστοκλείτῳ.
ταῦτα δὲ σχεδιάσαι ἔοικεν· εἰ γὰρ ἦν γεγονὼς δοῦλος
καὶ μάγειρος Ἱέρωνος, οὐκ ἂν ἀπέκρυψαν οἱ κωμικοὶ
πολλάκις αὐτοῦ μεμνημένοι ἐφ' οἷς ἐκαινούργησε
κλάσας τὴν ᾠδὴν παρὰ τὸ ἀρχαῖον ἔθος, ὡς Ἀριστο-
φάνης φησὶ καὶ Φερεκράτης (Burges: Ἀριστοκράτης
codd.).
971b ἦν δὲ γύννις καὶ ψυχρός.

cf. Sud. Φ 761, Poll. 4.66

3 Aristot. Metaph. a 1. 993b. 15 (p. 34 Jaeger)

εἰ μὲν γὰρ Τιμόθεος μὴ ἐγένετο, πολλὴν ἂν μελο-
ποιίαν οὐκ εἴχομεν· εἰ δὲ μὴ Φρῦνις, Τιμόθεος οὐκ ἂν
ἐγένετο.

PHRYNIS

Scholiast on the passage

Phrynis was a cithara-singer from Mytilene. He seems to have been the first to win the Panathenaic cithara-singing prize in Athens in the archonship of Callimachus[1] (446/5 B.C.). He was a pupil of Aristocleitus, who was descended from Terpander and flourished in Greece at the time of the Persian Wars: he took over Phrynis, who had previously sung to pipe accompaniment, and taught him cithara-playing. Ister[2] says he was Hiero's cook and was given to Aristocleitus along with some others; but he seems to have invented the story, for if Phrynis had really been Hiero's slave and cook, the comic poets would not have concealed the fact, and they often mention him for the innovations with which he changed the character of ancient song and made it effeminate: see Aristophanes and Pherecrates.[3]

[1] 'Callias' in mss.; see J. A. Davison, *J.H.S.* 78 (1958) 40 f.
[2] 3rd c. B.C. Attic historian from Cyrene, in his work *On the Lyric Poets.*   [3] 'Aristocrates' in mss. The scholiast adds that Phrynis was himself effeminate and 'cold', i.e. a feeble composer.

3 Aristotle, *Metaphysics*

For if there had been no Timotheus, we should be without much lyric poetry; but if there had been no Phrynis, there would have been no Timotheus.

4 [Plut.] *Mus.* 6. 1133b (p. 113 Lasserre, vi 3. 5s. Ziegler)

τὸ δ' ὅλον ἡ μὲν κατὰ Τέρπανδρον κιθαρῳδία καὶ
μέχρι τῆς Φρύνιδος ἡλικίας παντελῶς ἁπλῆ τις οὖσα
διετέλει· οὐ γὰρ ἐξῆν τὸ παλαιὸν οὕτως ποιεῖσθαι τὰς
κιθαρῳδίας ὡς νῦν οὐδὲ μεταφέρειν τὰς ἁρμονίας καὶ
τοὺς ῥυθμούς· ἐν γὰρ τοῖς νόμοις ἑκάστῳ διετήρουν
τὴν οἰκείαν τάσιν.

5 Procl. *Chrest.* (ap. Phot. *Bibl.* p. 320b Bekker, v 160s.
Henry)

δοκεῖ δὲ Τέρπανδρος μὲν πρῶτος τελειῶσαι τὸν
νόμον, ἡρῴῳ μέτρῳ χρησάμενος, ἔπειτα Ἀρίων ὁ
Μηθυμναῖος οὐκ ὀλίγα συναυξῆσαι, αὐτὸς καὶ ποιητὴς
καὶ κιθαρῳδὸς γενόμενος. Φρῦνις δὲ ὁ Μιτυληναῖος
ἐκαινοτόμησεν αὐτόν· τό τε γὰρ ἑξάμετρον τῷ λελυ-
μένῳ συνῆψε καὶ χορδαῖς τῶν ζ' πλείοσιν ἐχρήσατο.
Τιμόθεος δὲ ὕστερον εἰς τὴν νῦν αὐτὸν ἤγαγε τάξιν.

6 Plut. *Prof. Virt.* 13. 84a (Paton-Wegehaupt i 167)

Φρῦνιν μὲν γὰρ οἱ ἔφοροι ταῖς ἑπτὰ χορδαῖς δύο
παρεντεινάμενον ἠρώτων πότερον τὰς ἄνωθεν ἢ τὰς
κάτωθεν ἐκτεμεῖν αὐτοῖς ἐθέλει παρασχεῖν.

4 'Plutarch', *On Music*

To put it briefly, cithara-singing in the style of Terpander continued to be completely simple right down to the time of Phrynis; for in the olden days it was not allowed to sing to the cithara as they do now, nor to modulate the tunings and rhythms: in each of the nomes they kept to the pitch that belonged to it.

5 Proclus, *Chrestomathy*

Terpander seems to have been the first to perfect the nome by his use of the heroic metre; next, Arion of Methymna, both poet and cithara-singer, seems to have made important developments. Phrynis of Mytilene made innovations in it: he combined the hexameter with loose rhythm, and he used more strings than the traditional seven. Timotheus later brought it to its present form.

6 Plutarch, *How a man may sense his progress in virtue*

When Phrynis added two strings to the traditional seven, the ephors asked him whether he wished to have them cut out the top two or the bottom two.[1]

[1] Cf. *Agis* 10. 4, where Plut. says that the ephor Ecprepes cut out two strings with an adze and that the ephors did the same to Timotheus. See also *Apoph. Lac.* 8. 220c and *Inst. Lac.* 17. 238c (= Tim. test. 7).

7 Athen. 14. 638bc (iii 409 Kaibel)

καὶ μοχθηρῶν δὲ ᾀσμάτων γεγόνασι ποιηταί, περὶ
ὧν φησι Φαινίας ὁ Ἐρέσιος ἐν τοῖς πρὸς τοὺς σοφιστὰς
(F.H.G. ii 299; fr. 10 Wehrli) γράφων οὕτως· ʽΤελέ-
νικος ὁ Βυζάντιος, ἔτι δὲ Ἀργᾶς ποιηταὶ μοχθηρῶν
ὄντες νόμων πρὸς μὲν τὸν ἴδιον χαρακτῆρα τῆς ποιή-
σεως εὐπόρουν, τῶν δὲ Τερπάνδρου καὶ Φρύνιδος νό-
μων οὐδὲ κατὰ μικρὸν ἠδύναντο ἐπιψαῦσαι.ʼ

PHRYNIS

7 Athenaeus, *Scholars at Dinner*

There have also been composers of indecent songs: Phaenias of Eresus says of them in his work *Against the Sophists*, 'Telenicus of Byzantium and also Argas, composers of indecent nomes, were successful enough in their own style of poetry but came nowhere near the nomes of Terpander and Phrynis.'

TIMOTHEUS

TESTIMONIA VITAE ATQUE ARTIS

1 Pherecrates fr. 155 Kassel-Austin = [Plut.] *Mus.* 30. 1141f–42a

ὁ δὲ Τιμόθεός μ', ὦ φιλτάτη, κατορώρυχε
20 καὶ διακέκναικ' αἴσχιστα. (Δικ.) ποῖος οὑτοσὶ
<ὁ> Τιμόθεος; (Μουσ.) Μιλήσιός τις πυρρίας.
κακά μοι παρέσχεν οὗτος, ἅπαντας οὓς λέγω
παρελήλυθεν, ἄγων ἐκτραπέλους μυρμηκιάς.
κἂν ἐντύχῃ πού μοι βαδιζούσῃ μόνῃ,
25 ἀπέδυσε κἀνέλυσε χορδαῖς δώδεκα

ἐξαρμονίους ὑπερβολαίους τ' ἀνοσίους
καὶ νιγλάρους, ὥσπερ τε τὰς ῥαφάνους ὅλην
καμπῶν με κατεμέστωσε.

25 ἀπέδυσε Wyttenbach: ἀπέλυσε codd.   28 Elmsley: κάμπτων codd.

TIMOTHEUS

LIFE AND WORK[1]

1 Pherecrates, *Cheiron*[2]

Music. Timotheus on the other hand, my dear, dug me deep and ruined me shamefully.

Justice. Which Timotheus is this?

Music. A red-haired Milesian. *He* brought me trouble, far worse than all those others, with his outlandish ant-runs[3]; and if he met me walking somewhere on my own, he stripped me and slackened me with his twelve strings[4]; ... exharmonic, high-pitched, unholy trills, and filled me full of wrigglers[5] like a cabbage.

[1] See also Phrynis test. 3; fr. 791. 202 ff. [2] Continued from Phrynis test. 1. [3] I.e. his meandering melodies. [4] The text of 'Plutarch' goes on to mention Aristophanes' mockery of Philoxenus (see Philox. test. 5), and it is uncertain whether the words 'exharmonic ... cabbage' refer to Timotheus or to Philoxenus. [5] The word means both 'twists' (i.e. modulations: see Cinesias test. 1 n. 2) and 'caterpillars'.

2 *Sud.* T 620 (iv 556s. Adler)

Τιμόθεος, Θερσάνδρου ἢ Νεομούσου ἢ Φιλοπόλιδος, Μιλήσιος, λυρικός· ὃς τὴν ι΄ καὶ ια΄ χορδὴν προσέθηκε καὶ τὴν ἀρχαίαν μουσικὴν ἐπὶ τὸ μαλακώτερον μετήγαγεν. ἦν δὲ ἐπὶ τῶν Εὐριπίδου χρόνων τοῦ τραγικοῦ, καθ᾽ οὓς καὶ Φίλιππος ὁ Μακεδὼν ἐβασίλευεν· καὶ ἐτελεύτησεν ἐτῶν ϙζ΄, γράψας δι᾽ ἐπῶν νόμους μουσικοὺς ιθ΄, προοίμια λς΄, Ἄρτεμιν, διασκευὰς η΄, ἐγκώμια, Πέρσας [[ἢ del. Bernhardy]] Ναύπλιον, Φινείδας, Λαέρτην, διθυράμβους ιη΄, ὕμνους κα΄ καὶ ἄλλα τινά.

3 Diod. Sic. 14. 46. 6 (iii 256 Vogel)

ἤκμασαν δὲ κατὰ τοῦτον τὸν ἐνιαυτὸν οἱ ἐπισημότατοι διθυραμβοποιοί, Φιλόξενος Κυθήριος, Τιμόθεος Μιλήσιος, Τελέστης Σελινούντιος, Πολύειδος ὃς καὶ ζωγραφικῆς καὶ μουσικῆς εἶχεν ἐμπειρίαν.

2 Suda

Timotheus: son of Thersander or of Neomusus or of Philopolis,[1] from Miletus, lyric poet. He added the tenth and eleventh strings to the lyre, and he made the old-fashioned music more effeminate. He lived at the time of the tragedian Euripides,[2] when Philip of Macedon was king.[3] He died at the age of ninety-seven, having written 19 musical nomes in hexameters, 36 preludes, the *Artemis*,[4] 8 adaptations, encomia, *The Persians*,[5] *Nauplius*,[6] *The Sons of Phineus*, *Laertes*, 18 dithyrambs, 21 hymns and other works.

[1] The last two are unlikely to be authentic. [2] C. 485–c. 406 B.C. See test. 6 and the epitaph attributed to T. [3] Philip II, king 359–336 B.C. For T.'s exchange with Archelaus (king 413–399) see fr. 801. [4] See fr. 778. [5] See frr. 788–91. [6] See fr. 785.

CHRONOLOGY[1]

3 Diodorus Siculus, *World History*

In that year (398 B.C.) the most distinguished dithyrambic poets were in their prime, Philoxenus of Cythera, Timotheus of Miletus, Telestes of Selinus and Polyidus, who was also an expert in painting and music.

[1] See also test. 2.

4 *Marm. Par.* Ep. 76 (p. 19 Jacoby)

ἀφ᾽ οὗ Τιμόθεος βιώσας ἔτη ΓΔΔΔΔ ἐτελεύτησεν,
ἔτ[η . . .

5 Steph. Byz. (p. 452s. Meineke)

Μίλητος· . . . ὁ πολίτης Μιλήσιος. οὕτω καὶ Θαλῆς
Ἐξαμύου πατρὸς Μιλήσιος ἐχρημάτιζε καὶ Φωκυλίδης
καὶ Τιμόθεος κιθαρῳδός, ὃς ἐποίησε νόμων κιθαρῳδι-
κῶν βίβλους ὀκτωκαίδεκα εἰς ἐπῶν ὀκτακισχιλίων τὸν
ἀριθμόν, καὶ προνόμια ἄλλων χίλια. θνῄσκει δ᾽ ἐν
Μακεδονίᾳ. ἐπιγέγραπται δ᾽ αὐτῷ τόδε (*F.G.E.* anon.
cxxiv a)·

πάτρα Μίλητος τίκτει Μούσαισι ποθεινὸν
    Τιμόθεον κιθάρας δεξιὸν ἡνίοχον.

6 P. Oxy. 1176 fr. 39 col. xxii

. . . [καταφρονουμένου e.g. Edmonds] τοῦ Τιμοθέου
παρὰ τ[οῖ]ς Ἕλλη[σι]ν διὰ [τ]ὴν ἐν τῆι μου[σι]κῆ[ι]
καινοτομίαν καὶ καθ᾽ ὑπερβολὴν ἀθυμήσαντος ὥστε
κα[ὶ] τὰς χεῖρας ἑαυτῶι διεγνωκέναι προσφέρειν,
μόνος Εὐριπίδης ἀνάπαλιν τῶν μὲν θεατῶν καταγελά-
σαι, τὸν δὲ Τιμόθεον α[ἰσ]θόμενος ἡλίκος ἐστὶν ἐν τῶι

4 *Parian Marble*

From the time when Timotheus died, having lived ninety years, . . .[1]

[1] The figure is lost, but the date lies between 366/5 and 357/6.

BIRTHPLACE[1]

5 Stephanus of Byzantium, *Places and Peoples* (on Miletus)

The inhabitants are called Milesian, e.g. Thales, son of Examyas, and Phocylides and Timotheus the cithara-singer, who composed 18 books of nomes for cithara-singing, 8,000 hexameters in all, and pro-nomes, another 1,000 lines. He died in Macedonia, and his epitaph is as follows: 'Miletus was the motherland of Timotheus whom the Muses loved, skilful charioteer of the lyre.'

[1] For a statue-base inscribed 'Timotheus of Miletus', found in Pergamum, see G. M. A. Richter, *The Portraits of the Greeks* i 145.

TIMOTHEUS AND EURIPIDES

6 Satyrus, *Life of Euripides*

When Timotheus (was despised?) among the Greeks for his musical innovation and was so deeply depressed that he had decided to take his own life, Euripides was the only one to laugh at the audiences instead, and realising how great a composer

γένει παραμυθήσασθαί τε λόγους διεξιὼν ὡς οἷόν τε
παρακλητικωτάτους καὶ δὴ καὶ τὸ τῶν Περσῶν προ-
οίμιον συγγράψαι, τῶι (Wilamowitz: τοῦ pap.) τε
νικῆ[σ]αι παύσασθ[αι] καταφ[ρ]ο[νούμ]ενον [. . . . .
τὸ]ν Τι[μόθεον . . .

7 Plut. *Inst. Lac.* 17. 238c (ii 209 Nachstädt)

Τιμοθέου δ᾽ ἀγωνιζομένου τὰ Κάρνεια, εἷς τῶν
ἐφόρων μάχαιραν λαβὼν ἠρώτησεν αὐτὸν ἐκ ποτέρου
τῶν μερῶν ἀποτέμῃ τὰς πλείους τῶν ἑπτὰ χορδῶν.

---

[1] See also Melanippides test. 6, Philoxenus test. 6, Polyidus testt.
2, 3.   [2] Continued from Terpander test. 17, where Plut. says
the ephors fined Terp. for adding one string; see also Phrynis test.
6.   [3] For T. and Sparta see fr. 791. 206 ff.; T. speaks of his 11
strings (*ibid.* 230): so Paus. 3. 12. 10, Nicomachus 4 (*Mus. Scr. Gr.*

8 [Plut.] *Mus.* 12. 1135cd (p. 116 Lasserre, vi 3. 11
Ziegler)

ἔστι δὲ <καὶ> τις Ἀλκμανικὴ καινοτομία καὶ Στη-
σιχόρειος, καὶ αὗται οὐκ ἀφεστῶσαι τοῦ καλοῦ. Κρέξος
δὲ καὶ Τιμόθεος καὶ Φιλόξενος καὶ οἱ κατὰ ταύτην τὴν
ἡλικίαν γεγονότες ποιηταὶ φορτικώτεροι καὶ φιλόκαι-
νοι γεγόνασι, τὸ (Ziegler: τὸν codd.) φιλάνθρωπον καὶ
θεματικὸν νῦν ὀνομαζόμενον διώξαντες (ἐκδιώξαντες
Na)· τὴν γὰρ ὀλιγοχορδίαν (Valgulius: -χορείαν
codd.) τε καὶ τὴν ἁπλότητα καὶ σεμνότητα τῆς μουσι-
κῆς παντελῶς ἀρχαϊκὴν εἶναι συμβέβηκεν.

Timotheus was in his chosen genre he encouraged him with the most comforting arguments possible[1] and even composed the prelude to *The Persians*, with the result that Timotheus won the prize and was despised no longer.

[1] Cf. Plut. *an seni* 23.

MUSIC AND METRE[1]

7 Plutarch, *Spartan Customs*[2]

When Timotheus was competing at the Carnea, one of the ephors took a knife and asked him from which end he should cut off the strings that exceeded the traditional seven.[3]

p. 274 Jan); the text of Pherecrates attributes 12 to both T. (test. 1) and Melanippides (test. 6); see also Cic. *Leg.* 2. 15. 39, Pliny *N.H.* 7. 56. 204, Dio Chrys. 33. 57, 'Plutarch' *Mus.* 30. 1141c (= Terp. test. 16), Athen. 14. 636ef, 'Censorinus', *Gramm. Lat.* vi 610 Keil, Boethius *Mus.* 1. 1. 182.

8 'Plutarch', *On Music*

There is also a certain originality (sc. in metre) in Alcman and Stesichorus, although their innovations do not abandon the noble manner either; but Crexus, Timotheus, Philoxenus and the other poets of their time were more vulgar and fond of novelty, aiming for what is now called the popular and money-spinning style: the use of few strings and simplicity and dignity in music have dropped out of fashion completely.

9 [Plut.] *Mus.* 4. 1132e (p. 113 Lasserre, vi 3. 4 Ziegler)

ὅτι δ' οἱ κιθαρῳδικοὶ νόμοι οἱ πάλαι ἐξ ἐπῶν
συνίσταντο Τιμόθεος ἐδήλωσε· τοὺς γοῦν πρώτους
νόμους ἐν ἔπεσι διαμιγνύων διθυραμβικὴν λέξιν ᾖδεν,
ὅπως μὴ εὐθὺς φανῇ παρανομῶν εἰς τὴν ἀρχαίαν
μουσικήν.

10 Dion. Hal. *Comp.* 19 (vi 85s. Usener-Radermacher)

οἱ μὲν οὖν ἀρχαῖοι μελοποιοί, λέγω δὲ Ἀλκαῖόν τε
καὶ Σαπφώ, μικρὰς ἐποιοῦντο στροφάς, ὥστ' ἐν ὀλί-
γοις τοῖς κώλοις οὐ πολλὰς εἰσῆγον μεταβολάς, ἐπῳ-
δοῖς τε πάνυ ἐχρῶντο ὀλίγοις. οἱ δὲ περὶ Στησίχορόν
τε καὶ Πίνδαρον μείζους ἐργασάμενοι τὰς περιόδους εἰς
πολλὰ μέτρα καὶ κῶλα διένειμαν αὐτὰς οὐκ ἄλλου
τινὸς ἢ τῆς μεταβολῆς ἔρωτι. οἱ δέ γε διθυραμβοποιοὶ
καὶ τοὺς τρόπους μετέβαλλον, Δωρίους τε καὶ Φρυ-
γίους καὶ Λυδίους ἐν τῷ αὐτῷ ᾄσματι ποιοῦντες· καὶ
τὰς μελῳδίας ἐξήλλαττον, τοτὲ μὲν ἐναρμονίους ποι-
οῦντες, τοτὲ δὲ χρωματικάς, τοτὲ δὲ διατόνους· καὶ
τοῖς ῥυθμοῖς κατὰ πολλὴν ἄδειαν ἐνεξουσιάζοντες
διετέλουν, οἵ γε δὴ κατὰ Φιλόξενον καὶ Τιμόθεον καὶ
Τελέστην· ἐπεὶ παρά γε τοῖς ἀρχαίοις τεταγμένος ἦν
καὶ ὁ διθύραμβος.

9 'Plutarch', *On Music*

That the ancient nomes for cithara-singing were composed in hexameters was shown by Timotheus: at any rate he sang his first nomes in hexameters with a mixture of dithyrambic diction, so that it would not be obvious from the outset that he was a transgressor against the laws of ancient music.[1]

[1] For T.'s nomes see also Phrynis test. 5, Clem. Alex. *Strom.* 1. 16. 78. 5.

10 Dionysius of Halicarnassus, *On Literary Composition*

The ancient lyric poets, I mean Alcaeus and Sappho, made their stanzas short, so they did not introduce many variations in their few colons, and they used the 'epode' or shorter line very sparingly. But Stesichorus, Pindar and the like made their periods longer and divided them into many metres and colons for the sheer love of variety. The dithyrambic poets actually changed the tunings also, using Dorian, Phrygian and Lydian in the same song; they varied the melodies, making them now enharmonic, now chromatic, now diatonic; and in the matter of rhythm they always went their own way and used great licence. The poets I mean are the school of Philoxenus and Timotheus and Telestes: among the ancients the dithyramb too had been composed in accordance with strict rules.

11 Heph. *Poem.* iii (3) (p. 64s. Consbruch)

ἀπολελυμένα δὲ ἃ εἰκῆ γέγραπται καὶ ἄνευ μέτρου ὡρισμένου, οἷοί εἰσιν οἱ νόμοι οἱ κιθαρῳδικοὶ Τιμοθέου.

12 Themist. *Or.* 26. 316e (p. 382 Dindorf, ii 127 Norman)

καὶ τῇ γραφικῇ οὐδὲν εἰσήνεγκεν Ἀπέλλης οὐδὲ Τέρπανδρος τῇ κιθάρᾳ οὐδὲ Τιμόθεος τοῖς αὐλοῖς;

13 Polyb. 4. 20. 8–9 (ii 27 Büttner-Wobst)

ταῦτα γὰρ πᾶσίν ἐστι γνώριμα καὶ συνήθη διότι σχεδὸν παρὰ μόνοις Ἀρκάσι πρῶτον μὲν οἱ παῖδες ἐκ νηπίων ᾄδειν ἐθίζονται κατὰ νόμους τοὺς ὕμνους καὶ παιᾶνας οἷς ἕκαστοι κατὰ τὰ πάτρια τοὺς ἐπιχωρίους ἥρωας καὶ θεοὺς ὑμνοῦσι· μετὰ δὲ ταῦτα τοὺς Φιλοξένου καὶ Τιμοθέου νόμους μανθάνοντες . . .

14 *C.I.G.* 3053 = Schwyzer 190

. . . ἐπεὶ . . . ἐπεδείξατο Μενεκλῆς μετὰ κιθάρας πλεονάκις τά τε Τιμοθέω καὶ Πολυΐδω καὶ τῶν ἁμῶν ἀρχαίων ποιητᾶν καλῶς καὶ ὡς προσῆκεν ἀνδρὶ πεπαιδευμένωι . . .

---

1 Commendation by Cnossus of Herodotus and Menecles, ambassadors sent to Crete from Teos.

11 Hephaestion, *On Poems*

'Free verse' is verse written at random and without definite metre, for example Timotheus' nomes for cithara-singing.

12 Themistius, *Orations*

Did Apelles make no contribution to painting, Terpander none to the cithara, Timotheus none to the pipes?

TIMOTHEUS IN THE 2ND CENTURY B.C.[1]

13 Polybius, *Histories* (on Arcadian virtue)

For everyone is familiar with the fact that in Arcadia and scarcely anywhere else the boys are trained from early childhood first of all to sing according to musical rules the hymns and paeans in which they celebrate in traditional fashion the heroes and gods of each locality; and later they learn the nomes of Philoxenus and Timotheus . . .

[1] For performances of his works in 319 and 207 B.C. see frr. 779, 788.

14 Inscription from Teos[1] (*c.* 170 B.C.)

. . . since . . . Menecles many times performed to his cithara the songs of Timotheus and Polyidus and our (i.e. Cnossian) ancient poets most beautifully and in a manner befitting an educated gentleman . . .

81

TIMOTHEUS

FRAGMENTA

ΑΙΑΣ ΕΜΜΑΝΗΣ

777 Lucian. *Harmonides* 1 (iii 375 Macleod)

... ὥσπερ ὅτε καὶ σύ, ὦ Τιμόθεε, τὸ πρῶτον ἐλθὼν οἴκοθεν ἐκ Βοιωτίας ἐπηύλησας τῇ Πανδιονίδι καὶ ἐνίκησας ἐν τῷ Αἴαντι τῷ ἐμμανεῖ, τοῦ ὁμωνύμου σοι ποιήσαντος τὸ μέλος, οὐδεὶς ἦν ὃς ἠγνόει τοὔνομα, Τιμόθεον ἐκ Θηβῶν.

ΑΡΤΕΜΙΣ

778 (a) Macrob. *Sat.* 5. 22. 4s. (i 342s. Willis)

Alexander Aetolus, poeta egregius, in libro qui inscribitur Musae refert quanto studio populus Ephesius dedicato templo Dianae curaverit praemiis propositis ut qui tunc erant poetae ingeniosissimi in deam carmina diversa componerent. in his versibus Opis non comes Dianae sed Diana ipsa vocitata est. loquitur autem, ut dixi, de populo Ephesio (fr. 4 Powell):

TIMOTHEUS

FRAGMENTS

THE MADNESS OF AJAX

777 Lucian, *Harmonides*[1]

. . . just as when you, Timotheus, first arrived from your home in Boeotia and played the accompaniment for *Pandion's Daughter* and won the prize with your performance of *The Madness of Ajax*, the music for which was composed by your namesake, there was no one who did not know the name of Timotheus of Thebes.

[1] The piper Harmonides is speaking to his teacher Timotheus (*fl.* 330 B.C.).

ARTEMIS[1]

778 (a) Macrobius, *Saturnalia*

The excellent poet Alexander of Aetolia in his book called *The Muses* tells how enthusiastically the people of Ephesus on the dedication of the temple to Diana[2] ensured by the offer of prizes that the most talented poets of the day should compose various songs in honour of the goddess. In Alexander's lines Opis is the name not of a companion of Diana but of Diana herself. He is speaking, as I

[1] See also test. 2.   [2] Perhaps after damage by fire; G. F. Brussich, *Q.U.C.C.* 34 (1990) 25 ff., argues that Tim. composed his poem in 397–396 or at the latest in 395.

ἀλλ' ὅγε πευθόμενος πάγχυ Γραικοῖσι μέλεσθαι
Τιμόθεον κιθάρης ἴδμονα καὶ μελέων
υἱὸν Θερσάνδρου <κλυ>τὸν ἤνεσεν ἀνέρα σίγλων
χρυσείων ἱερὴν δὴ τότε χιλιάδα
ὑμνῆσαι ταχέων τ' Ὦπιν βλήτειραν ὀϊστῶν
ἥ τ' ἐπὶ Κεγχρείῳ τίμιον οἶκον ἔχει,

et mox

μηδὲ θεῆς προλίπῃ Λητωίδος ἄκλεα ἔργα.

(b) Plut. de superstit. 10 (i 350 Paton-Wegehaupt)

τοῦ Τιμοθέου τὴν Ἄρτεμιν ᾄδοντος ἐν Ἀθήναις καὶ λέγοντος

θυιάδα φοιβάδα μαινάδα λυσσάδα

Κινησίας ὁ μελοποιὸς ἐκ τῶν θεατῶν ἀναστὰς 'τοιαύτη σοι' εἶπε
'θυγάτηρ γένοιτο.'

cf. de aud. poet. 4 (μ. θ. φ. λ.)

ΕΛΠΗΝΩΡ

779 C.I.A. 1246 = I.G. ii² 3055

Νι[κ]ί[α]ς Νι[κ]οδήμου Ξυ[π]εταιὼν ἀνέθηκε νικήσας χορηγῶν
Κεκροπίδι παιδων· [Πα]νταλέων Σικυώνιο[ς] ηὔλει, ᾆσμα Ἐλπή-
νωρ Τιμοθέου, Νέ[αιχ]μ[ο]ς ἦρχεν.

said, about the people of Ephesus: 'but hearing that the Greeks held Timotheus, son of Thersander, in high regard for his skill in the cithara and in song, they told the distinguished man to sing in return for gold shekels of the sacred millennium and of Opis the shooter of swift arrows, who has her honoured home on the Cenchreius;[3] and a few lines later, 'and not leave unsung the deeds of Leto's divine daughter.'

[3] River of Ephesus (Strabo 14. 1. 20).

(b) Plutarch, *On superstition*

When Timotheus was singing his *Artemis* in Athens and called the goddess

mantic, frantic, Bacchic, fanatic,[1]

Cinesias the lyric poet stood up in the audience and said, 'May you have a daughter like that!'

[1] The Greek adjectives have identical ending, accentuation and metrical pattern (dactyl).

ELPENOR[1]

779 Athenian inscription

Nicias son of Nicodemus of the deme Xypete made this dedication on his victory as boys' choregus for the tribe Cecropis. Pantaleon of Sicyon was the piper, the song was Timotheus' *Elpenor*, the archon was Neaechmus (320/319 B.C.).

[1] *P.M.G.* 925 was assigned to this poem by del Grande. Elpenor was a companion of Odysseus (*Od.* 10. 552 ff.).

GREEK LYRIC

ΚΥΚΛΩΨ

780 Athen. 11. 465c (iii 13 Kaibel)

Τιμόθεος δ᾽ ἐν Κύκλωπι·

ἔγχευε δ᾽ ἓν μὲν δέπας κίσσινον μελαίνας
σταγόνος ἀμβρότας ἀφρῷ βρυάζον,
εἴκοσιν δὲ μέτρ᾽ ἐνέχευ᾽, ἀνέμισγε
δ᾽ αἷμα Βακχίου νεορρύτοισιν
5 δακρύοισι Νυμφᾶν.

cf. Eustath. Od. 1631.61

1 Bergk: ἔχευεν cod. A   3s. Kaibel (-χευ᾽), Grotefend (αἷμα):
ἀνέχευαν ἔμισγε διαμα A, ἐνέχευεν ἀνέμισγε δ᾽ ἅμα E   4 Page:
νεωρυτως A, -τοις E   5 -ουσι A   νυμφᾶν A, πηγᾶν E

781 Chrysipp. π. ἀποφ. 10 (*S.V.F.* ii 54s. Arnim)

εἰ Κύκλωψ ὁ τοῦ Τιμοθέου πρός τινα οὕτως ἀπεφήνατο·

οὗτοι τόν γ᾽ ὑπεραμπέχοντ᾽ οὐρανὸν εἰσαναβήσει.

782 Aristot. *Poet.* 2. 1448a 11 (p. 5 Kassel)

Ὅμηρος μὲν βελτίους, Κλεοφῶν δὲ ὁμοίους, Ἡγήμων δὲ ὁ
Θάσιος <ὁ> τὰς παρῳδίας ποιήσας πρῶτος καὶ Νικοχάρης ὁ τὴν
Δειλιάδα χείρους· ὁμοίως δὲ καὶ περὶ τοὺς διθυράμβους καὶ περὶ
τοὺς νόμους, ὥσπερ †γᾶς† Κύκλωπας Τιμόθεος καὶ Φιλόξενος
μιμήσαιτο ἄν τις.

ὥσπερ <θεοὺς Ἀρ>γᾶς Castelvetro (Ἀργᾶς), Vahlen (θεοὺς)

TIMOTHEUS

CYCLOPS[1]

780 Athenaeus, *Scholars at Dinner*

Timotheus in his *Cyclops*:

And into it he[2] poured one ivy-wood cup of the dark immortal drops, teeming with foam, and then he poured in twenty measures,[3] and so he mingled the blood of the Bacchic god with the fresh-flowing tears of the Nymphs.

[1] See also *P.M.G.* 840.   [2] Odysseus serves the Cyclops the remarkable wine which he had been given by Maron, priest of Apollo at Ismarus (*Od.* 9. 208 ff.; for the ivy-wood cup cf. 9. 346).   [3] I.e. of water.

781 Chrysippus, *On Negatives*

If[1] Timotheus' Cyclops expressed himself to someone as follows:

Never will you climb up to the heavens that enclose us above.

[1] Part of a Stoic exercise in logic. The Cyclops may be assuring Odysseus that he cannot escape.

782 Aristotle, *Poetics*

Homer represents men as better than they are, Cleophon represents them as they are, Hegemon of Thasos, the first composer of parodies, and Nicochares, composer of the *Deiliad*, as worse. The same is true of dithyrambs and nomes, as in the representation[1] ... of the Cyclops by Timotheus and Philoxenus.

[1] Text defective: perhaps 'of the gods by Argas and of the Cyclops ...'

783 Schol. A Hom. *Il.* 9. 219b (ii 446 Erbse)

ὅτι θῦσαι οὐ σφάξαι, <ὡς> ὁ Τιμόθεος ὑπέλαβεν καὶ Φιλόξενος ὁμοίως τῇ ἡμετέρᾳ συνηθείᾳ, ἀλλὰ θυμᾶσαι.

ΛΑΕΡΤΗΣ

784 *Sud.* T 620 (= test. 2)

Τιμόθεος . . . γράψας . . . Λαέρτην . . .

ΝΑΥΠΛΙΟΣ?

785 *Sud.* T 620 (= test. 2)

Τιμόθεος . . . γράψας . . . Πέρσας, ⟦ἢ del. Bernhardy⟧ Ναύπλιον, Φινείδας, Λαέρτην . . .

Hegesand. *Hypomn.* *(F.H.G.* iv 416) ap. Athen. 8. 338a (ii 242 Kaibel)

ὁ αὐτὸς Δωρίων καταγελῶν τοῦ ἐν τῷ Τιμοθέου Ναυπλίῳ (Casaubon: Ναυτίλῳ codd.) χειμῶνος ἔφασκεν ἐν κακκάβᾳ ζεούσᾳ μείζονα ἑωρακέναι χειμῶνα.

TIMOTHEUS

783 Scholiast on *Iliad* 9. 219

θῦσαι ('to make sacrifice') does not mean 'to slit an animal's throat', as Timotheus and Philoxenus[1] took it just as in our usage, but 'to make a burnt offering'.

[1] Cf. Philox. 823. Bergk assigned the usage to T.'s *Cyclops*.

LAERTES[1]

784 : see *Suda* (test. 2)

[1] Father of Odysseus.

NAUPLIUS[1] ?

785 *Suda* (= test. 2)

(Timotheus wrote) *The Persians, Nauplius,*[2] *The Sons of Phineus, Laertes,* . . .

[1] An Argonaut, father of Palamedes.   [2] Mss. have '*The Persians* or *Nauplius*'.

Hegesander, *Commentaries* (in Athenaeus, *Scholars at Dinner*)

The same Dorion ridiculed the storm in Timotheus' *Nauplius*,[1] saying that he had seen a bigger storm in a boiling pot.

[1] Mss. have *Nautilus*.

NIOBH

786 Macho fr. 9. 81ss. Gow (ap. Athen. 8. 341cd)

ἀλλ' ἐπεὶ
ὁ Τιμοθέου Χάρων σχολάζειν οὐκ ἐᾷ,
οὐκ τῆς Νιόβης, χωρεῖν δὲ πορθμιδ᾽ ἀναβοᾷ,
καλεῖ δὲ μοῖρα νύχιος, ἧς κλύειν χρεών, . . .

cf. Stob. 3. 1. 98 (Teles) (iii 46 Hense) ἔμβα πορθμίδος ἔρυμα

πορθμιδ᾽ Casaubon, Meineke: πορθμὸν Athen. codd.

787 Diog. Laert. 7. 28 (ii 309 Long)

ἐτελεύτα δὴ οὕτως (sc. ὁ Ζήνων)· ἐκ τῆς σχολῆς ἀπιὼν
προσέπταισε καὶ τὸν δάκτυλον περιέρρηξε· παίσας δὲ τὴν γῆν τῇ
χερί φησι τὸ ἐκ τῆς Νιόβης·

ἔρχομαι· τί μ' αὔεις;

καὶ παραχρῆμα ἐτελεύτησεν ἀποπνίξας ἑαυτόν.

cf. 7. 31, *Sud.* A 4420, [Lucian.] *Macrob.* 19, Stob. 3. 7. 44

ΠΕΡΣΑΙ

788 Plut. *vit. Philopoem.* 11 (ii 2. 14 Ziegler)

ἄρτι δ' αὐτῶν εἰσεληλυθότων, κατὰ τύχην Πυλάδην τὸν κιθα-
ρῳδὸν ᾄδοντα τοὺς Τιμοθέου Πέρσας ἐνάρξασθαι·

TIMOTHEUS

NIOBE

786 Machon, *Philoxenus*[1]

'But since Timotheus' Charon, the one in his *Niobe*, does not let me dally but shouts that the ferry-boat is leaving,[2] and gloomy Fate, who must be obeyed, is summoning me, ...'

[1] The speaker in the anecdote is Philoxenus, the dithyrambic poet.   [2] Or 'shouts to me to board the ferry'; a phrase from Teles in Stobaeus, 'board the ferry's ramparts', was ascribed to Timotheus' poem by Bergk.

787 Diogenes Laertius, *Life of Zeno the Stoic*

He died in the following manner: as he was leaving the school he stumbled and broke his toe; striking the ground with his hand he spoke the words from the *Niobe*[1]:

I am coming: why do you call me?

and immediately he died by suffocating himself.

[1] Nauck ascribed the words to Timotheus' *Niobe*, Brunck to Sophocles', Hermann to Aeschylus'.

THE PERSIANS[1]

788 Plutarch, *Life of Philopoemen*

When they had just entered,[2] it happened that the cithara-singer Pylades was performing *The Persians* of Timotheus and began,[3]

[1] See also fr. 1027(f).   [2] Philopoemen, general of the Achaean confederacy, visited the theatre at Nemea with his troops in 207 B.C., shortly after his defeat of the Spartans at Mantinea.   [3] The hexameter may be the first line of the prelude, for which see test. 6.

GREEK LYRIC

κλεινὸν ἐλευθερίας τεύχων μέγαν Ἑλλάδι κόσμον,

ἅμα δὲ τῇ λαμπρότητι τῆς φωνῆς τοῦ περὶ τὴν ποίησιν ὄγκου συμ-
πρέψαντος, ἐπίβλεψιν γενέσθαι τοῦ θεάτρου πανταχόθεν εἰς τὸν
Φιλοποίμενα καὶ κρότον μετὰ χαρᾶς, τῶν Ἑλλήνων τὸ παλαιὸν
ἀξίωμα ταῖς ἐλπίσιν ἀναλαμβανόντων καὶ τοῦ τότε φρονήματος
ἔγγιστα τῷ θαρρεῖν γινομένων.

cf. Paus. 8. 50. 3 (ᾄδοντος Τιμοθέου νόμον τοῦ Μιλησίου Πέρσας καὶ
καταρξαμένου τῆς ᾠδῆς, κλεινὸν . . . κόσμον)

789 Plut. *de aud. poet.* 11 (i 65 Paton-Wegehaupt)

ἀφ' ὧν καὶ Τιμόθεος ὁρμηθεὶς οὐ κακῶς ἐν τοῖς Πέρσαις τοὺς
Ἕλληνας παρεκάλει·

σέβεσθ' αἰδῶ συνεργὸν ἀρετᾶς δοριμάχου.

cf. *de fort. Rom.* 11

790 Plut. *vit. Agesil.* 14. 4 (iii 2. 210 Ziegler)

πολλοῖς ἐπῄει τὰ τοῦ Τιμοθέου λέγειν·

Ἄρης τύραννος· χρυσὸν Ἑλλὰς οὐ δέδοικε.

cf. *vit. Demetr.* 42, Zenob. Ath. ii 47 (Miller, *Mélanges* p. 363),
Menand. fr. 189 Körte, Macar. *cent.* ii 39, *Sud.* A 3853, Hsch. A
7174

δ' Ἑλλὰς codd., δ' del. G. S. Farnell

Fashioning[4] for Greece the great and glorious ornament of freedom;

and thanks to the splendid voice of the singer and the equally conspicuous majesty of the poetry, all the spectators turned their eyes towards Philopoemen, and the Greeks broke into joyful applause, since in their hopes they were recovering their ancient prestige and in their confidence coming close to the spirit of those earlier days.[5]

[4] The reference may be to Themistocles or to the people of Athens. [5] Pausanias, telling the same story, calls the song 'The Persians, a nome of Timotheus the Milesian'.

789 Plutarch, *How the young man should study poetry*

Timotheus based on these lines (*Il.* 16. 422, 13. 121 f.) the splendid exhortation[1] of the Greeks in his *Persians*:

have respect for Shame, the helpmate of spear-fighting Valour.

[1] Perhaps from the speech by Themistocles (Hdt. 8. 83) or from the great shout (of Athena?) heard at Salamis (Aes. *Pers.* 402 ff., Hdt. 8. 84. 2).

790 Plutarch, *Life of Agesilaus*[1]

Many (sc. of the Greeks in Asia Minor) were moved to quote the words of Timotheus:

Ares is lord: Greece has no fear of gold.[2]

[1] Spartan king who defeated Tissaphernes in Phrygia in 395 B.C. [2] This too may be from Themistocles' exhortation. 'Ares is lord' became proverbial.

791 P. Berol. 9875

(col. i) fr. 4. 3 νυμφα.[,　4 ἐπ᾽ [ε]ὐκυκλ[,] ου
ῥόθωι[,　5 ἐπ᾽ [ε]ὐθυφ[,] σκοπεῖν[,　6 συ[ν]-
δρομ[,　12]παλιμμ[　fr. 3. 3]στοιχο[
fr. 7. 4]ε ὀξυ[　fr. 8. 5] ρου κοιλ[　6]λίνοιο
δ . . [,　　8]γυῖα　　fr. 9. 9]ας εἶχον[

[. .] [. .] . [. . . . . .]αντ[ ]νων[ ] . . | σὺν
[ἐμ]βόλο[ι]σι γειτ[. . .]σ[. .]υ[. . . . . . .]αν-
τιαι[. . . . .]πρι[. . .]ν ἐ|χάρα[ξ]αν πο ι δὲ
γε[. . .]λογχο[. . . .] ἀμφέθ[ε]ντ᾽ ὀδόντων |
στο . [.] αιδ[.] κυρτοῖ[σι] κρασὶν [. . . . . . .
5　　　　　　]μεναι [χε]ῖ-
ρας παρέσυρον ἐλα[τίνα]ς·
ἀλλ᾽ εἰ μὲν [ἐ]νθένδ᾽ [ἀπρόσο]ισ-
τος ἐπ[ιφ]έροιτο πλαγὰ
ῥηξί[κωπ]ος, πάντες [ἐπ]ανέ-
10　 πι[πτον] ἐκεῖσε να[ῦ]ται·
εἰ δ᾽ ἀντίτοιχος ἀκτ[ὰ
μῆχ]ος ἄξειεμ [πο]λυκρότο[ιο
πλώ]σιμον πεύκας, πάλιν ἐφέροντο·

omnia suppl. et corr. ed. pr. (Wilamowitz) exceptis quae notan-
tur　3 πο[σ]ὶ Wilamowitz, πο[τ]ὶ Danielsson　7 αδλει pap.
ἀπρόσο]ιστος ci. Page　9 -[κωπ]ος Page　9s. Daniels-
son　11, 12 init., fin., 13 Page

---

1 Of rams?　　2 I.e. the Greek ships would sweep away the
enemy oars.　　3 The oar.

TIMOTHEUS

791 Berlin papyrus (4th c. B.C.)

*Found at Abusir in 1902; first edition by Wilamowitz
(1903). Of the six columns of the roll the first is almost com-
pletely destroyed, the second (vv. 1–59) is badly damaged,
the rest are well preserved; the sixth contains only the final
lines of the poem (vv. 235–240). Since a fragment contain-
ing the upper left-hand corner of col. i shows no title, the
beginning of the poem must have been contained in another
roll: that roll (which would have included frr. 788–790)
must have held about 350 verses, so that the total length of
The Persians will have been about 650 verses. (The figure
assumes only one lost roll.) The text was written continu-
ously as prose: Wilamowitz set it out as 253 verses, Page
(whose line-numbering is used in the present edition) as
240. The most badly damaged portions of coll. ii and iii
(vv. 1–4, 52–59, 110–113) are printed as prose. The theme
of the poem, as in The Persians of Aeschylus, is the Greek
victory at Salamis; much is obscure.*

. . . nymph . . . well-rounded . . . surge . . . straight
. . . look . . . running together . . . back again . . .
column (of ships?) . . . sharp . . . flax (= sail-cloth?)
. . . limbs . . . they had . . .

(there is a gap of several lines)

. . . by means of rams . . . neighbouring . . . facing . . .
(they) furrowed (the water?) . . . spear . . . (they) put
round themselves . . . of teeth . . . bulging heads[1] . . .
they would sweep away the firwood arms[2]; but if an
(irresistible?) oar-smashing blow was inflicted on
one side, the sailors would all tumble back there,
while if a headland opposite the ships' sides snapped
the sailing device of the noisy pine,[3] back they came

95

αἱ δ' ε[ὖτ' ἀν]αιδῆ γυῖα [δ]ιαφέρουσα[ι
15 πλ]ευρὰς λι[νο]ζώστους ἔφαι-
νον, τὰς μ[έν, αἰόλας ὕβρε]ις
σκηπτ[ῶν] ἐπεμβάλλ[ο]ντες ἀνε-
[χ]αίτιζον, αἱ δὲ πρα[νέες
            ] [. .]ας ἀπηγ<λ>αϊ-
20 σμένα[ι] σιδα[ρ]<έ>ωι κράνει·
ἴσος δὲ πυρὶ δαμ[ασίφως
Ἄρης] ἀγκυλένδετος
μεθίετο χερσίν, ἐν δ' ἔπιπτε γυίοις
αἰθε[ροφόρητος, σ]ῶμα διακραδαίνων·
25 στερεοπαγῆ δ' ἐφέρετο φόνι-
α[. . . . .]α[. .]τά τε περίβολα
πυρὶ φλεγ[όμ]εν' ἐν ἀποτομάσι
βουδ[ροισι· τῶν δὲ] βίοτος
ἐθύετ' ἀδιν[ὸ]ς ὑπὸ τανυπτέ-
30 ροισι χαλκόκρασι νευρε[   ],
σμαραγδοχαίτας δὲ πόν-
τος ἄλοκα ναΐοις ἐφοι-
νίσσετο σταλά[γμασι,
κρ]αυγᾶι βοὰ δὲ [πα]μμι[γ]ὴς κατεῖχεν·
35 ὁμοῦ δὲ νάϊος στρατὸς
βάρβαρος ἀμμι[γ . . . . .]
ἀντεφέρετ' ἐ[π' ἰχ]θυ[ο]-
στέφεσι μαρμαροπ[τύχ]ο[ι]ς
κόλποισιν ['Αμφιτρίτ]ας.
40   ἔνθα τοι τ[ις Φρυγιο]πέδιος
ἀνὴρ ἁμεροδρόμοι-
ο χώρας ἄναξ [. . .
δυσο]μβρίαν α . ω[. . .

again; and when the other ships[4] by tearing apart
the (shameless?) limbs[5] revealed the flax-bound
sides, the crews would capsize some ships by hurl-
ing on them (the flashing outrages of) dolphin-
weights; other ships (sank) face-downwards,
stripped of their ornament by the iron helmet[6]; and
like fire the man-slaying thong-bound (warlord)[7]
was hurled from hands and airborne fell on men's
limbs, shaking their bodies violently; and solid-hard
murderous (missiles) were rushing ..., and ...
wrapped flaming with fire on ox-flaying splints of
wood[8]; and their lives were being sacrificed in great
number under long-winged bronze-headed (arrows
shot by bowstrings); and the emerald-haired sea had
its furrow reddened by the drops of naval blood, and
shouting mingled with screaming prevailed; and
together the barbarian naval host was driven back
in confusion on the fish-wreathed bosom of Amphi-
trite with its gleaming folds.

At this point a man from the (Phrygian?) plain, a
lord of the land that takes a day to cross, ... striking

---

[4] The Greek ships. [5] The hulls of ships (now shamelessly
exposed?). [6] The ram. [7] 'Ares', of a javelin.
[8] I.e. fire-darts.

---

14 init., 16, 17 init. ci. Page   18 fin. Page   19 βάπτουσι δέμ]ας
ci. Page   24 -φόρητος Jannsen   27 -τομεσι pap.
28 -σι· τῶν Page   33 Page   34 [πα]μμι[γ]ὴς Diehl
36 ἀμμί[γδην vel ἄμμι[γ(α)   37 ἰχ]θυ[ο- Diehl
38 van Leeuwen   40 ἀμετρο]πέδιος ci. Page   43 Page

ποσί τε χ]ερσίν τε παί-
45 ω[ν ἔ]πλει νησίω-
τας [ποντίαι]ς θεινόμε[νος ἄ-
ταις, δ]ιεξόδους μ[ατεύω]ν
ἰσόρροπά τε παλευό[μενος
       ]ηλ[   ]ων
50 κάλει θ[αλάσ]ιον θεὸν
πατέρα τ[
. . . .] . νο[. . .]φι[   ] . κεπ[. .] . . [. . .
. . . .]λασσων . [| . . . . . .]σπ[.]τε[
. . .] . γαν[. .]ον[. . . . . .]α Περσᾶν |
. . . .] . εφασ[. .]ρ[   ]αντεκεκρατ[. . . . . .
. . . .]νιν κελαι | . . . ἀμ]βλὺ δ' ὠ[χ]ρὸν[
. .]ς κατεσσφρα[. . . . .] . στα | . . .
. .]πεπα[. .]ολλ[   ]υτεκ . τοσ[. . . . . .
. .]νωτου | . . . . .]ε διαπαλεύων[
]που βάσιμον[. . . . .]ν δίοδον | . . .
. δ]εσμ[ὸ]ς [ἄπ]ειρος[   ]φι ναίοις
τρυ[. . . . ἑ]λιχθείς |]υλα[
]φον[. .]ευμα . [   ] ·
60 ὅ]τε δὲ τᾶι λείποιεν αὖραι
τᾶι δ' ἐπεισέπιπτον, ἀφρῶι
δ' <ὕ> ἀβακχίωτος ὄμ-
βρος, εἰς δὲ τρόφιμον ἄγγος
ἐχεῖτ' · ἐπεὶ δ' ἀμβόλιμος ἅλ-
65 μα στόματος ὑπερέθυιεν,
ὀξυπαραυδήτωι
φωνᾶι παρακόπωι τε δόξαι φρενῶν
κατακορὴς ἀπείλει

the wretched water with his feet and hands was floating, an islander now, battered (by the sea's destruction?), seeking ways of escape and equally entrapped (by them) ... (he) called on the sea-god, the father ... Persians ... (black?) ... blunt, pale ... sealed ... trapping ... where ... a way through to tread on ... imprisonment unending ... naval ... rolling (?) ...; and whenever the winds dropped in one place to attack in another, water devoid of Bacchus rained down with foam and poured into his alimentary vessel[9]; and as the surging brine bubbled over from his mouth, with shrill distorted voice and wits deranged, sated by it all, he would make

[9] His stomach.

---

44 ποσί τε Page
62, 69 Page

46, 47 init., 48 Page

55 κατεσφρα[γισ- ?

γόμφοις<ιν> ἐμπρίων
70 †μιμούμενος† λυμεώ-
νι σώματος θαλάσσαι·
'ἤδη θρασεῖα καὶ πάρος
λάβρον αὐχέν' ἔσχες ἐμ
πέδαι καταζευχθεῖσα λινοδέτωι τεόν·
75 νῦν δέ σ' ἀναταράξει
ἐμὸς ἄναξ ἐμὸς πεύ-
καισιν ὀριγόνοισιν, ἐγ-
κλήισει δὲ πεδία πλόϊμα νομάσι ναύταις,
οἰστρομανὲς παλεομί-
80 σημ' ἄπιστόν τ' ἀγκάλι-
σμα κλυσιδρομάδος αὔρας.'
φατ' ἄσθματι στρεύγομενος,
βλοσυρὰν δ' ἐξέβαλλεν ἄ-
χναν ἐπανερεύγομενος
85 στόματι βρύχιον ἅλμαν.
φυγᾶι δὲ πάλιν ἵετο Πέρ-
σης στρατὸς βάρβαρος ἐπισπέρχων·
ἄλλα δ' ἄλλαν θραῦεν σύρτις
μακραυχενό-
90 πλους, χειρῶν δ' ἔγβαλλον ὀρεί-
ους πόδας ναός, στόματος
δ' ἐξήλλοντο μαρμαροφεγ-
γεῖς παῖδες συγκρουόμενοι·
κατάστερος δὲ πόντος ἐγ
95 λιποπνόης αὐγ[ο]στερέσιν
ἐγάργαιρε σώμασιν,
ἐβρίθοντο δ' ἀϊόνες.
ο[ἱ] δ' ἐπ' ἀκταῖς ἐνάλοις

100

threats gnashing his teeth (in anger?) against the sea, the destroyer of his body: 'Once before for all your audacity you were yoked and found your turbulent neck in a flaxen fetter[10]; and now my lord, yes mine, will stir you up with his mountain-born pines[11] and enclose your navigable plains with his roaming seamen, you crazed victim of the gadfly, hateful thing of old, treacherous darling of the wind that races to dash you.' He spoke in distress from his choking and spat out a grim froth, belching from his mouth the deep-sea brine.

And backwards in flight went the barbarian Persian host, racing along; and various destructions[12] shattered their ships as they sailed the long neck of the sea, and from their hands they dropped their ship's mountain feet,[13] and from their mouths jumped their bright-shining children,[14] smashed together; and the sea, star-sprinkled (?), swarmed with bodies (sunlight-)robbed from failure of breath, and the shores were laden with them; and others,

[10] When Xerxes bridged the Hellespont the previous year (Hdt. 7. 34 ff.).   [11] His oars or ships.   [12] Literally, 'shoals'.
[13] Their oars.   [14] Their teeth.

70 θυμούμενος van Leeuwen   71 θαλασας pap.   78 Wilamowitz (νομάσι), Danielsson, Croiset, Sitzler (ναύταις): νομμασιναυγαις pap.   82 αθματι pap.   87 βάρβαρος del. Wilamowitz   94 κατάστορος Keil   95 ci. Page

ἥμενοι γυμνοπαγεῖς
100   αὐτᾶι τε καὶ δακρυ-
σταγεῖ [γ]όωι
στερνοκτύποι γοηταὶ
θρηνώδει κατείχοντ' ὀδυρμῶι·
ἅμα δὲ [γᾶν] πατρίαν ἐπανε-
105   κα[λ]έοντ'· 'ιὼ Μύσιαι
δενδροέθειραι πτυχαί,
[ῥύσ]ασθέ μ' ἐνθέν[δ]ε· νῦν ἀήταις
φερόμεθ'· οὐ γὰρ ἔτι ποτ' ἁμὸν
[σῶ]μα δέξεται [πόλ]ις
κ[.] . εγ γὰρ χερὶ πα[.]ε[ι] νυμφαιογόνον |
[ἄβα]τον ἄντρον ο[. . .] . [. . .]διαστακαπε[. .
. . .] . ονειτεο βαθύ | [τ]ερον πόντοιο τ[. . .]α
ἄπεχε μαχιμο[. .] . [. .] | πλόϊμον Ἕλλαν
ευ[. . .]η
                        στέγην ἔδειμε
115   [τ]ῆλ[ε] τελεόπορον ἐμὸς
[δ]εσπότης· οὐ γὰρ ἄ[ν Τμῶ]λον οὐδ'
ἄστυ Λύδιον [λι]πὼν Σαρδέων
ἦλθον ['Ε]λλαν' ἀπέρξων Ἄρ[η·
νῦν δὲ πᾶι τις δυσέκφευκ[τ]ον εὕ-
120   ρηι γλυκεῖαν μόρου καταφυγήν;
'Ιλιοπόρος κακῶν λυαί-
α μόνα γένοιτ' ἄν, εἰ
δυνατά <τωι> πρὸς μελαμ-
πεταλοχίτωνα Ματρὸς οὐρείας
125   δεσπόσυνα γόνατα πεσεῖν

sitting in frozen nakedness on sea headlands, with shouts and tear-shedding wailing, breast-beating wailers, were gripped by dirge-like lamentation and appealed to their fatherland: 'Ho, you tree-tressed glens of Mysia, rescue me from this place, since as it is we are being swept along by the gales; for otherwise my city will never welcome my body again; for with hand ... the cave, (not to be entered,) birthplace of nymphs (from ancient times?), ... deeper ... (of) the sea ... ward off! ... warlike ... navigable Helle[15] ...; (would that) my master had (not) built far from home a cover to provide a crossing[16]; for then I should not have left Tmolus or the Lydian town of Sardis and come to fend off Greek Ares: as it is now, where is one to find sweet refuge, a hard task for the refugee, from doom? Troyward-conveying, she alone might be the deliverer from disaster, if one could fall at the queenly knees, black-leaf-robed, of the mountain Mother and cast-

[15] The Hellespont, in which Helle drowned.   [16] Xerxes' bridge.

---

102 -κτύπωι pap.   109 πόλ]ις Danielsson   πατρ]ίς Inama,
Sitzler   110 πα[λ]ε[ο]νυμφ. Wilamowitz   113 εἴ[θε μ]ὴ
Danielsson   117 Λυδὸν ci. Wilamowitz   118 ατερξων pap.
123 Wilamowitz (δυνατά), <τωι> Page: δυναστα pap.

εὐωλένους τε χεῖρας ἀμφιβάλλων
λίσσ<οιτο· "σῶσ>ον χρυσοπλόκαμε
θεὰ Μᾶτερ ἱκνοῦμαι
ἐμὸν ἐμὸν αἰῶνα δυσέκφευκτον," ἐπεί
130 μ' αὐτίκα λαιμοτόμωι τις ἀποίσεται
ἐνθάδε μήστορι σιδάρωι,
ἢ κατακυμοτακεῖς ναυσιφθόροι
αὖραι νυκτιπαγεῖ βορέαι δια-
ραίσονται· περὶ γὰρ κλύδων
135 ἄγριος ἀνέρρηξεν ἅπαγ
γυίων εἶδος ὑφαντόν·
ἔνθα κείσομαι οἰκτρὸς ὀρ-
νίθων ἔθνεσιν ὠμοβρῶσι θοίνα.'
      τοιάδ' ὀδυρόμενοι κατεδάκρυον·
140 ἐπεὶ δέ τις λαβὼν ἄγοι
πολυβότων Κελαινᾶν
οἰκήτορ' ὀρφανὸν μαχᾶν
σιδαρόκωπος Ἕλλαν,
ἄγεγ κόμης ἐπισπάσας,
145 ὁ δ' ἀμφὶ γόνασι περιπλεκεὶς
ἐλίσσετ', Ἑλλάδ' ἐμπλέκων
Ἀσιάδι φωνᾶι διάτορον
σφραγῖδα θραύων στόματος,
Ἰάονα γλῶσσαν ἐξιχνεύων·
150 'ἔπω μοί σοι κῶς καὶ τί πρᾶγμα;
αὖτις οὐδάμ' ἔλθω·
καὶ νῦν ἐμὸς δεσπότης
δεῦρό μ' ἐνθάδ' ἥξει·
τὰ λοιπὰ δ' οὐκέτι, πάτερ,
155 οὐκέτι μαχέσ' αὖτις ἐνθάδ' ἔρχω

ing one's beautiful arms about them might pray,
"Gold-tressed goddess Mother, save, I beseech you,
my life, yes mine, for which refuge is hard to find;"[17]
since otherwise someone will presently do away
with me here with the throat-slitting deviser, the
steel, or the winds, billow-dissolving, ship-wrecking,
will destroy me with night-freezing norther, since
the savage wave has torn away all the fair woven
warmth[18] for my limbs: here I shall lie, a pitiable
feast for the flesh-eating tribes of birds.'

Uttering such lamentations they wept bitterly;
and whenever some steel-bladed Greek seized
and carried off an inhabitant of rich-pasturing
Celaenae[19] bereft of his fighting powers, he would
carry him off dragging him by the hair; and he,
embracing his knees, would beseech him,
interweaving Greek speech with Asian, shattering
his mouth's seal in piercing cry, tracking down the
Ionian tongue: 'How me speak you, and what thing
speak?[20] Never again I come back. This time my
master, he brung me here to this place; but from
now on no more, father, no more I come again here

[17] Perhaps the appeal to the Mother goddess continues to the end
of their speech (v. 138). [18] $\epsilon \hat{\iota} \delta o \varsigma = \hat{\iota} \delta o \varsigma$ (West). [19] City
of Phrygia. [20] The Phrygian's meaning is not always clear.

127 λίσσ<οιτο· λῦσ>ον Page, λισσ<οίμαν ... σῶσ>ον West: λισσων
pap. 146 ελλαδι pap. 155 ενθδερχω pap.

ἀλλὰ κάθω.
ἐγώ σοι μὴ δεῦρ᾽, ἐγὼ
κεῖσε παρὰ Σάρδι, παρὰ Σοῦσα,
᾽Αγβάτανα ναίων·
160 Ἄρτιμις ἐμὸς μέγας θεὸς
παρ᾽ Ἔφεσον φυλάξει.᾽
οἱ δ᾽ ἐπεὶ παλίμπορον φυ-
γὴν ἔθεντο ταχύπορον,
αὐτίκα μὲν ἀμφιστόμους ἄ-
165 κοντας ἐχ χερῶν ἔριπτον,
δρύπτετο δὲ πρόσωπ᾽ ὄνυξι·
Περσίδα <δὲ> στολὴν περὶ στέρ-
νοις ἔρεικον εὐυφῆ,
σύντονος δ᾽ ἁρμόζετ᾽ ᾽Ασιὰς
170 οἰμωγὰ πολυ<γλώσσωι> στόνωι,
κτύπει δὲ πᾶσα Βασιλέως πανήγυρις
φόβωι τὸ μέλλον εἰσορώμενοι πάθος·
ὁ δὲ παλινπόρευτον ὡς ἐσ-
εῖδε Βασιλεὺς εἰς φυγὴν ὁρ-
175 μῶντα παμμιγῆ στρατόν,
γονυπετὴς αἴκιζε σῶμα,
φάτο δὲ κυμαίνων τύχαισιν·
᾽ἰὼ κατασκαφαὶ δόμων
σείραί τε νᾶες Ἑλλανίδες, αἱ
180 κατὰ μὲν ἥλικ᾽ ὠλέσαθ᾽ ἥ-
βαν νέων πολύανδρον·
νᾶες δ᾽ οὐκ ὀπισσοπόρευ-
τον †ἄξουσιμ, πυρὸς
δ᾽ αἰθαλόεμ μένος ἀγρίωι
185 σώματι φλέξει, στονόεντα δ᾽ ἄλγη

for fight: I sit still. I no come here to you, I go over there to Sardis, to Susa, Ecbatana dweller. Artimis, my great god, will guard me to Ephesus.'

And when they had completed their backward-moving swift-moving flight, they at once threw down from their hands the double-mouthed[21] javelins, and their faces were torn by their nails; and they rent their well-woven Persian dress about their breasts, and a high-pitched Asian wailing was attuned to their many-tongued lament, and the whole of the King's entourage clamoured as they gazed in fear on the coming disaster; and when the King had looked on his army rushing in confusion in backward-travelling flight, fallen to his knees he maltreated his body and said as he tossed in the billows of his misfortune, 'Oh, the ruination of my house! Oh, you scorching[22] Greek ships that destroyed the young men of my ships, a great throng of my contemporaries, so that the ships will not carry them away backward-travelling, but fire's smoky

---

[21] 'Biting' with two points.   [22] With reference to the fire-darts (see n. 8).

---

165 ἐρριπτον pap.   166 Blass, Sitzler: προσωπονονυξι pap.
167 Sitzler   170 ci. Page   177 τύχαις ci.
Maas   181 vel νέων   182s. ουκιοπισσ- pap.   post
νᾶες δὲ lacunam indicat Wilamowitz: δ' <ἁμέτεραί νιν> van
Leeuwen, <μ' ἀπ>άξουσιν ci. Page   185 φλεξεισστονο- pap.

ἔσται Περσίδι χώραι·
ἰὼ βαρεῖα συμφορά,
ἅ μ’ ἐς Ἑλλάδ’ ἤγαγες.
ἀλλ’ ἴτε, μηκέτι μέλλετε,
190   ζεύγνυτε μὲν τετράορον ἵππων
ὄχημ’, οἱ δ’ ἀνάριθμον ὄλ-
βον φορεῖτ’ ἐπ’ ἀπήνας·
πίμπρατε δὲ σκηνάς,
μηδέ τις ἡμετέρου γένοιτ’
195   ὄνησις αὐτοῖσι πλούτου.’

οἱ δὲ τροπαῖα στησάμενοι Διὸς
ἁγνότατον τέμενος, Παιᾶν’
ἐκελάδησαν ἰήιον
ἄνακτα, σύμμετροι δ’ ἐπε-
200   κτύπεον ποδῶν
ὑψικρότοις χορείαις.

ἀλλ’ ὦ χρυσεοκίθαριν ἀέ-
ξων μοῦσαν νεοτευχῆ,
ἐμοῖς ἔλθ’ ἐπίκουρος ὕμ-
205   νοις, ἰήιε Παιάν·
ὁ γάρ μ’ εὐγενέτας μακραί-
ων Σπάρτας μέγας ἀγεμὼν
βρύων ἄνθεσιν ἥβας
δονεῖ λαὸς ἐπιφλέγων
210   ἐλᾶι τ’ αἴθοπι μώμωι,
ὅτι παλαιοτέραν νέοις
ὕμνοις μοῦσαν ἀτιμῶ·
ἐγὼ δ’ οὔτε νέον τιν’ οὔ-
τε γεραὸν οὔτ’ ἰσήβαν
215   εἴργω τῶνδ’ ἑκὰς ὕμνων·

strength will burn them with its savage body, and lamentable sufferings will befall the Persian land! Oh, you heavy fate that brought me to Greece! But go, delay no longer, yoke my four-horsed chariot, and you, carry my countless riches on to the wagons; and burn the tents, and let them have no benefit from our wealth!'

But the other side set up trophies to establish a most holy sanctuary of Zeus and shouted on Paean, the healer lord, and with measured beat they set about stamping in the high-pounding dances of their feet.

You who foster the new-fashioned muse of the golden cithara, come, healer Paean, as helper to my songs; for Sparta's great leader, well-born, long-lived, the populace riotous with the flowers of youth,[23] buffets me, blazing hostility, and hounds me with fiery censure on the grounds that I dishonour the older muse with my new songs; but I

[23] I.e. the youthful aristocracy of Sparta: see test. 7.

186s. χωραιω pap.: fort. χώραι· ὦ   190 τετραον pap.
204s. υμνοισιν pap.

τοὺς δὲ μουσοπαλαιολύ-
μας, τούτους δ᾽ ἀπερύκω,
λωβητῆρας ἀοιδᾶν,
κηρύκων λιγυμακροφώ-
220 νων τείνοντας ἰυγάς.
πρῶτος ποικιλόμουσος Ὀρ-
φεὺς <χέλ>υν ἐτέκνωσεν
υἱὸς Καλλιόπα<ς ‿ –
– ‿ > Πιερίαθεν·
225 Τέρπανδρος δ᾽ ἐπὶ τῶι δέκα
ζεῦξε μοῦσαν ἐν ὠιδαῖς·
Λέσβος δ᾽ Αἰολία ν<ιν> Ἀν-
τίσσαι γείνατο κλεινόν·
νῦν δὲ Τιμόθεος μέτροις
230 ῥυθμοῖς τ᾽ ἑνδεκακρουμάτοις
κίθαριν ἐξανατέλλει,
θησαυρὸν πολύυμνον οἴ-
ξας Μουσᾶν θαλαμευτόν·
Μίλητος δὲ πόλις νιν ἁ
235 θρέψασ᾽ ἁ δυωδεκατειχέος
λαοῦ πρωτέος ἐξ Ἀχαιῶν.
ἀλλ᾽ ἑκαταβόλε Πύθι᾽ ἁγνὰν
ἔλθοις τάνδε πόλιν σὺν ὄλβωι,
πέμπων ἀπήμονι λαῶι
240 τῶιδ᾽ εἰρήναν θάλλουσαν εὐνομίαι.

221s. οριυσυνετεκνωσεν pap.   223s. καλλιοπαπιεριασενι pap.:
Καλλιόπα<ς> Πιερίας ἔπι Wilamowitz (qui lacunam non indicat);
lacunam metri causa indicat, Πιερίαθεν ci. Page   225 -δροσαεπι
pap.   226 τευξε pap.   227s. αιολιαναντισσαγεινατο pap.:
Λεσβὶς δ᾽ Αἰολίαι νιν Ἄντισσα γ. Maas   240 τωδ, ευνομιαν pap.

110

keep neither young man nor old man nor my peer at a distance from these songs of mine: it is the corrupters of the old muse that I fend off, debauchers of songs, uttering the loud shrieks of shrill far-calling criers. Orpheus, Calliope's son, he of the intricate muse, was the first to beget the tortoise-shell lyre in Pieria[24]; after him Terpander yoked his muse in ten songs[25]: Aeolian Lesbos bore him to give glory to Antissa; and now Timotheus brings to new life the cithara with eleven-stringed measures and rhythms, opening the Muses' chambered treasure with its abundance of song: it was the city of Miletus that nurtured him, the city of a twelve-walled people[26] that is foremost among the Achaeans.[27] Come, far-shooting Pythian, to this holy city[28] and bring prosperity with you, conveying to this people, that they be untroubled, peace that flourishes in good civic order.

[24] Birthplace of the Muses; text uncertain. See Terp. 15.
[25] Text and meaning uncertain; seven or eight nomes of Terp. were listed (Terp. test. 19).   [26] With reference to the Ionian confederacy of twelve cities.   [27] I.e. the Greeks.   [28] The place of performance, probably Athens: see S. E. Bassett, *Cl. Phil.* 26 (1931) 153 ff.

ΣΕΜΕΛΗΣ ΩΔΙΣ

792 Athen. 8. 352a (ii 271 Kaibel)

ἐπακούσας δὲ τῆς Ὠδῖνος τῆς Τιμοθέου, εἰ δ' ἐργολάβον, ἔφη (sc. ὁ Στρατόνικος), ἔτικτεν καὶ μὴ θεόν, ποίας ἂν ἠφίει φωνάς;

cf. Alc. Messen. x 2s. Gow-Page Δωρόθεος . . . ἔπνεε . . . Σεμέλας ὠδῖνα κεραύνιον, Dio. Chrys. 78. 32 (ii 271 de Budé) ὥσπερ αὐλοῦντα τὴν τῆς Σεμέλης ὠδῖνα, Boeth. Mus. 1. 1 (p. 182s. Friedlein)

ΣΚΥΛΛΑ

793 Aristot. poet. 15. 1454a 28 (p. 24 Kassel)

ἔστιν δὲ παράδειγμα . . . τοῦ δὲ ἀπρεποῦς καὶ μὴ ἁρμόττοντος ὅ τε θρῆνος Ὀδυσσέως ἐν τῇ Σκύλλῃ . . .

ibid. 26. 1461b 30 (p. 47 Kassel)

. . . πολλὴν κίνησιν κινοῦνται, οἷον οἱ φαῦλοι αὐληταὶ κυλιόμενοι ἂν δίσκον δέῃ μιμεῖσθαι καὶ ἕλκοντες τὸν κορυφαῖον ἂν Σκύλλαν αὐλῶσιν.

Mittheil. Samm. Pap. Erz. Rainer 1 (1887) 84ss. Gomperz: v. Oellacher, *Études de Papyrologie* 4 (1938) 135ss.

εἰσὶν δέ τινες οἳ ὃν μὲν προτίθενται οὐ μειμοῦνται [[δέ]], ἄλλον δὲ καὶ τοῦτον καλῶς, [οὗ τ]υγχάνομεν ἔχοντες ἔννοιαν καὶ παράδειγμα παρ' ἡμεῖν αὐτοῖς, ὥσπερ καὶ Τειμόθεος ἐν τῶι θρήνωι τοῦ Ὀδυσσέως εἰ μέν τινα μειμεῖται καὶ τὸ ὅμοιόν τινι οἶδεν ἀλλ[ὰ] τῶι Ὀδυσσεῖ [

TIMOTHEUS

THE BIRTH-PANGS OF SEMELE[1]

792 Athenaeus, *Scholars at Dinner*

When he heard Timotheus' *Birth-pangs*, Stratonicus said, 'If she had been giving birth to a contractor instead of a god, what would her screams have been like?'

[1] Alcaeus of Messene says the piper Dorotheus performed 'Semele's lightning-blasted Birth-pangs'; Dio Chrysostom, retelling the story of Alcmaeon's visit to Croesus' treasury (Hdt. 6. 125), says he staggered out with bulging cheeks as if he were a piper playing *The Birth-pangs of Semele*.

SCYLLA

793 Aristotle, *Poetics* 15

An example . . . of the unsuitable and inappropriate is the lament of Odysseus[1] in the *Scylla*.

[1] For his companions devoured by Scylla.

Aristotle, *Poetics* 26

. . . (tragic actors) indulge in much movement, like inferior pipers spinning round if they have to represent a discus or dragging the chorus-leader about if they are playing the *Scylla*.

Rainer papyrus (3rd c. A.D.)

There are some who do not represent the man they claim to represent but some other man, making a fine job of it: we can form an idea of this from an example at home here: Timotheus in the lament of Odysseus, if he is representing someone and understands what bears a likeness to him, but . . . to Odysseus . . .

113

GREEK LYRIC

794 Aristot. *Rhet.* 3. 14. 1415a 10 (p. 127 Römer, p. 176 Ross)

τὰ μὲν γὰρ τῶν διθυράμβων (sc. προοίμια) ὅμοια τοῖς ἐπι-
δεικτικοῖς·

> διὰ σε καὶ τεὰ δῶρα †ειτα† Σκύλλα

cf. comment. in Ar. graec. xxi 2 (p. 230 Rabe) οἷον· ἦλθον εἰς σὲ καὶ τὰ
τεὰ καὶ τὰ σὰ δῶρα καὶ εὐεργετήματα καὶ τὰ σκῦλα, ὦ θεὲ Διόνυσε.

ita cod. Paris.: εἴτε (εἴ τι) σκῦλα cett.

ΦΙΝΕΪΔΑΙ

795 *Sud.* T 620 (= test. 2)

Τιμόθεος . . . γράψας . . . Φινεΐδας . . .

796 Athen. 3. 122cd (i 279 Kaibel)

εἰ οὖν κἀγώ τι ἥμαρτον, ὦ καλλίστων ὀνομάτων καὶ ῥημάτων
θηρευτά, μὴ χαλέπαινε· κατὰ γὰρ τὸν Μιλήσιον Τιμόθεον τὸν
ποιητήν

> οὐκ ἀείδω τὰ παλαιά,
> καινὰ γὰρ ἀμὰ κρείσσω·
> νέος ὁ Ζεὺς βασιλεύει,
> τὸ πάλαι δ' ἦν Κρόνος ἄρχων·
> 5 ἀπίτω Μοῦσα παλαιά.

cf. Eust. *Od.* 1422. 50

1 ἄδω G. S. Farnell   2 καινὰ γὰρ κ. codd. CE, Eust.   καὶ
ταγὰρ ἅμα κ. cod. A   ἀμὰ Wilamowitz   καινὰ γὰρ μάλα κ.
Bergk   4 Meineke: τὸ παλαιὸν codd.

794 Aristotle, *Rhetoric*

For the preludes of dithyrambs are like the introductions to declamatory speeches:

Because of you and your gifts . . . Scylla . . .[1]

[1] Text insecure: most mss. have σκῦλα, 'spoils'. The scholiast, amplifying the text, seems to point to a different interpretation: 'I came to you because of you and your gifts and kindnesses and spoils, god Dionysus.'

THE SONS OF PHINEUS[1]

795 : see *Suda* (test. 2)

[1] Thracian king who blinded his sons (or condoned the deed) when they were slandered by their stepmother; as punishment, the Harpies seized all his food until the Argonauts rescued him; details vary.

Frr. 796–804 are from unidentified poems

796 Athenaeus, *Scholars at Dinner* (Cynulcus to Ulpian)

So if I too have gone wrong, you hunter of the finest nouns and verbs, do not be angry; for in the words of the poet Timotheus of Miletus,

I do not sing the ancient songs, for my new ones are better. The young Zeus is king, and it was in ancient times that Cronus was ruler. Let the ancient Muse depart!

797 Athen. 10. 433c (ii 442 Kaibel)

οὐκ ἂν ἁμάρτοι δέ τις καὶ τὸ ποτήριον αὐτοῦ (sc. τοῦ Νέστορος) λέγων φιάλην Ἄρεως κατὰ τὸν Ἀντιφάνους Καινέα, ἐν ᾧ λέγεται οὕτως (fr. 110 K.-A.)·

εἶτ' ἤδη δὸς

φιάλην Ἄρεως

κατὰ Τιμόθεον ξυστόν τε βέλος.

cf. 11. 502b, Aristot. *Poet.* 1457b 22, *Rhet.* 3. 1407a 16, 1412b 35 (= adesp. 951 *P.M.G.*)

Koppiers: φιάλην τὸ ὅπλον Ἄρεως codd.

798 Athen. 10. 455f (ii 490s. Kaibel)

Ἀναξανδρίδης Αἴσχρᾳ (fr. 6 K.-A.)· ἀρτίως διηρτάμηκε καὶ τὰ μὲν διανεκῆ | σώματος μέρη δαμάζετ'

ἐν πυρικτίτῳ στέγᾳ·

| Τιμόθεος ἔφη ποτ', ἄνδρες, τὴν χύτραν οἶμαι λέγων.

Kock: δαμάζετε ἐν πυρικτίτοισι γᾶς cod. A (η sup. a scr.)

799 *Et. Gen.* B (p. 227 Miller, *Mélanges*) = *Et. Mag.* 630. 40 + cod. Paris. 2720 (ap. *Anecd. Par.* iv 12 Cramer)

ὀρίγανον· ... ὥς φησιν Ὠριγένης, εὕρηται ἐν συστολῇ ἡ ρι συλλαβῇ ὡς παρὰ Τιμοθέῳ τῷ κιθαρῳδῷ, οἷον·

τεταμένον ὀρίγανα διὰ μυελοτρεφῆ.

σύγκειται δ' οὗτος ὁ στίχος ἀπὸ προκελευσματικῶν, ὁ δὲ τελευταῖος ποὺς ἀνάπαιστος.

τεταμένα *Et. Gen., Anecd. Par., Et. Mag.* cod. M   μυελ/τροφῆ *Et. Mag.* cod. M   δμοελοτρεφῆ *Anecd. Par.*

116

TIMOTHEUS

797 Athenaeus, *Scholars at Dinner*

One would not go wrong in calling Nestor's cup 'the goblet of Ares',[1] as Antiphanes has it in his *Caeneus*, where he says, 'Then give me at once my

goblet of Ares,[2]

in the words of Timotheus, and my whittled javelin.'

[1] Since he took it with him to Troy (*Il.* 11. 632 ff.).   [2] I.e. my shield (saucer-shaped like the *phiale*).

798 Athenaeus, *Scholars at Dinner* (on riddles)

Anaxandrides in his *Aeschra*: 'He has newly chopped it up and is subduing the chine-cut parts of the carcass

in the fire-made shelter;

so Timotheus once put it, gentlemen, meaning, I suppose, the pot.'

799 *Etymologicum Genuinum* s.v. ὀρίγανον ('dittany')

According to Origen,[1] the second syllable is found shortened, as in Timotheus the cithara-singer:

stretched out over marrow-fed dittany.[2]

The line is composed of proceleusmatics ($\cup\cup\cup\cup$)[3] with the last foot an anapaest ($\cup\cup-$).

[1] An error for Orus?   [2] Of a corpse on a bier? Cf. Ar. *Eccl.* 1030. But why 'marrow-fed'?   [3] I.e. resolved anapaests.

GREEK LYRIC

800 Macrob. *Sat.* 1. 17. 19s. (i 86s. Willis)

Apollodorus in libro quarto decimo περὶ θεῶν (244 F95. 19s. Jacoby) Ἰήιον solem scribit: ita appellari Apollinem ἀπὸ τοῦ κατὰ τὸν κόσμον ἵεσθαι καὶ ἰέναι, quod sol per orbem impetu fertur. sed Timotheus ita:

> σύ τ᾽ ὦ τὸν ἀεὶ πόλον οὐράνιον
> λαμπραῖς ἀκτῖσ᾽ Ἅλιε βάλλων,
> πέμψον ἑκαβόλον ἐχθροῖσ<ι> βέλος
> σᾶς ἀπὸ νευρᾶς, ὦ ἰὲ Παιάν.

3 Crusius

801 Plut. *de fort. Alex.* 1 (ii 2. 94 Nachstädt)

Ἀρχελάῳ δὲ δοκοῦντι γλισχροτέρῳ περὶ τὰς δωρεὰς εἶναι Τιμόθεος ᾄδων ἐνεσήμαινε πολλάκις τουτὶ τὸ κομμάτιον·

> σὺ δὲ τὸν γηγενέταν ἄργυρον αἰνεῖς·

ὁ δ᾽ Ἀρχέλαος οὐκ ἀμούσως ἀντεφώνησε· σὺ δέ γ᾽ αἰτεῖς.

cf. *reg. apophth.* 177b

σὺ δὲ reg.   σὺ δὴ Alex.

802 Plut. *de laude ipsius* 1 (iii 372 Pohlenz-Sieveking)

ἦ καὶ τὸν Τιμόθεον ἐπὶ τῇ κατὰ Φρύνιδος νίκῃ γράφοντα·

> μακάριος ἦσθα, Τιμόθε᾽, ὅτε κᾶρυξ
> εἶπε· νικᾷ Τιμόθεος
> Μιλήσιος τὸν Κάμωνος τὸν ἰωνοκάμπταν,

εἰκότως δυσχεραίνομεν ὡς ἀμούσως καὶ παρανόμως ἀνακηρύττοντα τὴν ἑαυτοῦ νίκην.

1 Τιμόθεε codd., -θεος ci. Hartung   ὅτε codd., εὖτε ci. Wilamowitz   3 Bergk: ὁ Μιλ. τὸν κάρβωνος (κάρωνος) codd.

118

800 Macrobius, *Saturnalia*

Apollodorus in Book 14 of his work *On the Gods* calls the sun Ἰήιος, saying that Apollo is so called because he moves (ἴεσθαι) and goes (ἰέναι) through the universe, since the sun races over the world. But Timotheus has

And you, Sun, who strike with your bright rays the everlasting heavenly vault, send on our enemies a far-shot arrow from your bowstring, oh ië Paean![1]

[1] Perhaps taken to mean 'oh shoot it (ἴε), Paean!' Since the Greeks sang a paean at daybreak before the battle of Salamis (Aes. *Pers.* 386 ff.), Edmonds assigned the lines to T.'s *Persians*.

801 Plutarch, *On the Fortune of Alexander*

When Archelaus[1] seemed rather sticky-fingered in the matter of his gifts Timotheus would often sing this phrase to bring it to his attention:

but you commend earth-born silver;

to which Archelaus made this witty rejoinder, 'But you demand it.'

[1] King of Macedon, died 399 B.C.

802 Plutarch, *On praising oneself inoffensively*

So when Timotheus writes of his victory over Phrynis,

You were blessed, Timotheus, when the herald said, 'Timotheus of Miletus is victorious over Camon's son,[1] the modulator[2] of Ionian melody,'

we have good reason to be disgusted at his tasteless and irregular heralding of his own victory.

[1] Cf. Pollux 4. 66, 'Phrynis, Camon's son': *Suda* s.v. Phrynis has 'Canops' son'.   [2] Literally 'twister': see Phrynis testt. 1, 2.

803 Plut. *quaest. conviv.* 3. 10. 3 (iv 115 Hubert)

Τιμόθεος δ' ἀντικρύς φησιν·

διὰ κυάνεον πόλον ἄστρων
διά τ' ὠκυτόκοιο σελάνας.

cf. *aet. Rom.* 77, Macrob. *Sat.* 7. 16. 28

κυάνεον Plut.   λαμπρὸν Macrob.

804 Stob. 1. 49 (περὶ ψυχῆς) 61 (i 448 Wachsmuth)

τοῦ αὐτοῦ (sc. Πορφυρίου ἐκ τῶν περὶ Στυγός)
... Ἠλύσιον μὲν πεδίον εἰκότως προσειπὼν (Hom. *Od.* 4.
563ss.) τὴν τῆς σελήνης ἐπιφάνειαν ὑπὸ ἡλίου καταλαμπομένην,

ὅτ' αὔξεται ἡλίου αὐγαῖς,

ὥς φησι Τιμόθεος.

ἀέξεται ci. Meineke   ἡλίου, ἠελίου codd.

F.G.E. p. 307s.   *Vit. Eur.* (p. 3 Schwartz)

ἐτάφη δ' ἐν Μακεδονίᾳ, κενοτάφιον δ' αὐτοῦ Ἀθήνησιν ἐγένετο
καὶ ἐπίγραμμα ἐπεγέγραπτο Θουκυδίδου τοῦ ἱστοριογράφου ποιή-
σαντος ἢ Τιμοθέου τοῦ μελοποιοῦ·

μνῆμα μὲν Ἑλλὰς ἅπασ' Εὐριπίδου, ὀστέα δ' ἴσχει
   γῆ Μακεδών, ᾗπερ δέξατο τέρμα βίου.
πατρὶς δ' Ἑλλάδος Ἑλλάς, Ἀθῆναι· πλεῖστα δὲ Μού-
      σαις
   τέρψας ἐκ πολλῶν καὶ τὸν ἔπαινον ἔχει.

cf. *Anth. Pal.* 7. 45 (Θουκυδίδου τοῦ ἱστορικοῦ) (Plan.), Athen. 5. 187d

1 μνᾶμα Anth., Plan.   2 ἢ γὰρ Anth., Plan.   3 πολλὰ δὲ
vit. cod. P   Μούσαις Anth., vit. cod. P, Μούσας Plan., vit. codd.
rell.

803 Plutarch, *Table-talk*

Timotheus says outright:

Through the blue-black vault of the stars and of the moon who gives swift childbirth.[1]

[1] Plut. assumes here that T. identifies the moon with Artemis; in *Roman Questions* he compares the moon to Juno Lucina (see also Macrobius).

804 Stobaeus, *Anthology* (on the soul)

From Porphyry, *On the Styx*
Homer reasonably gives the name 'Elysian plain' to the appearance of the moon illuminated by the sun,

when she grows with the sun's rays,

as Timotheus says.

F.G.E. p. 307f.　　*Life of Euripides*

He was buried in Macedonia, but his cenotaph was in Athens[1] and had an epigram inscribed on it, the work either of Thucydides the historian or of Timotheus the lyric poet[2]:

All Greece is the monument of Euripides, although his bones lie in the land of Macedon, where he met the end of his life. His native city was Athens, the Greece of Greece. He gave much pleasure by his poetry, and he enjoys the praise of many.

[1] Cf. Paus. 1. 2. 2.　　[2] The *Palatine Anthology* and Athenaeus attribute it to Thuc.; we cannot say who wrote it. For T.'s friendship with Eur. see test. 6.

121

TELESTES

TESTIMONIA VITAE ATQUE ARTIS

1 *Sud.* T 265 (iv 518 Adler)

Τελέστης, κωμικός. τούτου δράματά ἐστιν Ἀργὼ καὶ Ἀσκληπιός, ὥς φησιν Ἀθήναιος ἐν τῷ ιδ' τῶν Δειπνοσοφιστῶν.

2 *Marm. Par.* Ep. 65 (p. 18 Jacoby)

ἀφ' οὗ Τελέστης Σελινούντιος ἐνίκησεν Ἀθήνησιν, ἔτη ΗΔΔΔΓΙΙΙΙ, ἄρχοντος Ἀθήνησιν Μίκωνος.

3 Plut. *vit. Alex.* 8. 3 (ii 2. 161 Ziegler) = Onesicritus, *F.Gr.H.* 134 F38

τῶν δ' ἄλλων βιβλίων οὐκ εὐπορῶν ἐν τοῖς ἄνω τόποις Ἅρπαλον ἐκέλευσε πέμψαι, κἀκεῖνος ἔπεμψεν αὐτῷ τάς τε Φιλίστου βίβλους καὶ τῶν Εὐριπίδου καὶ Σοφοκλέους καὶ Αἰσχύλου τραγῳδιῶν συχνὰς καὶ Τελέστου καὶ Φιλοξένου διθυράμβους.

TELESTES

1 *Suda*

Telestes, comic poet.[2] His plays are the *Argo* and *Asclepius*, as Athenaeus says in *Scholars at Dinner*, book 14.[3]

[1] See also Melanippides test. 1 n. 5, Timotheus testt. 3, 10.
[2] An error; both 'plays' were probably dithyrambs.   [3] See frr. 805, 806.

2 *Parian Marble*

From the time when Telestes of Selinus was victorious in Athens 139 years[1]; Micon was archon at Athens.

[1] I.e. 402/401 B.C., 139 years before 264/263.

3 Plutarch, *Life of Alexander*[1]

And when he was short of other books up-country[2] he ordered Harpalus to send them; and Harpalus sent him the books of Philistus and many of the tragedies of Euripides and Sophocles and Aeschylus and dithyrambs of Telestes and Philoxenus.

[1] Material taken from the History of Onesicritus, Alex.'s contemporary.   [2] I.e. in the interior of Asia.

123

4 Plin. *N.H.* 35. 36. 109 (v 269s. Mayhoff)

nec fuit alius in ea arte velocior. tradunt namque conduxisse pingendum ab Aristrato, Sicyoniorum tyranno, quod is faciebat Telesti poetae monimentum, praefinito die intra quem perageretur, nec multo ante venisse, tyranno in poenam accenso, paucisque diebus absolvisse et celeritate et arte mira.

5 Apollon. *Hist. Mir.* 40 (p. 53 Keller, p. 136s. Giannini)

Ἀριστόξενος ὁ μουσικὸς ἐν τῷ Τελέστου βίῳ φησὶν (fr. 117 Wehrli) ᾧπερ ἐν Ἰταλίᾳ συνεκύρησεν, ὑπὸ τὸν αὐτὸν καιρὸν γίγνεσθαι πάθη, ὧν ἓν εἶναι καὶ τὸ περὶ τὰς γυναῖκας γενόμενον ἄτοπον. ἐκστάσεις γὰρ γίγνεσθαι τοιαύτας ὥστε ἐνίοτε καθημένας καὶ δειπνούσας ὡς καλοῦντός τινος ὑπακούειν, εἶτα ἐκπηδᾶν ἀκατασχέτους γιγνομένας καὶ τρέχειν ἐκτὸς τῆς πόλεως. μαντευομένοις δὲ τοῖς Λοκροῖς καὶ Ῥηγίνοις περὶ τῆς ἀπαλλαγῆς τοῦ πάθους εἰπεῖν τὸν θεὸν παιᾶνας ᾄδειν ἐαρινοὺς ⟦δωδεκάτης⟧ ἡμέρας ξʹ, ὅθεν πολλοὺς γενέσθαι παιανογράφους ἐν τῇ Ἰταλίᾳ.

δώδεκα τῆς ἡμέρας ⟨ἐπὶ ἡμέρας⟩ ξʹ ci. West

4 Pliny, *Natural History* (on the painter Nicomachus)

No painter worked more quickly: they say that he accepted a commission from Aristratus, tyrant of Sicyon,[1] to paint a monument that he was erecting to the poet Telestes, the date for completion being stipulated, and that he arrived shortly before the deadline, by which time the tyrant was angry and threatening a penalty, and carried out his commission in a few days with wonderful speed and artistry.

[1] A supporter of Philip of Macedon, *c.* 360–340 B.C.

5 Apollonius, *Marvellous Stories*

The musician Aristoxenus says in his *Life of Telestes* that at the time of his visit to Italy strange things were happening. One odd one concerned the women: they were seized by such distraction that sometimes when seated at supper they would answer as if someone were calling and then dash out uncontrollably and run outside the city. When the Locrians and Rhegines consulted the oracle about relief from the condition, the god told them to sing spring paeans for sixty days.[1] That, he says, is why there were many paean-writers in Italy.

[1] M. L. West, *C.Q.* 40 (1990) 286 f., emends the text so as to read 'twelve paeans a day for sixty days'.

TELESTES

FRAGMENTA

ΑΡΓΩ

805 Athen. 14. 616f–617a (iii 360s. Kaibel)

πρὸς ὃν ἀντιλέγων ἄλλος ἔφη· ἀλλ' ὅ γε Σελινούντιος Τελέστης τῷ Μελανιππίδῃ ἀντικορυσσόμενος ἐν Ἀργοῖ ἔφη· ὁ δὲ λόγος ἐστὶ περὶ τῆς Ἀθηνᾶς·

(a) †ὃν† σοφὸν σοφὰν λαβοῦσαν οὐκ ἐπέλπομαι νόῳ
　　　δρυμοῖς ὀρείοις ὄργανον
　　　δίαν Ἀθάναν δυσόφθαλμον αἶσχος ἐκφοβη-
　　　　　θεῖσαν αὖθις χερῶν ἐκβαλεῖν
　　　νυμφαγενεῖ χειροκτύπῳ φηρὶ Μαρσύᾳ κλέος·
5　τί γάρ νιν εὐηράτοιο κάλλεος ὀξὺς ἔρως ἔτειρεν,
　　　ᾇ παρθενίαν ἄγαμον καὶ ἄπαιδ' ἀπένειμε Κλω-
　　　　　θώ;

ὡς οὐκ ἂν εὐλαβηθείσης τὴν αἰσχρότητα τοῦ εἴδους διὰ τὴν παρθενίαν, ἑξῆς τέ φησι·

(b) ἀλλὰ μάταν ἀχόρευτος ἅδε ματαιολόγων
　　　φάμα προσέπταθ' Ἑλλάδα μουσοπόλων
　　　σοφᾶς ἐπίφθονον βροτοῖς τέχνας ὄνειδος.

(a) 1 τὰν, mox σοφὰν σοφῶν (post Bergk transp. Wilamowitz) ci. Page　　2 Musurus: ὀριοις cod.　　3 Wilamowitz: ἐκ χερ. βαλ. codd.　　4 χοροκτύπῳ ci. Meineke, χοροιτύπῳ anon. 6 Schweighäuser (ᾇ γὰρ): αιγὰρ cod.　　Casaubon: ἀγανὸν cod. (b) 1 Grotefend: αναχορευτος codd.

126

TELESTES

ARGO

805 Athenaeus, *Scholars at Dinner*[1]

Another guest disagreed and said, 'But Telestes of Sel-
inus took up the cudgels against Melanippides and said in
his *Argo* with reference to Athena,

(a) I do not believe in my heart that the clever
one, divine Athena, took the clever instrument in
the mountain thickets and then in fear of eye-
offending ugliness threw it from her hands to be the
glory of the nymph-born, hand-clapping beast[2] Mar-
syas; for why should a keen yearning for lovely
beauty distress her, to whom Clotho had assigned a
marriageless and childless virginity?

He implies that because of her virginity she would not
have taken care to avoid physical ugliness; and he goes on
to say,

(b) No, this is a tale that idly flew to Greece, told
by idly-talking Muse-followers, a tale unsuited to
the choral dance, an invidious reproach brought
among mortals against a clever skill.

[1] Continued from Melanippides 758.   [2] Marsyas was a satyr.

μετὰ ταῦτα δὲ ἐγκωμιάζων τὴν αὐλητικὴν λέγει·

(c) ἃν συνεριθοτάταν Βρομίῳ παρέδωκε σεμνᾶς
δαίμονος ἀερθὲν πνεῦμ' αἰολοπτέρυγον
σὺν ἀγλαᾶν ὠκύτατι χειρῶν.

(c) 1 (λέγει·) ἃν Kaibel: λεγεγαν cod.   Hecker: συμεριθ-
cod.   2 ἀερόεν ci. Bergk   Hartung: -πτερύγων cod.

ΑΣΚΛΗΠΙΟΣ

806 Athen. 14. 617b (iii 361 Kaibel)

κομψῶς δὲ κἀν τῷ Ἀσκληπιῷ ὁ Τελέστης ἐδήλωσε τὴν τῶν
αὐλῶν χρείαν ἐν τούτοις·

ἢ Φρύγα καλλιπνόων αὐλῶν ἱερῶν βασιλῆα,
Λυδὸν ὃς ἅρμοσε πρῶτος
Δωρίδος ἀντίπαλον μούσας νόμον αἰολομόρφοις
πνεύματος εὔπτερον αὔραν ἀμφιπλέκων καλάμοις.

2 Huschke (Λυδὸν), Grotefend (ἥρμοσε): ἀνδον ὃς ηροσε cod.   3
Musurus: δουρ- cod.   4 Dobree (νόμον), Wilamowitz (αἰολομόρ-
φοις): νομοαίολον ὀρφναι cod.   αἰόλον ὀμφᾷ Schweighäuser

807 = Cinesias 774

cf. Philodem. de piet. p. 17 Gomperz

ΥΜΕΝΑΙΟΣ

808 Athen. 14. 637a (iii 406 Kaibel)

Τελέστης δ' ἐν Ὑμεναίῳ διθυράμβῳ πεντάχορδόν φησιν αὐτὴν
(sc. τὴν μάγαδιν) εἶναι διὰ τούτων·

128

Next he sings the praises of pipe-music and says,

(c) it was handed over as a most helpful servant to Bromius[3] by the uplifted wing-flashing breath of the august goddess along with the swiftness of her glorious hands.

[3] Dionysus, god of the dithyramb.

ASCLEPIUS

806 Athenaeus, *Scholars at Dinner*[1]

In his *Asclepius* too Telestes elegantly indicated the use of the pipes in these lines:

or the Phrygian king[2] of the fair-breathing holy pipes, who was the first to tune the Lydian strain, rival of the Dorian muse, weaving about the quivering[3] reeds the fair-winged gust of his breath.

[1] Continued from 805.   [2] Presumably Olympus, pupil (or son) of Marsyas: see Olympus testt. 1–3, 6.   [3] Text uncertain.

807 = Cinesias 774

HYMENAEUS

808 Athenaeus, *Scholars at Dinner*

Telestes in his dithyramb *Hymenaeus* says the magadis is five-stringed[1] in these lines:

[1] An error: 'five-staffed' (v. 3) describes the framework of the instrument: see G. Comotti, *Q.U.C.C.* n.s. 15 (1983) 57–71.

ἄλλος δ᾽ ἄλλαν κλαγγὰν ἱεὶς
κερατόφωνον ἐρεθίζε μάγαδιν
πενταρράβδῳ χορδᾶν ἀρθμῷ
χέρα καμψιδίαυλον ἀναστρωφῶν τάχος.

cf. Eust. *Il.* 1108. 1 (v. 4)

3 Dindorf: ἐν πεντ. cod. A   -ράβδωι A, -ρόδω E, -ράδωι C
Bergk: ἀριθμῷ codd.   4 Wilamowitz: χεῖρα Athen., Eust.

ΔΙΟΣ ΓΟΝΑΙ?

809 Philodem. *De Piet.* (p. 23 Gomperz: v. A. Henrichs,
Cron. ercol. 5 (1975) 18s.)

καὶ Τελέσ[της ἐν Διὸ]ς γονα<ῖ>ς το[. . . . (.) κ]αὶ Ῥέαν στ[

τὸ [αὐτὸ] Philippson

810 Athen. 14. 625e–626a (iii 380s. Kaibel)

τὴν δὲ Φρυγιστὶ καὶ τὴν Λυδιστὶ παρὰ τῶν βαρβάρων οὔσας
γνωσθῆναι τοῖς Ἕλλησιν ἀπὸ τῶν σὺν Πέλοπι κατελθόντων εἰς τὴν
Πελοπόννησον Φρυγῶν καὶ Λυδῶν. . . . διὸ καὶ Τελέστης ὁ Σελι-
νούντιός φησιν·

πρῶτοι παρὰ κρατῆρας Ἑλλάνων ἐν αὐλοῖς
συνοπαδοὶ Πέλοπος Ματρὸς ὀρείας
Φρύγιον ἄεισαν νόμον·
τοὶ δ᾽ ὀξυφώνοις πηκτίδων ψαλμοῖς κρέκον
5 Λύδιον ὕμνον.

1 Bergk: Ἑλλήν- Athen.   4 Musurus: τοῖς δ᾽ Athen.
fort. πακτ-   ψαλμοὶ Athen., corr. codd. recc.

and sending forth each a different clamour they were rousing the horn-voiced[2] magadis, swiftly turning to and fro their lap-rounding[3] hands on the five-staffed jointing of the strings.

[2] I.e. resonant like the military instrument.   [3] The hand resembles a runner completing a double course, there and back.

BIRTH OF ZEUS?

809 Philodemus, *On Piety*[1]

and Telestes in his *Birth of Zeus* (says the same thing and that Rhea . . . ?)[2]

[1] Continued from Melanippides 764.   [2] Perhaps that like Demeter she was the same as the Mother of the gods.

810 Athenaeus, *Scholars at Dinner*

The Phrygian and Lydian tunings originated with the barbarians and came to be known to the Greeks from the Phrygians and Lydians who settled in the Peloponnese with Pelops. . . . That is why Telestes of Selinus says,

The first to sing to the pipes the Phrygian tune of the mountain Mother beside the mixing-bowls of the Greeks[1] were the companions of Pelops; and the Greeks began to twang the Lydian hymn with the shrill-voiced plucking of the pectis.[2]

[1] I.e. at Greek drinking-parties.   [2] A lyre like the magadis: see Terpander test. 12.

811 Athen. 11. 501f–502a (iii 107 Kaibel)

καὶ Θεόπομπος δ᾽ ἐν Ἀλθαίᾳ (fr. 4 K.-A.) ἔφη·

λαβοῦσα πλήρη χρυσέαν μεσόμφαλον
φιάλην· Τελέστης δ᾽ ἄκατον ὠνόμαζέ νιν·

ὡς τοῦ Τελέστου

ἄκατον

τὴν φιάλην εἰρηκότος.

ἄκρατον (Theopomp. v. 2) cod. A, corr. Porson   τοῦ Τ. ἄκατον, ρ
supra κ scr. cod. A

812 Philodem. *De Piet.* p. 18 Gomperz

Αἰσχύλος δ[. . . . .] καὶ Εἴβ[υκος (fr. 292) καὶ Τε]λέστης
[. . . . .] τὰς Ἁρπ[υίας . . .

ποιοῦσιν] τὰς Ἁρπ[υίας θνησκ]ούσας ὑπ[ὸ τῶν Βορέου παί]δων suppl.
Gomperz

132

TELESTES

811 Athenaeus, *Scholars at Dinner*

And Theopompus said in his *Althaea*, 'She, taking a full golden mid-bossed goblet—but Telestes called it a boat,' for Telestes used the term

boat

for goblet (*phiale*).

812 Philodemus, *On Piety*

Aeschylus ... and Ibycus and Telestes (represent) the Harpies (as being killed by the sons of Boreas?).

ARIPHRON

TESTIMONIUM VITAE

1 *I.G.* ii 3. 1280

Μνησίμαχος Μνησιστράτου Θεότιμος Διοτίμου ἐχορήγουν, Ἀρί-
φρων ἐδίδασκεν, Π[ολυχ]άρης Κώμω[ν]ος ἐ[δίδ]ασκεν.

PAEAN

813 Athen. 15. 701f–702b (iii 559s. Kaibel)

τὸν εἰς τὴν Ὑγίειαν παιᾶνα ᾄσας τὸν ποιηθέντα ὑπὸ Ἀρίφρο-
νος τοῦ Σικυωνίου τόνδε ·

Ὑγίεια βροτοῖσι πρεσβίστα μακάρων, μετὰ σεῦ
ναίοιμι τὸ λειπόμενον βιοτᾶς, σὺ δέ μοι πρόφρων
ξυνείης ·

cf. *I.G.*[2] ii 4533 (lapis Cass.), iv 1. 132 (lapis Epidaur.), cod. Ottob.
gr. 59 ii fol. 31v, Plut. *virt. mor.* 10, *de frat. am.* 2, Luc. *de lapsu* 6
(τὸ γνωριμώτατον ἐκεῖνο καὶ πᾶσι διὰ στόματος), Max. Tyr. 7. 1a, Sext.
Emp. *adv. math.* 11. 49, Stob. 4. 27. 9

1 βροτοῖσι Cass., Ottob., Epidaur.: om. Athen., Luc., Max.   σεῦ
Epidaur., Luc.: σοῦ Cass., Ottob., Athen., Max.   2 βιοτᾶς
Athen., Luc., Max.: βίου Cass., βὶ Ottob.   ξυνείης Ottob., Epi-
daur. ut vid.: ζυγείην Cass.   σύνοικος εἴης Athen., ξύνοικον
ἐλθεῖν in paraphrasi Max.

ARIPHRON

1 Attic inscription (early 4th c. B.C.)

Mnesimachus son of Mnesistratus and Theotimus son of Diotimus were the *chorēgoi*, Ariphron trained the chorus, and Polychares son of Comon trained the chorus.

PAEAN TO HEALTH

813 Athenaeus, *Scholars at Dinner*

He sang the paean to Health that was composed by Ariphron of Sicyon, as follows[1]:

Health, most revered of the blessed ones among mortals, may I dwell with you for what is left of my life, and may you graciously keep company with me:

[1] The paean is preserved on an Athenian stone dated *c.* 200 A.D. (now in Kassel) and on a very fragmentary stone from the Asclepieum at Epidaurus. Lucian calls it 'very well known, on everyone's lips', and Maximus of Tyre shows that it was still sung in their day; see also Licymnius 769.

εἰ γάρ τις ἢ πλούτου χάρις ἢ τεκέων
ἢ τᾶς ἰσοδαίμονος ἀνθρώποις βασιληΐδος ἀρχᾶς ἢ
πόθων

5 οὓς κρυφίοις Ἀφροδίτας ἔρκεσιν θηρεύομεν,
ἢ εἴ τις ἄλλα θεόθεν ἀνθρώποισι τέρψις ἢ πόνων
ἀμπνοὰ πέφανται,
μετὰ σεῖο, μάκαιρ᾽ Ὑγίεια,
τέθαλε καὶ λάμπει Χαρίτων ὀάροις·

10 σέθεν δὲ χωρὶς οὔτις εὐδαίμων ἔφυ.

3 εἰ γάρ τις ἢ Ottob., Athen. cod. E: ἢ γάρ τις Athen. cod. A, ηδαυθιση
Cass., τίς γὰρ Sext., οὔτε γὰρ Plut. in paraphrasi   χάριν Cass.,
Plut.   4 ηδαυθισευδαιμονος Cass., τᾶς εἰσοδαίμονος, om. ἢ,
Athen.   4s. αρχασηποιφρονζυγιησαφροδειτασ Cass.   5 ἔρκεσι
Ottob.: ελκεσι Cass., ἄρκυσι Epid., ἀρκουσι Athen.   6 ἢ εἰ
Athen.: η Ottob., η[.]σ Cass.   7 ἀμπνοὰ Ottob., Athen.: ακμα[.]
Cass.   πέφανται: τεθαλται Cass.   8 σεῖο: θια Cass.
9 τέθαλε Ottob., Cass.: τέθαλε πάντα Athen., Epidaur. ut vid.
ὀάροις Ottob.: ὄαροι vel ἔαροι Athen. cod. A, ὄαρι γρ. ὄαρ Athen. cod. E,
οαο[..] Cass.   10 ἔφυ om. Athen.

136

for any joy in wealth or in children or in a king's godlike rule over men or in the desires which we hunt with the hidden nets of Aphrodite, any other delight or respite from toils that has been revealed by the gods to men, with you, blessed Health, it flourishes and shines in the converse of the Graces; and without you no man is happy.

PHILOXENUS CYTHERIUS

TESTIMONIA VITAE ATQUE ARTIS

1 *Sud.* Φ 393 (iv 728s. Adler)

Φιλόξενος, Εὐλυτίδου, Κυθήριος, λυρικός. ἔγραψε διθυράμβους κδ'· τελευτᾷ δὲ ἐν Ἐφέσῳ. οὗτος ἀνδρα-ποδισθέντων τῶν Κυθήρων ὑπὸ Ἀθηναίων (Reinesius: Λακεδαιμονίων codd.) ἠγοράσθη ὑπὸ Ἀγεσύλου τινὸς καὶ ὑπ' αὐτοῦ ἐτράφη καὶ Μύρμηξ ἐκαλεῖτο. ἐπαι-δεύθη δὲ μετὰ τὸν θάνατον Ἀγεσύλου, Μελανιππίδου πριαμένου αὐτὸν τοῦ λυρικοῦ. Καλλίστρατος δὲ Ἡρα-κλείας αὐτὸν γράφει Ποντικῆς. ἔγραψε δὲ μελικῶς Γενεαλογίαν τῶν Αἰακιδῶν.

---

[1] See also Melanippides test. 1 n. 5.   [2] In 424 B.C. The mss. read 'by the Spartans'.   [3] Hesychius Δ 2261 says that some-one (a comic poet? See fr. anon. CXXII Meineke, 74 Kock) called

2 *Marm. Par.* Ep. 69 (p. 18 Jacoby)

ἀφ'] οὗ Φιλόξενος διθυραμβοποιὸς τελευτᾶι βιοὺς ἔτη ΓᴬΓ, ἔτη ΗΔΓΙ, ἄρχοντος Ἀθήνησιν Πυθέου.

---

[1] Diodorus put his *floruit* in 398: see Timotheus test. 3. Schol. Theocr. 4. 31 says he was older than the musician Pyrrhus.   [2] I.e. 380/379, 116 years before 264/263; the year of his birth is 435/434.

138

PHILOXENUS OF CYTHERA

LIFE AND WORK[1]

1 *Suda*

Philoxenus, son of Eulytides, from Cythera, lyric poet. He wrote 24 dithyrambs, and he died in Ephesus. When Cythera was enslaved by the Athenians,[2] he was bought[3] by a certain Agesylus, brought up by him, and known as Myrmex ('Ant').[4] After the death of Agesylus he received his education when he was bought by Melanippides the lyric poet. Callistratus wrote that he belonged to Pontic Heraclea.[5] He wrote a lyric poem, *The Genealogy of the Aeacids.*

him Doulon because he had been a slave (*doulos*).   [4] Cf. Timotheus test. 1 n. 3, Ar. *Thesm.* 100 (the 'ant-paths' of Agathon). [5] Wrongly, it seems. Domitius Callistratus (1st c. B.C.?) wrote an account of Pontic Heraclea (*F.Gr.H.* 433).

CHRONOLOGY[1]

2 *Parian Marble*

From the time when Philoxenus the dithyrambic poet died at the age of fifty-five 116 years[2]; Pytheas was archon at Athens.

GREEK LYRIC

3 Diod. Sic. 15. 6 (iii 366ss. Vogel)

κατὰ δὲ τὴν Σικελίαν Διονύσιος ὁ τῶν Συρακοσίων τύραννος ἀπολελυμένος τῶν πρὸς Καρχηδονίους πολέμων πολλὴν εἰρήνην καὶ σχολὴν εἶχεν. διὸ καὶ ποιήματα γράφειν ὑπεστήσατο μετὰ πολλῆς σπουδῆς, καὶ τοὺς ἐν τούτοις δόξαν ἔχοντας μετεπέμπετο καὶ προτιμῶν αὐτοὺς συνδιέτριβε καὶ τῶν ποιημάτων ἐπιστάτας καὶ διορθωτὰς εἶχεν. ὑπὸ δὲ τούτων διὰ τὰς εὐεργεσίας τοῖς πρὸς χάριν λόγοις μετεωριζόμενος ἐκαυχᾶτο πολὺ μᾶλλον ἐπὶ τοῖς ποιήμασιν ἢ τοῖς ἐν πολέμῳ κατωρθωμένοις. τῶν δὲ συνόντων αὐτῷ ποιητῶν Φιλόξενος ὁ διθυραμβοποιός, μέγιστον ἔχων ἀξίωμα κατὰ τὴν κατασκευὴν τοῦ ἰδίου ποιήματος, κατὰ τὸ συμπόσιον ἀναγνωσθέντων τῶν τοῦ τυράννου ποιημάτων μοχθηρῶν ὄντων ἐπηρωτήθη περὶ τῶν ποιημάτων τίνα κρίσιν ἔχοι. ἀποκριναμένου δ᾽ αὐτοῦ παρρησιωδέστερον, ὁ μὲν τύραννος προσκόψας τοῖς ῥηθεῖσι, καὶ καταμεμψάμενος ὅτι διὰ φθόνον ἐβλασφήμησε, προσέταξε τοῖς ὑπηρέταις παραχρῆμα ἀπάγειν εἰς τὰς λατομίας. τῇ δ᾽ ὑστεραίᾳ τῶν φίλων παρακαλούντων συγγνώμην δοῦναι τῷ Φιλοξένῳ, διαλλαγεὶς αὐτῷ πάλιν τοὺς αὐτοὺς παρέλαβεν ἐπὶ τὸ συμπόσιον. προβαίνοντος δὲ τοῦ πότου, καὶ πάλιν τοῦ Διονυσίου καυχωμένου περὶ τῶν ἰδίων ποιημάτων, καί τινας στίχους τῶν δοκούντων ἐπιτετεῦχθαι προενεγκαμένου, καὶ ἐπερωτῶντος 'ποῖά τινά σοι φαίνεται τὰ ποιήματα ὑπάρχειν;' ἄλλο

---

1 See also frr. 816, 819, Cicero, *Att.* 4. 6. 2, Plut. *Tranq.* 12, Paus. 1. 2. 3, Lucian, *Cal.* 14, Aelian, *V.H.* 12. 44, schol. Ar. *Plut.* 179, Tzetz. *Chil.* 5. 23. 152 ff.

140

PHILOXENUS OF CYTHERA

PHILOXENUS AND DIONYSIUS[1]

3 Diodorus Siculus, *World History*

In Sicily[2] Dionysius, the tyrant of Syracuse, no longer embroiled in the wars against Carthage, was enjoying peace and leisure. He began writing poetry with great enthusiasm, sending for the famous poets, spending his time with them and showering honours on them, and using them as supervisors and reviewers of his poetry. His generosity led to flattery on the part of these grateful critics, and removed from reality by it he bragged more of his poetry than of his military successes. One of the poets at his court was Philoxenus, the composer of dithyrambs, who had a high reputation for his own style of composition, and at the drinking-party when the tyrant's wretched poems were read he was asked his opinion of them; he gave a rather frank reply, and the tyrant took offence, faulted him for slandering him out of envy, and told his attendants to take him off at once to the quarries. Next day his friends begged him to pardon Philoxenus, so he made it up with him and invited the same company to the drinking-party. As the drinking progressed, Dionysius again began to brag of his poetry and cited some lines which he regarded as particularly successful; but when he asked Philoxenus what he thought of them, his only response was to summon

[2]Diod. sets the incident in 386 B.C., probably a few years too late.

μὲν οὐδὲν εἶπε, τοὺς δ' ὑπηρέτας τοῦ Διονυσίου προσ-
καλεσάμενος ἐκέλευσεν αὐτὸν ἀπαγαγεῖν εἰς τὰς λατο-
μίας. τότε μὲν οὖν διὰ τὴν εὐτραπελίαν τῶν λόγων
μειδιάσας ὁ Διονύσιος ἤνεγκε τὴν παρρησίαν, τοῦ
γέλωτος τὴν μέμψιν ἀμβλύνοντος· μετ' ὀλίγον δὲ τῶν
γνωρίμων ἅμ' ἐκείνου καὶ τοῦ Διονυσίου παραιτουμέ-
νων τὴν ἄκαιρον παρρησίαν, ὁ Φιλόξενος ἐπηγγείλατο
παράδοξόν τινα ἐπαγγελίαν. ἔφη γὰρ διὰ τῆς ἀποκρί-
σεως τηρήσειν ἅμα καὶ τὴν ἀλήθειαν καὶ τὴν εὐδόκη-
σιν τοῦ Διονυσίου, καὶ οὐ διεψεύσθη. τοῦ γὰρ τυράννου
προενεγκαμένου τινὰς στίχους ἔχοντας ἐλεεινὰ πάθη,
καὶ ἐρωτήσαντος 'ποῖά τινα φαίνεται τὰ ποιήματα;'
εἶπεν 'οἰκτρά,' διὰ τῆς ἀμφιβολίας ἀμφότερα τηρήσας.
ὁ μὲν γὰρ Διονύσιος ἐδέξατο τὰ οἰκτρὰ εἶναι ἐλεεινὰ
καὶ συμπαθείας πλήρη, τὰ δὲ τοιαῦτα εἶναι ποιητῶν
ἀγαθῶν ἐπιτεύγματα, ὅθεν ὡς ἐπηνεκότα αὐτὸν ἀπε-
δέχετο· οἱ δ' ἄλλοι τὴν ἀληθινὴν διάνοιαν ἐκδεξάμενοι
πᾶν τὸ οἰκτρὸν ἀποτεύγματος φύσιν εἰρῆσθαι διελάμ-
βανον.

4 *Sud.* Φ 397 (iv 729s. Adler)

Φιλοξένου γραμμάτιον· ἐπὶ τῶν μὴ πειθομένων ἐφ'
οἷς παρακαλοῦνται ἀλλ' ἀπαγορευόντων μᾶλλον·
Φιλόξενος γὰρ ὁ Κυθήριος διαφυγὼν τὰς εἰς Συρακού-
σας λιθοτομίας εἰς ἃς ἐνέπεσεν ὅτι τὰς τοῦ Διονυσίου

the attendants and tell them to take him off to the quarries.[3] At the time Dionysius smiled at the wittiness of the reply and put up with his frankness: laughter took the edge off fault-finding; but soon after when the friends of each party asked Dionysius to excuse his untimely frankness, Philoxenus made the strange offer that his answer would preserve both the truth and Dionysius' reputation; and he kept his promise, because when the tyrant cited some lines which described lamentable events[4] and asked what he thought of them, Philoxenus said, 'Tragic', using the ambiguity to preserve the truth together with the tyrant's reputation: Dionysius took 'tragic' to mean 'lamentable and full of pathos', and knowing that good poets excelled in such writing accepted it as praise from Philoxenus; but the rest of the company picked up the true meaning and saw that the term 'tragic' had been used only to brand a failure.

[3] 'Take me off to the quarries' became proverbial: *Suda* A 2862, EI 291, Stob. 3. 13. 31, App. Prov. 2. 26.   [4] Lucian, *Adv. Indoct.* 15, referring to the story, says D. wrote tragedy; cf. also Eust. *Od.* 1691. 32, test. 4.

4 *Suda*

'The letter of Philoxenus': applied to those who do not accept the terms of an invitation but refuse it. Philoxenus of Cythera on escaping the Syracusan quarries into which he had been thrown for refusing to praise the tragedies of the tyrant Dionysius was

τοῦ τυράννου τραγῳδίας οὐκ ἐπῄνει διέτριβεν ἐν
Τάραντι τῆς Ἰταλίας (Kuster: Σικελίας codd.). μετα-
πεμπομένου δὲ Διονυσίου αὐτὸν καὶ ἀξιοῦντος διὰ
γραμμάτων ἐλθεῖν, Φιλόξενος ἀντιγράψαι μὲν οὐκ
ἔγνω, λαβὼν δὲ βιβλίον τὸ ο (codd. AV: ου GM) στοι-
χεῖον ἔγραψε μόνον πολλάκις ἐν αὐτῷ, διὰ τούτου
δηλώσας ὅτι τὴν παράκλησιν διωθεῖται.

5 [Plut.] *Mus.* 30. 1142a (p. 125 Lasserre, vi 3. 26 Ziegler)

καὶ Ἀριστοφάνης ὁ κωμικὸς (fr. dub. 953 K.-A.)
μνημονεύει Φιλοξένου καί φησιν ὅτι εἰς τοὺς κυκλίους
χοροὺς μέλη[1] εἰσηνέγκατο. ἡ δὲ Μουσικὴ λέγει ταῦτα·
ἐξαρμονίους κτλ. (v. Timoth. test. 1).

[1]<μονῳδικὰ> μέλη Westphal, <προβατίων αἰγῶν τε> μέλη Weil-
Reinach, <ἄμουσα> vel <ἄτοπα> vel <περίεργα> μέλη Fritzsche

living in Tarentum[1] in Italy. When Dionysius wrote asking him to return, Philoxenus decided not to give a direct answer, but instead took a scroll and wrote on it the letter οὖ (omicron) several times over,[2] thus indicating that he rejected the request.[3]

[1] Croton, according to the scholiast on Aristides 46. 309 Dindorf. Plut. *Vit. Aer. Al.* 8 says he had a farm 'in a Sicilian colony'.
[2] Concentric o's according to the scholiast, who explains that Phil. meant, 'I don't care about you,' 'I don't wish to come to you,' 'Go to hell!' etc., omicron being the first letter of these expressions and οὖ being also the negative, 'not'. [3] See also Apostol. 6. 68, Diogen. 8. 54, App. Prov. 5. 16.

MUSIC[1]

5 'Plutarch', *On Music*

Further, Aristophanes the comic poet mentions Philoxenus and says he introduced songs[2] into his cyclic choruses.[3] Music speaks as follows: '... exharmonic etc.'

[1] See also frr. 825, 826, Melanippides test. 6, Timotheus testt. 8, 10, Aelian *H.A.* 2. 11. [2] Perhaps this can mean that he introduced solo songs into his (choral) dithyrambs. Editors propose 'monodic songs' or 'the songs of sheep and goats' (see frr. 819, 820) or 'tasteless' or 'strange' or 'superfluous songs'. [3] The sentence, which seems misplaced, follows the long excerpt from Pherecrates: see Timotheus test. 1 with n. 4.

6 [Plut.] *Mus.* 31. 1142bc (p. 126 Lasserre, vi 3. 26s. Ziegler)

ὅτι δὲ παρὰ τὰς ἀγωγὰς καὶ τὰς μαθήσεις διόρθωσις ἢ διαστροφὴ γίγνεται, δῆλον Ἀριστόξενος ἐποίησε (fr. 76 Wehrli). τῶν γὰρ κατὰ τὴν αὐτοῦ ἡλικίαν φησὶ Τελεσία τῷ Θηβαίῳ συμβῆναι νέῳ μὲν ὄντι τραφῆναι ἐν τῇ καλλίστῃ μουσικῇ, καὶ μαθεῖν ἄλλα τε τῶν εὐδοκιμούντων καὶ δὴ καὶ τὰ Πινδάρου, τά τε Διονυσίου τοῦ Θηβαίου καὶ τὰ Λάμπρου καὶ τὰ Πρατίνου καὶ τῶν λοιπῶν ὅσοι τῶν λυρικῶν ἄνδρες ἐγένοντο ποιηταὶ κρουμάτων ἀγαθοί· καὶ αὐλῆσαι δὲ καλῶς καὶ περὶ τὰ λοιπὰ μέρη τῆς συμπάσης παιδείας ἱκανῶς διαπονηθῆναι· παραλλάξαντα δὲ τὴν τῆς ἀκμῆς ἡλικίαν, οὕτω σφόδρα ἐξαπατηθῆναι ὑπὸ τῆς σκηνικῆς τε καὶ ποικίλης μουσικῆς, ὡς καταφρονῆσαι τῶν καλῶν ἐκείνων ἐν οἷς ἀνετράφη, τὰ Φιλοξένου δὲ καὶ Τιμοθέου ἐκμανθάνειν, καὶ τούτων αὐτῶν τὰ ποικιλώτατα καὶ πλείστην ἐν αὑτοῖς ἔχοντα καινοτομίαν· ὁρμήσαντά τ' ἐπὶ τὸ ποιεῖν μέλη καὶ διαπειρώμενον ἀμφοτέρων τῶν τρόπων, τοῦ τε Πινδαρείου καὶ τοῦ Φιλοξενείου, μὴ δύνασθαι κατορθοῦν ἐν τῷ Φιλοξενείῳ γένει· γεγενῆσθαι δ' αἰτίαν τὴν ἐκ παιδὸς καλλίστην ἀγωγήν.

7 Philod. *Mus.* 1. 23 (IX 67 fr. 5) (p. 133 Rispoli)

κ[αὶ τοὺ]ς δειθυραμβικοὺς δὲ τρόπους εἴ τις συγκρίναι, τόν τε κατὰ Πίνδαρον καὶ τὸν κατὰ Φιλόξενον, μεγάλην εὑρεθήσεσθαι τὴν διαφορὰν τῶν ἐπιφαινομένων ἠθῶν, τὸν αὐτὸν δ' εἶναι τρόπον.

6 'Plutarch', *On Music*

That training and teaching are responsible for the proper practice or the perversion of music was made clear by Aristoxenus, who says that among his contemporaries Telesias[1] of Thebes was brought up in his youth on the most beautiful music and learned the works of the distinguished poets, in particular Pindar, Dionysius of Thebes, Lamprus,[2] Pratinas and all the other lyric poets who composed good music for the lyre; in addition, he was a fine piper and was well instructed in all the other branches of a complete musical education; but when he left his youth behind him he was so completely seduced by the elaborate music of the theatre that he came to despise the fine composers on whom he had been brought up and began learning by heart the works of Philoxenus and Timotheus—and the most elaborate and innovative works at that; but when he tried his hand at composition and attempted both styles, the Pindaric and the Philoxenean, he failed to achieve success in the Philoxenean, simply because of the fine training he had had since his boyhood.

[1] Unknown.   [2] = Lamprus test. 1. All four composed in the 5th c.

7 Philodemus, *On Music*

If the dithyrambic styles of Pindar and Philoxenus are compared, it will be found that there is a great difference in the characters represented, but the style is the same.

8 Athen. 8. 352c (ii 272 Kaibel)

ζηλωτὴς δὲ <διὰ> τῶν εὐτραπέλων λόγων τούτων
ἐγένετο ὁ Στρατόνικος Σιμωνίδου τοῦ ποιητοῦ, ὥς
φησιν Ἔφορος ἐν δευτέρῳ περὶ εὑρημάτων (*F.Gr.H.* 70
F2), φάσκων καὶ Φιλόξενον τὸν Κυθήριον περὶ τὰ
ὅμοια ἐσπουδακέναι.

9 (a) Stob. 2. 31 (περὶ ἀγωγῆς καὶ παιδείας) 86 (ii 216 Wachs-
muth)

Φιλόξενος ὁ μουσικός, ἐρωτηθεὶς τί μάλιστα συνερ-
γεῖ παιδείᾳ, εἶπε ʻχρόνοςʼ.

(b) *Flor. Mon.* 260 (iv 289 Meineke, *Stobaeus*)

Φιλόξενος παρῄνει προτιμᾶν τῶν γονέων τοὺς διδα-
σκάλους, ὅτι οἱ μὲν γονεῖς τοῦ ζῆν μόνον, οἱ δὲ διδά-
σκαλοι τοῦ καλῶς ζῆν αἴτιοι γεγόνασιν.
261 (ibid.) ὁ αὐτὸς πρὸς μειράκιον ἐρυθριᾶσαν ἔφη,
ʻθάρρει· τοιοῦτον γὰρ ἡ ἀρετὴ ἔχει τὸ χρῶμα.ʼ

10 Athen. 8. 341e (ii 250 Kaibel)

περὶ δὲ τοῦ Φιλοξένου καὶ ὁ παρῳδὸς Σώπατρος
λέγων φησί (fr. 23 Kaibel, Olivieri)·

δισσαῖς γὰρ ἐν μέσαισιν ἰχθύων φοραῖς
ἧσται τὸν Αἴτνης ἐς μέσον λεύσσων σκοπόν.

---

[1] There may be confusion with Phil. of Leucas, author of the *Ban-
quet* (836 *P.M.G.*); see also fr. 816 with n. 1, fr. 828.   [2] The
passage follows test. 11.   [3] *C.* 300 B.C.

PHILOXENUS OF CYTHERA

APOPHTHEGMS

8 Athenaeus, *Scholars at Dinner*

In the matter of these witticisms Stratonicus tried to emulate the poet Simonides,[1] as Ephorus says in book 2 of his work *On Inventions*, alleging that Philoxenus of Cythera had the same ambition.[2]

[1] See Sim. test. 47. [2] Diogenes Laertius gives an example (4. 6. 11): Phil. found brickmakers singing one of his songs badly, trampled on their bricks and said, 'As you destroy my work, so I destroy yours.'

9 (a) Stobaeus, *Anthology* (on training and education)

The musician Philoxenus, asked what is the greatest aid to education, said 'Time'.

(b) *Munich Anthology*

(i) Philoxenus used to advise men to honour their teachers more than their parents, since parents are responsible only for life, teachers for a good life.
(ii) To a youth who had crimsoned Philoxenus said, 'Cheer up! That is virtue's colour.'

PHILOXENUS THE FISH-EATER[1]

10 Athenaeus, *Scholars at Dinner*[2]

The parodist Sopater[3] says of Philoxenus, 'Between two courses of fish he sits gazing at the lookout half-way up Etna.'

11 Athen. 8. 341a–d (ii 249s. Kaibel)

περὶ δὲ Φιλοξένου τοῦ Κυθηρίου διθυραμβοποιοῦ
Μάχων ὁ κωμῳδιοποιὸς τάδε γράφει (fr. 9 Gow)·

> ὑπερβολῇ λέγουσι τὸν Φιλόξενον
> τῶν διθυράμβων τὸν ποιητὴν γεγονέναι
> ὀψοφάγον. εἶτα πουλύποδα πηχῶν δυεῖν
> ἐν ταῖς Συρακούσαις ποτ' αὐτὸν ἀγοράσαι
> 5 καὶ σκευάσαντα καταφαγεῖν ὅλον σχεδόν
> πλὴν τῆς κεφαλῆς, ἁλόντα δ' ὑπὸ δυσπεψίας
> κακῶς ἔχειν σφόδρ'· εἶτα δ' ἰατροῦ τινος
> πρὸς αὐτὸν εἰσελθόντος ὃς φαύλως πάνυ
> ὁρῶν φερόμενον αὐτὸν εἶπεν, 'εἴ τί σοι
> 10 ἀνοικονόμητόν ἐστι διατίθου ταχύ,
> Φιλόξεν', ἀποθανῇ γὰρ ὥρας ἑβδόμης.'
> κἀκεῖνος εἶπε, 'τέλος ἔχει τὰ πάντα μοι,
> ἰατρέ,' φησί, 'καὶ δεδώκηται πάλαι.
> τοὺς διθυράμβους σὺν θεοῖς καταλιμπάνω
> 15 ἠνδρωμένους καὶ πάντας ἐστεφανωμένους,
> οὓς ἀνατίθημι ταῖς ἐμαυτοῦ συντρόφοις
> Μούσαις. Ἀφροδίτην καὶ Διόνυσον ἐπιτρόπους—
> ταῦθ' αἱ διαθῆκαι διασαφοῦσιν, ἀλλ' ἐπεί
> ὁ Τιμοθέου Χάρων σχολάζειν οὐκ ἐᾷ,
> 20 οὑκ τῆς Νιόβης, χωρεῖν δὲ πορθμὸν ἀναβοᾷ,
> καλεῖ δὲ μοῖρα νύχιος ἧς κλύειν χρεών,
> ἵν' ἔχων ἀποτρέχω πάντα τἀμαυτοῦ κάτω
> τοῦ πουλύποδός μοι τὸ κατάλοιπον ἀπόδοτε.'

κἀν ἄλλῳ δὲ μέρει φησί·

> Φιλόξενός ποθ', ὡς λέγουσ', ὁ Κυθήριος

PHILOXENUS OF CYTHERA

11 Athenaeus, *Scholars at Dinner*

Of the dithyrambic poet Philoxenus of Cythera Machon, the comic poet,[1] writes as follows: 'They say that Philoxenus, the composer of dithyrambs, was an excessively enthusiastic fish-eater. Once in Syracuse he bought an octopus three feet wide, prepared it and ate nearly all of it except the head. Seized by dyspepsia, he was very seriously ill, and a doctor arrived, who on seeing his poor condition said, "If any of your affairs are not in order, Philoxenus, see to them at once, since you will die before the seventh hour." Philoxenus replied, "Everything is complete, doctor, and has been in order for a long time. By the gods' grace I leave my dithyrambs behind grown to manhood and crowned with garlands, all of them, and I dedicate them to the Muses with whom I was brought up; Aphrodite and Dionysus as their guardians — my will makes all this clear. But since Timotheus' Charon, the one in his *Niobe*,[2] does not let me dally but shouts that the ferry-boat is leaving, and gloomy Fate, who must be obeyed, is summoning me[3] — so that I may have all my belongings with me when I run off down below, fetch me the remains of that octopus!"' Elsewhere he writes, 'Philoxenus of Cythera, they say, once

---

[1] C. 250 B.C.   [2] Fr. 786.   [3] According to the *Suda* Phil. died in Ephesus. The tale is likely to be apocryphal.

ηὔξατο τριῶν σχεῖν τὸν λάρυγγα πήχεων,
'ὅπως καταπίνω', φησίν, 'ὅτι πλεῖστον χρόνον
καὶ πάνθ' ἅμα μοι τὰ βρώμαθ' ἡδονὴν ποιῇ.'

12 Athen. 14. 643de (iii 422 Kaibel)

ταῦτα καὶ ὁ Κυθήριος Φιλόξενος, ὃν ἐπαινῶν Ἀντι-
φάνης ἐν τῷ Τριταγωνιστῇ φησι (fr. 207 K.-A.)·

   πολύ γ' ἐστὶ πάντων τῶν ποιητῶν διάφορος
   ὁ Φιλόξενος. πρώτιστα μὲν γὰρ ὀνόμασιν
   ἰδίοισι καὶ καινοῖσι χρῆται πανταχοῦ,
   ἔπειτα <τὰ> μέλη μεταβολαῖς καὶ χρώμασιν
5 ὡς εὖ κέκραται. θεὸς ἐν ἀνθρώποισιν ἦν
   ἐκεῖνος, εἰδὼς τὴν ἀληθῶς μουσικήν.
   οἱ νῦν δὲ κισσόπλεκτα καὶ κρηναῖα καὶ
   ἀνθεσιπότατα μέλεα μελέοις ὀνόμασι
   ποιοῦσιν ἐμπλέκοντες ἀλλότρια μέλη.

prayed to get a throat four feet long "so that I may have the longest possible time for swallowing and my foods may give me pleasure all at the same time.'"

THE VERDICT OF ANTIQUITY[1]

12 Athenaeus, *Scholars at Dinner*

These[2] are the lines of Philoxenus of Cythera, in praise of whom Antiphanes[3] says in his *Third Actor*: 'Far superior to all other poets is Philoxenus. In the first place, he always uses new words of his own, and, secondly, what a fine blend his songs are of modulations and chromatics! A god among men he was, and he knew true poetry and music. But poets nowadays compose ivy-twined, fountain stuff, flower-flitting, wretched songs with wretched words, into which they weave other men's melodies.'

[1] See also Timotheus test. 13, Telestes test. 3. [2] Athen. has cited fr. 836(e) from the *Banquet* (by Phil. of Leucas). [3] Prolific comic poet, first play produced in 385 B.C.

PHILOXENUS CYTHERIUS

FRAGMENTA

ΓΕΝΕΑΛΟΓΙΑ ΤΩΝ ΑΙΑΚΙΔΩΝ

814 v. test. 1.

ΚΥΚΛΩΨ ἢ ΓΑΛΑΤΕΙΑ

815 Hermesianax fr. 7. 69ss. Powell (*Coll. Alex.* p. 100)
(ap. Athen. 13. 598e)

> ἄνδρα δὲ τὸν Κυθέρηθεν ὃν ἐθρέψαντο τιθῆναι
> Βάκχου καὶ λωτοῦ πιστότατον ταμίην
> Μοῦσαι παιδευθέντα Φιλόξενον, οἷα τιναχθεὶς
> Ὀρτυγίῃ ταύτης ἦλθε διὰ πτόλεως
> γιγνώσκεις, ἀίουσα μέγαν πόθον ὃν Γαλατείᾳ
> αὐτοῖς μηλείοις θήκαθ᾽ ὑπὸ προγόνοις.

PHILOXENUS OF CYTHERA

FRAGMENTS

GENEALOGY OF THE AEACIDS

814 : See test. 1.

CYCLOPS *or* GALATEA[1]

815 Hermesianax, *Leontium*[2]

And you know how the man from Cythera, whom the Muses reared as his nurses, taught to be the most trusty steward of Bacchus and the pipe,[3] Philoxenus, came through this city[4] after a great battering in Ortygia[5]; for you have heard of his passionate longing, which Galatea ranked lower than the very first-born lambs.

[1] See also Timotheus 782, Oeniades 840, *P.M.G.* 966, Aelian *V.H.* 12. 44 (Phil. composed the dithyramb in the quarries). *Pap. Rainer* n.s. 1932 p. 140 fr. bIII seems to be a commentary on a *Cyclops*. [2] Herm. is listing for his mistress Leontium the loves of poets and philosophers. [3] As dithyrambic composer. [4] Presumably Colophon, Herm.'s city. [5] I.e., battered by his love for Galatea in Syracuse. Text uncertain.

GREEK LYRIC

816 Athen. 1. 6e–7a (i 13s. Kaibel)

Φαινίας δέ φησιν (fr. 13 Wehrli) ὅτι Φιλόξενος ὁ Κυθήριος ποιητής, περιπαθὴς ὢν τοῖς ὄψοις, δειπνῶν ποτε παρὰ Διονυσίῳ ὡς εἶδεν ἐκείνῳ μὲν μεγάλην τρῖγλαν παρατεθεῖσαν, ἑαυτῷ δὲ μικράν, ἀναλαβὼν αὐτὴν εἰς τὰς χεῖρας πρὸς τὸ οὖς προσήνεγκε. πυθομένου δὲ τοῦ Διονυσίου τίνος ἕνεκεν τοῦτο ποιεῖ, εἶπεν ὁ Φιλόξενος ὅτι γράφων τὴν Γαλάτειαν βούλοιτό τινα παρ᾽ ἐκείνης τῶν κατὰ Νηρέα πυθέσθαι· τὴν δὲ ἠρωτημένην ἀποκεκρίσθαι διότι νεωτέρα ἁλοίη· διὸ μὴ παρακολουθεῖν· τὴν δὲ τῷ Διονυσίῳ παρατεθεῖσαν πρεσβυτέραν οὖσαν εἰδέναι πάντα σαφῶς ἃ βούλεται μαθεῖν. τὸν οὖν Διονύσιον γελάσαντα ἀποστεῖλαι αὐτῷ τὴν τρῖγλαν τὴν παρακειμένην αὐτῷ. συνεμέθυε δὲ τῷ Φιλοξένῳ ἡδέως ὁ Διονύσιος. ἐπεὶ δὲ τὴν ἐρωμένην Γαλάτειαν ἐφωράθη διαφθείρων, εἰς τὰς λατομίας ἐνεβλήθη· ἐν αἷς ποιῶν τὸν Κύκλωπα συνέθηκε τὸν μῦθον εἰς τὸ περὶ αὐτὸν γενόμενον πάθος, τὸν μὲν Διονύσιον Κύκλωπα ὑποστησάμενος, τὴν δ᾽ αὐλητρίδα Γαλάτειαν, ἑαυτὸν δ᾽ Ὀδυσσέα.

817 Schol. Theocr. 6(f) (p. 189 Wendel)

Δοῦρίς φησι (F.Gr.H. 76 F58) διὰ τὴν εὐβοσίαν τῶν θρεμμάτων καὶ τοῦ γάλακτος πολυπλήθειαν τὸν Πολύφημον ἱδρύσασθαι ἱερὸν παρὰ τῇ Αἴτνῃ Γαλατείας· Φιλόξενον δὲ τὸν Κυθήριον ἐπιδημήσαντα καὶ μὴ δυνάμενον ἐπινοῆσαι τὴν αἰτίαν ἀναπλάσαι ὡς ὅτι Πολύφημος ἤρα τῆς Γαλατείας.

PHILOXENUS OF CYTHERA

816 Athenaeus, *Scholars at Dinner*[1]

Phaenias[2] says that the poet Philoxenus of Cythera, who was extremely fond of fish, was dining once with Dionysius when he saw that a large mullet had been served to the tyrant and a small one to himself. He took the fish and put it to his ear; and when Dionysius asked why he was doing that, he replied that he was writing his *Galatea* and wanted some information about Nereus[3] from the mullet, but she had replied that she was too young when she was caught and so could not follow what he said, but that the fish that had been served to Dionysius was older and had a clear understanding of all he wanted to know; at which the tyrant laughed and sent him the mullet that was at his place. Dionysius used to enjoy getting drunk with Philoxenus; but when the poet was caught in the act of seducing the tyrant's mistress Galatea, he was thrown into the quarries. There he wrote his *Cyclops* and adapted the plot to his own unhappy fate, making Dionysius the Cyclops, the pipe-girl Galatea and himself Odysseus.

[1] Cf. *Suda* Φ 395 (s.v. Philoxenus, son of Leucadius).
[2] Presumably in his work *On the Sicilian Tyrants*; *floruit* 320 B.C.
[3] Sea-god, father of the nymph Galatea.

817 Scholiast on Theocritus 6

Duris[1] says that Polyphemus built a shrine to Galatea near Mount Etna in gratitude for the rich pasturage for his flocks and the abundant supply of milk,[2] but that Philoxenus of Cythera when he paid his visit and could not think of the reason for the shrine invented the tale that Polyphemus was in love with Galatea.

[1] Tyrant of Samos and historian, *c.* 340–*c.* 260 B.C.   [2] Greek *gala*.

157

818 Synes. *Epist.* 121 (*Patr. Gr.* 66. 1500b–d Migne, Hercher, *Epist. Gr.* p. 711s.)

Ἀθανασίῳ ὑδρομίκτῃ. Ὀδυσσεὺς ἔπειθε τὸν Πολύφημον διαφεῖναι αὐτὸν ἐκ τοῦ σπηλαίου· 'γόης γάρ εἰμι καὶ ἐς καιρὸν ἄν σοι παρείην οὐκ εὐτυχοῦντι τὰ εἰς τὸν θαλάττιον ἔρωτα· ἀλλ' ἐγώ τοι καὶ ἐπῳδὰς οἶδα καὶ καταδέσμους καὶ ἐρωτικὰς καταναγκας, αἷς οὐκ εἰκὸς ἀντισχεῖν οὐδὲ πρὸς βραχὺ τὴν Γαλάτειαν. μόνον ὑπόστηθι σὺ τὴν θύραν ἀποκινῆσαι, μᾶλλον δὲ τὸν θυρεὸν τοῦτον· ἐμοὶ μὲν γὰρ καὶ ἀκρωτήριον εἶναι φαίνεται· ἐγὼ δὲ ἐπανήξω σοι θᾶττον ἢ λόγος τὴν παῖδα κατεργασάμενος· τί λέγω κατεργασάμενος; αὐτὴν ἐκείνην ἀποφανῶ σοι δεῦρο πολλαῖς ἴυγξι γενομένην ἀγώγιμον. καὶ δεήσεταί σου καὶ ἀντιβολήσει, σὺ δὲ ἀκκιῇ καὶ κατειρωνεύσῃ. ἀτὰρ μεταξύ μέ τι καὶ τοιοῦτον ἔθραξε, μὴ τῶν κῳδίων ὁ γράσος ἀηδὴς γένηται κόρῃ τρυφώσῃ καὶ λουμένῃ τῆς ἡμέρας πολλάκις· καλὸν οὖν εἰ πάντα εὐθετήσας ἐκκορήσειάς τε καὶ ἐκπλύνειας καὶ ἐκθυμιάσαις (Diggle: -πλυνεῖς καὶ ἐνθυμι-codd.) τὸ δωμάτιον· ἔτι δὲ κάλλιον εἰ καὶ στεφάνους παρασκευάσαιο κιττοῦ τε καὶ μίλακος, οἷς σαυτόν τε καὶ τὰ παιδικὰ ἀναδήσαιο. ἀλλὰ τί διατρίβεις; οὐκ ἐγχειρεῖς ἤδη τῇ θύρᾳ;' πρὸς οὖν ταῦτα ὁ Πολύφημος ἐξεκάγχασέ τε ὅσον ἠδύνατο μέγιστον καὶ τὼ χεῖρε ἐκρότησε. καὶ ὁ μὲν Ὀδυσσεὺς ᾤετο αὐτὸν ὑπὸ χαρμονῆς οὐκ ἔχειν ὅ τι ἑαυτῷ χρήσαιτο κατελπίσαντα τῶν παιδικῶν περιέσεσθαι. ὁ δὲ ὑπογενειάσας αὐτόν, 'ὦ Οὖτι,' ἔφη, 'δριμύτατον μὲν ἀνθρώπιον ἔοικας εἶναι καὶ ἐγκατατετριμμένον ἐν πράγμασιν. ἄλλο μέντοι τι ποίκιλλε· ἐνθένδε γὰρ οὐκ ἀποδράσεις.'

ὁ μὲν οὖν Ὀδυσσεύς, ἠδικεῖτο γὰρ ὄντως, ἔμελλεν ἄρα τῆς πανουργίας ὀνήσεσθαι· σὲ δέ, Κύκλωπα μὲν ὄντα τῇ τόλμῃ, Σίσυφον δὲ τοῖς ἐγχειρήμασι, δίκη μετῆλθε καὶ νόμος καθεῖρξεν, ὧν μή ποτε σὺ καταγελάσειας. εἰ δὲ δεῖ πάντως ὑπερέχειν σε τῶν νόμων, ἀλλὰ μὴ ἔγωγε εἴην ὁ παραλύων αὐτοὺς καὶ τὰς θύρας καταρρηγνὺς τοῦ ἐπὶ τοῖς δεσμώταις οἰκήματος· καὶ γὰρ εἰ μὲν ἦν ἐπὶ τοῖς ἱερεῦσιν ἡ πολιτεία, κτλ.

---

[1] The first half of the letter is probably derived, directly or indirectly, from Philoxenus' poem.

PHILOXENUS OF CYTHERA

818 Synesius, *Letter*[1]

To Athanasius, diluter of wine. Odysseus was trying to persuade Polyphemus to let him out of the cave: 'for I am a sorcerer,' he said, 'and I could give you timely help in your unsuccessful marine love: I know incantations and binding charms and love spells which Galatea is unlikely to resist even for a short time. For your part, just promise to move the door — or rather this door-stone: it seems as big as a promontory to me — and I'll return more quickly than it takes to tell, after winning the girl over. Winning her over, do I say? I'll produce her here in person, made compliant by many enchantments. She'll beg and beseech you, and you will play coy and hide your true feelings. But one thing worries me in all this: I'm afraid the goat-stink of your fleecy blankets may be offensive to a girl who lives in luxury and washes many times a day. So it would be a good idea if you put everything in order and swept and washed and fumigated your room, and better still if you prepared wreaths of ivy and bindweed to garland yourself and your darling girl. Come on, why waste time? Why not put your hand to the door now?' At this Polyphemus roared with laughter and clapped his hands, and Odysseus imagined he was beside himself with joy at the thought that he would win his darling; but instead he stroked him under the chin and said, 'No-man, you seem to be a shrewd little fellow, a smooth businessman; start work on some other elaborate scheme, however, for you won't escape from here.'

Now Odysseus, who was being genuinely wronged, was destined in the end to profit from his cleverness; whereas you, a Cyclops in your boldness and a Sisyphus in your endeavours, have been overtaken by justice and imprisoned by the law — and may you never laugh at these; but if you must at all events have the better of the laws, then I hope I may not be the one to undo them and break down the doors of the building that houses the prisoners. If the governing of the state were in the hands of the priests, . . .

819 Ar. *Plut.* 290ss.

ΚΑ. καὶ μὴν ἐγὼ βουλήσομαι

θρεττανελό

τὸν Κύκλωπα / μιμούμενος καὶ τοῖν ποδοῖν ὡδὶ παρενσαλεύων /
ὑμᾶς ἄγειν·

ἀλλ' εἶα τέκεα θαμίν' ἐπαναβοῶντες /

βληχώμενοί τε προβατίων / αἰγῶν τε κιναβρώντων μέλη / ἔπεσθ'
ἀπεψωλημένοι· τράγοι δ' ἀκρατιεῖσθε.

Schol. ad loc. (p. 341 Dübner): ... διασύρει δὲ Φιλόξενον τὸν
τραγικόν, ὃς εἰσήγαγε κιθαρίζοντα τὸν Πολύφημον. τὸ δὲ 'θρεττα-
νελό' ποιὸν μέλος καὶ κρουμάτιόν ἐστι· τὸ δὲ 'ἀλλ' εἶα τέκεα
θαμίν' ἐπαναβοῶντες' ἐκ τοῦ Κύκλωπος Φιλοξένου ἐστί. Φιλόξε-
νον τὸν διθυραμβοποιὸν ἢ τραγῳδοδιδάσκαλον διασύρει, ὃς ἔγραψε
τὸν ἔρωτα τοῦ Κύκλωπος τὸν ἐπὶ τῇ Γαλατείᾳ. εἶτα κιθάρας ἦχον
μιμούμενος ἐν τῷ συγγράμματι, τοῦτό φησι τὸ ῥῆμα 'θρεττανελό'·
ἐκεῖ γὰρ εἰσάγει τὸν Κύκλωπα κιθαρίζοντα καὶ ἐρεθίζοντα τὴν
Γαλάτειαν.... ἄλλως· ὁ Φιλόξενος ὁ διθυραμβοποιὸς ἐν Σικελίᾳ
ἦν παρὰ Διονυσίῳ· λέγουσι δὲ ὅτι ποτὲ Γαλατείᾳ τινὶ παλλακίδι
Διονυσίου προσέβαλε· καὶ μαθὼν Διονύσιος ἐξώρισεν αὐτὸν εἰς
λατομίαν. φεύγων δὲ ἐκεῖθεν ἦλθεν εἰς τὰ ὄρη τῶν Κυθήρων καὶ
ἐκεῖ δρᾶμα τὴν Γαλάτειαν ἐποίησεν, ἐν ᾧ εἰσήνεγκε τὸν Κύκλωπα
ἐρῶντα τῆς Γαλατείας· τοῦτο δὲ αἰνιττόμενος εἰς Διονύσιον· ἀπεί-
κασε γὰρ αὐτὸν τῷ Κύκλωπι ἐπεὶ καὶ αὐτὸς ὁ Διονύσιος οὐκ ὠξυ-
δόρκει.

cf. Sud. Θ 475 (ii 727 Adler)

θρεττανελό, -λώ codd.

PHILOXENUS OF CYTHERA

819 Aristophanes, *Plutus*

> *Cario.* Now then, I want to imitate the Cyclops —
>
> threttaneló —
>
> and lead you along, swaying like this on my two feet:
>
> come on, my children, shout again and again
>
> and bleat the songs of sheep and stinking goats, and follow me, foreskins drawn back, and you'll breakfast like billy-goats.

Scholiast on the passage: (1) Aristophanes is mocking the tragic poet[1] Philoxenus, who introduced Polyphemus playing the lyre. The word 'threttaneló' is a kind of musical sound representing a stringed instrument. The phrase 'come on, my children, shout again and again' is from the *Cyclops* of Philoxenus. He is mocking the dithyrambic or tragic poet Philoxenus, who wrote of the love of the Cyclops for Galatea; and to imitate the sound of the cithara in his writing he uses this expression 'threttaneló', for in that work he introduces the Cyclops playing the cithara and challenging Galatea.... (2) Philoxenus the dithyrambic poet was in Sicily with Dionysius. They say that he once assaulted Galatea, a mistress of Dionysius, and when the tyrant heard of it he sent him off to the quarry. But in his exile he went from there to the hills of Cythera and there composed his play *Galatea*, in which he introduced the Cyclops in love with Galatea. This was a riddling reference to Dionysius, whom he likened to the Cyclops since the tyrant's own eyesight was poor.

[1] An error for 'the dithyrambic poet': cf. the reference to 'the play *Galatea*' below.

GREEK LYRIC

820 Ar. *Plut.* 296ss.

ΧΟΡ. ἡμεῖς δέ γ' αὖ ζητήσομεν θρεττανελὸ τὸν Κύκλωπα /
βληχώμενοι σὲ τουτονὶ πινῶντα καταλαβόντες /

πήραν ἔχοντα λάχανά τ' ἄγρια δροσερὰ

κραιπαλῶντα / ἡγούμενον τοῖς προβατίοις / εἰκῆ δὲ καταδαρθόντα
που / μέγαν λαβόντες ἡμμένον σφηνίσκον ἐκτυφλῶσαι.

Schol. ad loc. (p. 342 Dübner): (RV) 'πήραν ἔχοντα'· Φιλοξέ-
νου ἐστὶ παρηγμένον καὶ τοῦτο τὸ ῥητόν. . . . (Junt.) ἐνταῦθα ὁ
ποιητὴς παιγνιωδῶς ἐπιφέρει τὰ τοῦ Φιλοξένου εἰπόντος πήραν
βαστάζειν τὸν Κύκλωπα καὶ λάχανα ἐσθίειν. οὕτω γὰρ πεποίηκε
τὸν τοῦ Κύκλωπος ὑποκριτὴν εἰς τὴν σκηνὴν εἰσαγόμενον.
ἐμνήσθη δὲ καὶ τῆς τυφλώσεως ὡς οὔσης ἐν τῷ ποίημα. ταῦτα δὲ
πάντα διασύρων τὸν Φιλόξενον εἶπεν ὡς μὴ ἀληθεύοντα· ὁ γὰρ
Κύκλωψ, ὥς φησιν Ὅμηρος, κρέα ἤσθιε καὶ οὐ λάχανα· ἃ τοίνυν
ἔφησεν ἐκεῖ ὁ Φιλόξενος, ταῦτα ὁ χορὸς εἰς τὸ μέσον ἀναφέρει.

821 Athen. 13. 564ef (iii 245 Kaibel)

ὁ δὲ τοῦ Κυθηρίου Φιλοξένου Κύκλωψ ἐρῶν τῆς Γαλατείας καὶ
ἐπαινῶν αὐτῆς τὸ κάλλος προμαντευόμενος τὴν τύφλωσιν πάντα
μᾶλλον αὐτῆς ἐπαινεῖ ἢ τῶν ὀφθαλμῶν μνημονεύει, λέγων ὧδε·

ὦ καλλιπρόσωπε χρυσεοβόστρυχε ⟦Γαλάτεια⟧
χαριτόφωνε θάλος Ἐρώτων.

τυφλὸς ὁ ἔπαινος καὶ κατ' οὐδὲν ὅμοιος τῷ Ἰβυκείῳ ἐκείνῳ (fr.
288).

cf. Eust. *Od.* 1558. 15

1 χρυσο- ci. Bergk   Γαλάτεια om. Eust., del. Wilamowitz
2 Bergk (θάλος Jacobs, Fiorillo): κάλλος codd., Eust.

162

820 Aristophanes, *Plutus* (continued)

Chorus. No, we'll try to catch you while we bleat—
threttaneló—you filthy old Cyclops

with your leather bag and its dewy wild herbs,

leading your sheep drunk, and when you've tumbled down
somewhere for a sleep we'll get a great burning wedge and
blind you.

Scholiast on the passage: (1) 'with your leather bag': this
expression too is introduced from Philoxenus. (2) Here the
poet playfully attacks the passage in Philoxenus where he
says that the Cyclops carries a leather bag and eats herbs,
for that is how he equipped the actor who played the part
of the Cyclops. Aristophanes mentions the blinding too,
since it was in the poem. All this he said to mock Philo-
xenus for not telling the truth: for the Cyclops, as Homer
tells, ate meat,[1] not herbs; and what Philoxenus said in his
poem the chorus now repeats on the stage.

[1] Regularly? The meat at *Od.* 9. 295 is the flesh of Odysseus' com-
panions.

821 Athenaeus, *Scholars at Dinner*

But when the Cyclops of Philoxenus of Cythera is in
love with Galatea and is praising her beauty, he praises
everything else about her but makes no mention of her
eyes, since he has a premonition of his own blindness. He
addresses her as follows:

Fair-faced, golden-tressed, Grace-voiced offshoot
of the Loves.

This praise is blind and not in the least like the famous
words of Ibycus (fr. 288).

822 Plut. *Quaest. Conviv.* 1. 5. 1 (iv 25 Hubert)

ἐζητεῖτο παρὰ Σοσσίῳ Σαπφικῶν τινων ᾀσθέντων ὅπου καὶ τὸν Κύκλωπα

Μούσαις εὐφώνοις

ἰᾶσθαί φησι τὸν ἔρωτα Φιλόξενος.

Schol. Theocr. 11. 1–3b (p. 241 Wendel)

καὶ Φιλόξενος τὸν Κύκλωπα ποιεῖ παραμυθούμενον ἑαυτὸν ἐπὶ τῷ τῆς Γαλατείας ἔρωτι καὶ ἐντελλόμενον τοῖς δελφῖσιν ὅπως ἀπαγγείλωσιν αὐτῇ ὅτι ταῖς Μούσαις τὸν ἔρωτα ἀκεῖται.

cf. Plut. *Amator.* 18 (iv 372 Hubert) (Σάπφω) Μούσαις εὐφώνοις ἰωμένη τὸν ἔρωτα κατὰ Φιλόξενον.

823 *Sud.* E 336 (ii 211s. Adler)

ἔθυσας, ἀντιθύσῃ.

τοῦτο παρὰ Φιλοξένῳ ὁ Κύκλωψ λέγει πρὸς τὸν Ὀδυσσέα. ἀπεκδέχονται γὰρ τὸ 'ἔνθα δὲ πῦρ κείαντες ἐθύσαμεν' παρὰ τῷ ποιητῇ (*Od.* 9. 231) εἰρῆσθαι ἐπὶ τῶν ἀρνῶν, οὐχὶ δὲ τὸ †'ἀπεθύσαμεν'† (ἐθυμιάσαμεν ci. Bernhardy) νοεῖσθαι.

cf. Zonar. 625, *App. Prov.* 2. 10 (i 395 Leutsch-Schneidewin)

ἀντιθύσῃ *Sud.* codd. AM, *App. Prov.*: ἀντὶ τοῦ θύσῃ *Sud.* rell., Zonar.

824 Zenob. 5. 45 (i 139 Leutsch-Schneidewin)

οἵῳ μ᾽ ὁ δαίμων τέρατι συγκαθεῖρξεν.

ἐπὶ τῶν δυσανασχετούντων ἐπί τινι δυσχερεῖ πράγματι λέγεται ἡ παροιμία· Κύκλωψ γάρ ἐστι δρᾶμα Φιλοξένου τοῦ ποιητοῦ ἐν ᾧ ὁ Ὀδυσσεὺς περισχεθεὶς τῷ τοῦ Κύκλωπος σπηλαίῳ λέγει 'οἵῳ κτλ.'

cf. Diogenian. 7.19, Arsen. = Apostol. 12.52 (i 289, ii 554 L.-S.)

PHILOXENUS OF CYTHERA

822 Plutarch, *Table-talk*

At Sossius' house when some lines of Sappho had been sung the question arose as to where Philoxenus says that the Cyclops tries to cure his love

with the tuneful Muses.

Scholiast on Theocritus 11

Philoxenus makes the Cyclops console himself for his love of Galatea and tell the dolphins to report to her that he is healing his love with the Muses.[1]

[1] Cf. Plut. *Amator.* 18, Callimachus *Epigr.* III. 1 ff. Gow-Page, Philodemus, *Mus.* 4. xv. 1 ff. (p. 58 Neubecker) (the line acceptable if Phil. meant not music but poetry!).

823 *Suda*

You sacrificed: you shall be sacrificed in turn.

The Cyclops says this to Odysseus in Philoxenus. They misinterpret Homer's 'Then we lit a fire and sacrificed' (*Od.* 9. 231) as a reference to the lambs instead of taking it as 'We made burnt offering.'[1]

[1] I.e. Homer's verb means not that they slit the throats of the Cyclops' lambs (as Philoxenus and others take it), but that they burned his cheeses. See also Timotheus 783.

824 Zenobius, *Proverbs*

With what a monster has God imprisoned me!

The proverb is used of people who are distressed by some vexatious circumstance: the *Cyclops* is a play[1] by the poet Philoxenus in which Odysseus speaks the words after being shut in the Cyclops' cave.

[1] See fr. 819 n. 1.

GREEK LYRIC

ΚΩΜΑΣΤΗΣ?

825 *Sud.* A 2657 (i 235 Adler)

Ἀντιγενίδης, Σατύρου, Θηβαῖος μουσικὸς αὐλῳδὸς Φιλοξένου·
οὗτος ὑποδήμασι Μιλησίοις πρῶτος ἐχρήσατο καὶ κροκωτὸν ἐν τῷ
Κωμαστῇ περιεβάλλετο ἱμάτιον· ἔγραψε μέλη.

ΜΥΣΟΙ?

826 Aristot. *Pol.* 8. 7. 1342b (p. 290 Immisch)

<δηλοῖ δ᾽ ἡ ποίησις> οἷον ὁ διθύραμβος ὁμολογουμένως εἶναι
δοκεῖ Φρύγιον. καὶ τούτου πολλὰ παραδείγματα λέγουσιν οἱ περὶ
τὴν σύνεσιν ταύτην ἄλλα τε καὶ ὅτι Φιλόξενος ἐγχειρήσας ἐν τῇ
δωριστὶ ποιῆσαι διθύραμβον τοὺς Μυσοὺς (Schneider: μύθους
codd.) οὐχ οἷός τ᾽ ἦν, ἀλλ᾽ ὑπὸ τῆς φύσεως αὐτῆς ἐξέπεσεν εἰς τὴν
φρυγιστὶ τὴν προσήκουσαν ἁρμονίαν πάλιν.

ΣΥΡΟΣ?

827 Hsch. M 900 (ii 651 Latte) (Hdn. ii 550 Lentz)

Ἀριστοφάνης φησί (fr. 745 K.-A.)· μεσαύχενας νέκυας τοὺς
ἀσκούς (Dobree: ν. ἀσώτους cod.). διὰ τοῦ μ γραπτέον, μεσαύχε-
νες, ὅτι μέσον τὸν αὐχένα ἀσκοῦ (Schmidt: αὐτοῦ cod.) πιέζει ὁ
(Bergk: πεζεῖ cod.) περιεβάλλοντο (Dobree: παρεβάλλοντο τὸ
cod.) σχοινίον. παρατραγῳδεῖ (Bergk: τραγῳδεῖ cod.) δὲ τὰ ἐν τῷ
Φιλοξένου (-νω cod.) Σύρῳ. ἔνιοι δὲ διὰ τοῦ δ γράφουσι, δεσαύχε-
νες, [[καὶ]] οὐ καλῶς.

Σύρῳ: Σατύρῳ ci. Bergk, Σισύφῳ vel Σκίρῳ Berglein

---

1 Did Phil. apply the adjective to corpses hung by the neck? Editors
emend *Syrus* ('The Syrian') to *Satyrus, Sisyphus* or *Scirus*.

PHILOXENUS OF CYTHERA

THE REVELLER?

825 *Suda*

Antigenides, son of Satyrus, Theban musician, pipe-singer of Philoxenus.[1] He was the first to wear Milesian shoes and wore a yellow cloak in *The Reveller*.[2] He wrote songs.

[1] See also *P.M.G.* 840 (Oeniades).   [2] Berglein suggested that this was a dithyramb by Philoxenus.

THE MYSIANS?

826 Aristotle, *Politics*

Composition shows how the dithyramb is generally agreed to be a Phrygian form. The experts in the field give many examples and in particular tell how Philoxenus tried to compose his dithyramb *The Mysians*[1] in the Dorian *harmonia* but failed: nature herself forced him back to the appropriate *harmonia*, the Phrygian.

[1] The title is the result of an emended text. See also 'Plutarch' *Mus.* 33. 1142 f for a possible reference to the *harmoniai* of this dithyramb.

SYRUS?

827 Hesychius, *Lexicon*

μεσαύχενες ('mid-neck'): Aristophanes uses the expression 'mid-neck corpses' of wineskins. It should be written with the μ, μεσαύχενες, since the middle of the wine-skin's neck is squeezed by the cord they used to put round it. Aristophanes is parodying the words in the *Syrus* of Philoxenus.[1] Some write δεσαύχενες ('tied-neck') with the δ, wrongly.

ΥΜΕΝΑΙΟΣ

828 Athen. 1. 5f–6b (i 11s. Kaibel)

τὰ δ' αὐτὰ καὶ περὶ τοῦ Κυθηρίου Φιλοξένου ἱστοροῦσι.... Κλέαρχος δέ φησι (fr. 57 Wehrli) Φιλόξενον προλουόμενον <ἐν τῇ πατρίδι κἂν ἄλλαις πόλεσι> περιέρχεσθαι τὰς οἰκίας ἀκολουθούντων αὐτῷ παίδων καὶ φερόντων ἔλαιον οἶνον γάρον ὄξος καὶ ἄλλα ἡδύσματα· ἔπειτα εἰσιόντα εἰς τὰς ἀλλοτρίας οἰκίας τὰ ἑψόμενα τοῖς ἄλλοις ἀρτύειν ἐμβάλλοντα ὧν ἐστι χρεία, κᾆθ' οὕτως ἀνακάψαντα (Müller: Athen. ἀνακάμψαντα, Sud. εἰς ἑαυτὸν κύψαντα) εὐωχεῖσθαι. οὗτος εἰς Ἔφεσον καταπλεύσας εὑρὼν τὴν ὀψοπώλιδα κενὴν ἐπύθετο τὴν αἰτίαν· καὶ μαθὼν ὅτι πᾶν εἰς γάμους συνηγόρασται λουσάμενος παρῆν ἄκλητος ὡς τὸν νυμφίον. καὶ μετὰ τὸ δεῖπνον ᾄσας ὑμέναιον οὗ ἡ ἀρχὴ

Γάμε θεῶν λαμπρότατε

πάντας ἐψυχαγώγησεν· ἦν δὲ διθυραμβοποιός. καὶ ὁ νυμφίος 'Φιλόξενε,' εἶπε, 'καὶ αὔριον ὧδε δειπνήσεις;' καὶ ὁ Φιλόξενος 'ἂν ὄψον', ἔφη, 'μὴ πωλῇ τις.'

cf. Sud. Φ 395 s.v. Φιλόξενος Λευκαδίου

829 Antig. Caryst. *Mir.* 127 (141) (p. 31s. Keller)

οἱ Δελφοὶ δὲ λέγουσιν ὅτι ἐν τῷ Παρνασσῷ κατά τινας χρόνους τὸ Κωρύκιον φαίνεσθαι χρυσοειδές· διὸ καὶ τὸν Φιλόξενον οὐδεὶς ἂν εἰκονολογεῖν εἴποι λέγονθ' οὕτως·

αὐτοὶ γὰρ διὰ Παρνασσοῦ
χρυσορόφων Νυμφέων εἴσω
θαλάμων

168

PHILOXENUS OF CYTHERA

WEDDING-SONG

828 Athenaeus, *Scholars at Dinner*

They tell the same story[1] about Philoxenus of Cythera.... Clearchus[2] says that Philoxenus would wash and then go round the houses in his own city and others accompanied by slaves carrying olive oil, wine, fish paste, vinegar and other relishes, and going into other men's houses would add the necessary seasoning to what was being boiled; then he gulped it down and had a feast. Once when he landed at Ephesus he found the fish-market empty and on asking the reason was told that the fish had all been bought up for a wedding. So he washed and turned up uninvited at the bridegroom's house; after the banquet he sang a wedding-song which begins

> Marriage, most radiant of gods!

and beguiled everyone, for he was a dithyrambic poet. When the bridegroom said, 'Will you dine here tomorrow too?' he replied, 'Yes, if there is no fish on sale.'

[1] That like Phil. of Leucas he practised eating his food so hot that he got the lion's share: cf. *Sud.* O 1091.   [2] Peripatetic scholar, c. 340–c. 250 B.C.

The following fragments are from unidentified poems.

829 Antigonus of Carystus, *Marvels*

The Delphians say that at certain times on Mt. Parnassus the Corycian cave shines like gold. So no one should say that Philoxenus was only speaking figuratively when he says,

> For they themselves on Parnassus within the gold-roofed chambers of the Nymphs . . .

169

830 Ar. *Nub.* 335

ΣΤ. ταῦτ' ἄρ' ἐποίουν 'ὑγρᾶν Νεφελᾶν στρεπταίγλαν δάϊον
ὁρμάν.'

Schol. ENM ad loc. (i 84 Holwerda)

ταῦτα εἰς Φιλόξενον τὸν διθυραμβοποιόν· τὸ γὰρ

στρεπταίγλαν

αὐτὸς εἶπεν.

831 Athen. 2. 35d (i 82 Kaibel)

ὁ δὲ Κυθήριος Φιλόξενος λέγει·

εὑρείτας οἶνος πάμφωνος.

cf. Eust. *Od.* 1770. 9

832 Athen. 10. 446ab (ii 469s. Kaibel)

ὁ αὐτός φησιν Ἀντιφάνης ἐν τῷ Τραυματίᾳ (fr. 205 K.-A.)·
... παραδίδου δ' ἑξῆς ἐμοὶ / [[οἶνον]]

<τὸν> ἀρκεσίγυιον

ὡς ἔφασκ' Εὐριπίδης. / — Εὐριπίδης γὰρ τοῦτ' ἔφασκεν; — ἀλλὰ
τίς; / — Φιλόξενος δήπουθεν. — οὐθὲν διαφέρει, / ὦ τᾶν· ἐλέγχεις
μ' ἕνεκα συλλαβῆς μιᾶς.

830 Aristophanes, *Clouds*

Strepsiades. So that's why they[1] wrote 'the destructive twist-flashing onset of the moist Clouds'.

Scholiast on the passage

This alludes to Philoxenus the dithyrambic poet,[2] for it was he who said

twist-flashing.

[1] Socrates has just referred to dithyrambic poets.　　[2] The chronology is wrong: Phil. was only 12 when *Clouds* was produced in 423 (revised version 418–416). Perhaps he used the epithet later.

831 Athenaeus, *Scholars at Dinner*

Philoxenus of Cythera says

fair-flowing wine, all-expressive.

832 Athenaeus, *Scholars at Dinner*

The same Antiphanes[1] says in his *Wounded Man*, 'And next hand me

the limb-helper,[2]

as Euripides put it. — As Euripides put it? — Well, who then? — Philoxenus, of course. — Makes no difference, my friend. You're putting me in the wrong for the sake of one syllable.

[1] See test. 12 with n. 3.　　[2] Wine.

833 Athen. 15. 692d (iii 531 Kaibel)

ἐπεὶ δ' ἐνταῦθα τοῦ λόγου ἐσμέν,

συμβαλοῦμαί τι μέλος ὑμῖν εἰς ἔρωτα

κατὰ τὸν Κυθήριον ποιητήν.

cf. 6. 271b, Plat. *Symp.* 185c, Dion. Hal. *Comp.* 1.6, *App. Prov.* 4. 77 (i 453 Leutsch-Schneidewin)

834 Plin. *N.H.* 37. 31 (v 393s. Mayhoff)

Phaethontis fulmine icti sorores luctu mutatas in arbores populos lacrimis electrum omnibus annis fundere iuxta Eridanum amnem, quem Padum vocavimus, electrum appellatum, quoniam sol vocitatus sit elector, plurimi poetae dixere, primique ut arbitror Aeschylus (*Heliades*, fr. 73 Radt), Philoxenus, Euripides (*Hipp.* 737ss.), Nicander (*Heteroeumena*, fr. 63 Schneider), Satyrus (v. *R.E.* Satyros 20).

835 Theophrast. *De Ventis* 38 (iii 107 Wimmer)

πνεῖ δ' ἐνιαχοῦ μὲν χειμέριος (sc. ὁ Ζέφυρος), ὅθεν καὶ ὁ ποιητὴς δυσαῆ προσηγόρευσεν (*Il.* 23. 200, *Od.* 5. 295)· ἐνιαχοῦ δὲ μετρίως καὶ μαλακῶς, διὸ καὶ Φιλόξενος

ἡδεῖαν

αὐτοῦ πεποίηκε τὴν πνοήν.

Meineke: ἰδίαν cod.

172

833 Athenaeus, *Scholars at Dinner*

Since we have reached this point in our discussion,

I shall contribute for you[1] a song to love,

as the poet of Cythera puts it.

[1] Plural 'you'.

834 Pliny, *Natural History*

When Phaethon was struck by the thunderbolt, his sisters were changed into poplar trees in their grief and every year shed tears of amber by the banks of the river Eridanus, which we call the Padus (Po); the amber is known as *electrum*, since the Sun[1] is called Elector (ἠλέκτωρ, the shiner). Many poets have told of this, the first of whom, I believe, were Aeschylus, Philoxenus, Euripides, Nicander and Satyrus.

[1] Father of Phaethon, who fell from the Sun's chariot into the Eridanus, and of his sisters the Heliades; see J. Diggle, *Euripides: Phaethon* 4 f.

835 Theophrastus, *On Winds*

In some places the Zephyr is a stormy wind, which explains why Homer called it 'ill-blowing' (*Il.* 23. 200, *Od.* 5. 295); in others it blows moderately and gently, and that is why Philoxenus makes its breath

sweet.

GREEK LYRIC

EPIGRAMMA

8D. *Anth. Pal.* 9. 319 = Philoxenus i Gow-Page (*H.E.* i 165)

Τληπόλεμος ὁ Μυρεὺς Ἑρμᾶν ἀφετήριον ἕρμα
ἱροδρόμοις θῆκεν παῖς ὁ Πολυκρίτεω
δὶς δέκ᾽ ἀπὸ σταδίων, ἐναγώνιον· ἀλλὰ πονεῖτε
μαλθακὸν ἐκ γονάτων ὄκνον ἀπωσάμενοι.

PHILOXENUS OF CYTHERA

EPIGRAM

8D. *Palatine Anthology*: Philoxenus[1]

Tlepolemus of Myra, son of Polycrites, dedicated this Hermes, god of games, as starting-post for the sacred races to mark his twice ten sprints[2]: work hard, you runners, driving soft timidity from your knees.

---

[1] Authorship uncertain; if Tlepolemus is the Olympic rider known from Paus. 5. 8. 11 as winner in 256 B.C., Phil. is excluded.

[2] I.e. the twenty victories of his career as sprinter.

PHILOXENUS LEUCADIUS

TESTIMONIA VITAE ATQUE ARTIS

1 Athen. 1. 5b–f (i 10s. Kaibel)

τοῦ Φιλοξένου δὲ τοῦ Λευκαδίου Δείπνου Πλάτων ὁ
κωμῳδιοποιὸς μέμνηται (fr. 189 K.-A.)·

       ἐγὼ δ᾽ ἐνθάδ᾽ ἐν τῇ ἐρημίᾳ
τουτὶ διελθεῖν βούλομαι τὸ βιβλίον
πρὸς ἐμαυτόν.   (B.) ἔστι δ᾽, ἀντιβολῶ σε, τοῦτο τί;
(A.) Φιλοξένου καινή τις ὀψαρτυσία.
(B.) ἐπίδειξον αὐτὴν ἥτις ἔστ᾽.   (A.) ἄκουε δή.
ἄρξομαι ἐκ βολβοῖο, τελευτήσω δ᾽ ἐπὶ θύννον . . .

(5d) ἀπὸ τούτου τοῦ Φιλοξένου καὶ Φιλοξένειοί τινες
πλακοῦντες ὠνομάσθησαν. περὶ τούτου Χρύσιππός
φησιν· ᾽ἐγὼ κατέχω τινὰ ὀψοφάγον . . .᾽ τὰ δ᾽ αὐτὰ
καὶ περὶ τοῦ Κυθηρίου Φιλοξένου ἱστοροῦσι καὶ Ἀρχύ-
του καὶ ἄλλων πλειόνων . . .

PHILOXENUS OF LEUCAS

LIFE AND WORK[1]

1 Athenaeus, *Scholars at Dinner*

Plato the comic poet[2] mentions the *Banquet* of Philoxenus of Leucas:

A. And in this deserted spot here I propose to read this book to myself.

B. Tell me, what book is it?

A. A new cookery-book of Philoxenus.

B. Show me what it's like.

A. Listen then. 'I shall begin with the onion and end with the tunny . . .'.[3]

From this Philoxenus Philoxenean cakes got their name.[4] Chrysippus[5] says of him, 'I remember a gourmet who . . .'[6] They tell the same story about Philoxenus of Cythera,[7] Archytas and several others. . . .

---

[1] The *Suda* gives two anecdotes s.v. Philoxenus son of Leucadius (*sic*): see frr. 828, 816 above.   [2] In his *Phaon*, dated to 391 B.C.; see also fr. 836(b).   [3] Plato's 14 lines of parody are in hexameters, whereas the *Banquet* is in dactylo-epitrites.   [4] Cf. *Sud.* O 1091.   [5] Stoic philosopher, *c.* 280–207 B.C.   [6] He practised eating his food so hot that he got the lion's share.
[7] Continued at fr. 828.

2 Athen. 1. 6d (i 13 Kaibel)

ἄλλοι δὲ φίλιχθυν τὸν Φιλόξενόν φασιν· Ἀριστο-
τέλης δὲ φιλόδειπνον ἁπλῶς, ὃς καὶ γράφει που ταῦτα
(fr. 63 Rose)· 'δημηγοροῦντες ἐν τοῖς ὄχλοις κατατρί-
βουσιν ὅλην τὴν ἡμέραν ἐν τοῖς θαύμασι καὶ πρὸς τοὺς
ἐκ τοῦ Φάσιδος ἢ Βορυσθένους καταπλέοντας, ἀνεγνω-
κότες οὐδὲν πλὴν εἰ τὸ Φιλοξένου Δεῖπνον οὐχ ὅλον.'

PHILOXENUS OF LEUCAS

2 Athenaeus, *Scholars at Dinner*

Others call Philoxenus[1] a fish-lover, but Aristotle calls him simply a banquet-lover; somewhere he writes, 'They spend the whole day giving speeches where there are crowds, among the jugglers or to people who sail in from the Phasis or the Borysthenes; and yet they have read nothing except the *Banquet* of Philoxenus, and not all of that!'[2]

[1] The last Philoxenus mentioned was 'Phil. the son of Eryxis', a notorious glutton (*R.E.* 5) who is sometimes identified with Phil. of Leucas. Confusion is deepened by the stories which make Phil. of Cythera a great fish-eater (testt. 10, 11). [2] Continued at fr. 816.

PHILOXENUS LEUCADIUS

FRAGMENTA

ΔΕΙΠΝΟΝ

836 (a) Athen. 15. 685d (iii 516 Kaibel)

Φιλόξενος δ᾽ ὁ διθυραμβοποιὸς ἐν τῷ ἐπιγραφομένῳ Δείπνῳ
ἀρχὴν ποιεῖται τὸν στέφανον τῆς εὐωχίας οὑτωσὶ λέγων·

1   κατὰ χειρὸς δ᾽

2 ἦλυθ᾽ ὕδωρ· ἁπαλὸς
     παιδίσκος ἐν ἀργυρέᾳ
       πρόχῳ φορέων ἐπέχευεν·

3 εἶτ᾽ ἔφερε στέφανον
     λεπτᾶς ἀπὸ μυρτίδος εὐ-
       γνήτων κλαδέων δισύναπτον.

2 ἦλιθ᾽ ci. Page   Page: προχοω φέρων cod. A   3 Grote-
fend, Fiorillo: στεφανολεπτας ἀπὸ μυρτίδων A   Bergk: κλάδων A

(b) Athen. 4. 146f–147e (vv. 1–40) + 9. 409e (vv. 40–43) (i
332ss. + ii 392s. Kaibel)

Φιλόξενος δ᾽ ὁ Κυθήριος ἐν τῷ ἐπιγραφομένῳ Δείπνῳ, εἴπερ
τούτου καὶ ὁ κωμῳδιοποιὸς Πλάτων ἐν τῷ Φάωνι ἐμνήσθη (fr. 189
Κ.-Α.) καὶ μὴ τοῦ Λευκαδίου Φιλοξένου, τοιαύτην ἐκτίθεται παρα-
σκευὴν δείπνου·

180

PHILOXENUS OF LEUCAS

FRAGMENTS

THE BANQUET

836 (a) Athenaeus, *Scholars at Dinner*

Philoxenus the dithyrambic poet[1] in his work entitled *The Banquet* makes the garland the beginning of the feast in these words:

And water came for our hands: a tender young boy poured it, carrying it in a silver jug; then he brought a garland double-woven from vigorous twigs of slender myrtle.

[1] I.e. Phil. of Cythera; but *The Banquet,* which is certainly not a dithyramb, is best attributed to Phil. of Leucas.

(b) Athenaeus, *Scholars at Dinner*

Philoxenus of Cythera in his work entitled *The Banquet* — if indeed it was he whom the comic poet Plato mentioned in his *Phaon*[1] and not the Leucadian Philoxenus — gives the following account of the arrangements for a banquet:

[1] See Phil. of Leucas test. 1 with n. 2.

1 εἰς δ' ἔφερον διπλόοι
  παῖδες λιπαρῶπα τράπεζαν

2 ἄμμ', ἑτέραν δ' ἑτέροις,
  ἄλλοις δ' ἑτέραν, μέχρις οὗ
  πλήρωσαν οἶκον·

3 ταὶ δὲ πρὸς ὑψιλύχνους
  ἔστιλβον αὐγὰς

4 εὐστέφανοι λεκάναις
  παροψίσι τ' ὀξυβάφων <τε>
  πλήθεϊ σύν τε χλιδῶσαι

5 παντοδαποῖσι τέχνας
  εὑρήμασι πρὸς βιοτάν,
  ψυχᾶς δελεασματίοισι·

6 πάρφερον ἐν κανέοις
  μάζας χιονόχροας ἄλλοι·

7 <τοῖς> δ' ἐπὶ πρῶτα παρῆλθ'
  οὐ κάκκαβος, ὦ φιλότας,
  ἀλλ' †ἀλλοπλατεῖς τὸ† μέγιστον

8 †πάντ' ἔπαθεν λιπαροντες
  εγχελεατινες ἄριστον†

9 †γόγγροιτοιωνητεμων†
  πλῆρες θεοτερπές· ἐπ' αὐτῷ

10 δ' ἄλλο παρῆλθε τόσον,
   βατὶς δ' ἐνέην ἰσόκυκλος·

11 μικρὰ δὲ κακκάβι' ἧς
   ἔχοντα τὸ μὲν γαλεοῦ
   τι, ναρκίον ἄλλο <   >

12 <   > παρῆς ἕτερον
   πίων ἀπὸ τευθιάδων
   καὶ σηπιοπουλυποδείων

PHILOXENUS OF LEUCAS

And a pair of boys brought in a shining-faced
table for us and a second for others and another for
others again, until they had filled the room; and
those tables gleamed in the lamplight high above,
laden with plates and side-dishes and a pile of
saucers and revelling in every skilful invention for
good living, enticements for the spirit. Others
served snow-white loaves in baskets; and after them
arrived not a three-legged pot, dear friend,[2] but (? a
huge wide platter with shining eels and congers),[3] a
full plate that would delight the gods. After it,
another arrived, equally big, with a perfectly round
skate on it; and there were small pots, one with a
piece of dogfish, another with a ray . . . ; another was
there with rich squid and many-armed cuttlefish,

[2] The poem is addressed to a male friend: see v. 16.   [3] Text
uncertain here and elsewhere.

---

2 Bergk, Kaibel: ἄμμι ἑτέραν δ᾿ ἕτεροι ἄλλοι δ᾿ ἑτέραν codd. AE
μέχρι A   4 Bergk: ἐστεφάνοι λαχάνοις A   τε   πλήθεϊ
Kaibel: πλήρεις A   5 Bergk: -δαποις A   6 Bergk: παρέφε-
ρον ἐν κανέοισι A   7 Hartung, Bergk: ἐπεὶ A   παρῆλθεν A
10 Bergk (-έης): βαστιανεην A   11 Bergk: κακκαβίης A
11s. Bergk, qui lacunam stat.: ἄλλου A   12 Bergk: τευθιάδα A
Bergk: σηπίου πολυποδίων A

13   <τῶν> ἀπαλοπλοκάμων·
       θερμὸς μετὰ ταῦτα παρῆλθεν

14   ἰσοτράπεζος ὅλος
       νῆστις συνόδων πυρὸς <   >

15   †ἔπειτα βαθμοὺς† ἀτμί-
       ζων ἔτι, τῷ δ' ἐπὶ πασταὶ

16   τευθίδες, ὦ φίλε, κά-
       ξανθισμέναι καρῖδες αἱ
           κυφαὶ παρῆλθον·

17   θρυμματίδες δ' ἐπὶ ταύ-
       ταις εὐπέταλοι χλοεραί
           τε †δηφαρυγες†

18   πύρνων τε στεγαναὶ
       φυσταὶ μέγαθος κατὰ κάκ-
           καβον γλυκυόξεες, <οἷος>

19   ὀμφαλὸς θοίνας καλεῖται
       παρά γ' ἐμὶν καὶ τίν, σάφ' οἶδα.

20   εἶτα δὲ ναὶ μὰ θεοὺς
       ὑπερμέγεθές τι θέμος
           θύννου μόλεν ὀπτὸν ἐκεῖθεν

21   θερμανθὲν γλυφίσιν
       τετμημένον εὐθὺς ἐπ' αὐτὰς

22   τὰς ὑπογαστρίδας, <αἷς>
       διανεκέως ἐπαμύνειν

23   εἴπερ ἐμίν τε μέλοι
       καὶ τίν, μάλα κεν κεχαροίμεθ'.

24   ἀλλ' ὅθεν ἐλλίπομεν,
       θοίνα παρέης †ὅτε παλάξαι†

25   †δύνατ' ἐπικρατέως†
       ἔγωγ' ἔτι, κοὔ κε λέγοι τις

the soft-tentacled ones; next arrived hot a whole
empty-bellied[4] bream, as big as the table, ... fire ...
steps (?) ..., still steaming; and after it floured
squid arrived and browned prawns, hump-backed;
and after these, crumpets leaf-thin, and yellow ...,
and coated wine-cakes of wheat grains, as big as a
three-legged pot, sweet-and-sharp, such as are
called 'the navel of the feast' at your house and
mine, as I well know. Next—it's true, by the
gods!—an outsized serving of broiled tunny came
from there, heated up, carved by the knife right to
the belly-cuts: if it were up to you and me to help
them along nonstop, we should greatly enjoy our-
selves.

But to resume where we left off, a feast was there
... I for my part still ... (mightily?), and no one

4 For the empty belly see D'A. W. Thompson, *Greek Fishes* 255.

---

13 suppl. Bergk   14 Schweighäuser: μνήστης A   15 Meineke:
ἐπὶ τῷδ' ἐπιπύσται A   16 Dindorf: φίλαι A   Bergk: καὶ ξανθαὶ
μελικαρίδες αἱ κοῦφαι A ('nihil mutandum' Page)   17 χλωραί A
18 Bergk: πυριων A   Schmidt: στεγναι βύσται A   Edmonds, Page:
κακὰ κακκάβου A   Schmidt: γλυκυου ὀξιος A   fin. suppl. Ed-
monds   19 Meineke: θοιναας A   Koen: καπιν A   Jacobs:
σαφνοιδα A   20 Schmidt: εσταδα A   Schmidt: θυγμοῦ A   21 Page:
θερμὸν ὅθεν γλυφις A   Schmidt: τετμενον A   22 suppl.
Page   Bergk: διανεκεος ἐπαμυν A   23 Bergk (εἴπερ): επ A
24 Bergk: οὐθὲν ἐλλείπ- A   25 Bergk: καὶ λέγοι A

26 πάνθ᾿ ἃ παρῆν ἐτύμως
 ἄμμιν, παρέπεισε δὲ θερμὸν

27 σπλάγχνον· ἔπειτα δὲ νή-
 στις δέλφακος οἰκετικᾶς

28 καὶ νωτί᾿ ἐσῆλθε καὶ ὀσ-
 φῦς καὶ μινυρίγματα θερμά,

29 καὶ κεφάλαιον ὅλον
 διαπτυχὲς ἑφθὸν †ἀπερ-
 πευθηνος ἀλεκτοτρόφου†
 πνικτᾶς ἐρίφου παρέθηκε.

30 εἶτα δίεφθ᾿ ἀκροκώ-
 λια σχελίδας τε μετ᾿ αὐτῶν

31 λευκοφορινοχρόους,
 ῥύγχη κεφάλαια πόδας
 τε χναυμάτιόν τε σεσιλ-
 φιωμένον·

32 ἑφθά τ᾿ ἔπειτα κρέ᾿ ὀπ-
 τά <τ᾿> ἀλλ᾿ ἐρίφων τε καὶ ἄρνων

33 ἅ θ᾿ ὑπερωμόκρεως
 χορδὰ γλυκίστα

34 μιξεριφαρνογενής,
 ἃν δὴ φιλέοντι θεοί·

35 τουτ<   >, ὦ φιλότας,
 ἔσθοις κε· λαγῷά τ᾿ ἔπειτ᾿
 ἀλεκτρυόνων τε νεοσσοί,

36 περδίκων φάσσεων
 τε †χύδαν ἤδη δὲ παρεβάλλετο θερμὰ πολλὰ†

26 Kaibel: πάντα παρῆν A   Meineke: ὔμμιν A   Page:
παρέπεσαι A   28 Bergk, Kaibel: νώτιος εἴληφε A   Musu-
rus: ἰσφῦς A   29 θηλογαλακτοτρόφου ci. Kaibel   31 Dobree:

could truly tell all that was there for us, but my rash heart has persuaded me. Next the intestine of a stall-fed pig and its back arrived and its loin and its warblings,[5] all hot; and a boy served the whole head, cooked and split open, of a (milk-nourished?) kid killed by strangling[6]; then well-boiled meat-ends and ribs with them, white with fat: snouts, head-parts and feet and titbits prepared with silphium[7]; then other boiled and roasted flesh of kids and lambs and the sweetest shoulder-meat kid-and-lamb sausages, just what the gods love: you, dear friend, would eat it . . .; then hares and young cockerels, and great quantities of partridges and pigeons were lavishly heaped hot before us, and of

---

[5] A colloquial term? The lungs? [6] To save the blood.
[7] For its uses in cooking see J. Edwards, *The Roman Cookery of Apicius* xxiv.

ρύγχη καὶ κεφαλαὶ ἄποδος τεχνάματι ὄντες ἐσιλφωμένον A   32
suppl. Bergk   33s. Bergk: αθυπερωμακαρὸς χορδὴ γλυκὺς ταμιξ A
35 Dindorf: τουτωφιλετας A   Bergk: ἔσθοις καὶ A
36 εἰδη pro ἤδη Kaibel   δὲ seclusit Bergk

187

37 καὶ μαλακοπτυχέων
  ἄρτων· ὁμοσύζυγα δὲ
    ξανθόν τ’ ἐπεισῆλ-
      θεν μέλι καὶ γάλα σύμπακ-
        τον, τό κε τυρὸν ἅπας τις

38 ἦμεν ἔφασχ’ ἁπαλόν,
  κηγὼν ἐφάμαν· ὅτε δ’ ἤδη

39 βρωτύος ἠδὲ ποτᾶ-
  τος ἐς κόρον ἦμεν ἑταῖροι,

40 τῆνα μὲν ἐξαπάει-
  ρον δμῶες, ἔπειτα δὲ παῖ-
    δες νίπτρ’ ἔδοσαν κατὰ χειρῶν

41 σμήμασιν ἰρινομίκ-
  τοις χλιεροθαλπὲς ὕδωρ
    ἐπεγχέοντες

42 τόσσον ὅσον <τις> ἔχρῃζ’,
  ἐκτρίμματά τ(ε) <   > λαμπρὰ

43 σινδονυφῆ, δίδοσαν
  <δὲ> χρίματά τ’ ἀμβροσίο-
    δμα καὶ στεφάνους ἰοθαλέας.

37 Dindorf: καὶ τυρὸν A   38 Dindorf: ἔφασκεν A
39 Schweighäuser: ἑταῖροι ἥμεν A   40 Bergk: -είρεον A
41 Schweighäuser: χαιερο- A   42 suppl. Bergk   Bergk: ἔχρη-
ζεν A   Musurus: ἐκτρίμμά τε A   lacunam stat. Bergk
43 suppl. Bergk   Villebrun: χρίματ’ ἀμβρ. A

cf. Eust. Od. 1388. 64 λιπαρώψ, οὗ χρῆσις παρὰ Φιλοξένῳ ἐν τῷ (v. 1),
1887. 50 Φιλόξενος δὲ ὁ Κυθήριος ἔκτριμμα (v. 42)

softly-folded loaves; and to keep them company yellow honey arrived and curded milk which everyone declared to be soft cheese, as indeed I did; and when we friends had finally reached our fill of food and drink, attendants cleared away,[8] and then boys gave us water to wash our hands,[9] pouring it comfortably warm over soap-powders mixed with iris-oil, as much as one wished, and they gave us shining linen towels ... and ointments, ambrosia-perfumed, and garlands of fresh violets.

[8] The quotation in Book 9 of Athenaeus begins here ('Phil. in the work entitled *The Banquet* says ...').   [9] The quotation in Book 4 ends here.

GREEK LYRIC

(c) Athen. 11. 487ab (iii 73 Kaibel)

Φιλόξενος δ᾽ ὁ διθυραμβοποιὸς ἐν τῷ ἐπιγραφομένῳ Δείπνῳ μετὰ τὸ ἀπονίψασθαι τὰς χεῖρας προπίνων τινί φησι·

1   σὺ δὲ τάνδ᾽
      ἐν βακχίᾳ
2 εὔδροσον πλή-
      ρη μετανιπτρίδα δέξαι·
3 πραῢ τί τοι Βρόμιος
      γάνος τόδε δοὺς ἐπὶ τέρψιν
      πάντας ἄγει.

1 Bergk: ἐκβακχια A   3 Meineke: ἅπαντας A

(d) Athen. 11. 476de (iii 48 Kaibel)

τοὺς δὲ Παιόνων βασιλεῖς φησι Θεόπομπος ἐν δευτέρᾳ Φιλιππι-κῶν (F.Gr.H. 115 F38), τῶν βοῶν τῶν παρ᾽ αὐτοῖς γινομένων μεγάλα κέρατα φυόντων ὡς χωρεῖν τρεῖς καὶ τέτταρας χόας, ἐκπώ-ματα ποιεῖν ἐξ αὐτῶν, τὰ χείλη περιαργυροῦντας καὶ χρυσοῦντας· καὶ Φιλόξενος δ᾽ ὁ Κυθήριος ἐν τῷ ἐπιγραφομένῳ Δείπνῳ φησίν·

1 πίνετο νεκτάρεον
      πῶμ᾽ ἐν χρυσέαις προτομαῖς
2 τελέων κεράτων, ἐβρέχοντο
      δ᾽ οὐ κατὰ μικρόν.

1 Meineke: ἐπίνετο A   Fiorillo: πόμ᾽ A   Meineke: χρυ-σαῖς A   2 Page: τε ἄλλων A   Meineke (δ᾽ αὖ), Hartung: ἔβρεχον δὲ κατὰ μ. A

(e) Athen. 14. 642f–643d (iii 420ss. Kaibel)

ἐπεὶ δὲ καὶ ὁ Κυθήριος Φιλόξενος ἐν τῷ Δείπνῳ δευτέρων τρα-πεζῶν μνημονεύων πολλὰ καὶ τῶν ἡμῖν παρακειμένων ὠνόμασεν, φέρε καὶ τούτων ἀπομνημονεύσωμεν·

190

(c) Athenaeus, *Scholars at Dinner*

Philoxenus the dithyrambic poet in his work entitled *The Banquet* after the washing of the hands drinks to someone's health[1] with the words:

Accept this after-washing cup, full and well-bedewed,[2] in our Bacchic revel: Bromius[3] by his gift of this, a gentle joy, draws all men on to delight.

[1] To the health of the friend addressed in (b) above.   [2] With the appropriate mixture of water?   [3] Dionysus, god of wine.

(d) Athenaeus, *Scholars at Dinner*

Theopompus in book 2 of his *Philippics* says that in Paeonia[1] the oxen grow horns so large that they hold three or four *choes*,[2] and the kings make drinking-cups from them, overlaying the rims with silver or gold; and Philoxenus of Cythera says in his poem entitled *The Banquet*,

The draught of nectar was drunk from gold goblets, whole horns that had been lopped, and the guests quickly became soaked.

[1] Region of Macedonia.   [2] 18–24 pints.

(e) Athenaeus, *Scholars at Dinner*

Since Philoxenus of Cythera when he mentioned 'second tables' in his *Banquet* named many of the foods that have been served to us, let's recite them:

1 τὰς δὲ δὴ πρόσθεν μολούσας
    <   > λιπαραυγεῖς

2 πορθμίδας πολ-
    λῶν ἀγαθῶν πάλιν εἴσφε-
    ρον γεμούσας,

3 τὰς ἐφήμεροι καλέοντι
    νῦν τραπέζας <δευτέρας>,

4 ἀθάνατοι δέ τ' Ἀμαλθεί-
    ας κέρας· ταῖς δ' ἐν μέσαισιν

5 ἐγκαθιδρύ-
    θη μέγα χάρμα βροτοῖς, λευ-
    κὸς μυελὸς γλαγερός,

6 λεπτᾶς ἀράχνας ἐναλιγκί-
    οισι πέπλοις

7 συγκαλύπτων ὄψιν αἰσχύ-
    νας ὕπο, μὴ κατίδῃ τις

8 πῶυ τὸ μαλογενὲς λι-
    πόντ' ἀνάγκᾳ

9 ξηρὸν ἐν ξηραῖς Ἀρισταί-
    ου παλιρρύτοισι παγαῖς·

10 τῷ δ' ὄνομ' ἧς ἄμυλος,
    χερσὶν δ' ἐπέθεντο <τότ' οὐ-
    κέτι> στόμιον μαλεραῖς

11 <   >
    ταν δεξαμέναν ὅ τι κεν
    διδῷ τις, ἃ Ζανὸς καλέοντι

12 τρώγματ'· ἔπειτ' ἐπένειμεν
    ἐγκατακνακομιγὲς
    πεφρυγμένον

192

And the freighters[1] that had departed earlier ...
they now brought in again, bright-shining, laden
with many good things: creatures of a day now call
them 'second tables',[2] but the immortals call them
'the horn of Amalthea'[3]; and in the middle of the
tables had been placed, great joy for mortals, a
white milky custard,[4] hiding its face for shame
under a veil that resembled a spider's fine web, lest
anyone should see that it had of necessity left the
sheep-born flock dry in the dry backward-flowing
fountains of Aristaeus[5]: *amylos* was its name[6]; and
they set no curb on their greedy hands[7] ... when it
had accepted whatever was offered: they call it the
dessert of Zeus. Then a boy distributed, mixed well
with safflower-seed[8] and toasted, biscuits of wheat,

---

[1] The portable tables.   [2] Cf. Lat. *mensae secundae*, 'dessert'.
[3] The horn of plenty, *cornu copiae*; Amalthea was the goat who
nursed the baby Zeus: ambrosia flowed from one horn, nectar from
the other.   [4] *myelos*, normally 'marrow'; the reference is to
beestings, the first milk produced by the sheep or goat after birth,
used for a dessert since regarded as too rich for the young
animal.   [5] The milked udders? Text and interpretation un-
certain. Aristaeus was god of shepherds.   [6] Very odd: *amylos*
was a cake made of fine 'un-milled' meal, as in v. 18 below; ἄμυλον
(Lat. *amylum*), starch, was used to bind and thicken.   [7] The
gap may be quite large.   [8] See J. Edwards, loc. cit. 9.

---

1 lacun. stat. Meineke   2 Meineke: εἰσεφ- A   3 Meineke:
ἐφημέριοι AE   suppl. Bergk   4 Meineke: σταῖσι (ταῖσι E)
δ' ἐν μέσαις AE   5 Kaibel: γλυκερός A   7 Casaubon:
-καλύπτον A   dett., Bergk: κατίδης A   8 dett.: μολογ- A
Meineke, Edmonds: μ. πῶν λιπὼν ταῖς ἀνάγκαις A   9 Meineke:
ξηροῖς A   μελι- Meineke, πολυ- Bergk   10 Meineke:
τὸ δ' A   Musurus: ἐπίθεντο A   lacun. stat. Kaibel, suppl.
Page   11 lacun. stat. Bergk   Page: καὶ A, κα Dindorf

13 πυρβρομολευκερεβινθο-
  ξάνθωμ' ἔκκριτον ἁδὺ
  βρῶμα τὸ παντανάμικτον.

14 †ἀμπυκικηροιδηστί-
  χας† παρεγίνετο τούτοις

15 σταιτινοκογχομαγὴς
  τε καὶ ζεσελαιο<   >
  ξανθεπιπαγκαπύρ<ω-
  τ>ος χοιρίνας,

16 ἁδέα δε<   >
  κυκλώθ' ὁλόφωκτ' ἀνάριθμα

17 καὶ μελίπακτα τετυγμέν'
  ἄφθονα σασαμόφωκτα·

18 τυρακίνας δὲ γάλακτι
  καὶ μέλι συγκατάφυρτος
  ἦς ἄμυλος πλαθανίτας·

19 σασαμοτυροπαγῆ δὲ
  καὶ ζεσελαιοπαγῆ
  πλατύνετο σασαμόπαστα

20 πέμματα, κᾆτ' ἐρέβινθοι
  κνακομιγεῖς ἁπαλαῖς θάλ-
  λοντες ὥραις,

21 ᾠά τ' ἀμαγδαλίδες <τε>
  τᾶν μαλακοφλοΐδων
  <   >τετο τρωκτά τε παισὶν

22 ἁδυεδῆ κάρυ', ἄλλα
  θ' ὅσσα πρέπει παρὰ θοίναν

23 ὀλβιόπλουτον <ἔμεν>·
  πόσις δ' ἐπεραίνετο κότ-
  ταβοί τε λόγοι τ' ἐπὶ κοινᾶς·

PHILOXENUS OF LEUCAS

oats and white chickpea[9] done golden-brown, a
choice and sweet food, the mix of all sorts. . . . honey-
comb . . . there turned up beside these a kneaded ris-
sole of spelt-dough and boiled beans, fried crackly
and gold in boiling oil, and countless round sweet . . .
roasted whole, and honey-cakes, sesame-sprinkled
and toasted, prepared in abundance; and there was
a cheese-cake, well mixed with milk and honey,
made of fine flour and baked in a mould; and
sesame-sprinkled cakes lay flat,[10] a sesame-cheese
mixture done in boiling oil; and then chickpeas
mixed with safflower-seed and flourishing in their
tender youth; and eggs and almonds, soft-skinned
ones . . . and the sweet walnuts nibbled by children,
and everything else that befits a feast of blessed
opulence; and the drinking drew to an end
and the cottabus[11] and the general conversation;

[9] The sweetest chickpea (Theophr. *On Plants* 8. 5. 1).
[10] Translation insecure; πλάτυσμα was the name of a flat cake.
[11] The game in which drinkers aimed the last drops of wine at a
target.

---

13 Meineke: πῦρ ὄβρομ- A   Bergk: -ερεβινθοακανθουμικτριτυαδυ A
14 -κηριο- ci. Meineke   15 Meineke: ταιτινοκογχομανὴς A
Meineke, Page: τοξαισελαιο- A   -πύρωτος suppl. Meineke
Meineke: χοιρινις A   16 lacun. suspic. Meineke   Bergk:
κυκλωτα ομοφλωκτα A, ὁμόφωκτ' Meineke, ὀπό- Kaibel   17
Meineke: -φλωκτα A   18 Bergk: τε A   Meineke:
πλατανις A   19 Schmidt: -ρυτοπαγη A   Meineke:
πλατυντο A   20 Meineke, Schmidt: καὶ τερεβινθοκνακοσυμμιγεις A
21 suppl. Meineke   Bergk: μαλακόφλοια ὦν A   lacun.
stat. Meineke   22 Fiorillo: αδυιδη A   suppl. Bergk

195

24 ἔνθα τι καινὸν ἐλέχθη
    κομψὸν ἀθυρμάτιον, καὶ
      θαύμασαν αὖτ᾽ ἐπί τ᾽ ἤνη-
    σαν <   >

ταῦτα καὶ ὁ Κυθήριος Φιλόξενος . . .

24 Dalecamp: κηνον A   Meineke: ἐθαύμασαν αὐτὸ ἔπειτ᾽ A

(f) Plut. *De aud. poet.* 1 (i 28 Paton-Wegehaupt)

εἰ μέν, ὡς Φιλόξενος ὁ ποιητὴς ἔλεγεν, τῶν κρεῶν τὰ μὴ κρέα
ἥδιστά ἐστι καὶ τῶν ἰχθύων οἱ μὴ ἰχθύες, . . .

then a new witty joke was told, and they admired it and commended it. . . .

These are the lines of Philoxenus of Cythera . . .[12]

[12] Continued at Phil. of Cythera test. 12.

(f) Plutarch, *How the young man should study the poets*

If, as Philoxenus the poet said, the most delicious meats are not meats and the most delicious fish not fish, . . .

POLYIDUS

TESTIMONIA VITAE ATQUE ARTIS

1 *Marm. Par.* Ep. 68 (p. 18 Jacoby)

ἀφ' οὗ Πολύιδος Σηλυμβριανὸς διθυράμβωι ἐνίκη-
σεν Ἀθήνησιν, ἔτη ΗΔ[

2 [Plut.] *Mus.* 21. 1138ab (p. 120 Lasserre, vi 3. 17 Zie-
gler)

καθόλου δ' εἴ τις τῷ μὴ χρῆσθαι τεκμαιρόμενος
καταγνώσεται τῶν μὴ χρωμένων ἄγνοιαν, πολλῶν ἂν
τι φθάνοι καὶ τῶν νῦν καταγιγνώσκων, οἷον ... τῶν δὲ
κιθαρῳδῶν τοῦ Τιμοθείου τρόπου (sc. καταφρονούν-
των)· σχεδὸν γὰρ ἀποπεφοιτήκασιν εἴς τε τὰ καττύ-
ματα (κατατύμματα Lasserre) καὶ εἰς τὰ Πολυείδου
ποιήματα.

POLYIDUS

LIFE AND WORK[1]

1 *Parian Marble*

From the time when Polyidus of Selymbria was victorious in Athens with a dithyramb, [ ] years.[2]

---

[1] See also Timotheus test. 14.   [2] The year falls between 399/398 and 380/379. Diodorus put his *floruit* in 398, describing him as painter and musician as well as dithyrambic poet: see Timotheus test. 3.

2 'Plutarch', *On Music*

In general, if anyone argues that those who do not follow a certain practice are acting out of ignorance, he will be making a hasty judgement against many of our contemporaries[1]; for example, ... against the cithara-singers who scorn the style of Timotheus, which they have pretty well abandoned in favour of the 'patchwork' music[2] and the compositions of Polyidus.[3]

---

[1] I.e. late 4th c. contemporaries of Aristoxenus, source of the present passage.   [2] Literally, leather patches stitched to the soles of shoes; perhaps 'medleys' (Barker). E. K. Borthwick, *Hermes* 96 (1968) 61 f., suggested καρταρτύματα 'confections', or καταχύ(σ)ματα, 'sweetmeats'.   [3] 'Censorinus' said Timotheus and Polyidus used the free rhythms of Pindar (*Gramm. Lat.* vi 608 Keil).

3 Athen. 8. 352b (ii 271 Kaibel)

Πολυίδου δὲ σεμνυνομένου ὡς ἐνίκησε Τιμόθεον ὁ μαθητὴς αὐτοῦ Φιλώτας, θαυμάζειν ἔφη (sc. ὁ Στρατόνικος) 'εἰ ἀγνοεῖς ὅτι αὐτὸς μὲν ψηφίσματα ποιεῖ, Τιμόθεος δὲ νόμους.'

3 Athenaeus, *Scholars at Dinner*

When Polyidus was boasting that his pupil Philotas had defeated Timotheus, Stratonicus said, 'I am surprised that you don't know that Philotas makes decrees, but Timotheus makes laws.'[1]

[1] More permanent than decrees; but νόμοι, 'laws', also means the musical compositions, 'nomes'.

POLYIDUS

FRAGMENTUM

837 *Et. Mag.* 164. 20

Ἄτλας· ὄρος Λιβύης. Πολύιδος δὲ ὁ διθυραμβοποιὸς παρίστησιν αὐτὸν ποιμένα γεγονέναι καί φησιν ὅτι παραγενόμενος ὁ Περσεὺς ἐπερωτώμενός τε ὑπ' αὐτοῦ τίς εἴη καὶ πόθεν ἀφίκ<οι>το, ἐπειδὴ λέγων οὐκ ἔπειθεν, ἀνάγκη ἔδειξεν αὐτῷ τὸ τῆς Γοργόνος πρόσωπον καὶ ἀπελίθωσεν αὐτόν· καὶ ἀπ' αὐτοῦ τὸ ὄρος Ἄτλας ἐκλήθη. οὕτως Λυκόφρονος ἐν ὑπομνήματι (Tzetz. *Lycophr.* 879).

cf. Tzetz. *Exeg. Il.* 132.18

POLYIDUS

FRAGMENT[1]

837 *Etymologicum Magnum*

Atlas: a mountain in Africa. Polyidus the dithyrambic poet makes Atlas a shepherd: according to him, Perseus arrived on the scene, and Atlas asked who he was and where he had come from; and when Perseus' words failed to persuade him (to allow him to pass), he was compelled to show him the Gorgon's face and turned him to stone; and the mountain was called Atlas after him. So the commentary on Lycophron.[2]

---

[1] There are two doubtful fragments, rejected by Page: (1) Aristotle, *Poetics* 16 and 17, mentions 'Polyidus the sophist' in connection with the recognition scene between Iphigenia and Orestes: see *T.G.F.* i 248 f. (Snell); (2) Schol. *Il.* 24. 804a (v 643 Erbse) says Polyidus used τάφος in the sense of 'tomb'; Erbse suggests Pindar (cf. *Isthm.* 8. 57, *Pae.* 6. 99).

CLEOMENES

TESTIMONIA VITAE ATQUE ARTIS

1 Chionides, Πτωχοί fr. 4 K.-A. (Athen. 14. 638d)

ταῦτ' οὐ μὰ Δία Γνήσιππος οὐδ' ὁ Κλεομένης
ἐν ἐννέ' ἂν χορδαῖς κατεγλυκάνατο.

2 Epicrates, *Antilais* fr. 4 K.-A. (Athen. 13. 605e)

τἀρωτίκ' ἐκμεμάθηκα ταῦτα παντελῶς
Σαπφοῦς, Μελήτου, Κλεομένους, Λαμυνθίου.

FRAGMENTUM

ΜΕΛΕΑΓΡΟΣ

838 Athen. 9. 402a (ii 376 Kaibel)

ἐπεὶ δὲ σὺ καὶ τὸ προβληθέν σοι ἀποπροσπεποίησαι περὶ τῆς
χρόας τοῦ Καλυδωνίου συός, εἴ τις αὐτὸν ἱστορεῖ λευκὸν τὴν χρόαν
γεγονότα, ἐροῦμεν ἡμεῖς τὸν εἰπόντα, τὸ δὲ μαρτύριον ἀνίχνευσον
σύ· πάλαι γὰρ τυγχάνω ἀνεγνωκὼς τοὺς Κλεομένους τοῦ Ῥηγίνου
διθυράμβους, ὧν ἐν τῷ ἐπιγραφομένῳ Μελεάγρῳ τοῦτο ἱστόρηται.

CLEOMENES

1 Chionides, *Beggars*

By god, neither Gnesippus[1] nor Cleomenes could have made this seem sweet on his nine-stringed lyre.

[1] Composer of love-songs; see Alcman test. 24.

2 Epicrates, *Anti-lais*

I have thoroughly learned all these love-songs by Sappho, Meletus, Cleomenes and Lamynthius.

FRAGMENT

MELEAGER

838 Athenaeus, *Scholars at Dinner*

But since you have declined to answer the question put to you about the colour of the Calydonian boar, namely whether anyone says it was white, I shall tell you who said it, and you must track down the testimony: a long time ago I read the dithyrambs of Cleomenes of Rhegium, and the information is given in the one entitled *Meleager*.

LAMYNTHIUS

TESTIMONIUM VITAE ATQUE ARTIS

1 Phot. s.v. (p. 207 Porson, i 374 Naber)

Λαμύνθιος· ποιητὴς ἐρωτικῶν μελῶν.

FRAGMENTUM

ΛΥΔΗ

839 Athen. 13. 596f–597a (iii 315s. Kaibel)

ἀλλὰ μικροῦ, ἔφη, ἄνδρες φίλοι, ἐξελαθόμην ὑμῖν εἰπεῖν τήν τε
Ἀντιμάχου Λύδην (test. 8 West), προσέτι δὲ καὶ τὴν ὁμώνυμον
ταύτης ἑταίραν Λύδην ἣν ἠγάπα Λαμύνθιος ὁ Μιλήσιος· ἑκάτερος
γὰρ τούτων τῶν ποιητῶν, ὥς φησι Κλέαρχος ἐν τοῖς Ἐρωτικοῖς
(fr. 34 Wehrli), τῆς (del. Wilamowitz) βαρβάρου Λύδης εἰς ἐπι-
θυμίαν καταστὰς ἐποίησεν ὁ μὲν ἐν ἐλεγείοις, ὁ δ' ἐν μέλει τὸ
καλούμενον ποίημα Λύδην.

LAMYNTHIUS

LIFE AND WORK[1]

1 Photius, *Lexicon*

Lamynthius: composer of love-songs.

[1] See also Cleomenes test. 2.

FRAGMENT

LYDE

839 Athenaeus, *Scholars at Dinner* (on famous courtesans)

'But, my friends,' he said, 'I nearly forgot to tell you of the Lyde of Antimachus,[1] and also of her namesake, the courtesan who was loved by Lamynthius of Miletus. Each of these poets, according to Clearchus[2] in his *Erotica*, fell in love with a foreign girl, Lyde, and composed his poem called *Lyde*, the former in elegiac couplets, the latter in lyric verse.'

[1] Elegiac poet, 5th-4th c. B.C.; for the fragments of *Lyde* see West, *I.E.G.* ii 38 ff.   [2] Scholar from Soli in Cyprus, c. 340–c. 250 B.C.

OENIADES

TESTIMONIUM VITAE ATQUE ARTIS

1 *I.G* ii^2 3064

Οἰ]νιάδης Προνόμου ηὔλει.

FRAGMENTUM

840 Didymus in [Demosth.] 11. 22, col. 12. 43ss. *B.K.T.* i
59s. (p. 45s. Pearson-Stephens)

περὶ μ(ὲν) γ(ὰρ) τὴν Μεθώνης πολιορκίαν τὸν δεξιὸν ὀφθαλ-
μ[ὸ]ν ἐξεκόπη (sc. ὁ Φίλιππος). . . . τὰ μ(ὲν) γ(ὰρ) περὶ τῶν
αὐλητ(ῶν) ὁμολογεῖται κ(αὶ) παρὰ Μαρσύαι (*F.Gr.H.* 135/6
F17), διότι συντελοῦντι μουσικοὺς ἀγῶνας αὐτῶι μικρὸν ἐπάνω
τῆς συμφορ(ᾶς) κ(ατὰ) δαίμονα συνέβη τὸν Κύκλωπα πάντας
αὐλῆσαι, Ἀντιγενείδην μ(ὲν) τὸν Φιλοξένου, Χρυσόγονον δ(ὲ) τὸν
[Στ]ησιχόρου, Τιμόθεον δ(ὲ) τὸν Οἰνιάδου (Οἰνιάδην . . . τὸν Τιμο-
θέου ci. Foucart)

OENIADES

LIFE AND WORK

1 Inscription from Athens (384/3 B.C.)

Oeniades son of Pronomus[1] was the piper.

[1] For Pronomus son of Oeniades, piper and poet, see *P.M.G.* 767 above.

FRAGMENT

840 Didymus on 'Demosthenes', *Answer to Philip's Letter*

At the siege of Methone[1] Philip lost his right eye. . . . The story[2] about the pipers is told in the same terms by Marsyas[3]: when Philip was holding musical competitions shortly before his accident it happened by a strange coincidence that all the pipers performed the *Cyclops*, Antigenides that of Philoxenus,[4] Chrysogonus that of Stesichorus,[5] Timotheus that of Oeniades.[6]

[1] In 354 B.C.   [2] See Duris of Samos, *F.Gr.H.* 76 F36.   [3] Historian from Pella, late 4th c., or 'the younger Marsyas' from Philippi.
[4] See Philox. frr. 815–824, 825.   [5] See Stesichorus II below.   [6] Foucart emended the text to read 'Oeniades that of Timotheus': cf. Oen. test. 1, Timotheus frr. 780–783. For the piper Timotheus of Thebes see Timotheus fr. 777.

STESICHORUS II

TESTIMONIUM VITAE ATQUE ARTIS

1 *Marm. Par.* Ep. 73 (p. 18 Jacoby)

ἀφ' οὗ Στησίχορος ὁ Ἱμεραῖος ὁ δεύτερος ἐνίκησεν
Ἀθήνησιν, καὶ οἰκίσθη Μεγάλη πόλις[

FRAGMENTUM

841 v. Oeniades fr. 840.

STESICHORUS II

LIFE AND WORK

1 *Parian Marble*

From the time when the second Stesichorus of Himera[1] was victorious in Athens and Megalopolis was founded [[2]

---

[1] An assumed name? Himera was destroyed by Carthage in 409 B.C.   [2] The number of years is lost, but the date was 370/69 or 369/68.

FRAGMENT

841 See Oeniades fr. 840 above.

ARISTOTELES

TESTIMONIUM VITAE

1 *Sud.* A 3929 (i 357 Adler)

Ἀριστοτέλης, υἱὸς Νικομάχου καὶ Φαιστιάδος ... ·
ἐκ Σταγείρων, πόλεως τῆς Θράκης, φιλόσοφος, μαθη-
τὴς Πλάτωνος. . . . ἦρξε δὲ ἔτη ιγ' τῆς Περιπατητι-
κῆς κληθείσης φιλοσοφίας διὰ τὸ ἐν περιπάτῳ ἤτοι
κήπῳ διδάξαι ἀναχωρήσαντα τῆς Ἀκαδημίας, ἐν ᾗ
Πλάτων ἐδίδαξεν. ἐγεννήθη δὲ ἐν τῇ ϙθ' Ὀλυμπιάδι
καὶ ἀπέθανεν ἀκόνιτον πιὼν ἐν Χαλκίδι, διότι ἐκα-
λεῖτο πρὸς εὐθύνας ἐπειδὴ ἔγραψε παιᾶνα εἰς Ἑρμείαν
τὸν εὐνοῦχον· οἱ δέ φασι νόσῳ αὐτὸν τελευτῆσαι βιώ-
σαντα ἔτη ο'.

ARISTOTLE

BIOGRAPHY

1 *Suda*

Aristotle, son of Nicomachus and Phaestias ...;
born in Stageira, a city of Thrace; philosopher, pupil
of Plato. ... For 13 years he was head of the philo-
sophic school known as the Peripatetic because he
taught in the walk (*peripatos*) or garden after leav-
ing the Academy in which Plato had taught. He was
born in the 99th Olympiad (384/380 B.C.) and died in
Chalcis after drinking aconite because he was
charged with writing a paean for Hermeias the
eunuch (842 *P.M.G.* below); others say that he died
of disease at the age of 70.[1]

[1] Diog. Laert. 5. 10 says he died a natural death aged 63, and the
dates 384–322 are universally accepted.

ARISTOTELES

POEMATA

842 Athen. 15. 696a–697b (iii 541ss. Kaibel) = Hermippus fr. 48 Wehrli

τούτων λεχθέντων ὁ Δημόκριτος ἔφη· ʼἀλλὰ μὴν καὶ τὸ
ὑπὸ τοῦ πολυμαθεστάτου γραφὲν Ἀριστοτέλους εἰς Ἑρμείαν τὸν
Ἀταρνέα οὐ παιάν ἐστιν, ὡς ὁ τὴν τῆς ἀσεβείας κατὰ τοῦ φιλο-
σόφου γραφὴν ἀπενεγκάμενος Δημόφιλος ἐξέδωκε (Bergk: εἰς
αἰδῶτε codd.) παρασκευασθεὶς ὑπʼ Εὐρυμέδοντος, ὡς ἀσεβοῦντος
καὶ ᾄδοντος ἐν τοῖς συσσιτίοις ὁσημέραι εἰς Ἑρμείαν παιᾶνα. ὅτι δὲ
παιᾶνος οὐδεμίαν ἔμφασιν παρέχει τὸ ᾆσμα ἀλλὰ τῶν σκολίων ἕν τι
καὶ αὐτὸ εἶδός ἐστιν ἐξ αὐτῆς τῆς λέξεως φανερὸν ὑμῖν ποιήσω·

> Ἀρετὰ πολύμοχθε γένει βροτείῳ,
>   θήραμα κάλλιστον βίῳ,
> σᾶς πέρι, παρθένε, μορφᾶς
>   καὶ θανεῖν ζηλωτὸς ἐν Ἑλλάδι πότμος
> 5 καὶ πόνους τλῆναι μαλερούς ἀκάμαντας·
>   τοῖον ἐπὶ φρένα βάλλεις
>   καρπὸν ἰσαθάνατον χρυσοῦ τε κρείσσω

cf. Diog. Laert. 5.6ss. (i 199s. Long) ὁ δὲ ὕμνος ἔχει τοῦτον τὸν τρόπον
(vv. 1–21), Did. in Demosth. 10.32, col. 6.18ss. *B.K.T.* i 25 (p. 19ss.
Pearson-Stephens) (= pap.) [ὁ] γραφεὶς ἐπʼ αὐτῶι [παι]ὰν . . .· κοὐκ ἂν
[ἔ]χ[ο]ι φαύλως αὐτὸν ἀναγρά[ψαι δι]ὰ τὸ μὴ πολλοῖς πρὸ χειρὸς (εἶναι),
ἔχοντα [ο]ὕ(τως)· (vv. 1–21).

de lectionibus D.L. et Athen. v. A.Gercke, *Hermes* 37 (1902) 424s.
1 βροτεωι pap.   5 ακαμαντος pap.: ἀκαμάτους Athen.

214

ARISTOTLE

SCOLION?

842 Athenaeus, *Scholars at Dinner*[1]

When these scolia had been recited, Democritus spoke: 'What's more, the poem written by the learned Aristotle for Hermeias of Atarneus[2] is not a paean, as was claimed by Demophilus who, suborned by Eurymedon, brought a charge of impiety against the philosopher,[3] alleging that he displayed impiety by singing a paean to Hermeias every day in the common dining-room.[4] The song in fact shows none of the characteristics of a paean, but belongs to these scolia as a unique type. I shall give you clear proof from the text itself:

Virtue, you who bring many labours for the race of mortals, fairest quarry for a man's life, for the sake of your beauty, maiden, even to die is an enviable fate in Greece, or to endure cruel unresting toils: such a fruition, as good as immortal, do you

---

[1] Athen.'s source is Hermippus, 3rd B.C. biographer of Aristotle (fr. 48 Wehrli).   [2] Became tyrant of Atarneus (on the Aeolian coast of Asia Minor opposite Lesbos) *c.* 355 B.C.; patron of philosophers including Aristotle, who married his niece and adopted daughter; tortured and executed by the Persian King Artaxerxes III in 341.   [3] On Alexander's death in 323.   [4] Of the Lyceum.

---

7 ἰσαθάνατον pap. (ci. Bergk, Wilamowitz): τ᾽ ἀθ. Athen., εἰς ἀθ. D.L. κρεῖσσον D.L.

215

καὶ γονέων μαλακαυγήτοιό θ' ὕπνου.
σεῦ δ' ἕνεκεν <καὶ> ὁ δῖος

10   Ἡρακλῆς Λήδας τε κοῦροι
πόλλ' ἀνέτλασαν ἐν ἔργοις
σὰν ἀγρεύοντες δύναμιν·
σοῖς τε πόθοις Ἀχιλεὺς Αἴ-
ας τ' Ἀΐδαο δόμους ἦλθον·

15   σᾶς δ' ἕνεκεν φιλίου μορφᾶς Ἀταρνέος
ἔντροφος ἀελίου χήρωσεν αὐγάς.
τοιγὰρ ἀοίδιμος ἔργοις,
ἀθάνατόν τέ μιν αὐξήσουσι Μοῦσαι,
Μναμοσύνας θύγατρες, Δι-

20   ὸς ξενίου σέβας αὔξου-
σαι φιλίας τε γέρας βεβαίου.

ἐγὼ μὲν οὐκ οἶδα εἴ τίς τι κατιδεῖν ἐν τούτοις δύναται παιανικὸν
ἰδίωμα, σαφῶς ὁμολογοῦντος τοῦ γεγραφότος τετελευτηκέναι τὸν
Ἑρμείαν δι' ὧν εἴρηκεν· σᾶς γὰρ φιλίου μορφᾶς Ἀταρνέος ἔντρο-
φος ἠελίου χήρωσεν αὐγάς (v. 15s.). οὐκ ἔχει δ' οὐδὲ τὸ παιανικὸν
ἐπίρρημα.... ἀλλὰ μὴν καὶ αὐτὸς Ἀριστοτέλης ἐν τῇ Ἀπολογίᾳ
τῆς Ἀσεβείας (fr. 645 Rose), εἰ μὴ κατέψευσται ὁ λόγος, φησίν·
οὐ γὰρ ἄν ποτε Ἑρμείᾳ θύειν ὡς ἀθανάτῳ προαιρούμενος ὡς θνητῷ
μνῆμα κατεσκεύαζον, καὶ ἀθανατίζειν τὴν φύσιν βουλόμενος ἐπι-
ταφίοις ἂν τιμαῖς ἐκόσμησα τὸ <σῶμα>.'

8 -αυγητου pap.   9 Page: οουγενειοσοδειος pap., σεῦ δ' ἕνεκεν
(ἕνεχ' cod. E) ὁ δῖος Athen., σοῦ δ' ἕνεκ' ἐκ διὸς D.L., ἕνεχ' οὐκ Διὸς
ci. Brunck   10 -κλέης D.L.   κ[ό]ρ[οι pap. ut vid.   11 πολληνε-
πλασαν pap.   ἐν add. nescio quis   12 Athen.: [. . . .]επουν-
τε[. . . .]μιν pap. (= σὰν ἐφέποντες δ. ?), ἀναγορεύοντες δ. D.L.
13 δὲ Athen.   Ἀχιλλ- Athen., D.L.   14 τ' Ἀΐδα
δόμον ci. Wilamowitz   15 φιλίας, -ία, -ίου D.L. codd.   16 D.L.:
ἠελ- Athen., ἀλ[ίου vel ἠλίου pap.   χωρη[pap.   αὐγάς,
αὐγᾶς codd.   17 D.L.: -μον Athen., pap.   18 ἀθάνατοι D.L.

bestow on the mind, better than gold or parents or soft-eyed sleep; on your account noble Heracles and the sons of Leda endured much in their exploits, (hunting?)[5] your power; in their desire for you Achilles and Ajax went to the dwelling of Hades; and on account of your dear beauty the nursling of Atarneus left desolate the rays of the sun. Therefore he is glorified in song for his exploits, and the Muses, daughters of Memory, will exalt him to immortality, exalting the majesty of Zeus, god of hospitality, and the privilege of secure friendship.[6]

Now I do not know if anyone can see in these lines anything that belongs peculiarly to the paean: the writer clearly admits that Hermeias is dead when he says, "for your dear beauty the nursling of Atarneus left desolate the rays of the sun." Besides, the poem does not have the paeanic refrain.... Moreover Aristotle himself in his Defence against the charge of Impiety says, unless the speech is spurious, "For if my intention had been to sacrifice to Hermeias as an immortal, I should never have erected a tomb to him as a mortal; and if I had wanted to make an immortal of him, I should never have honoured his body with burial rites.'"

[5] Same metaphor as in 'quarry' above? Text uncertain.   [6] On the poem see R. Renehan, *G.R.B.S.* 23 (1982) 251 ff.

672 Rose = West   Diog. Laert. 5. 27 (i 211 Long)

ἔπη, ὧν ἀρχή·

  ἁγνὲ θεῶν πρέσβισθ᾽ ἑκατηβόλε

ἐλεγεῖα, ὧν ἀρχή·

  καλλιτέκνου μητρὸς θύγατερ

cf. Hesych. Mil. vit. (I. Düring, *Aristotle in the Biographical Tradition* 87, no. 139)

673 Rose = West   Olympiod. in Plat. *Gorg.* (p. 215
Westerink)

οὐ μόνον δὲ ἐγκώμιον ποιήσας αὐτοῦ ἐπαινεῖ αὐτόν, ἀλλὰ καὶ ἐν
τοῖς ἐλεγείοις τοῖς πρὸς Εὔδημον αὐτὸν ἐπαινῶν Πλάτωνα ἐγκω-
μιάζει, γράφων οὕτως·

  ἐλθὼν δ᾽ ἐς κλεινὸν Κεκροπίης δάπεδον
  εὐσεβέως σεμνῆς φιλίης ἱδρύσατο βωμὸν
    ἀνδρὸς ὃν οὐδ᾽ αἰνεῖν τοῖσι κακοῖσι θέμις,
  ὃς μόνος ἢ πρῶτος θνητῶν κατέδειξεν ἐναργῶς
5   οἰκείῳ τε βίῳ καὶ μεθόδοισι λόγων
  ὡς ἀγαθός τε καὶ εὐδαίμων ἅμα γίνεται ἀνήρ·
    οὐ νῦν δ᾽ ἔστι λαβεῖν οὐδενὶ ταῦτά ποτε.

cf. Aristotelis vitas ap. West, *I.E.G.* ii 45, Gentili-Prato ii 127

ARISTOTLE

ELEGIACS

672 Rose = West   Diogenes Laertius, *Life of Aristotle*[1]

Hexameters beginning

Holy one, chief of gods, far-darting . . .[2]

Elegiac couplets beginning

Daughter of a mother of fair children . . .

[1] The last two items in a long list of Aristotle's writings.
[2] Apollo.

673 Rose = West   Olympiodorus on Plato, *Gorgias*

Not only does Aristotle praise Plato in the encomium he
composed on him, but he also delivers an encomium on him
in the elegiacs addressed to Eudemus[1] when he is praising
the latter;

and coming to the famous plain of Cecropia[2] he[3]
piously established an altar to honour the holy
friendship of a man[4] whom it is not right for the
wicked even to praise, a man who was the only one
or the first among mortals to show clearly both by
his own life and by the investigations of his
discourses that the good man is also a happy man;
no one can ever attain that now.

[1] Eudemus of Cyprus, friend of Aristotle, rather than Eudemus of
Rhodes, his pupil.   [2] Attica.   [3] Eudemus. Biographers
of Aristotle changed the text to make it Aristotle who established
the altar.   [4] Plato.

GREEK LYRIC

F.G.E. i (p. 32) Diog. Laert. 5. 5s. (i 198s. Long)

ὁ δ᾽ οὖν Ἀριστοτέλης ἐλθὼν εἰς τὰς Ἀθήνας καὶ τρία πρὸς τοῖς δέκα τῆς σχολῆς ἀφηγησάμενος ἔτη ὑπεξῆλθεν εἰς Χαλκίδα, Εὐρυμέδοντος αὐτὸν τοῦ ἱεροφάντου δίκην ἀσεβείας γραψαμένου, ἢ Δημοφίλου ὥς φησι Φαβωρῖνος ἐν Παντοδαπῇ Ἱστορίᾳ (fr. 68 Barigazzi), ἐπειδήπερ τὸν ὕμνον ἐποίησεν εἰς τὸν προειρημένον Ἑρμίαν (842 *P.M.G.* supra), ἀλλὰ καὶ ἐπίγραμμα ἐπὶ τοῦ ἐν Δελφοῖς ἀνδριάντος τοιοῦτον

τόνδε ποτ᾽ οὐχ ὁσίως παραβὰς μακάρων θέμιν ἁγνὴν
ἔκτεινεν Περσῶν τοξοφόρων βασιλεύς,
οὐ φανερᾷ λόγχῃ φονίοις ἐν ἀγῶσι κρατήσας
ἀλλ᾽ ἀνδρὸς πίστει χρησάμενος δολίου.

cf. Did. in Demosth. 10. 32, col. 6. 36ss. *B.K.T.* i 27 (p. 21 Pearson-Stephens) (vv. 1–4) (= pap.), Himer. *or.* 40. 45 Colonna

3 Diels: φα]νερας [λογ]χη[ς pap., φανερῶς λόγχῃ D.L.

220

ARISTOTLE

EPIGRAM

***F.G.E.* i**   Diogenes Laertius, *Life of Aristotle*

Aristotle, then, came to Athens and was in charge of his school for thirteen years; and then he withdrew to Chalcis, indicted for impiety by the hierophant Eurymedon or, according to Favorinus in his *Miscellaneous History*, by Demophilus, the charge being that he composed his hymn for the aforesaid Hermeias (842 *P.M.G.* above), as well as the following inscription for his statue at Delphi:

This man was once impiously slain by the king of the bow-bearing Persians in transgression of the holy law of the blessed gods; he overcame him not with an open spear in murderous fight but by using the faith of a guileful man.[1]

[1] Mentor, a Rhodian mercenary leader in the service of the Persians: he arrested Hermeias by treachery and handed him over to the King. See 842 *P.M.G.* n. 2 above.

LYCOPHRONIDES

FRAGMENTA

843 Athen. 13. 564ab (iii 243 Kaibel)

καὶ γὰρ τὸ παλαιὸν παίδων ἤρων, ὡς καὶ ὁ Ἀρίστων ἔφη (fr. 17 Wehrli), ὅθεν καὶ καλεῖσθαι τοὺς ἐρωμένους συνέβη παιδικά. πρὸς ἀλήθειαν γάρ, καθάπερ φησὶ Κλέαρχος ἐν τῷ πρώτῳ τῶν ἐρωτικῶν (fr. 22 Wehrli), Λυκοφρονίδην εἰρηκέναι φησίν·

οὔτε παιδὸς ἄρρενος οὔτε παρθένων
τῶν χρυσοφόρων οὐδὲ γυναικῶν βαθυκόλπων
καλὸν τὸ πρόσωπον, ἀλλ' ὃ κόσμιον πεφύκει·
ἡ γὰρ αἰδὼς ἄνθος ἐπισπείρει.

3 Page: ἀλλὰ κ. Athen.   πέφυκεν Schaefer

844 Athen. 15. 670d–f (iii 482 Kaibel) = Clearchus fr. 24 Wehrli

ἢ μᾶλλον ὑφ' ὧν οἴονταί τε καὶ πρὸς ἀλήθειαν τὸν τῆς ψυχῆς κόσμον ἐσκύλευνται, [[καὶ]] τούτοις καὶ τὸν τοῦ σώματος κόσμον ὑπὸ τοῦ πάθους ἐξαγόμενοι [[καὶ]] σκυλεύοντες ἑαυτοὺς ἀνατιθέασιν. πᾶς δ' ὁ ἐρῶν τοῦτο δρᾷ μὲν <παρόντος>, μὴ παρόντος δὲ τοῦ ἐρωμένου τῷ (Edmonds: τοῦ cod.) ἐμποδὼν ποιεῖται τὴν ἀνάθεσιν. ὅθεν Λυκοφρονίδης τὸν ἐρῶντα ἐκεῖνον αἰπόλον ἐποίησε λέγοντα·

LYCOPHRONIDES

843 Athenaeus, *Scholars at Dinner*

In olden days they used to love boys, as Ariston[1] said,
so that the loved ones came to be known as *paidika*, 'boy-
favourites'. For truthfully, as Clearchus[2] says in book 1 of
his *Erotica*, citing Lycophronides,

> neither in boy nor in gold-wearing girls nor in
> deep-bosomed women is the face beautiful unless it
> is modest; for it is decorous behaviour that sows the
> seed of beauty's bloom.

[1] Ariston of Ceos, Peripatetic writer, late 3rd c. B.C., author of *Erotic Likenesses*.   [2] Clearchus of Soli, an earlier Peripatetic, *c.* 340–*c.* 250 B.C.

844 Athenaeus, *Scholars at Dinner*[1] ('Why if men's gar-
lands come apart do we say they are in love?')

Or rather, since they see themselves as despoiled of
their soul's ornament,[2] as has indeed happened, they are
carried away by their passion and despoil themselves to
dedicate to the despoilers their body's ornament also.
Every lover does this if the beloved is present; and if he is
not, he makes his dedication to whoever is. That is why
Lycophronides made his lovesick goatherd say,

[1] This material too is taken from Clearchus, *Erotica* book 1.
[2] The word also means 'orderliness'.

τόδ᾽ ἀνατίθημί σοι ῥόδον,
καλὸν ἄνθημα, καὶ πέδιλα καὶ κυνέαν
καὶ τὰν θηροφόνον λογχίδ᾽, ἐπεί μοι νόος ἄλλᾳ
  κέχυται
ἐπὶ τὰν Χάρισιν φίλαν παῖδα καὶ καλάν.

1 ῥόπαλον ci. K. F. Hermann   2 Casaubon: κ. νόημα cod.
4 Fiorillo: Χάρισι cod.

LYCOPHRONIDES

I dedicate to you this rose,[3] a beautiful dedication, and these shoes and cap and beast-slaying javelin, since my thoughts are spilled out elsewhere, towards the girl who is dear to the Graces and beautiful.

[3] Or, with emended text, 'this club'.

CASTORION

FRAGMENTA

845 = 312 *Suppl. Hell.*   Athen. 12. 542e (iii 196 Kaibel)

ἐν δὲ τῇ πομπῇ τῶν Διονυσίων, ἣν ἔπεμψεν ἄρχων γενόμενος
(sc. Δημήτριος ὁ Φαληρεύς), ᾖδεν ὁ χορὸς εἰς αὐτὸν ποίημα τὸ
(Page: ποιήματα Athen.) Καστορίωνος (Leopardi: Σείρωνος
Athen. cod. A, om. cod. E) τοῦ Σολέως, ἐν ᾧ (Page: οἷς codd.)
ἡλιόμορφος προσηγορεύετο·

> ἐξόχως δ' εὐγενέτας ἡλιόμορφος ζαθέοις
> ἄρχων τιμαῖς σε γεραίρει.

cf. Eust. *Od.* 1558. 1 (χορὸς . . . ἡλιόμορφον ἐκεῖνον ἐξόχως τε εὐγενέταν
προσηγόρευσε)

1 δὲ A, τε E   Kuhn (cf. Eust.): ἠπιόμοιρος A, E(?)   2 Page:
σε τιμαῖς A

310 *Suppl. Hell.*   Athen. 10. 454f–455b (ii 488s. Kaibel)

τὸ δὲ Καστορίωνος τοῦ Σολέως, ὡς ὁ Κλέαρχός φησιν (fr. 88
Wehrli), εἰς τὸν Πᾶνα ποίημα τοιοῦτόν ἐστι· τῶν ποδῶν ἕκαστος
ὅλοις ὀνόμασιν περιειλημμένος πάντας ὁμοίως ἡγεμονικοὺς καὶ
ἀκολουθητικοὺς ἔχει τοὺς πόδας, οἷον·

CASTORION

FRAGMENTS

845 = 312 *Suppl. Hell.* Athenaeus, *Scholars at Dinner* (on the lavish expenditure of Demetrius of Phalerum)[1]

In the procession at the Dionysia which he marshalled on becoming archon[2] the chorus sang in his honour a poem by Castorion of Soli in which he was called Sun-like[3]:

and the archon, well-born above all others, Sun-like, venerates you[4] with divine honours.

[1] The material (= Dem. Phal. fr. 34 Wehrli) is taken from the historian Duris (*F.Gr.H.* 76 F10).   [2] In 309/8 B.C.   [3] His blond hair-dye, rouge and other ointments have just been mentioned.   [4] Dionysus; the poem was presumably a dithyramb.

310 *Suppl. Hell.*[1]   Athenaeus, *Scholars at Dinner*

The poem to Pan by Castorion of Soli is like this, as Clearchus[2] says: each of its *metra*, being self-contained, may equally lead or follow[3]:

[1] See also fr. 311, where an emended text of the Berne commentary on Lucan 3. 402 runs, 'Pindar (fr. 100) and Castorion (*cateri* cod.) call Pan the son of Apollo and Penelope.'   [2] See Lycophr. 842 n. 2.   [3] The text is confused but means that the position of each of the three *metra* ('feet' in the text) in the iambic trimeters is interchangeable.

σὲ τὸν βολαῖς νιφοκτύποις δυσχείμερον
ναίονθ' ἕδραν, θηρονόμε Πάν, χθόν' 'Αρκάδων
κλήσω γραφῇ τῇδ' ἐν σοφῇ πάγκλειτ' ἔπη
συνθείς, ἄναξ, δύσγνωτα μὴ σοφῷ κλύειν,
5 μωσοπόλε θήρ, κηρόχυτον ὃς μείλιγμ' ἱείς . . .

καὶ τὰ λοιπὰ τὸν αὐτὸν τρόπον. τούτων δὲ ἕκαστον τῶν ποδῶν ὡς
ἂν τῇ τάξει θῇς, τὸ αὐτὸ μέτρον ἀποδώσει, οὕτως·

σὲ τὸν βολαῖς νιφοκτύποις δυσχείμερον,
νιφοκτύποις σὲ τὸν βολαῖς δυσχείμερον.

καὶ ὅτι τῶν ποδῶν ἕκαστός ἐστι⟨ν⟩ ⟨ἐν⟩δεκαγράμματος.

1 Meineke: βολοις cod. A (ter)   2 Casaubon: νεονθ' A
Cobet: ὁδος A   Casaubon: χθὼν A   3 Porson: τῇδε σοφῇ ἱ
πάγκλητ' A   4 Meineke: σοφοῖς A   5 Cobet: μουσο- A

228

You who dwell in the land of the Arcadians, an abode wintry with battering snowstorms, beast-tending Pan, I shall glorify, putting together all-glorious lines in this skilful composition, lord, lines hard for the unskilled to understand, you beast who serve the Muses, who utter soothing song, wax-poured[4] . . . :

and so on in the same way. Each of these *metra*, wherever you place it in the line, will produce the same rhythm:

σὲ τὸν βολαῖς νιφοκτύποις δυσχείμερον

and

νιφοκτύποις σὲ τὸν βολαῖς δυσχείμερον.

Note also that each of the *metra* has eleven letters.[5]

---

[4] From Pan's pipes, fastened together with wax.   [5] Iota subscript counts as a letter.

HERMOLOCHUS

FRAGMENTUM

846 Stob. 4. 34. 66 (v 845 Hense) (περὶ τοῦ βίου ὅτι βραχὺς κτλ)

Ἑρμολόχου·

ἀτέκμαρτος ὁ πᾶς βίος οὐδὲν ἔχων πιστὸν
πλανᾶται
συντυχίαις· ἐλπὶς δὲ φρένας παραθαρσύνει· τὸ
δὲ μέλλον ἀκριβῶς
οἶδεν οὐδεὶς θνατὸς ὅπα φέρεται·
θεὸς δὲ πάντας †ἐν κινδύνοις θνατούς† κυβερνᾷ·
5 ἀντιπνεῖ δὲ πολλάκις εὐτυχίᾳ δεινά τις αὔρα.

lemma Ἑρμολόχου codd. MA (cf. Phot.), Ἑρμολάου cod. S
2 φρένα A   3 Pflugk: ὁ θάνατος ὅπη codd.   4 ἐν γε κ. κυβ.
(del. θνατοὺς) ci. Page   4 post 5 posuit Bergk
5 Pflugk, Schneidewin: ἀτυχίας codd.

230

HERMOLOCHUS

FRAGMENT

846 Stobaeus, *Extracts* (that life is short, worthless and full of cares)

From Hermolochus[1]:

Man's whole life is baffling, without security, sent astray by events. Hope comforts his heart; but as for the future no mortal knows for certain where he is bound, and it is God who steers all men amid dangers, and often a grim breeze blows in the face of success.

[1] So in two mss. and in Photius' list of the poets used by Stob. (*Bibl.* 167, ii 157 Henry); one ms. has 'Hermolaus'. Stob. included the extract among prose passages.

CARMINA POPULARIA

847 Athen. 3. 109ef (i 251 Kaibel)

ἀχαΐνας· τούτου τοῦ ἄρτου μνημονεύει Σῆμος ἐν η' Δηλιάδος (*F.Gr.H.* 396 F14) λέγων ταῖς θεσμοφόροις γίνεσθαι. εἰσὶ δὲ ἄρτοι μεγάλοι, καὶ ἑορτὴ καλεῖται Μεγαλάρτια ἐπιλεγόντων τῶν φερόντων·

ἀχαΐνην στέατος ἔμπλεων τράγον.

cf. Hsch. χαΐνας (sic)· στέαρ

848 Athen. 8. 360b–d (ii 287ss. Kaibel)

κορωνισταὶ δὲ ἐκαλοῦντο οἱ τῇ κορώνῃ ἀγείροντες ... καὶ τὰ ἀδόμενα δὲ ὑπ' αὐτῶν κορωνίσματα καλεῖται, ὡς ἱστορεῖ Ἀγνοκλῆς ὁ Ῥόδιος ἐν Κορωνισταῖς· καὶ χελιδονίζειν δὲ καλεῖται παρὰ Ῥοδίοις ἀγερμός τις ἄλλος, περὶ οὗ φησι Θέογνις ἐν β' περὶ τῶν ἐν Ῥόδῳ θυσιῶν (*F.Gr.H.* 526 F1), γράφων οὕτως· εἶδος δέ τι τοῦ ἀγείρειν χελιδονίζειν Ῥόδιοι καλοῦσιν, ὃ γίνεται τῷ Βοηδρομιῶνι μηνί· χελιδονίζειν δὲ λέγεται διὰ τὸ εἰωθὸς ἐπιφωνεῖσθαι·

ἦλθ' ἦλθε χελιδὼν
καλὰς ὥρας ἄγουσα
καὶ καλοὺς ἐνιαυτούς,
ἐπὶ γαστέρα λευκά
5 κἀπὶ νῶτα μέλαινα.

---

[1] Unknown. [2] Historian, date unknown. [3] I.e. February-March:

FOLK SONGS

Frr. 847–883 are folk songs in the alphabetical order of the authors who quote them.

847 Athenaeus, *Scholars at Dinner* (on kinds of bread)

achaïnē: this loaf is mentioned by Semus[1] in his *Delias*, book 8; he says it is made for the Lawgivers.[2] They are big loaves, and there is a festival called Big-Loaves at which those who bring them say

munch the *achaïnē* full of lard.

[1] Antiquarian of Delos, *c.* 200 B.C.   [2] Demeter and Persephone.

848 Athenaeus, *Scholars at Dinner*

The name 'crow-men' was used for those who went round begging for the crow ... and their songs are called 'crow-songs', as Hagnocles[1] of Rhodes says in his *Crowmen*. Another kind of begging is called 'singing the swallow-song' on Rhodes: Theognis[2] in book 2 of his *Festivals on Rhodes* writes about it as follows: 'The Rhodians call a certain kind of begging 'singing the swallow-song'; it takes place in the month of Boedromion,[3] and it is so named because of the song they used to sing while they begged:

The swallow has come, the swallow has come, bringing the fine weather and the fine time of year, white on its belly and black on its back. Won't you

cf. E. J. Bickerman, *Chronology of the Ancient World* 20.

233

παλάθαν οὐ προκυκλεῖς
ἐκ πίονος οἴκου
οἴνου τε δέπαστρον
τυροῦ τε κάνυστρον
10   καὶ πυρῶν; ἁ χελιδών
καὶ λεκιθίταν οὐκ ἀπωθεῖται.
    πότερ' ἀπίωμες ἢ λαβώμεθα;
εἰ μέν τι δώσεις· εἰ δὲ μή, οὐκ ἐάσομες·
ἢ τὰν θύραν φέρωμες ἢ τὸ ὑπέρθυρον
15   ἢ τὰν γυναῖκα τὰν ἔσω καθημέναν·
μικρὰ μέν ἐστι, ῥᾳδίως νιν οἴσομες.
ἂν δή τι φέρῃς, μέγα δή τι φέροις·
ἄνοιγ' ἄνοιγε τὰν θύραν χελιδόνι·
οὐ γὰρ γέροντές ἐσμεν, ἀλλὰ παιδία.

τὸν δὲ ἀγερμὸν τοῦτον κατέδειξε πρῶτος Κλεόβουλος ὁ Λίνδιος ἐν
Λίνδῳ χρείας γενομένης συλλογῆς χρημάτων.

cf. Eust. *Od.* 1914. 45

6 σὺ προκύκλει Hermann   9 τυρῶ Athen. cod. A, corr. C
13 ἐάσομεν codd.   16 μικρὰ μιν Athen.   17 Page: φέρῃς τι
Athen.

849 Athen. 14. 618de (iii 364 Kaibel)

Σῆμος δ' ὁ Δήλιος ἐν τῷ περὶ Παιάνων φησί (*F.Gr.H.* 396
F23)· τὰ δράγματα τῶν κριθῶν αὐτὰ καθ' αὑτὰ προσηγόρευον
ἀμάλας, συναθροισθέντα δὲ καὶ ἐκ πολλῶν μίαν γενόμενα δέσμην
οὔλους καὶ ἰούλους· καὶ τὴν Δήμητρα ὁτὲ μὲν Χλόην, ὁτὲ δὲ
Ἰουλώ· ἀπὸ τῶν οὖν τῆς Δήμητρος εὑρημάτων τούς τε καρποὺς καὶ
τοὺς ὕμνους τοὺς εἰς τὴν θεὸν οὔλους καλοῦσι καὶ ἰούλους· δημή-
τρουλοι καὶ καλλίουλοι· καὶ

πλεῖστον οὖλον οὖλον ἵει, ἴουλον ἵει.

234

roll out a fruit-cake from your wealthy house and a cup of wine and a basket of cheese and wheat? The swallow doesn't refuse pulse-bread either. Are we to go away or are we to get something? If you mean to give us something, that's fine; if you don't, we shan't leave you in peace: we'll take your door or your lintel or your wife sitting inside: she's little, we'll carry her easily. If you fetch us something, we hope you fetch us something big. Open up, open up your door to the swallow! We're not old men, we're little children.[4]

Cleobulus[5] of Lindus was the first to introduce this begging at Lindus when there was need for a collection of money.'

[4] For the metre of the song, ionic rather than aeolic, see West, *Greek Metre* 147.   [5] Tyrant of Lindus *c.* 600 B.C., sometimes listed as one of the Seven Sages.

849 Athenaeus, *Scholars at Dinner*

Semus[1] of Delos says in his work *On Paeans* that they used to call the individual handfuls of barley *amalai*, but when they were gathered and bound together into a single[2] sheaf *ouloi* and *iouloi*; and they sometimes called Demeter *Chloe*,[3] sometimes *Ioulo*. So from Demeter's inventions they call both the grain and the hymns to the goddess *ouloi* and *iouloi*, as in Demetr-ouloi and Calli-ouloi; cf. too

Send a large sheaf, a sheaf (*oulos*), send a sheaf (*ioulos*).

[1] See fr. 847 n. 1.   [2] From *oulos* = whole.   [3] Verdant, from the young green crop.

GREEK LYRIC

ἄλλοι δέ φασιν ἐριουργῶν εἶναι τὴν ᾠδήν.

cf. Eust. *Il.* 1162. 42 (iv 253 van der Valk), schol. Ap. Rhod. 1. 972a
(p. 85 Wendel), Phot. s.v. ἴουλος (i 295 Naber), Polluc. 1. 38 (i 11
Bethe)

850 Athen. 14. 619cd (iii 365s. Kaibel)

Κλέαρχος δ' ἐν πρώτῳ Ἐρωτικῶν (fr. 32 Wehrli) νόμιον
καλεῖσθαί τινά φησιν ᾠδὴν ἀπ' Ἠριφανίδος, γράφων οὕτως· Ἠρι-
φανὶς ἡ μελοποιὸς Μενάλκου κυνηγετοῦντος ἐρασθεῖσα ἐθήρευεν
μεταθέουσα ταῖς ἐπιθυμίαις. φοιτῶσα γὰρ καὶ πλανωμένη πάντας
τοὺς ὀρείους ἐπεξῄει δρυμούς, ὡς μῦθον εἶναι τοὺς λεγομένους Ἰοῦς
δρόμους· ὥστε μὴ μόνον τῶν ἀνθρώπων τοὺς ἀστοργίᾳ διαφέροντας
ἀλλὰ καὶ τῶν θηρῶν τοὺς ἀνημερωτάτους συνδακρῦσαι τῷ πάθει,
λαβόντας αἴσθησιν ἐρωτικῆς ἐλπίδος. ὅθεν ἐποίησέ τε καὶ ποιή-
σασα περιῄει κατὰ τὴν ἐρημίαν, ὥς φασιν, ἀναβοῶσα καὶ ᾄδουσα τὸ
καλούμενον νόμιον, ἐν ᾧ ἐστιν·

> μακραὶ δρύες, ὦ Μέναλκα.

851 Athen. 14. 622a–d (iii 371s. Kaibel)

Σῆμος δ' ὁ Δήλιος ἐν τῷ περὶ Παιάνων ... οἱ δὲ ἰθύφαλλοι,
φησί (*F.Gr.H.* 396 F24), καλούμενοι προσωπεῖα μεθυόντων ἔχου-
σιν καὶ ἐστεφάνωνται, χειρίδας ἀνθίνας ἔχοντες· χιτῶσι δὲ χρῶνται
μεσολεύκοις καὶ περιέζωνται ταραντῖνον καλύπτον αὐτοὺς μέχρι
τῶν σφυρῶν. σιγῇ δὲ διὰ τοῦ πυλῶνος εἰσελθόντες, ὅταν κατὰ μέσην
τὴν ὀρχήστραν γένωνται, ἐπιστρέφουσιν εἰς τὸ θέατρον λέγοντες·

---

[1] See fr. 847 n. 1.   [2] Named from the erect phallus which
they escorted into the theatre; Semus does not say in which city or
cities they and the phallus-bearers performed. See Pickard-
Cambridge, *D.T.C.*[2] 140 ff.   [3] A diaphanous robe, often worn
by women.

Others say that the song is sung by wool-workers.[4]

[4] Since *oulos* = woolly; cf. Eratosthenes fr. 10 Powell, Tryphon in Athen. loc. cit.

850 Athenaeus, *Scholars at Dinner*

Clearchus[1] in Book 1 of his *Erotica* says that a certain song is called the pastoral after the story of Eriphanis. He writes as follows: Eriphanis, the lyric poetess, fell in love with Menalcas as he was hunting and went chasing after him, pursuing him in her desire. Wandering up hill and down dale she traversed all the mountain copses, putting into the shade the so-called courses of Io. The result was that not only those human beings who were conspicuously lacking in affection but also the most savage of beasts wept in sympathy with her plight when they sensed the fond hope of her love. So it was that she composed the so-called pastoral and after composing it wandered throughout the wilderness, so they say, shouting aloud and singing it. In it are the words

> The oaks are tall, Menalcas.

[1] See fr. 843 n. 2. The characters in the tale have no historical reality.

851 Athenaeus, *Scholars at Dinner* (on entertainments and ceremonies)

Semus[1] of Delos says in his work *On Paeans* ...: the so-called *ithyphalloi*[2] wear masks representing drunk men, are garlanded and have flowered sleeves; their tunics have a wide stripe, and they wear a Tarentine[3] which covers them down to their ankles. They enter the theatre silently through the gateway, but when they reach the middle of the *orchestra* they turn to the spectators with the words:

237

(a) ἀνάγετ᾽, εὐρυχωρίαν
　　τῷ θεῷ ποιεῖτε·
　　θέλει γὰρ ὁ θεὸς ὀρθὸς ἐσφυδωμένος
　　διὰ μέσου βαδίζειν.

οἱ δὲ φαλλοφόροι, φησίν, προσωπεῖον μὲν οὐ λαμβάνουσιν, προσκό-
πιον (Kaibel: προπόλιον Athen.) δ᾽ ἐξ ἑρπύλλου περιτιθέμενοι καὶ
παιδέρωτος ἐπάνω τούτου ἐπιτίθενται στέφανον [[τε]] δασὺν ἴων
καὶ κιττοῦ· καυνάκας τε περιβεβλημένοι παρέρχονται οἱ μὲν ἐκ
παρόδου, οἱ δὲ κατὰ μέσας τὰς θύρας, βαίνοντες ἐν ῥυθμῷ καὶ
λέγοντες·

(b) σοί, Βάκχε, τάνδε μοῦσαν ἀγλαΐζομεν,
　　ἁπλοῦν ῥυθμὸν χέοντες αἰόλῳ μέλει,
　　καινὰν ἀπαρθένευτον, οὔ τι ταῖς πάρος
　　κεχρημέναν ᾠδαῖσιν, ἀλλ᾽ ἀκήρατον
　5 κατάρχομεν τὸν ὕμνον·

εἶτα προστρέχοντες ἐτώθαζον οὓς [[ἂν]] προέλοιντο, στάδον δὲ
ἔπραττον· ὁ δὲ φαλλοφόρος ἰθὺ βαδίζων καταπασθεὶς (Kaibel:
καταπλησθεὶς Athen.) αἰθάλῳ.

(a) 2 Porson: ποιεῖτε τῷ θεῷ A, ποιεῖτε (om. τῷ θεῷ) E
3 Meineke: ἐθέλει AE　　　ὀρθὸς om. E　　　Meineke: ἐσφυρ- AE
(b) 3 Hemsterhuys: καὶ μὰν A　　　　4 Porson: κεχρημεναν A

852 Athen. 14. 629e (iii 389 Kaibel)

ἦν δὲ καὶ παρὰ τοῖς ἰδιώταις (sc. ἡ ὄρχησις) ἡ καλουμένη
ἄνθεμα· ταύτην δὲ ὠρχοῦντο μετὰ λέξεως τοιαύτης μιμούμενοι καὶ
λέγοντες·

　1 ποῦ μοι τὰ ῥόδα, ποῦ μοι τὰ ἴα,
　　　ποῦ μοι τὰ καλὰ σέλινα;
　2 ταδὶ τὰ ῥόδα, ταδὶ τὰ ἴα,
　　　ταδὶ τὰ καλὰ σέλινα.

(a) Stand back, make plenty of room for the god!
For the god, erect and at bursting-point, wishes to
pass through your midst.

The phallus-bearers,[4] he says, wear no mask, but put on a
visor made of thyme and boy-love[5] and on top of it a thick
garland of violets and ivy. Wearing *kaunakai*[6] they enter,
some by the *parados*, others through the central doors,
marching in step and saying,

(b) To you, Bacchus, we give glory with this
music, pouring forth a simple measure[7] with chang-
ing melody, new music, virginal, not using previous
songs: the hymn we strike up is undefiled.

Then they used to run up and make fun of anyone they
chose, standing still as they did it; but the phallus-bearer
walked straight on, smeared with soot.

[4] Semus lists three groups: *autokabdaloi* ('improvisers'), *ithyphal-
loi* and phallus-bearers, one of whom carried the phallic emblem:
see below.   [5] *paideros*, a shrub with oak-shaped leaves, said
by Paus. 2. 10. 5 to grow only at the sanctuary of Aphrodite in
Sicyon.   [6] Thick woollen cloaks; see MacDowell on Ar. *Wasps*
1137.   [7] Iambic trimeters, perhaps modelled on Eur. *Hipp.* 73 ff.

852 Athenaeus, *Scholars at Dinner* (on dances)

In private life there was also the one called *Flowers*,
which they danced putting actions to the following words:

Where are my roses, where are my violets, where
are my beautiful celery-flowers?
— Here are your roses, here are your violets, here
are your beautiful celery-flowers.

---

2 censor Ienensis: ποῦ μοι ταδὶ τὰ ῥ. Athen.

GREEK LYRIC

853 Athen. 15. 697bc (iii 543s. Kaibel)

οὗτος γὰρ (sc. Οὐλπιανὸς) τὰς καπυρωτέρας ᾠδὰς ἀσπάζεται μᾶλλον τῶν ἐσπουδασμένων, οἷαί εἰσιν αἱ Λοκρικαὶ καλούμεναι, μοιχικαί τινες τὴν φύσιν ὑπάρχουσαι, ὡς καὶ ἥδε·

> ὦ τί πάσχεις; μὴ προδῷς ἄμμ᾽, ἱκετεύω·
> πρὶν καὶ μολεῖν κεῖνον ἀνίστω,
> μὴ κακόν <σε> μέγα ποιήσῃ
> κἀμὲ τὰν δειλάκραν.
> 5 ἁμέρα καὶ δή· τὸ φῶς
> διὰ τᾶς θυρίδος οὐκ εἰσορῇς;

τοιούτων γὰρ ᾀσμάτων αὐτοῦ πᾶσα πλήρης ἡ Φοινίκη . . .

2 μολιν A   3 Bergk: μὴ κ. μ. ποιήσης A   5 Bergk: καὶ ἤδη A
6 Meineke: ἐκορης A

854 Marc. Aurel. 5. 7 (i 78 Farquharson, p. 38 Dalfen)

εὐχὴ Ἀθηναίων·

> ὗσον ὗσον ὦ φίλε
> Ζεῦ κατὰ τῆς ἀρούρας
> 2 †τῆς Ἀθηναίων καὶ τῶν πεδίων.†

ἤτοι οὐ δεῖ εὔχεσθαι ἢ οὕτως ἁπλῶς καὶ ἐλευθέρως.

855 Demosth. *De Corona* 259 (p. 181s. Goodwin)

ἀνὴρ δὲ γενόμενος τῇ μητρὶ τελούσῃ τὰς βίβλους ἀνεγίγνωσκες καὶ τἆλλα συνεσκευωροῦ, τὴν μὲν νύκτα νεβρίζων καὶ κρατηρίζων καὶ καθαίρων τοὺς τελουμένους καὶ ἀπομάττων τῷ πηλῷ καὶ τοῖς πιτύροις καὶ ἀνιστὰς ἀπὸ τοῦ καθαρμοῦ κελεύων λέγειν·

FOLK SONGS

853 Athenaeus, *Scholars at Dinner*

For Ulpian here welcomes the more frivolous songs rather than the serious ones, the so-called Locrian songs for example, randy like this one:

Oh, what's the matter with you? Don't give us away, I beg you. Get up before he[1] comes, in case he does great harm to you and to me, poor wretch! Look, it's day! Don't you see the light through the window?

Ulpian's country Phoenicia is full of this sort of song.

[1] The singer's husband.

854 Marcus Aurelius, *Meditations*

A prayer of the Athenians:

Rain, rain, dear Zeus, on the fields of the Athenians and their plains.[1]

One should either pray simply and freely like this or not pray at all.

[1] Text uncertain: the last words are not metrical. Paus. 1. 24. 3 reports from the acropolis of Athens a statue of Earth praying to Zeus to rain on her.

855 Demosthenes, *On the Crown*

When you[1] reached manhood, you would read the books for your mother while she performed initiation rites and organise matters in general: at night you wrapped the candidates in fawnskins, plied them with the wine-bowl, cleansed them, scoured them with mud and bran and made them get up after their cleansing, telling them to say,

[1] Aeschines.

ἔφυγον κακόν, εὗρον ἄμεινον.

cf. Zenob. *Cent.* 3. 98 (i 82s. Leutsch-Schneidewin) = 'Plut.' *Cent.* 1. 16 (i 323s. L.-S.), Diogenian. *Cent.* 4. 74 (i 243 L.-S.), Hsch. E 7546 (ii 248 Latte), *Sud.* E 3971 (ii 491 Adler), Eust. *Od.* 1726. 19, Arsen. = Apostol. *Cent.* 8. 16 (ii 429 L.-S.), Porphyr. *de abstin.* 1. 1 (p. 85 Nauck)

856 Dio Chrys. *Or.* 2. 59 (i 28s. von Arnim)

ἔτι δὲ οἶμαι (sc. τὴν ᾠδὴν) τὴν παρακλητικήν, οἵα ἡ τῶν Λακωνικῶν ἐμβατηρίων, μάλα πρέπουσα τῇ Λυκούργου πολιτείᾳ καὶ τοῖς ἐπιτηδεύμασιν ἐκείνοις·

    ἄγετ᾽ ὦ Σπάρτας εὐάνδρου
    κοῦροι πατέρων πολιητᾶν,
    λαιᾷ μὲν ἴτυν προβάλεσθε,
    δόρυ δ᾽ εὐτόλμως πάλλοντες,
5   μὴ φειδόμενοι τᾶς ζωᾶς·
    οὐ γὰρ πάτριον τᾷ Σπάρτᾳ.

schol. ad loc. παρακλητικὰ ἐκ τῶν Τυρταίου

cf. Tzetz. *Chil.* 1. 699ss., Mar. Vict. *Art. Gram.* 2. 10 (vi 98 Keil) ite o Spartae primores fauste nunc †parcas† ducentes

4 Luzac: βάλλοντες, βάλλοντε codd.

857 Heph. *Ench.* 8. 4 (p. 25s. Consbruch)

τὸ μέντοι (sc. τὸ ἀναπαιστικὸν τὸ τετράμετρον καταληκτικὸν εἰς συλλαβήν) τὸν σπονδεῖον ἔχον ἀλλὰ μὴ τὸν ἀνάπαιστον παραλήγοντα εἰσὶν οἳ Λακωνικὸν καλοῦσι, προφερόμενοι παράδειγμα τὸ

    ἄγετ᾽ ὦ Σπάρτας ἔνοπλοι κοῦροι
    ποτὶ τὰν Ἄρεως κίνασιν.

Ἄρεος codd. DI

242

I have escaped the bad, I have found the better.[2]

[2] A proverbial expression in paroemiac rhythm, said to have been spoken at Athenian weddings.

856 Dio Chrysostom, *On Kingship*

Or again, I imagine, he[1] might allow the hortatory song like that in the Spartan marching-songs, well suited to the constitution of Lycurgus and the practices of that city:

Come, youths of Sparta, rich in men, you sons of citizen fathers, with your left hand hold your shield before you, and brandish your spear boldly, not sparing your life — that is not the Spartan way.[2]

[1] Alexander is recommending to Philip songs appropriate for a king.   [2] The scholiast and Tzetzes ascribe the lines to Tyrtaeus.

857 Hephaestion, *Handbook on Metre*

The anapaestic tetrameter catalectic with a spondee rather than an anapaest in its second-last foot some call 'Spartan',[1] giving as an example:

Come, armed youths of Sparta, to the dance of Ares.

[1] Because the Spartan Alcman used it, acc. to scholiast (see Alcm. test. 18); in Bergk the fragment is Tyrtaeus 16.

858 P. Argent. W.G. 306ᵛ col. ii, ed. Snell, *Herm*. Einzel-schrift v (1937) 90s.

```
 1  ]παρ[ . . . . ]ρ[ . ]ας ἀντ’ ἀλκᾶς
 2  ]κυαναρου[      4 ]ναστρο[
 7  τὺ δεπα[
    πέφαται παν[
    μετάδος πω . . ρασκ[
10  ἵει νυν οὖρον ἐπαγρ[
    πολεμ . . μονον . [
```

desunt iii vv.

```
15  αρη[
    λιαρὸν ῥηέθροις Εὐρο[
    Εὐρ’ ὦ σωτὴρ τᾶς Σπάρτας
    κατὰ πάντα μόλοις μετὰ νίκας·
    ἰὲ Παιὰν ἰήιε Παιάν.
```

1 ἐ]παρ[ηκτο]ρ[ί]ας ? Snell   10 ἐπ’ ἀγρ[ούς ? Snell

859 Festus (p. 414 Lindsay)

stri(gem, ut ait Verr)ius, Graeci στρίγγα (Scaliger, Müller: συρνια cod. F) ap(pellant . . .)t maleficis mulieribus nomen inditum est, quas volaticas etiam vocant. itaque solent his verbis eas veluti avertere Graeci:

```
στρίγγ’ ἀποπομπεῖν νυκτιβόαν,
στρίγγ’ ἀπὸ λαῶν
ὄρνιν ἀνωνύμιον
ὠκυπόρους ἐπὶ νῆας.
```

1 Bergk: συρριντα πομπειεν F   Turnebus (cf. Hsch. Σ 2004
Schmidt, Γ 609 Latte): νυκτικομαν F   2 Haupt: στρωτατολαον F
3 ἀνώνυμον <ἐχθρῶν> Bergk

FOLK SONGS

858 Strasbourg papyrus[1] (2nd c. B.C.)

In return for valour ... dark (?) ... you (?) ... has been slain ... all ... grant a share ...! Send a breeze, then, over (the fields?) ... enemy ...! ... soft (wind) ... streams ... Eurus: Eurus, saviour of Sparta, may you come with victory at all times! Iě Paean, iēiě Paean!

[1] A Spartan paean, included in a Hellenistic anthology; it is addressed to Eurus, the East wind, whose cult in Sparta is attested.

859 Festus, *On the Meaning of Words*

The *strix* (a kind of owl) is called στρίξ by the Greeks, as Verrius[1] says ... The name is given to evil-doing women, whom they also call 'fliers'.[2] So the Greeks are accustomed to ward them off, as it were, with these words:

Cast out the owl, the night-screeching owl, that ill-omened bird, from the people on to the swift-faring ships.[3]

[1] Verrius Flaccus, Augustan scholar whose work was epitomised by Festus.   [2] Pliny *N.H.* 11. 232 says the *strix* was under a curse.   [3] Text and colometry very uncertain.

860 Heracl. *Alleg. Hom.* 6. 6 (p. 7 Buffière)

ὅτι μὲν τοίνυν ὁ αὐτὸς Ἀπόλλων ἡλίῳ καὶ θεὸς εἷς δυσὶν ὀνό-
μασι κοσμεῖται σαφὲς ἡμῖν ἔκ τε τῶν μυστικῶν λόγων, οὓς αἱ ἀπόρ-
ρητοι τελεταὶ θεολογοῦσι, καὶ τὸ δημῶδες ἄνω καὶ κάτω θρυλού-
μενον·

ἥλιος Ἀπόλλων, ὁ δέ γ᾽ Ἀπόλλων ἥλιος.

cf. Procl. *Theolog. Plat.* 6. 12 (p. 376 Aem. Portus), ps.-Eratosth.
Catast. 24 (*Myth. Gr.* iii 1. 29 Olivieri), schol. Pl. *Resp.* 6. 509c
(p. 245 Greene), schol. Demosth. *Meid.* 9 (39b, ii 161 Dilts), Iulian.
Or. 4. 149d (i 194 Hertlein), Fest. (p. 420 Lindsay)

861 Hsch. E 3502 (ii 115 Latte)

ἐξάγω χωλὸν τραγίσκον,

παιδιᾶς εἶδος παρὰ Ταραντίνοις.

Salmasius: τραγίσκιον cod.

862 Hippol. *Haer.* 5. 8. 40 (p. 96 Wendland, p. 163 Marco-
vich)

ὁ δὲ στάχυς οὗτός ἐστι καὶ παρὰ Ἀθηναίοις ὁ παρὰ τοῦ ἀχαρα-
κτηρίστου φωστὴρ τέλειος μέγας, καθάπερ αὐτὸς ὁ ἱεροφάντης, οὐκ
ἀποκεκομμένος μὲν ὡς ὁ Ἄττις, εὐνουχισμένος δὲ διὰ κωνείου καὶ
πᾶσαν ἀπηρτημένος τὴν σαρκικὴν γένεσιν, νυκτὸς ἐν Ἐλευσῖνι ὑπὸ
πολλῷ πυρὶ τελῶν τὰ μεγάλα καὶ ἄρρητα μυστήρια βοᾷ καὶ
κέκραγε λέγων·

ἱερὸν ἔτεκε Πότνια Κοῦρον
Βριμὼ Βριμόν,

τούτεστιν ἰσχυρὰ ἰσχυρόν.

βριμόν Miller: βριμή cod.

246

FOLK SONGS

860 Heraclitus, *Homeric Allegories*

That Apollo is the same as the sun and that one god is furnished with two names is made clear to us by the mystical words spoken in the secret initiation rites and by the popular refrain which can be heard everywhere:

The sun is Apollo and Apollo is the sun.

861 Hesychius, *Lexicon*

I lead out a little lame goat:

a kind of game played at Tarentum.

862 Hippolytus, *Refutation of all the Heresies*[1]

This ear of corn[2] is in Athens too the great complete light-giver sent by the Inexpressible, inasmuch as the Hierophant[3] himself, not castrated like Attis but made impotent by hemlock and removed from fleshly procreation, carries out the great secret mysteries at Eleusis by night to the light of a great fire and cries aloud and shouts the words,

Our Lady has borne a holy Son, *Brimo Brimos,*

i.e. the strong mother a strong son.[4]

[1] Hippolytus is quoting a Gnostic, a Naassene.   [2] Displayed at the climax of the Mysteries.   [3] 'Revealer of the holy', the high priest.   [4] Demeter and her son Ploutos, the wealth of the earth (Hes. *Theog.* 969 ff.); see N. J. Richardson, *Hom. Hymn to Demeter* 26 ff., 316 ff.

247

863 Iulian. *Caes.* 318d (i 409 Hertlein)

Ἑρμῆς δὲ ἐκήρυττεν·

ἄρχει μὲν ἀγών, τῶν καλλίστων
ἄθλων ταμίας, καιρὸς δὲ καλεῖ
μηκέτι μέλλειν.

1 Bergk: ἀγώνων τῶν codd.

864 Lucian. *Saltat.* 11 (iii 31s. Macleod)

τοιγαροῦν καὶ τὸ ᾆσμα ὃ μεταξὺ ὀρχούμενοι ᾄδουσιν (sc. οἱ
Λάκωνες) Ἀφροδίτης ἐπίκλησίς ἐστι καὶ Ἐρώτων, ὡς συγκωμά-
ζοιεν αὐτοῖς καὶ συνορχοῖντο· καὶ θάτερον δὲ τῶν ᾀσμάτων, δύο γὰρ
ᾄδεται, καὶ διδασκαλίαν ἔχει ὡς χρὴ ὀρχεῖσθαι· πόρρω γάρ, φασίν,
ὦ παῖδες κτλ.

πόρρω γάρ, ὦ παῖδες, πόδα
μετάβατε καὶ κωμάξατε
βέλτιον,

τουτέστιν ἄμεινον ὀρχήσασθε.

1 fort. γὰρ Luciani   2 κωμάξατε, κωμάσατε codd.

865 Lucian. *Demon.* 65 (i 56s. Macleod)

ὅτε δὲ συνῆκεν οὐκέθ' οἷός τε ὢν αὑτῷ ἐπικουρεῖν, εἰπὼν πρὸς
τοὺς παρόντας τὸν ἐναγώνιον τῶν κηρύκων πόδα·

λήγει μὲν ἀγών, τῶν καλλίστων
ἄθλων ταμίας, καιρὸς δὲ καλεῖ
μηκέτι μέλλειν·

καὶ πάντων ἀποσχόμενος ἀπῆλθεν τοῦ βίου φαιδρός ...

cf. Philostrat. *Gymn.* 7 (ii 264 Kayser)

248

863 Julian, *The Caesars*

Hermes made the proclamation[1]:

The contest begins, the steward of the finest prizes, and the moment calls that there be no more delay.[2]

[1] At a feast of gods and emperors a contest was proposed to see whether the emperors could challenge Alexander the Great in their achievements.   [2] Cf. fr. 865.

864 Lucian, *On Dancing*

That is why the song sung by the Spartans while dancing is an invitation to Aphrodite and the Loves to revel and dance along with them; and one of the two songs they sing gives instruction on how to dance: their words are,

Put your foot well forward, boys, and hold a finer revel,

i.e. dance better.

865 Lucian, *Life of Demonax*

When he realised that he was no longer able to fend for himself, he quoted to those who were present the contest 'foot' that the heralds recite[1]:

The contest ends, the steward of the finest prizes, and the moment calls that there be no more delay;

and after abstaining from all nourishment he departed this life cheerfully . . .

[1] Cf. fr. 863; the 'foot', i.e. the metrical period, is mentioned also by Galen, *Epidem.* 6, *Mot. Musc.* 2. 9, Pollux 4. 91, Philostratus, *Gymn.* 7 (who quotes the beginning of fr. 865), Ammianus 24. 6. 10 (pedis anapaesti).

866 Moeris (p. 193 Bekker)

βαλβῖδες αἱ ἐπὶ τῶν ἀφέσεων βάσεις ἐγκεχαραγμέναι, αἷς ἐπέβαινον οἱ δρομεῖς ἵν' ἐξ ἴσου ἵσταιντο. διὸ καὶ οἱ κήρυκες ἐπὶ τῶν τρεχόντων

†βαλβῖδα ποδὸς† θέτε πόδα παρὰ πόδα

καὶ νῦν ἔτι λέγουσιν. Ἀττικοί, ὕσπληξ δὲ κοινόν.

βαλβῖδα πόδας θέντες codd. Pricaei, Vossii: βαλβῖδι Bergk, πέλας Headlam

867 Plut. *Vit. Lys.* 18. 5 (iii 2. 114 Ziegler)

πρώτῳ μὲν γάρ, ὡς ἱστορεῖ Δοῦρις (*F.Gr.H.* 76 F71), Ἑλλήνων ἐκείνῳ βωμοὺς αἱ πόλεις ἀνέστησαν ὡς θεῷ καὶ θυσίας ἔθυσαν, εἰς πρῶτον δὲ παιᾶνες ᾔσθησαν, ὧν ἑνὸς ἀρχὴν ἀπομνημονεύουσι τοιάνδε·

τὸν Ἑλλάδος ἀγαθέας
στραταγὸν ἀπ' εὐρυχόρου Σπάρτας
ὑμνήσομεν, ὢ ἰὲ Παιάν.

cf. Athen. 15. 696e

2 Naeke: -χώρου codd.   3 Iuntina: -σωμεν codd.   Page: ὠιὴ codd.

868 Plut. *Vit. Thes.* 16. 2 (i 1. 12s. Ziegler)

Ἀριστοτέλης (fr. 485 Rose) δὲ καὶ αὐτὸς ἐν τῇ Βοττιαίων πολιτείᾳ δῆλός ἐστιν οὐ νομίζων ἀναιρεῖσθαι τοὺς παῖδας ὑπὸ τοῦ Μίνω, ἀλλὰ θητεύοντας ἐν τῇ Κρήτῃ καταγηράσκειν· καί ποτε Κρήτας εὐχὴν παλαιὰν ἀποδιδόντας ἀνθρώπων ἀπαρχὴν εἰς Δελφοὺς ἀποστέλλειν, τοῖς δὲ πεμπομένοις ἀναμειχθέντας ἐκγόνους ἐκείνων συνεξελθεῖν· ὡς δ' οὐκ ἦσαν ἱκανοὶ τρέφειν ἑαυτοὺς αὐτόθι, πρῶτον μὲν εἰς Ἰταλίαν διαπερᾶσαι κἀκεῖ κατοικεῖν περὶ τὴν Ἰαπυγίαν, ἐκεῖθεν δ' αὖθις εἰς Θρᾴκην κομισθῆναι καὶ κληθῆναι

FOLK SONGS

866 Moeris, *Attic Usage*

Balbides are the grooves cut at the starting-lines on which the runners stepped for a fair start. That is why the heralds still say with regard to the runners,

On the mark (*balbis*) set foot by foot!

This is the Attic word: the *koine* is *husplex*.[1]

[1] See Waldo E. Sweet, *Sport and Recreation in Ancient Greece* 28 f.

867 Plutarch, *Life of Lysander*

Lysander was the first Greek, as Duris[1] says, to whom the cities set up altars as to a god and made sacrifices. He was the first also in whose honour paeans were sung; the beginning of one of them is passed down as follows:

Of the commander of holy Greece from wide-spaced Sparta shall we sing, o iĕ Paean!

[1] Historian of Samos, *c.* 340–*c.* 260 B.C.; acc. to Athen. 15. 696e Duris said the paean was sung at Samos.

868 Plutarch, *Life of Theseus*

Aristotle himself in his *Constitution of the Bottiaeans* clearly does not believe that the children[1] were put to death by Minos but rather that they grew old as slaves in Crete; and on one occasion, he says, the Cretans in fulfilment of an ancient vow sent a human sacrificial offering to Delphi, and descendants of the Athenians left Crete with the group; and when they were unable to support themselves there, they first of all crossed to Italy and settled in the region of Iapygia, and then moved again to Thrace and were called Bottiaeans; and that is why

[1] The Athenian youths sent as tribute to Minos.

Βοττιαίους· διὸ τὰς κόρας τῶν Βοττιαίων θυσίαν τινὰ τελούσας
ἐπᾴδειν·

ἴωμεν εἰς Ἀθάνας.

cf. *Quaest. Graec.* 35

Ἀθήνας codd.

869 Plut. *Sept. Sap. Conv.* 14 (i 323 Paton-Wegehaupt)

ὁ μὲν Θαλῆς ἐπισκώπτων εὖ φρονεῖν ἔφη τὸν Ἐπιμενίδην ὅτι
μὴ βούλεται πράγματα ἔχειν ἀλῶν τὰ σιτία καὶ πέττων ἑαυτῷ
καθάπερ Πιττακός. ἐγὼ γάρ, εἶπε, τῆς ξένης ἤκουον ἀδούσης πρὸς
τὴν μύλην ἐν Ἐρέσῳ γενόμενος·

ἄλει μύλα ἄλει·
καὶ γὰρ Πιττακὸς ἄλει
μεγάλας Μυτιλήνας βασιλεύων.

cf. Diog. Laert. 1. 81, Aelian. *V.H.* 7. 4, Clem. Alex. *Paed.* 3. 10. 50,
Isid. Pelus. *Ep.* 1. 470

1 fort ἄλει μύλ' ἄλει   3 μιτυλάνας, μυτηλάνας, μιτυλήνας codd.

870 Plut. *Apophth. Lac.* 15 (ii 208 Nachstädt-Sieveking-
Titchener)

τριῶν οὖν χορῶν ὄντων κατὰ τὰς τρεῖς ἡλικίας καὶ συνισταμέ-
νων ἐν ταῖς ἑορταῖς ὁ μὲν τῶν γερόντων ἀρχόμενος ᾖδεν·

1 ἁμές ποκ' ἦμες ἄλκιμοι νεανίαι,

εἶτα ὁ τῶν ἀκμαζόντων ἀνδρῶν ἀμειβόμενος [[ἔλεγεν]]·

2 ἁμὲς δέ γ' εἰμές· αἰ δὲ λῆς, αὐγάσδεο·

cf. *Vit. Lycurg.* 21, *de laude ipsius* 15, *Consol. Apoll.* 15, anon. ap.
Miller, *Mélanges* 367, Poll. 4. 107, schol. Pl. *Legg.* 633a, Diogenian.
2. 30, 5. 3, Zenob. 1. 82, Greg. Cypr. 1. 48, Arsen. = Apostol. 2. 72

the Bottiaean girls sing in the performance of a certain sacrifice,

> Let us go to Athens.

869 Plutarch, *Dinner-party of the Seven Sages*

Thales facetiously remarked that Epimenides displayed good sense in that he had no wish to give himself trouble grinding and baking his own food like Pittacus; when I was in Eresus, he said, I used to hear my hostess singing to her handmill,

> Grind, mill, grind: Pittacus used to grind[1] while ruling great Mytilene.

[1] Or 'grinds'; with reference to P.'s 'grinding' oppression of the people, or perhaps to his sexual activity; Clearchus (in Diog. Laert. 1. 81) said it was P.'s daily exercise; other writers followed.

870 Plutarch, *Spartan Sayings*

So there were three choirs[1] based on the three age-groups and formed at the festivals: the choir of old men would begin and sing,

> We were once valiant youths[2];

then the choir of men in their prime would answer,

> And we are valiant youths; look, if you please;

[1] Pollux 4. 71 ascribes the triple choir to Tyrtaeus. [2] 'We were once' became proverbial.

---

1 (et 2) ἄμες, ἅμες, ἄμμες Plut. codd.   ποτ' (ποθ' anon. ap. Miller) codd. omn.   ἦμεν codd. plerique   2 εἰμές Diogenian.: εἰμὲν, ἐσμὲν rell.   αἰ δὲ λῇς: ἢν θέλῃς *de laude* codd. nonnulli   αὐγάσδεο: πεῖραν λαβέ *Lyc.* codd., *de laude* codd. nonnulli, schol. Pl., Apostol.

ὁ δὲ τρίτος ὁ τῶν παίδων·

3 ἁμὲς δέ γ᾽ ἐσσόμεσθα πολλῷ κάρρονες.

3 ἐσσόμεσθα, ἐσσόμεθα, ἐσόμεθα codd.   κρείσσονες, κάρρωνες codd.

871 Plut. *Quaest. Graec.* 36 (ii 353 Nachstädt-Sieveking-Titchener)

διὰ τί τὸν Διόνυσον αἱ τῶν Ἠλείων γυναῖκες ὑμνοῦσαι παρακα-
λοῦσι βοέῳ ποδὶ παραγίνεσθαι πρὸς αὐτάς; ἔχει δ᾽ οὕτως ὁ ὕμνος·

      ἐλθεῖν ἥρω Διόνυσε
      Ἀλείων ἐς ναὸν
      ἁγνὸν σὺν Χαρίτεσσιν
      ἐς ναὸν
   5 τῷ βοέῳ ποδὶ θύων,

εἶτα δὶς ἐπᾴδουσιν

      ἄξιε ταῦρε,
      ἄξιε ταῦρε.

1 ἥρως Schneidewin, de ἥρω Διόνυσον cogit. Bergk, ἵρ᾽ ὦ West
2 Bergk: ἄλιον codd.   5 δύων codd. ut vid.

872 Plut. *Quaest. Conviv.* 3. 6. 4 (iv 103 Hubert)

καὶ ἡμᾶς οὔπω παντάπασιν ἡ Ἀφροδίτη πέφευγεν, ἀλλὰ καὶ
προσευχόμεθα δήπουθεν αὐτῇ λέγοντες ἐν τοῖς τῶν θεῶν ὕμνοις·

      ἀνάβαλλ᾽ ἄνω τὸ γῆρας,
      ὦ καλὰ Ἀφροδίτα.

cf. Hsch. A 4189 ἀναβαλλόγηρας· φάρμακόν τι, καὶ λίθος ἐν Σάμῳ, Paus.
3. 18. 1 Ἀμβολογήρας Ἀφροδίτης ἄγαλμα

1 ἀνάβαλ᾽ ci. Bergk

and the third choir, the boys' choir, would answer,

And we shall be better by far.

871 Plutarch, *Greek Questions*

Why do the women of Elis when singing their hymn to Dionysus invite him to come to them 'with ox foot'? The hymn runs as follows[1]:

Come, hero Dionysus, to the holy temple of the Eleans along with the Graces, to the temple, raging[2] with your ox foot,

then they add the double refrain,

Worthy bull, worthy bull!

[1] Text uncertain: 'hero' is hard to accept, and the metre difficult to analyse; see C. Brown, *G.R.B.S.* 23 (1982) 305 ff., West, *Greek Metre* 146 f.   [2] Paus. 6. 26. 1 says that the Elean festival was called the Thuia (cf. *thuo*, 'rage').

872 Plutarch, *Table-talk*

And Aphrodite has not yet fled from us for good; rather we pray to her, I imagine, in the words of the hymns to the gods:

Postpone old age, beautiful Aphrodite[1]!

[1] In Sparta there was a statue of Aphrodite, Postponer of Old Age (Paus. 3. 18. 1); Crusius ascribed the fragment to Alcman.

873 Plut. *Amator.* 17 (iv 367s. Hubert)

Ἀριστοτέλης δὲ (fr. 98 Rose) τὸν μὲν Κλεόμαχον ἄλλως ἀπο-
θανεῖν φησι κρατήσαντα τῶν Ἐρετριέων τῇ μάχῃ· τὸν δ' ὑπὸ τοῦ
ἐρωμένου φιληθέντα τῶν ἀπὸ Θράκης Χαλκιδέων γενέσθαι,
πεμφθέντα τοῖς ἐν Εὐβοίᾳ Χαλκιδεῦσιν ἐπίκουρον· ὅθεν ᾄδεσθαι
παρὰ τοῖς Χαλκιδεῦσιν·

> ὦ παῖδες <ὅσ>οι Χαρίτων τε καὶ πατέρων
> λάχετ' ἐσθλῶν
> μὴ φθονεῖθ' ὥρας ἀγαθοῖσιν ὁμιλεῖν·
> σὺν γὰρ ἀνδρείᾳ καὶ ὁ λυσιμελὴς
> Ἔρως ἐνὶ Χαλκιδέων θάλλει πόλεσιν.

Ἄντων ἦν ὄνομα τῷ ἐραστῇ, τῷ δ' ἐρωμένῳ Φίλιστος . . .

1 ὅσοι Bergk   Meineke: ἐλάχετε codd.   2 Bergk: ὁμιλίαν codd.
3 Stephanus: ἀνδρία codd.   4 Bernadakis: ἐπὶ codd.

874 Plut. *Aet. Phys.* 16 (v 3. 14 Hubert)

διὰ τί λέγεται·

> σῖτον ἐν πηλῷ φύτευε, τὴν δὲ κριθὴν ἐν κόνει;

Bergk: φυτεύετε codd., exc. Est. 145 φυτεύειν (quod ci. Headlam)

875 Poll. 9. 113 (ii 178s. Bethe)

ἡ δὲ χυτρίνδα, ὁ μὲν ἐν μέσῳ κάθηται καὶ καλεῖται χύτρα, οἱ δὲ
τίλλουσιν ἢ κνίζουσιν ἢ καὶ παίουσιν αὐτὸν περιθέοντες. ὁ δ' ὑπ'
αὐτοῦ περιστρεφομένου ληφθεὶς ἀντ' αὐτοῦ κάθηται. ἔσθ' ὅτε ὁ
μὲν ἔχεται τῆς χύτρας κατὰ τὴν κεφαλὴν τῇ χειρὶ τῇ λαιᾷ περι-
θέων ἐν κύκλῳ, οἱ δὲ παίουσιν αὐτὸν ἐπερωτῶντες

> τίς τὴν χύτραν;

FOLK SONGS

873 Plutarch, *Dialogue on Love*

But Aristotle says that Cleomachus died in different circumstances after defeating the Eretrians in the battle,[1] and that the one who was kissed by his beloved boy was from Thracian Chalcidice, sent to fight for the Euboean Chalcidians; this, he says, is why the song in Chalcis runs:

You boys who possess the Graces and noble fathers, do not grudge your youthful beauty in converse with good men; for together with bravery Love, loosener of limbs, flourishes in the cities of the Chalcidians.

The lover was called Anton, the boy Philistus ...

[1] In the Lelantine War (late 8th c. B.C.); Plut. has told how Cleomachus of Pharsalus was watched by his *eromenos* as he led the Chalcidians to victory but lost his life. The Aristotle may be the historian from Chalcis (4th c. B.C.? *F.Gr.H.* 423).

874 Plutarch, *Causes of Natural Phenomena*

Why does the saying run,

Plant wheat in mud but barley in dust?

875 Pollux, *Vocabulary*

The pot-game: one sits in the middle and is called 'pot', while the others run round him pulling his hair or tickling him or even hitting him; and when 'pot' turns round and catches one of them, he sits down in his place. Sometimes one holds 'the pot' by the head with his left hand as he runs round him, and the others hit him and ask,

Who has the pot?

κἀκεῖνος ἀποκρίνεται

ἀναζεῖ·

ἤ

τίς περὶ χύτραν;

κἀκεῖνος ἀποκρίνεται

ἐγὼ Μίδας·

οὗ δ' ἂν τύχῃ τῷ ποδί, ἐκεῖνος ἀντ' αὐτοῦ περὶ τὴν χύτραν περιέρχεται.

876 Poll. 9. 122ss. (ii 180s. Bethe)

εἰσὶ δὲ καὶ ἄλλαι παιδιαί . . . · ἡ δὲ χαλκῆ μυῖα, ταινίᾳ τὼ ὀφθαλμὼ περισφίγξαντος ἑνὸς παιδός, ὁ μὲν περιστρέφεται κηρύττων

(a) χαλκῆν μυῖαν θηράσω,

οἱ δ' ἀποκρινόμενοι

θηράσεις, ἀλλ' οὐ λήψει,

σκύτεσι βυβλίνοις αὐτὸν παίουσιν ἕως τινὸς αὐτῶν λάβηται. ἡ δ'

(b) ἔξεχ' ὦ φίλ' ἥλιε

παιδιὰ κρότον ἔχει τῶν παίδων σὺν τῷ ἐπιβοήματι τούτῳ ὁπόταν νέφος ἐπιδράμῃ τὸν θεόν· ὅθεν καὶ Στράττις ἐν Φοινίσσαις (fr. 48 K.-A.)· εἶθ' ἥλιος μὲν πείθεται τοῖς παιδίοις | ὅταν λέγωσιν ἔξεχ' ὦ φίλ' ἥλιε. . . .

---

[1] 'Ancient Greek (and modern Cretan) boys used to tie a lighted taper of wax to a bronze-coloured flying-beetle, which they then chased in the dark' (H. W. Smyth ad loc.).   [2] Athenian comic poet, late 5th–early 4th c.

and he answers,

> The pot's boiling;

or they say,

> Who's going round the pot?

and he answers,

> I, Midas;

and whoever he touches with his foot takes his place going round 'the pot'.[1]

[1] See also Hsch. X 50, *Sud.* X 619.

876 Pollux, *Vocabulary*

There are other games: . . . in Bronze Fly one boy blindfolds himself with a cloth and turns round and round calling

> (a) I'll hunt a bronze fly,[1]

and the others answer

> You'll hunt it but you won't catch it,

hitting him with whips of papyrus till he grabs one of them.

The game

> (b) Come out, dear sun!

has the boys clapping their hands and shouting these words whenever a cloud passes over the sun-god; whence the lines of Strattis[2] in his *Phoenician Women*: 'And so the sun obeys the children when they say, "Come out, dear sun!"'

ἡ δὲ χελιχελώνη, παρθένων ἐστὶν ἡ παιδιά, παρόμοιόν τι
ἔχουσα τῇ χύτρᾳ· ἡ μὲν γὰρ κάθηται καὶ καλεῖται χελώνη, αἱ δὲ
περιτρέχουσιν ἀνερωτῶσαι·

(c) χελιχελώνα, τί ποιεῖς ἐν τῷ μέσῳ;

ἡ δὲ ἀποκρίνεται

    ἔρια μαρύομαι καὶ κρόκαν Μιλησίαν.

εἶτ᾽ ἐκεῖναι πάλιν ἐκβοῶσιν

    ὁ δ᾽ ἔκγονός σου τί ποιῶν ἀπώλετο;

ἡ δέ φησι

    λευκᾶν ἀφ᾽ ἵππων εἰς θάλασσαν ἅλατο.

cf. (a) Eust. *Il.* 1243. 29, Suet. *Paed.* 17 (p. 72 Taillardat), (b) Eust.
Il. 881. 42, *Sud.* E 1684, Ar. fr. 404 K.-A., Telesill. 718, (c) Eust. *Od.*
1914. 56, Suet. *Paed.* 19 (p. 72s. T.), Hsch. X 320

(c) 1 χέλει χ. Eust.   -χελώνη codd.   2 vid. West, *Greek*
Metre 147   κρόκην, κρόκον codd.   3 ἔγγονός Eust.

877 Procl. in Hes. *Op.* 389 (p. 136 Pertusi)

οἱ δὲ ἀρχαῖοι καὶ πρωαίτερον ἔσπειρον, καὶ δῆλον ἐκ τῶν Ἐλευ-
σινίων τελετῶν, ἐν οἷς ἐλέγετο (Bergk: ἔλεγε τοῦ codd.)·

    παράθει, Κόρη, γέφυραν· ὅσον οὔπω τρίπολον δή.

West (e.g.): πῆθι (πάριθι vel πέριθι Pertusi) codd. AQ, πάριθι Bergk
Wilamowitz: τριπόλε cum compendio A, τριπόλεον QR, τρὶς πολέουσιν
Bergk   Bergk: δέ codd.

878 Schol. M Aes. *Pers.* 940 (p. 252 Dähnhardt) (Μαριαν-
δυνοῦ θρηνητῆρος)

Καλλίστρατος ἐν δευτέρῳ περὶ Ἡρακλείας (*F.Gr.H.* 433
F3(a)) Τιτυοῦ τρεῖς παῖδας εἶναι, Πρίολαν Μαριανδυνὸν
<Βῶρ>μον, ὃν κυνηγετοῦντα ἀπολέσθαι, καὶ μέχρι νῦν Μαριανδυ-

Torti-tortoise, a girls' game, is rather like The Pot (see fr. 875): one girl sits and is called 'tortoise', and the others run round her asking

(c) Torti-tortoise, what are you doing in the middle?

and she answers

I'm weaving a web of Milesian wool.

Then they shout back

And how did your son die?

and she says

He jumped from white horses[3] into the sea.[4]

[3] I.e. from a horse-drawn chariot. [4] See R. D. Griffith–G. D'A Griffith, *Maia* 43 (1991) 83 ff.

877 Proclus on Hesiod, *Works and Days* ('sow naked')

The ancients used to sow earlier, as is made clear by the Eleusinian rites in the words used there:

Run across the bridge, Maiden: the ground is almost thrice-worked.[1]

[1] Text and translation uncertain; the Maiden is Persephone, the bridge that across the Attic Cephisus, used by the initiates travelling from Athens to Eleusis. Fallow land was turned over three times before the autumn sowing.

878 Scholiast on Aeschylus, *Persians* ('Mariandynian mourner')

Callistratus in Book 2 of his work *On Heraclea*[1] says Tityus had three sons, Priolas, Mariandynus and Bormus, who was killed while hunting: even now, he says, the Mari-

[1] Heraclea Pontica, a Megarian and Boeotian colony in Bithynia in the land of the Mariandynians; Callistratus may belong to 1st c. B.C.

νοὺς ἀκμῇ θέρους θρηνεῖν αὐτόν. τὸν δὲ Μαριανδυνὸν αὐξῆσαι
μάλιστα τὴν θρηνητικὴν αὐλῳδίαν, καὶ διδάξαι Ὕαγνιν τὸν Μαρ-
σύου πατέρα. καὶ αὐλοὶ δέ τινές εἰσι Μαριανδυνοὶ ἐπιτηδειότητα
ἔχοντες εἰς τὰς θρηνῳδίας. καὶ τὸ περιφερόμενον·

> αὐλεῖ Μαριανδυνοῖς καλάμοις κρούων Ἰαστί,

ὡς τῶν Μαριανδυνῶν θρηνῳδῶν ὄντων.

879 (1) Schol. RV Ar. *Ran.* 479 (p. 290 Dübner) (ἐγκέχοδα·
κάλει θεόν)

ἐν τοῖς Ληναϊκοῖς ἀγῶσι τοῦ Διονύσου ὁ δᾳδοῦχος κατέχων
λαμπάδα λέγει·

> καλεῖτε θεόν·

καὶ οἱ ὑπακούοντες βοῶσι·

> Σεμελήι᾽ Ἴακχε πλουτοδότα

(2) Ar. *Pax* 967s.

ἀλλ᾽ εὐχώμεθα. / τίς τῇδε; ποῦ ποτ᾽ εἰσὶ πολλοὶ κἀγαθοί;

Schol. RV ad loc. (p. 146 Holwerda) = *Sud.* T 671 (iv 562
Adler)

σπένδοντες γὰρ ἔλεγον·

> τίς τῇδε;

ἀντὶ τοῦ ῾τίς πάρεστιν;᾽ εἶτα οἱ παρόντες εὐφημιζόμενοι ἔλεγον·

> πολλοὶ κἀγαθοί.

τοῦτο δὲ ἐποίουν οἱ σπένδοντες ἵνα οἱ συνειδότες τι ἑαυτοῖς ἄτοπον
ἐκχωροῖεν τῶν σπονδῶν.

andynians mourn his death in the height of summer. Mariandynus developed the pipe-song for use in mourning, and he was the teacher of Hyagnis, Marsyas' father. Certain pipes are known as Mariandynian and are suitable for songs of mourning; there is also the saying,

he pipes on Mariandynian reeds, playing in the Ionian tuning,

the Mariandynians being singers of mourning-songs.

879 (1) Scholiast on Aristophanes, *Frogs* ('I've shit myself: call the god!')

In the Lenaean festivals of Dionysus the torch-bearer, torch in hand, says,

Call the god!

and the audience shouts,

Semelean Iacchus, giver of wealth!

(2) Aristophanes, *Peace*

Let us pray, then. 'Who is here?' Where on earth are the 'many good men'?

Scholiast on the passage

When they made libation they used to say,

Who is here?

in the sense of 'Who is present?' Then those who were present spoke words of good omen:

Many good men.

Those making libation did this so that any who had wicked behaviour on their conscience might leave the ceremony.

(3) Schol. RV Ar. *Ran.* 479

ἢ πρὸς τὸ ἐν ταῖς θυσίαις ἐπιλεγόμενον· ἐπειδὰν γὰρ σπον-
δοποιήσωνται ἐπιλέγουσιν·

ἐκκέχυται· κάλει θεόν.

(1) Ἴακχ' ὦ ci. Bergk   (2) cf. App. Prov. 4. 90 (i 455 Leutsch-
Schneidewin), ubi καλοὶ κἀγαθοί

880 Schol. b Hom. *Il.* 18. 570 (iv 558 Erbse)

φασὶ δὲ αὐτὸν (sc. τὸν Λίνον) ἐν Θήβαις ταφῆναι καὶ τιμηθῆναι
θρηνώδεσιν ᾠδαῖς ἃς λινῳδίας ἐκάλεσαν. ἆρα οὖν ὁ νεανίας διὰ τῆς
μιμήσεως ταύτης τὰ κατὰ τὸν Λίνον ᾖδεν; ἐθρηνεῖτο γὰρ οὗτος
παρὰ τῶν Μουσῶν οὕτως·

†ὦ Λίνε θεοῖσι τετιμημένε, σοὶ γὰρ πρώτῳ μέλος
ἔδωκαν ἀθάνατοι ἀνθρώποισι φωναῖς λιγυραῖς ἀεῖσαι·
Φοῖβος δέ σε κότῳ ἀναιρεῖ, Μοῦσαι δέ σε θρηνέουσιν.†

cf. Schol. T (iv 556 Erbse), Eust. *Il.* 1163. 59 (iv 258 van der Valk)

881 (a) Schol. Pind. *Pyth.* 3. 32c (ii 67s. Drachmann)

τὸ 'ὑποκουρίζεσθαι ἀοιδαῖς' εἶπε διὰ τὸ τοὺς ὑμεναιοῦντας
(Bothe: ὑμνοῦντας codd.) ἐπευφημιζομένους λέγειν

σὺν κόροις τε καὶ κόραις.

FOLK SONGS

(3) (continued from (1) above)

Or the reference is to the phrase used in sacrifices: after making libation they say,

> It is poured: call the god!

880 Scholiast b on *Iliad* (in the vintage scene on Achilles' shield a boy 'was singing the linus-song beautifully with piping voice' to his lyre accompaniment)

They say that Linus was buried in Thebes and honoured in mourning-songs which they called linus-songs. The linus is a song of mourning sung in a thin voice. Was the youth singing the song about Linus in this representation? He was mourned by the Muses as follows:

> Oh Linus, honoured by the gods — for you were the first to whom the immortals gave a song for men to sing with clear voice; Phoebus killed you in anger,[1] but the Muses mourn for you.[2]

[1] For claiming that he could sing as well as the god (Paus. 9. 29. 6); cf. also Hes. frr. 305, 306 M.-W., *O.C.D.*[2] s.v. Linus.   [2] Schol. T and Eustathius give a hexameter version of the song, calling it a Theban inscription: the version in schol. b may in fact have been derived from it; see E. Maass, *Hermes* 23 (1888) 303 ff., M. van der Valk, *Researches* i 154 f.

881 (a) Scholiast on Pindar, *Pythian* 3. 19

Pindar said 'to use girlhood names (ὑπο-κουρίζεσθαι) in their songs' because those who sing the wedding-hymn use words of good omen,

> with both boys and girls.

265

Αἰσχύλος Δαναΐσι (fr. 43 Radt)· κἄπειτα δ᾽ εὖτε λαμπρὸν ἡλίου
φάος | ἕως ἐγείρῃ, πρευμενεῖς τοὺς νυμφίους | νόμοισι θέντων σὺν
κόροις τε καὶ κόραις. κἂν τῷ βίῳ †εὐκορεῖ ἀντὶ τοῦ κόρους κορώνας
παρατρέποντες† ἔνιοί φασιν·

ἐκκόρει κόρει κορώνας.

κόρει vel κόρους codd.

(b) Horapollo *Hierogl.* 1. 8 (p. 19 Sbordone)

τῆς δὲ τοιαύτης αὐτῶν (sc. τῶν κορωνῶν) ὁμονοίας χάριν μέχρι
νῦν οἱ Ἕλληνες ἐν τοῖς γάμοις

ἐκκορὶ κορὶ κορώνη

λέγουσιν ἀγνοοῦντες.

κορώνην cod. L

(c) Hsch. K 3856 (ii 521 Latte)

κουριζόμενος· ὑμεναιῶν (Radt: ὑμεναιούμενος cod.) διὰ τὸ
γαμουμέναις λέγειν (γαμ. διὰ τὸ λέγ. cod.)· σὺν κούροις τε καὶ
κόραις. ὅπερ νῦν παρεφθαρμένως ἐκκορεῖν λέγεται.

(d) Aelian. *H.A.* 3.9 (i 164ss. Scholfield)

ἀκούω δὲ τοὺς πάλαι καὶ ἐν τοῖς γάμοις μετὰ τὸν ὑμέναιον τὴν
κορώνην ᾄδειν, σύνθημα ὁμονοίας τοῦτο τοῖς συνιοῦσιν ἐπὶ τῇ
παιδοποιίᾳ διδόντας.

FOLK SONGS

So Aeschylus in his *Danaids*: 'and then, when dawn rouses the sun's bright light, after they have propitiated the bridegrooms with the strains "with both boys and girls"'. And in real life some pervert the phrase . . . and say,

> sweep out, sweep out the crows![1]

[1] Text and interpretation uncertain at several points; see (d) n. 1.

(b) Horapollo, *Hieroglyphics*

On account of this conjugal fidelity of crows the Greeks still say at weddings,

> *ekkori kori korōnē*,[1]

without understanding the meaning.

[1] *korōnē* is 'crow'; the rest might be a reduplication like 'torti-tortoise', fr. 876(c).

(c) Hesychius, *Lexicon*

κουριζόμενος = 'singing the wedding hymn' because of the words spoken to brides, 'with both boys and girls'. The expression is nowadays corrupted to *ek-korein*, 'sweep out'.

(d) Aelian, *On Animals* (on the conjugal bond of crows)

I have heard too that in ancient days at weddings they used to sing 'The Crow' after the wedding-hymn, offering this as a token of loyalty to the pair who were uniting for the procreation of children.[1]

[1] Two distinct sayings are alluded to: (a) and (c) give a prayer for fertility, 'with both boys and girls'; (a) (b) and (d) point to an obscure reference to the crow or crows: perhaps 'sweep out the crow', an indelicate injunction to the bridegroom (cf. Hsch. K 4731).

882 Prolegom. Theocr. B b (p. 3 Wendel)

τοὺς δὲ νενικημένους (sc. ἀγροίκους) εἰς τὰς περιοικίδας χωρεῖν
ἀγείροντας ἑαυτοῖς τὰς τροφάς· ᾄδειν (Schäfer: διδόναι codd.) δὲ
ἄλλα τε παιδιᾶς καὶ γέλωτος ἐχόμενα καὶ εὐφημοῦντας ἐπιλέγειν·

> δέξαι τὰν ἀγαθὰν τύχαν,
> δέξαι τὰν ὑγίειαν,
> ἃν φέρομες παρὰ τᾶς θεοῦ
> †ἃν ἐκλελάσκετο† τήνα.

3 φέρομες, φέρομεν codd.   Hermann: τῆς, τοῦ codd.   4 ἐκ-
λελάσκετο K, ἐκαλέσσατο rell.: ᾇ 'κελήσατο ci. Ahrens

883 Zenob. *Cent.* 4. 33 (i 93 Leutsch-Schneidewin)

> θύραζε Κᾶρες· οὐκέτ᾽ Ἀνθεστήρια.

οἱ μὲν διὰ πλῆθος οἰκετῶν Καρικῶν εἰρῆσθαί φασιν ὡς ἐν τοῖς Ἀν-
θεστηρίοις εὐωχουμένων αὐτῶν καὶ οὐκ ἐργαζομένων. τῆς οὖν ἑορ-
τῆς τελεσθείσης λέγειν ἐπὶ τὰ ἔργα ἐκπέμποντας αὐτούς· θύρ.—
Ἀνθ. τινὲς δὲ οὕτω τὴν παροιμίαν φασίν, ὅτι οἱ Κᾶρές ποτε μέρος
τῆς Ἀττικῆς κατέσχον· καὶ εἴ ποτε τὴν ἑορτὴν τῶν Ἀνθεστηρίων
ἦγον οἱ Ἀθηναῖοι, σπονδῶν αὐτοῖς μετεδίδοσαν καὶ ἐδέχοντο τῷ
ἄστει καὶ ταῖς οἰκίαις. μετὰ δὲ τὴν ἑορτὴν τινῶν ὑπολειμμένων
ἐν ταῖς Ἀθηναῖς, οἱ ἀπαντῶντες πρὸς τοὺς Κᾶρας παίζοντες
ἔλεγον· θύρ.—Ἀνθ.

adiunt codd. BV τινὲς δὲ οὕτως φασί· θυράζε Κῆρες, οὐκέτ᾽
(οὐκ ἔνι codd.) Ἀνθεστήρια.

cf. Phot. *Lex.* s.v. (i 286 Naber), *Sud.* Θ 598 (ii 738 Adler) ὡς κατὰ
τὴν πόλιν τοῖς Ἀνθεστηρίοις τῶν ψυχῶν περιερχομένων, Diogenian.
Cent. 5. 24 (i 255 L.-S.) (Κᾶρες), Hsch. Θ 923 (ii 336 Latte) (Κᾶρες),
Arsen. = Apostol. *Cent.* 8. 94 (ii 459 L.-S.) (Κᾶρας)

FOLK SONGS

882 Introduction to Theocritus (on the invention of bucolic poetry)

The defeated singers[1] went off to the nearby villages begging for food. After singing songs full of fun and laughter they added these words of good omen:

Receive the good fortune, receive the good health, which we bring from the goddess[2] (in accordance with her instructions?).

[1] The scholiast finds the origin of bucolic poetry in songs sung competitively by countrymen at a festival of Artemis in Syracuse.
[2] Artemis.

883 Zenobius, *Proverbs*

Out, Carians! The Feast of Flowers is over.

Some say the proverb originated with the large number of Carian slaves, who celebrated and did no work during the Feast of Flowers: so when the festival was finished they said as they sent them out to the fields, 'Out, Carians! The Feast of Flowers is over.' Others explain it as follows: the Carians once seized part of Attica, and whenever the Athenians held the Feast of Flowers they made a truce with them and welcomed them in the city and their homes; but after the festival some were left behind in Athens, and those who met them said jestingly to them, 'Out, Carians! The Feast of Flowers is over.'[1]

[1] Another version is mentioned: 'Out, Spirits (Kēres)!' with reference to ghosts roaming Athens at the Feast.

CARMINA CONVIVIALIA

TESTIMONIA

1 Ar. *Vesp.* 1216ss.

Βδελυκλέων, Φιλοκλέων

Β. ὕδωρ κατὰ χειρός· τὰς τραπέζας εἰσφέρειν·
δειπνοῦμεν· ἀπονενίμμεθ'· ἤδη σπένδομεν.

Φ. πρὸς τῶν θεῶν, ἐνύπνιον ἑστιώμεθα;

Β. αὐλητρὶς ἐνεφύσησεν. οἱ δὲ συμπόται
εἰσὶν Θέωρος, Αἰσχίνης, Φᾶνος, Κλέων,
ξένος τις ἕτερος πρὸς κεφαλῆς Ἀκέστορος.
τούτοις ξυνὼν τὰ σκόλι' ὅπως δέξει καλῶς.

Φ. ἄληθες; ὡς οὐδείς γε Διακρίων ἐγώ.

---

[1] See also Pindar fr. 122. 14, Aristophanes, *Banqueters* fr. 235 K.-A. (Alcaeus test. 27), *Clouds* 1364 with schol. (citing Dicaearchus

270

SCOLIA

884–908 are the Attic scolia given together with Hybrias'
song (909) by Athenaeus 15. 694c–696a; 910–916 are scolia
from other sources.

TESTIMONIA[1]

1 Aristophanes, *Wasps* (Bdelycleon teaches his father
how to behave elegantly at a dinner-party)

Bdelycleon. Water for our hands! Bring in the
   tables! We're having our dinner. We've washed
   our hands. Now we're pouring libation.

Philocleon. For heaven's sake, is the feast just a
   dream?

Bdel. The piper has begun her music. Your fellow-
   drinkers are Theorus, Aeschines, Phanus, Cleon,
   and another foreigner at Acestor's head. With
   these men for company see that you make a good
   job of taking up[2] the scolia.

Phil. Of course I will, better than any Diacrian.[3]

fr. 89 Wehrli), Aristotle *P.M.G.* 842, Didymus p. 371 Schmidt, Plu-
tarch, *Qu. Conv.* 1. 1. 5, Proclus, *Chrest.* ap. Photius, *Bibl.* 321a (v
162 Henry), Eustathius *Od.* 1574. 6 ff.   [2] Lit. 'receiving';
he was expected to continue or to cap the line.   [3] Men of
Diacris, district of N. Attica; they must have been fine singers.

B. τάχ' εἴσομαι. καὶ δὴ γάρ εἰμ' ἐγὼ Κλέων,
  ᾄδω δὲ πρῶτος Ἁρμοδίου, δέξει δὲ σύ.
  'οὐδεὶς πώποτ' ἀνὴρ ἔγεντ' Ἀθήναις —'
Φ. — οὐχ οὕτω γε πανοῦργος <οὐδὲ> κλέπτης.
B. τουτὶ σὺ δράσεις; παραπολεῖ βοώμενος·
  φήσει γὰρ ἐξολεῖν σε καὶ διαφθερεῖν
  κἀκ τῆσδε τῆς γῆς ἐξελᾶν.
Φ.   ἐγὼ δέ γε,
  ἐὰν ἀπειλῇ, νὴ Δί' ἑτέραν ᾄσομαι·
  'ὤνθρωφ', οὗτος ὁ μαιόμενος τὸ μέγα κράτος,
  ἀντρέψεις ἔτι τὰν πόλιν· ἁ δ' ἔχεται ῥοπᾶς.'
B. τί δ', ὅταν Θέωρος πρὸς ποδῶν κατακείμενος
  ᾄδῃ Κλέωνος λαβόμενος τῆς δεξιᾶς·
  ''Ἀδμήτου λόγον, ὦταιρε, μαθὼν τοὺς ἀγαθοὺς
    φίλει.'
  τούτῳ τί λέξεις σκόλιον;
Φ.   ὡδί πως ἐγώ·
  'οὐκ ἔστιν ἀλωπεκίζειν,
  οὐδ' ἀμφοτέροισι γίγνεσθαι φίλον.'
B. μετὰ τοῦτον Αἰσχίνης ὁ Σέλλου δέξεται,
  ἀνὴρ σοφὸς καὶ μουσικός, κᾆτ' ᾄσεται·
  'χρήματα καὶ βίον
    Κλειταγόρᾳ τε κἀ-
    μοι μετὰ Θετταλῶν —'
Φ. — πολλὰ δὴ διεκόμπασας σὺ κἀγώ.
B. τουτὶ μὲν ἐπιεικῶς σύ γ' ἐξεπίστασαι.
  ὅπως δ' ἐπὶ δεῖπνον εἰς Φιλοκτήμονος ἴμεν.

Bdel. I'll soon know. Now then, I'm Cleon and I begin by singing the Harmodius song, and you have to take it up: 'There was never any man in Athens'[4] —

Phil. — who was such a villain and a thief!

Bdel. That's what you're going to do? You'll be bawled to death: he'll say he's going to ruin you and destroy you and drive you out of this land.

Phil. Well, if he makes threats I'll sing another song, by Zeus. 'You, fellow, you who seek supreme power, you'll overturn the city yet; its fate is in the balance.'[5]

Bdel. And when Theorus, reclining at Cleon's feet, grasps his right hand and sings, 'Learn the story of Admetus, my friend, and love the good,'[6] what scolion will you sing in answer to him?

Phil. Oh, something along these lines: 'It's not possible to play the fox or be a friend to both sides.'[7]

Bdel. After him Aeschines, son of Swank, a clever, musical man, will take it up and sing, 'Money and means for Cleitagora and me along with the Thessalians'[8] —

Phil. — we've had a long boasting match, the pair of us.

Bdel. You've got the hang of that pretty well. Off we go to Philoctemon's for dinner.

[4] *P.M.G.* 911.   [5] Alcaeus 141.3–4.   [6] Praxilla 749, *P.M.G.* 897.   [7] *P.M.G.* 912(a).   [8] *P.M.G.* 912(b).

GREEK LYRIC

Schol. ad loc. (p. 192ss. Koster)

1222a. τὰ σκόλι' ὅπως δέξῃ καλῶς· ἀρχαῖον ἦν ἔθος
ἑστιωμένους ᾄδειν ἀκολούθως τῷ πρώτῳ, εἰ παύσαιτο
τῆς ᾠδῆς, τὰ ἑξῆς. καὶ γὰρ ὁ ἐξ ἀρχῆς δάφνην ἢ μυρ-
ρίνην κατέχων ᾖδε Σιμωνίδου ἢ Στησιχόρου μέλη
ἄχρις οὗ ἤθελεν, καὶ μετὰ ταῦτα ᾧ ἐβούλετο ἐδίδου,
οὐχ ὡς ἡ τάξις ἀπῄτει. καὶ ἔλεγεν ὁ δεξάμενος παρὰ
τοῦ πρώτου τὰ ἑξῆς, κἀκεῖνος ἐπεδίδου πάλιν ᾧ ἐβού-
λετο. διὰ τὸ πάντας οὖν ἀπροσδοκήτως ᾄδειν καὶ
λέγειν τὰ μέλη σκολιὰ εἴρηται διὰ τὴν δυσκολίαν.
1238c. (τούτῳ τί λέξεις σκόλιον;) ἀνάγκη τις ἦν τοῖς
ἐν συμποσίοις ἅπασιν ᾄδειν μετὰ λύρας· ὅσοι δὲ οὐκ
ἠπίσταντο λύρᾳ χρῆσθαι δάφνης ἢ μυρρίνης κλῶνας
λαμβάνοντες ᾖδον. τοῖς οὖν <οὐκ> ἐπισταμένοις
μέλος πρὸς λύραν ᾄδειν σκολιὰ ἐδόκει· ὅθεν καὶ σκόλια
ὠνομάσθησαν.

2 Schol. Pl. *Gorg.* 451e = Phot. *Lex.* s.v. σκολιόν (ii 164
Naber), *Sud.* Σ 645 (iv 383 Adler)

(a) (p. 134 Greene) σκόλιον λέγεται ἡ παροίνιος
ᾠδή, ὡς μὲν Δικαίαρχος ἐν τῷ περὶ μουσικῶν ἀγώνων
(fr. 88 Wehrli), ὅτι τρία γένη ἦν ᾠδῶν, τὸ μὲν ὑπὸ

SCOLIA

Scholiast on the passage

'see that you make a good job of taking up the scolia': it was an ancient custom at feasts that, when the first man stopped his song, a second should follow on with the sequel. The first held a twig of laurel or myrtle and sang a song of Simonides or Stesichorus, stopping when he wished, and then he offered the twig to anyone he chose, not as the seating order dictated. The man who took it from the first recited the sequel, then offered the twig to anyone he chose. Since everyone sang or recited the songs without notice, they were called scolia because of the difficulty (*dyscolia*).[1]

'what scolion will you sing in answer to him?': everyone at drinking-parties had to sing to the lyre; those who could not play the lyre held twigs of laurel or myrtle while they sang. Since those who could not sing to the lyre thought the songs 'crooked'[2] they got the name 'scolia'.

[1] Perverse etymology.   [2] Supposed to mean 'not straightforward and easy'; but again the explanation is wrong-headed.

2 Scholiast on Plato, *Gorgias* (Socrates refers to scolion 890 *P.M.G.*)

(a) The song sung over the wine is called a scolion for the following reason, according to Dicaearchus[1] in his work *On Musical Contests*: there were three

[1] Peripatetic scholar, *fl. c.* 326–296 B.C.

πάντων ἀδόμενον, <τὸ δὲ> καθ' ἕνα ἑξῆς, τὰ δ' ὑπὸ
τῶν συνετωτάτων, ὡς ἔτυχε τῇ τάξει· ὧ δὴ καλεῖσθαι
σκόλιον. ὡς δὲ Ἀριστόξενος (fr. 125 Wehrli) καὶ Φίλ-
λις ὁ μουσικός, ὅτι ἐν τοῖς γάμοις περὶ μίαν τράπεζαν
πολλὰς κλίνας τιθέντες, παρὰ μέρος ἑξῆς μυρρίνας
ἔχοντες ᾖδον γνώμας καὶ ἐρωτικὰ σύντονα. ἡ δὲ περί-
οδος σκολιὰ ἐγίνετο διὰ τὴν θέσιν τῶν κλινῶν. . . . οὐ
διὰ τὴν μελοποιίαν οὖν, διὰ δὲ τὴν μυρρίνης σκολιὰν
διάδοσιν ταύτῃ καὶ τὰς ᾠδὰς σκολιὰς καλεῖσθαι.

(b) (p. 462 Greene) Ἀθήνησιν ἐν τῷ πρυτανείῳ
παρὰ πότον σκόλια ᾔδετο εἴς τινας, ὥσπερ εἰς Ἁρμό-
διον, Ἄδμητον, Τελαμῶνα· εἰρῆσθαι δὲ αὐτὸ σκόλιον
κατ' ἀντίφρασιν, ὅτι ῥάδια καὶ ὀλιγόστιχα ὡς ἐπι-
γράμματα ᾔδετο, ἃ ἐκαλεῖτο σκόλια, ἀντιπροτεινόντων
ἀλλήλοις τῶν συμποτῶν, καὶ ἠλέγχοντο οἱ μὴ ἄδοντες
ὡς ἄμουσοι.

3 Athen. 15. 693f–694c (iii 535s. Kaibel)

ἐμέμνηντο δ' οἱ πολλοὶ καὶ τῶν Ἀττικῶν ἐκείνων σκολίων·
ἅπερ καὶ αὐτὰ ἄξιόν ἐστί σοι ἀπομνημονεῦσαι διά τε τὴν ἀρχαι-
ότητα καὶ ἀφέλειαν τῶν ποιησάντων, [[καὶ τῶν]] ἐπαινουμένων ἐπὶ
τῇ ἰδέᾳ ταύτῃ τῆς ποιητικῆς Ἀλκαίου τε καὶ Ἀνακρέοντος, ὡς
Ἀριστοφάνης παρίστησιν ἐν Δαιταλεῦσιν λέγων οὕτως (fr. 235
K.-A.)· ἆσον δή μοι σκόλιόν τι λαβὼν Ἀλκαίου κἀνακρέοντος. καὶ

_____

1 Perhaps 'take the myrtle twig': cf. Ar. fr. 444 K.-A., testt. 1
(schol.), 2.

kinds of song, the first sung by everyone, the second sung by individuals in sequence, the third sung by the most skilled performers in haphazard order—whence the name scolion ('crooked'); but Aristoxenus[2] and Phillis the musician[3] say it was because at weddings they put many couches round one table and holding myrtle-twigs took turns singing proverbs and serious love-songs, one after the other; the progress was 'crooked' because of the position of the couches. . . . So it was not because of their composition that the songs were called 'crooked'[4] but because of the crooked course of the myrtle as it was passed on.

(b) In the town-hall at Athens scolia were sung over the wine in honour of certain men, for example Harmodius, Admetus and Telamon.[5] They got the name by antiphrasis[6] because the scolia were easy to sing and like epigrams had few lines; the drinkers passed them on one to another, and those who did not sing were shown up as unmusical.

[2] Musical theorist, born 375–360 B.C.   [3] Samian writer on music, date unknown.   [4] Cf. test. 1 (schol.) n. 2.   [5] 893–6, 897, 898–9.
[6] The calling of something by its opposite: again see test. 1 (schol.) n. 2.

3 Athenaeus, *Scholars at Dinner*

Most of the dinner-guests made mention of the well-known Attic scolia, which are worth recalling to you because of their antiquity and the simple style of their composers. Alcaeus and Anacreon are commended for this type of poetry, as Aristophanes shows in his *Banqueters* when he says, 'Take[1] and sing me a scolion from Alcaeus

GREEK LYRIC

Πράξιλλα δ' ἡ Σικυωνία ἐθαυμάζετο ἐπὶ τῇ τῶν σκολίων ποιήσει. σκόλια δὲ καλοῦνται οὐ κατὰ τὸν τῆς μελοποιίας τρόπον ὅτι σκολιὸς ἦν — λέγουσιν γὰρ τὰ ἐν ταῖς ἀνειμέναις εἶναι σκόλια — ἀλλὰ τριῶν γενῶν ὄντων, ὥς φησιν Ἀρτέμων ὁ Κασανδρεὺς ἐν δευτέρῳ Βιβλίων Χρήσεως (F.H.G. iv 342), ἐν οἷς τὰ περὶ τὰς συνουσίας ἦν ᾀδόμενα, ὧν τὸ μὲν πρῶτον ἦν ὃ δὴ πάντας ᾄδειν νόμος ἦν, τὸ δὲ δεύτερον ὃ δὴ πάντες μὲν ᾖδον, οὐ μὴν ἀλλά γε κατά τινα περίοδον ἐξ ὑποδοχῆς, <τὸ> τρίτον δὲ καὶ τὴν ἐπὶ πᾶσι τάξιν ἔχον, οὗ μετεῖχον οὐκέτι πάντες ἀλλ' οἱ συνετοὶ δοκοῦντες εἶναι μόνοι, καὶ κατὰ τόπον τινὰ εἰ τύχοιεν ὄντες· διόπερ ὡς ἀταξίαν τινὰ μόνον παρὰ τἆλλα ἔχον τὸ μήθ' ἅμα μήθ' ἑξῆς γινόμενον ἀλλ' ὅπου ἔτυχεν εἶναι σκόλιον ἐκλήθη. τὸ δὲ τοιοῦτον ᾔδετο ὁπότε τὰ κοινὰ καὶ πᾶσιν ἀναγκαῖα τέλος λάβοι· ἐνταῦθα γὰρ ἤδη τῶν σοφῶν ἕκαστον ᾠδήν τινα καλὴν εἰς μέσον ἠξίουν προφέρειν. καλὴν δὲ ταύτην ἐνόμιζον τὴν παραίνεσίν τέ τινα καὶ γνώμην ἔχειν δοκοῦσαν χρησίμην [[τε]] εἰς τὸν βίον.

τῶν οὖν δειπνοσοφιστῶν ὁ μέν τις ἔλεγε τῶν σκολίων τόδε, ὁ δέ τις τόδε. πάντα δ' ἦν τὰ λεχθέντα ταῦτα·

---

884 Παλλὰς Τριτογένει' ἄνασσ' Ἀθηνᾶ,
ὄρθου τήνδε πόλιν τε καὶ πολίτας
ἄτερ ἀλγέων καὶ στάσεων
καὶ θανάτων ἀώρων, σύ τε καὶ πατήρ.

1 Ἀθάνα ci. Jacobs   3 Jacobs, Hermann: τε καὶ codd.

278

SCOLIA

(test. 27) or Anacreon.' Praxilla of Sicyon also (test. 2) was admired for her composition of scolia. They are called 'scolia' not for the 'crooked' character of their composition—they are in fact counted among the relaxed types of verse[2]—but because they were of three kinds, as Artemon of Cassandreia[3] says in Book 2 of his work *On the Use of Books*, which contains the songs sung at social gatherings: the first kind was that which it was customary for everyone to sing; the second was sung by everyone, certainly, but in a sort of sequence, one taking it over from another; in the third and most highly ranked kind not everyone took part but only those who were considered experts, wherever they happened to be reclining; so it was called 'scolion' or 'crooked song' because it alone displayed irregularity, being sung neither by all the guests together nor in sequence but in haphazard order. This kind was sung when the communal songs that everyone had to sing came to an end, for then they would request each of the skilled singers to offer a fine song to the company; by a 'fine' song they meant one that appeared to give some advice or maxim useful for a man's life.

So the scholars at dinner went on to recite now this scolion, now that, and all that were recited are set out here.

[2] Here again 'crooked' is wrongly interpreted as meaning 'difficult': see test. 1 (schol.) with nn. 1, 2.   [3] 2nd or 1st c. B.C.? He depends on Dicaearchus (see test. 2).

884

Pallas, Trito-born, queen Athena, uphold this city and its citizens, free from pains and strifes and untimely deaths—you and your father.

885 Πλούτου μητέρ᾽ Ὀλυμπίαν ἀείδω
Δήμητρα στεφανηφόροις ἐν ὥραις
σέ τε παῖ Διὸς Φερσεφόνη·
χαίρετον, εὖ δὲ τάνδ᾽ ἀμφέπετον πόλιν.

1 ειδω cod. A, corr. recc. 2 δημητραστε στε- A 4 τήνδ᾽
Bergk Canter: ἀμφετον A

886 ἐν Δήλῳ ποτ᾽ ἔτικτε τέκνα Λατώ,
Φοῖβον χρυσοκόμαν ἄνακτ᾽ Ἀπόλλω
ἐλαφηβόλον τ᾽ ἀγροτέραν
Ἄρτεμιν, ἃ γυναικῶν μέγ᾽ ἔχει κράτος.

1 τέκνα A, παῖδα E 2 Ilgen: ἀπόλλων᾽ A, -ωνα E

887 ὦ Πὰν Ἀρκαδίας μεδέων κλεεννᾶς,
ὀρχηστὰ βρομίαις ὀπαδὲ Νύμφαις,
γελάσειας ὦ Πὰν ἐπ᾽ ἐμαῖς
εὐφροσύναις, ἀοιδᾷ κεχαρημένος.

1 Hermann: ἴω πὰν AE 3 Valckenaer: γελασίαισίω A, tantum
ἰὼ E 4 Hermann (ἀοιδαῖς): εὐφρ. ταῖσδ᾽ ἀοιδαῖς ἀοιδε (ἄειδε E)
κεχ. codd. ἀοιδᾷ Page εὔφροσι ταῖσδ᾽ ἀοιδαῖς κεχ.
Wilamowitz

888 ἐνικήσαμεν ὡς ἐβουλόμεσθα
καὶ νίκην ἔδοσαν θεοὶ φέροντες
παρὰ Πανδρόσου †ὡς φίλην Ἀθηνᾶν†

1 Hermann: -όμεθα AE 3 παρὰ Πάνδροσον ὡς φίλην Ἀθηνᾷ ci.
Bergk

885

I sing of the mother of Wealth,[1] Olympian Deme-
ter, in the garland-wearing season,[2] and of you,
Persephone, child of Zeus: greetings, both! Tend
this city well.

[1] Cf. Hes. *Theog.* 969 ff.   [2] Perhaps at an Athenian festival,
the Anthesteria (Smyth) or the Aloa, a 'harvest home' festival
(Bowra), or simply 'in spring' (van der Valk).

886

In Delos Leto bore children once, gold-haired
Phoebus, lord Apollo, and the deer-shooting hun-
tress Artemis, who holds great power over women.

887

Pan, ruler of famous Arcadia,[1] dancer, compan-
ion of the bacchant Nymphs, laugh, Pan, at my mer-
riment, rejoicing in my song.

[1] Cf. Pind. fr. 95.

888

We were victorious as we wished, and the gods
granted victory, bringing it from Pandrosus[1] . . .

[1] The last two lines are mutilated: with Bergk's emendation,
'bringing it to Pandrosus as Athena's friend'. P. was daughter of
Cecrops; the sacred olive was in her shrine on the acropolis of
Athens.

GREEK LYRIC

889 εἴθ' ἐξῆν ὁποῖός τις ἦν ἕκαστος
τὸ στῆθος διελόντ', ἔπειτα τὸν νοῦν
ἐσιδόντα, κλείσαντα πάλιν,
ἄνδρα φίλον νομίζειν ἀδόλῳ φρενί.

cf. Eust. *Od.* 1574. 16

3 εἰσιδ- A, ἴδ- E, Eust.

890 ὑγιαίνειν μὲν ἄριστον ἀνδρὶ θνητῷ,
δεύτερον δὲ καλὸν φυὰν γενέσθαι,
τὸ τρίτον δὲ πλουτεῖν ἀδόλως,
καὶ τὸ τέταρτον ἡβᾶν μετὰ τῶν φίλων.

cf. Plat. *Legg.* 1. 631c, 2. 661a, Clem. Alex. *Strom.* 4. 5. 23, schol. Aristot. *Rhet.* 1394b 13 (*comment.* xxi 2. 301 Rabe), schol. Plat. *Gorg.* 451e (v. inf.), schol. Lucian. *de lapsu* 6, Theodoret. *gr. aff. cur.* 11. 14, Stob. 4. 39. 9, Apostol. *Cent.* 17. 48d

ᾀσθέντος δὲ τούτου καὶ πάντων ἡσθέντων ἐπ' αὐτῷ καὶ μνημονευσάντων ὅτι καὶ ὁ καλὸς Πλάτων αὐτοῦ μέμνηται ὡς ἄριστα εἰρημένου (*Gorg.* 451e) ὁ Μυρτίλος ἔφη Ἀναξανδρίδην αὐτὸ διακεχλευακέναι τὸν κωμῳδιοποιὸν ἐν Θησαυρῷ λέγοντα οὕτως (fr. 18 K.-A.)·

> ὁ τὸ σκόλιον εὑρὼν ἐκεῖνος, ὅστις ἦν,
> τὸ μὲν ὑγιαίνειν πρῶτον ὡς ἄριστον ὂν
> ὠνόμασεν ὀρθῶς· δεύτερον δ' εἶναι καλόν,
> τρίτον δὲ πλουτεῖν, τοῦθ', ὁρᾷς, ἐμαίνετο·
> μετὰ τὴν ὑγίειαν γὰρ τὸ πλουτεῖν διαφέρει·
> καλὸς δὲ πεινῶν ἐστιν αἰσχρὸν θηρίον.

ἑξῆς δ' ἐλέχθη καὶ τάδε·

889

If only it were possible to see what everyone is like by opening his breast and having looked at his mind to close it up again and regard the man as one's friend for his guileless heart.[1]

[1] Eustathius quotes the scolion, noting its didactic tone and adding that it is based on a fable of Aesop in which Momus, 'Blame', finds fault with Prometheus for making man without a door in his breast. Aristophanes parodies the lines in *Eccl.* 938 ff.

890

To be healthy is best for mortal man, second is to be handsome in body, third is to be wealthy without trickery, fourth, to be young with one's friends.

When this song had been sung and everyone had enjoyed it and commented that the excellent Plato mentions it as a splendid composition (*Gorg.* 451e),[1] Myrtilus pointed out that the comic poet Anaxandrides made fun of it in his *Treasure* in these lines: 'The man who devised the scolion, whoever he was, was right to name health first as the best thing; but when he put a handsome body second and wealth third he was out of his mind, of course, for wealth is next best to health: a handsome man who is hungry is an ugly beast.'

[1] The scholiast on Plato said it was sometimes attributed to Simonides (see fr. 651), sometimes to Epicharmus (cf. fr. 262 Kaibel); Clement of Alexandria ascribed it to Simonides and Aristotle, Stobaeus to an unknown Sclerias.

Next the following scolia were recited:

283

891 <καλὸν μὲν> ἐκ γῆς χρὴ κατίδην πλόον
εἴ τις δύναιτο καὶ παλάμην ἔχοι,
ἐπεὶ δέ κ᾽ ἐν πόντῳ γένηται
τῷ παρεόντι τρέχειν ἀνάγκη.

1 suppl. Page   3 καὶ ἐν AE, corr. recc.

892 ὁ δὲ καρκίνος ὧδ᾽ ἔφα
χαλᾷ τὸν ὄφιν λαβών·
‘εὐθὺν χρὴ τὸν ἑταῖρον ἐμ-
μεν καὶ μὴ σκολιὰ φρονεῖν.’

cf. Eust. Od. 1574. 15

1 δὲ om. Athen. codd. dett.   ἔφη codd.   2 χαλλιτον A,
corr. E (η sup. utrumque α scr.), Eust.   3 εὐθέα E, Eust.
3s. Casaubon: ἐνμὲν A, ἔμεν E, Eust.

893 ἐν μύρτου κλαδὶ τὸ ξίφος φορήσω
ὥσπερ Ἁρμόδιος κἀριστογείτων
ὅτε τὸν τύραννον κτανέτην
ἰσονόμους τ᾽ Ἀθήνας ἐποιησάτην.

891[1]

One should look out from land for (a fair) voyage if one can and has the skill; but when one is on the high seas it is necessary to run in the conditions that exist.

[1] The lines were found on a papyrus text of Alcaeus (fr. 249. 6–9).

892

The crab, seizing the snake in its claws, spoke thus: 'One's comrade should be straight[1] and not think crooked thoughts.'[2]

[1] 'The only straight snake is a dead snake' (Bowra).   [2] Cf. Aesop's fable (211 Hausrath).

893[1]

I shall carry my sword in a spray of myrtle, like Harmodius and Aristogeiton when they killed the tyrant[2] and made Athens a city of equal rights.

[1] We have four versions of the scolion (893–896: cf. 911), which show how one singer might cap another's lines. Many authors refer to it: see Ar. *Lys.* 632 with schol., Hsch. E 3180, *Suda* E 1384 (τὸ ξ. κρατήσω), Eust. *Od.* 1400.18; also to 'the Harmodius song': Ar. *Ach.* 980, *Storks* fr. 444 K.-A., Antiphanes fr. 85 K.-A., and collectors of proverbs, Diogenian *Cent.* 2. 68, Macarius *Cent.* 2. 32, Apostolius *Cent.* 3. 82; Hesychius A 7317 says it was composed by Callistratus (unknown).   [2] Hipparchus, killed in 514 B.C., was in fact brother of the tyrant Hippias.

894   φίλταθ' Ἁρμόδι', οὔ τί που τέθνηκας,
νήσοις δ' ἐν μακάρων σέ φασιν εἶναι,
ἵνα περ ποδώκης Ἀχιλεὺς
Τυδείδην τέ φασιν Διομήδεα.

cf. schol. Ar. *Ach.* 980 (p. 124 Wilson) = *Sud.* O 812, Π 737 (iii 579,
iv 64 Adler), schol. *Ach.* 1093a (p. 137 Wilson), Aristid. *Or.* 1. 133
Dindorf

1 ἁρμοδι' οὔ τί που schol. Ar., ἁρμοδίου πω Athen.   που, πω Aris-
tid. codd.   3 Lowth: Ἀχιλλεὺς Athen. AE   4 Lowth: Τ.
τέ φασι τὸν ἐσθλὸν Δ. Athen.

895   ἐν μύρτου κλαδὶ τὸ ξίφος φορήσω
ὥσπερ Ἁρμόδιος κἀριστογείτων
ὅτ' Ἀθηναίης ἐν θυσίαις
ἄνδρα τύραννον Ἵππαρχον ἐκαινέτην.

896   αἰεὶ σφῶν κλέος ἔσσεται κατ' αἶαν,
φίλταθ' Ἁρμόδιε κἀριστόγειτον,
ὅτι τὸν τύραννον κτανέτην
ἰσονόμους τ' Ἀθήνας ἐποιησάτην.

2 Ἁρμόδιος κ(αὶ) Ἀριστογείτων ci. Ilgen

897
Ἀδμήτου λόγον ὦ ἑταῖρε μαθὼν τοὺς ἀγαθοὺς φίλει,
τῶν δειλῶν δ' ἀπέχου γνοὺς ὅτι δειλοῖς ὀλίγη χάρις.

cf. Ar. *Vesp.* 1238 + schol., Praxill. 749, Ar. fr. 444 K.-A., Cratin. fr.
254 K.-A., Eust. *Il.* 326. 38ss. (i 509 van der Valk), Paus. *Lex. Att.* A
25 Erbse, Phot. *Lex.* p. 32 Reitzenstein, *Sud.* A 493, Π 737 (i 52, iv
64 Adler), Zenob. 1. 18

894

Dearest Harmodius,[1] you cannot be dead: no, they say you are in the isles of the blessed, where swift-footed Achilles is and, they say, Tydeus' son, Diomedes.

[1] Parodied at Ar. *Ach.* 1092.

895

I shall carry my sword in a spray of myrtle, like Harmodius and Aristogeiton when at the festival of Athena[1] they killed the tyrant Hipparchus.

[1] The Panathenaic festival.

896

You two will always have glory on the earth, dearest Harmodius and Aristogeiton, because you killed the tyrant and made Athens a city of equal rights.

897

Learn the story of Admetus, my friend, and love the good, and keep away from the worthless, knowing that the worthless have little gratitude.[1]

[1] The scholiast on Ar. *Wasps*, where v. 1 is quoted (see test. 1), says that some ascribe the scolion to Alcaeus or Sappho (see 'Sa. or Alc.' 25C), but that it is included in Praxilla's drinking-songs (fr. 749); Ar. refers to it also in *Storks*, Cratinus in *Chirons*.

GREEK LYRIC

898

παῖ Τελαμῶνος Αἶαν αἰχμητά, λέγουσί σε
ἐς Τροΐαν ἄριστον ἐλθεῖν Δαναῶν μετ' Ἀχιλλέα.

cf. Eust. *Il.* 285. 2 (i 438 van der Valk), Ar. *Lys.* 1236s. + schol.
(p. 262 Dübner), Theopomp. fr. 65 K.-A., Antiphan. fr. 85 K.-A.,
Phot. *Lex.* (p. 48 Reitzenstein), Hsch. A 1765 (i 63 Latte)

1 Fiorillo: λεγούσης Athen. A, λέγουσί σ' E, Eust.   2 Δαναῶν
Athen., Ἀχαιῶν Eust.   μετ' Ἀχ. Eust., καὶ Ἀχ. Athen.

899

τὸν Τελαμῶνα πρῶτον, Αἴαντα δὲ δεύτερον
ἐς Τροΐαν λέγουσιν ἐλθεῖν Δαναῶν μετ' Ἀχιλλέα.

2 Casaubon: Δαναῶν καὶ Ἀχ. Athen.

900

εἴθε λύρα καλὴ γενοίμην ἐλεφαντίνη
καί με καλοὶ παῖδες φέροιεν Διονύσιον ἐς χορόν.

cf. Dion. Chrys. *Or.* 2. 62 (i 30 von Arnim)

1 γενοίμαν Dio   2 φέροιεν Athen., Dion. codd. PW, φορέοιεν
Dion. UBV, φοροῖεν Stephanus

901

εἴθ' ἄπυρον καλὸν γενοίμην μέγα χρυσίον
καί με καλὴ γυνὴ φοροίη καθαρὸν θεμένη νόον.

cf. Dion. ibid. (εἴθ' – φοροίη)

1 γενοίμαν E, Dio   2 γυνὴ καλὴ Dio   φοροῖεν Dion. codd. UBV

288

SCOLIA

898

Son of Telamon, Ajax, warrior, they say that after Achilles you were the best of the Greeks to come to Troy.[1]

[1] Comic writers mention 'the Telamon song', Ar. in *Lys.*, Theopompus and Antiphanes; for 'Ajax, best after Achilles' see Alc. 387 and cf. *Il.* 2. 768 f., Pind. *Nem.* 7. 27.

899

Telamon, they say, was first among the Greeks who came to Troy, Ajax second, after Achilles.

900[1]

If only I could become a handsome ivory lyre, and handsome boys carried me to Dionysus' choral dance.[2]

[1] 900 and 901 are quoted also by Dio Chrysostom as examples of Attic scolia unsuitable for kings but fit for cheerful relaxed gatherings of members of demes or phratries; cf. Anacr. 357.   [2] A dithyrambic performance?

901

If only I could become a great handsome unfired golden bowl, and a handsome woman carried me[1] with pure thoughts in her mind.

[1] In the Panathenaic procession?

902

σύν μοι πῖνε συνήβα συνέρα συστεφανηφόρει,
σύν μοι μαινομένῳ μαίνεο, σὺν σώφρονι σωφρόνει.

cf. Eust. *Od.* 1574. 20

1 συγκανηφόρει Eust.   2 Canter: σὺν σωφρονήσω σώφρονι A,
συσσωφρόνει σώφρονι E, Eust.

903

ὑπὸ παντὶ λίθῳ σκορπίος ὦ ἑταῖρ᾽ ὑποδύεται.
φράζευ μή σε βάλῃ· τῷ δ᾽ ἀφανεῖ πᾶς ἕπεται δόλος.

904

ἁ ὗς τὰν βάλανον τὰν μὲν ἔχει, τὰν δ᾽ ἔραται λαβεῖν·
κἀγὼ παῖδα καλὴν τὴν μὲν ἔχω, τὴν δ᾽ ἔραμαι λαβεῖν.

1 ἁ δ᾽ ὗς? Page   2 ἔχων A, corr. recc.

905

πόρνη καὶ βαλανεὺς τωὐτὸν ἔχουσ᾽ ἐμπεδέως ἔθος·
ἐν ταὐτᾷ πυέλῳ τόν τ᾽ ἀγαθὸν τόν τε κακὸν λόει.

1–2 fort. aut πόρνα aut ταὐτῇ

906 ἔγχει καὶ Κήδωνι, διάκονε, μηδ᾽ ἐπιλήθου,
εἰ χρὴ τοῖς ἀγαθοῖς ἀνδράσιν οἰνοχοεῖν.

cf. Aristot. *Ath. Pol.* 20. 5 (ἐν τοῖς σκολίοις)

εἰ χρὴ Aristot., εἰ δὲ χρὴ Athen.

SCOLIA

902

Drink with me, be youthful with me, love with
me, wear garlands with me, be mad with me when I
am mad, sober with me when I am sober.

903

Under every stone, my friend, a scorpion lurks.[1]
Take care that it does not strike you: all manner of
guile accompanies what is unseen.

[1] Cf. Praxilla 750; the expression was proverbial.

904

The sow has one acorn but longs to get the other;
and I have one beautiful girl but long to get the
other.[1]

[1] The dialect changes from Doric (in a proverb?) to Attic (in
parody?).

905

The whore and the bathman always have the
same habit: they wash the good man and the bad
man in the same tub.

906

Fill a cup for Cedon too, attendant, and do not
forget him, if you are to pour wine for the good
men.[1]

[1] I.e. for the democrats: Cedon, one of the Alcmaeonids, made an
unsuccessful attack on the Peisistratid tyrants (Aristot. *Ath. Pol.*
20. 5).

907   αἰαῖ Λειψύδριον προδωσέταιρον,
οἵους ἄνδρας ἀπώλεσας, μάχεσθαι
ἀγαθούς τε καὶ εὐπατρίδας,
οἳ τότ' ἔδειξαν οἵων πατέρων ἔσαν.

cf. *Et. Gen.* B (p. 122 Miller) + *Et. Mag.* 361. 31, *Et. Sym.*, *Sud.* E 2440 (ii 367s. Adler), Eust. *Il.* 461. 26 (i 729s. van der Valk), Arsen. = Apostol. *Cent.* 7. 70 (ii 414s. L.-S.)

1 προδοσ- *Sud.* (προσδοσ- cod. A), Eust.   3 δ' ἀγαθούς γε καὶ *Sud.*, τ' ἀγ. καὶ Eust.   4 οἳ τότ': ὁπότ' *Sud.*, *Et. Mag.* cod. D ἔσαν: κύρησαν Athen.

Aristot. *Ath. Pol.* 19. 3 (p. 17 Chambers)

ἔν τε γὰρ τοῖς ἄλλοις οἷς ἔπραττον διεσφάλλοντο (sc. οἱ Ἀλκμεωνίδαι) καὶ τειχίσαντες ἐν τῇ χώρᾳ Λειψύδριον τὸ ὑπὲρ Πάρνηθος, εἰς ὃ ξυνεξῆλθόν τινες τῶν ἐκ τοῦ ἄστεως, ἐξεπολιορκήθησαν ὑπὸ τῶν τυράννων, ὅθεν ὕστερον μετὰ ταύτην τὴν συμφορὰν ᾖδον ἐν τοῖς σκολίοις· αἰαῖ—ἔσαν.

908
ὅστις ἄνδρα φίλον μὴ προδίδωσιν μεγάλην ἔχει
τιμὴν ἔν τε βροτοῖς ἔν τε θεοῖσιν κατ' ἐμὸν νόον.

2 τιμὰν A   μεγάλαν . . . τιμὰν Bergk   θεοῖς A, corr. recc.

907

Alas, Leipsydrion,[1] betrayer of comrades! What
men you destroyed, good fighters and nobly born,
who showed then of what stock they came!

[1] Strongpoint on Mt. Parnes, base of Alcmaeonid operations
against Hippias (between 514 and 510).

Aristotle, *Constitution of Athens*

The Alcmaeonids came to grief in various undertak-
ings, in particular when they fortified Leipsydrion under
Mt. Parnes in the countryside: some of the city-dwellers
gathered there and were forced to surrender by the
tyrants; after this disaster they used to sing as one of their
scolia, 'Alas, Leipsydrion . . . came!'

908[1]

The man who does not betray his friend has great
honour among both mortals and gods in my view.

[1] The last of the 25 Attic scolia quoted by Athenaeus.

σκόλιον δέ φασί τινες καὶ τὸ ὑπὸ Ὑβρίου τοῦ Κρητὸς (κριτὸς Α, corr. Ε) ποιηθέν. ἔχει δὲ οὕτως·

909 ἐστί μοι πλοῦτος μέγας δόρυ καὶ ξίφος
καὶ τὸ καλὸν λαισήϊον, πρόβλημα χρωτός·
τούτῳ γὰρ ἀρῶ, τούτῳ θερίζω,
τούτῳ πατέω τὸν ἁδὺν οἶνον ἀπ᾽ ἀμπέλων,
5 τούτῳ δεσπότας μνοίας κέκλημαι.

τοὶ δὲ μὴ τολμῶντ᾽ ἔχειν δόρυ καὶ ξίφος
καὶ τὸ καλὸν λαισήϊον, πρόβλημα χρωτός,
πάντες γόνυ πεπτηῶτες ἁμὸν
< — προσ>κυνέοντι δεσπόταν <ἐμὲ δεσποτᾶν>
10 καὶ μέγαν βασιλῆα φωνέοντες.

cf. Eust. Od. 1574. 7

1 μέγα Ε, Eust.   4 ἀμπέλου Eust.   6 Hermann: -μῶντες codd.
7 πρόβλημά τε χρ. ΑΕ, corr. recc.   8 -τηῶτες Eust., -τηότες ΑΕ
Hermann: ἐμὸν codd.   9 προσ- suppl. Bergk   ἐμὲ δ. suppl.
Crusius   10 Hermann: -λέα codd.   -έοντες ΑΕ, -έοντι Eust.

910 Athen. 14. 625c

φασὶ δὲ Πύθερμον τὸν Τήιον ἐν τῷ γένει τῆς ἁρμονίας τούτῳ
ποιῆσαι σκόλια (Casaubon: σκαιὰ Α) μέλη, καὶ διὰ τὸ εἶναι τὸν
ποιητὴν Ἰωνικὸν Ἰαστὶ κληθῆναι τὴν ἁρμονίαν. οὗτός ἐστι Πύθερ-
μος οὗ μνημονεύει Ἀνάνιος (fr. 2 West) ἢ Ἱππῶναξ ἐν τοῖς Ἰάμ-
βοις <... καὶ> ἐν ἄλλῳ οὕτως· χρυσὸν λέγει Πύθερμος ὡς οὐδὲν
τἆλλα. λέγει δ᾽ οὕτως ὁ Πύθερμος·

οὐδὲν ἦν ἄρα τἆλλα πλὴν ὁ χρυσός.

cf. Diogenian. Cent. 6. 94 (i 285 L.-S.) + schol., Sud. O 793 (iii 577
Adler), 'Plut.' Cent. 1. 96 (i 335 L.-S.)

ὁ om. Athen., Diogenian.

294

According to some authorities, the poem composed by Hybrias[1] the Cretan is a scolion. It runs as follows:

909

Great wealth for me is my spear and my sword and my fine hide-shield, defence of my skin: thanks to it I plough, thanks to it I reap, thanks to it I trample the sweet wine from the vines, thanks to it I am called master of the serfs.[2]

Those who do not dare to hold spear and sword and fine hide-shield, defence of the skin, prostrate themselves cowering at my knee, calling me master (of masters) and great king.[3]

[1] Presumably the Cretan Hibrias mentioned by Hesychius I 128.
[2] The public slaves in Crete. D. L. Page (*P.C.P.S.* 191, 1965, 64 f.) argues that 'H. is a man who rose from the class of public slave to that of professional soldier.'   [3] Athen. continues with Aristotle 842.

910 Athenaeus, *Scholars at Dinner*

They say that Pythermus of Teos[1] composed scolia in this kind of tuning, and that since the poet was from Ionia the tuning was called Ionian. This is the Pythermus who is mentioned by Ananius or Hipponax in his *Iambics*[2] ... and in another as follows: 'Pythermus says of gold that all else is nothing.' The words of Pythermus are

So all else is nothing apart from gold.

[1] Perhaps a 6th c. poet.   [2] The quotation is lost.

911 Ar. *Vesp.* 1225

ᾄδω δὲ πρῶτος Ἁρμοδίου, δέξει δὲ σύ·

οὐδεὶς πώποτ' ἀνὴρ ἔγεντ' Ἀθήναις

Bentley: ἐγένετ' Ἀθηναῖος codd.

912 Ar. *Vesp.* 1239ss.

— τούτῳ τί λέξεις σκόλιον; — ὡδί πως ἐγώ·

(a)   οὐκ ἔστιν ἀλωπεκίζειν
      οὐδ' ἀμφοτέροισι γίγνεσθαι φίλον.

— μετὰ τοῦτον Αἰσχίνης ὁ Σέλλου δέξεται,
ἀνὴρ σοφὸς καὶ μουσικός, κᾆτ' ᾄσεται·

(b)   χρήματα καὶ βίον Κλειταγόρᾳ τε κἀμοὶ μετὰ
      Θετταλῶν.

(b) Tyrrwhitt: βίαν codd.

Schol. ad loc. (1238a: p. 195 Koster)

Ἀμμώνιος (Susemihl: Ἁρμόδιος codd., Ἡρόδικος Dobree) δὲ ἐν τοῖς Κωμῳδουμένοις (*F.Gr.H.* 350 F2) καὶ τὸν Ἄδμητον ἀνάγει, γραφὴν παραθεὶς τοῦ Κρατίνου ἐκ Χειρώνων (fr. 254 K.-A.)·

Κλειταγόρας ᾄδειν, ὅταν Ἀδμήτου μέλος αὐλῇ.

(1246: p. 197 K.) αὕτη γυνὴ ποιήτρια Θετταλή.

911 Aristophanes, *Wasps*[1]

I begin by singing the Harmodius song, and you have to take it up:

There never was any man in Athens . . .

[1] See test. 1 for the context.

912 Aristophanes, *Wasps*[1]

— What scolion will you sing in answer to him?
— Oh, something along these lines:

(a) It's not possible to play the fox or to be a friend to both sides.

— After him Aeschines, son of Swank, a clever, musical man, will take it up and sing,

(b) Money and means[2] for Cleitagora and me along with the Thessalians.

[1] See test. 1 for the context.   [2] 'Force' in mss.; the sense of the scolion is quite uncertain.

Scholiast on the passage

Ammonius in his work *People mocked in Comedy* mentions the Admetus song too, adducing a passage from Cratinus' *Chirons*: 'to sing the Cleitagora song when the piper plays the Admetus song' . . . The woman was a poetess from Thessaly . . .

GREEK LYRIC

Ar. *Lys.* 1236ss.

ὥστ᾽ εἰ μέν γε τις

ᾄδοι Τελαμῶνος, Κλειταγόρας ᾄδειν δέον,
ἐπῃνέσαμεν ἄν . . .

Schol. ad loc. (p. 262 Dübner) (cf. *Sud.* K 1763)

ὁ δὲ νοῦς ὅτι τὰ ἐναντία λέγομεν ἑαυτοῖς καὶ πράττομεν· ὅταν γάρ τις ᾄσῃ ἀπὸ τῶν σκολίων Πινδάρου, λέγομεν ὅτι δεῖ μᾶλλον ᾄδειν ἀπὸ Κλειταγόρας τῆς ποιητρίας· ἡ γὰρ Κλειταγόρα ποιήτρια ἦν Λακωνική, ἧς μέμνηται καὶ ἐν Δαναΐσιν (fr. 271 K.-A.) Ἀριστοφάνης.

Hsch. K 2913 (ii 486 Latte)

Κλειταγόρα· ᾠδῆς τι εἶδος. καὶ Λεσβία τὸ γένος.

913 Athen. 11. 783e (iii 22s. Kaibel)

ἔπινον δὲ τὴν ἄμυστιν μετὰ μέλους μεμετρημένου πρὸς ὠκύτητα χρόνου, ὡς Ἀμειψίας (fr. 21 K.-A.)·

— αὔλει μοι μέλος·

σὺ δ᾽ ᾆδε πρὸς τήνδ᾽, ἐκπίομαι δ᾽ ἐγὼ τέως.
— αὔλει σύ, καὶ <σὺ> τὴν ἄμυστιν λάμβανε·

**οὐ χρὴ πόλλ᾽ ἔχειν θνητὸν ἄνθρωπον,
ἀλλ᾽ ἐρᾶν καὶ κατεσθίειν· σὺ δὲ κάρτα φείδῃ.**

1 οὖ <τι> χρὴ πόλλ᾽ ἔχειν θν. ἄ. <ὄντ᾽> Page, Meineke secutus
2 σὺ δὲ κάρτ᾽ ἀφειδής ci. Meineke

Aristophanes, *Lysistrata*

So if someone sang the Telamon song when he should have been singing the Cleitagora, we would commend him ...

Scholiast on the passage

The meaning is that we say and do things that contradict each other; for when someone sings one of Pindar's scolia, we say he ought rather to be singing one by the poetess Cleitagora. Cleitagora was a Spartan poetess whom Aristophanes mentions in his *Danaids*.

Hesychius, *Lexicon*

Cleitagora: a kind of song; she belonged to Lesbos.[1]

[1] The attempts to identify the woman are probably all guesswork, and 'Cleitagora's song' does not imply 'the song composed by C.' For a Cleitagora on a red-figured vase dated 450–430 B.C. see D. M. Robinson, *A.J.A.* 60 (1956) 22.

913 Athenaeus, *Scholars at Dinner*

They used to drink the *amystis*[1] to the accompaniment of a song sung rapidly to promote swift drinking; cf. Ameipsias: 'Pipe me a tune, and you sing to her music; and meanwhile I'll drink up.' 'You pipe, and you take the *amystis*:' (sings)

Mortal man does not need to have much except to love and to eat well; but you go very sparingly.

[1] A cup drunk without stopping for breath.

914 Hsch. B 818 (i 334 Latte)

Βορέας· σκόλιόν τι οὕτως ἀρχόμενον (Meineke: ᾀδόμενον codd., ᾀδ. οὕτως Latte) ἔλεγον.

915 *Sud.* Π 737 (iv 74 Adler)

. . . μέλος τι ʽΑρμόδιον καλούμενον (894). . . . ἦν δὲ καὶ ἕτερα μέλη, τὸ μὲν ᾽Αδμήτου (897) λεγόμενον, τὸ δὲ Λάμπωνος.

916 Ar. *Pax* 289ss.

νῦν τοῦτ᾽ ἐκεῖν᾽· ἥκει τὸ Δάτιδος μέλος,
ὃ δεφόμενός ποτ᾽ ᾖδε τῆς μεσημβρίας·
ʽὡς ἥδομαι καὶ χαίρομαι κεὐφραίνομαι.᾽

917 P. Berol. 270, *B.K.T.* v (2) (1907) 56; v. E. Pellizer, G. Tedeschi (edd.), *Q.F.C.* 4 (1983) 5–17

(a) MOΥΣΑΙ

[. . . .]αι θυγάτη[ρ
[ἄ].π.λ.ε.[τ.]α. σῖτα φέρων[
[.]αμοι τεμένη β . [. . . . .]ων

1 σεμν]αὶ θύγατρ[ες ? *Q.F.C.*   2 suppl. ed. pr. (Schubart, Wilamowitz)

SCOLIA

914 Hesychius, *Lexicon*

Boreas: the name they gave to a scolion that began with the word.[1]

[1] Text uncertain: perhaps 'that was sung'.

915 *Suda*

... a song called Harmodius (894) ...; there were other songs, one called Admetus (897), another Lampon.

916 Aristophanes, *Peace*

Here we are! The song of Datis[1] has arrived, the one he used to sing while masturbating at midday: 'How pleased I am, how rejoiced I am, how happy I am!'

[1] Perhaps a scolion, according to Page, but see Sommerstein's note on the passage.

917 Berlin papyrus (early 3rd c. B.C.)

(a)   MUSES[1]

... daughter ... (he/I) bringing food (in abundance?) ... sanctuaries ...

[1] The three titles are in the margin opposite (c) 3.

(b) ΕΥΦΩΡΑΤ[ΟΣ]

[ἐ]νκέρασον Χαρίτων κρατῆ[ρ]' ἐπιστ[ε]-
   φέα κρ[. . . . . . . π]ρόπι̣[ν]ε [λό]γον ·
σήμαιν' ὅτι Παρθένων
ἀπε[ί]ροσι πλέξομεν ὕμνοις
[τ]ὰν δορὶ σώματα κειραμέναν Τρ[οί]αν
καὶ [τ]ὸν παρὰ ναυσὶν ἀειμνά[σ]τοις ἁλόντα
νυκτιβάταν σκοπόν.

tit. suppl. Manteuffel   1 κρ[ήγυόν τε Schubart
4 Gianotti: σωματι pap.   cett. suppl. ed. pr.

(c) ΜΝΗΜΟΣΥΝΗ

ὦ Μοῦσ' ἀγανόμματε μᾶτερ,
συνίσπεο σῶν τέκνων [ἀγν]ῶι̣ γ[όν]ωι ·
ἄρτι βρύουσαν ἀοιδὰν
πρωτοπαγεῖ σοφίαι διαποικίλον ἐκφέρομεν ·
5 [νῆά τ]οι̣ τέγξαν Ἀχελώιου δρόσ[οι ·]
   [παῦε] παραπροϊών, ὑφίει π̣όδα,
   λῦ' ἑανοῦ πτέρυγα̣ς, τάχος ἵεσο
   λεπτολίθων [ψαμαθῶ]ν ·
   εὖ · καθόρα πέλαγος,
10 παρὰ γᾶν ἔκφευγε νότου χαλεπὰν
   φοβερὰ[ν διαπο]ντοπλανῆ μα̣νίαν.

1 Μουσᾶν ἀγ., 6 πέρα προϊών ci. ed. pr.   8 suppl. Page, cett. ed. pr.

SCOLIA

(b)   THE EASY PREY[1]

Mix a bowl of the Graces brimful and pledge[2] a (fine?) tale: proclaim that we shall inweave in the countless hymns of the Maidens Troy, her bodies[3] cut down by the spear, and the night-prowling scout[4] captured beside the ever-remembered ships.

[1] With reference to Dolon, the Trojan spy captured by Odysseus (*Il.* 10. 299 ff.).   [2] The verb is used of gifting the cup as well as the wine; cf. Anacr. 407, Dionys. Chalc. 1. 1–4 West.   [3] Text uncertain.   [4] Dolon.

(c)   MNEMOSYNE

Gentle-eyed mother Muse,[1] keep company with (the pure family) of your children: we bring out a complex song, newly flowering with fresh-built skill.

Look! The dews of Achelous[2] have drenched (the ship): (stop) running forward, loosen the sheet, unfasten the wings of linen,[3] quickly rush for the fine sands! Well done! Watch the sea! Close to dry land flee the harsh fearsome ocean-roaming madness of the south wind!

[1] Mnemosyne (Memory) is classed as a Muse, mother of the others. Edd. emend to read 'mother of the Muses'.   [2] Perhaps rains rather than sea-water.   [3] The sails.

FRAGMENTA ADESPOTA

918 (a) P. Oxy. 1788 fr. 9

$$\dot{\epsilon}]\kappa \ \theta\alpha\lambda\alpha[$$
$$]\pi\acute{\epsilon}\delta\iota o[$$
$$]\pi o\lambda\upsilon[$$

1 θαλάσσης (-ας)? θαλάμου?   2 πέδιο[ν ed. pr. (Grenfell, Hunt),
sed aliter supplere possis (Page)

(b) = Pindar *Paean* 22(h)

(c) = Pindar *Paean* 22(i)

919 = Sappho or Alcaeus 42 (Voigt): v. vol. i p. 454

920 Pap. R. Univ. Milano i (1937) n. 7 pp. 10–11

    fr. (a) 1 σμικρ[2 ταν σφ[3 πολλα[
4 πρὶγ γα[5 πολλαισ[6 των σφω[
7 ωδαμελ[8 χει[9 γοργ[
fr. (b) 1 εις κυπ[

ANONYMOUS FRAGMENTS

918–1045 are anonymous fragments: 918–931T are papyrus finds, 932–938 are inscriptions, 939–1022 are book-texts (in alphabetical order of author), 1023–1028 may be tragic, 1029–1037 may be Alexandrian, 1038 (i) and (ii) are ostraca, 1039–1045 may be hexameter.

918 (a) Oxyrhynchus papyrus

... from (the sea?) (the chamber?) ... (plain?)[1] ... much ...

[1] Perhaps a compound adjective, e.g. 'with wide plains'; cf. Timoth. 791. 40.

(b) = Pindar *Paean* 22(h)

(c) = Pindar *Paean* 22(i)

919 = Sappho or Alcaeus 42 (Voigt): see vol. i p. 454

920 Milan papyrus[1] (3rd c. B.C.)

... little ... many ... before ... many ...

[1] Line-beginnings from at least two poems.

921 P. Argentorat. inv. gr. 1406–9 ed. Snell, *Herm.* Einzelschr. 5 (1937) 98ss.

(a) 3]νος εὐτυχία   (b) (ii) 8 ἀθάνατος νιφ . [

15]υμν . . . [17 TIMO[18 σταδιε[ι   20 αρχαι . [

(iii) 1]ορημι   (iv) 4 . . . . ουμα . . ν ὄνομα

5 αδ[.] . . οως ἐφάνης   10 . . [. .]μόρω ψυχῆς

15 [.]Η   18 συνος δρόμον   (v) 2 αλλο[5 θυμο[

12]N   13] . Υ[.]ΟΣ   20 φόβος   21 καθ᾽ ἡμέω[ν

22 εὐμεμπτο[(c) (ii) 1 ΙΕΡ[Ω   3] . υπνο[

7]ζοφθωμα

922 P. Oxy. 660

fr. (a)   fr. (b)

[. .] . [. . .]χεοδ[. .]ν ἀπείρατ[   ]ον ἔσσεσθ[αι

ξας · ἰὲ παιῆον ἀναρσίων τ[   ]άμμορον [

ὀιστῶν δούρων τε σιδαρο[   ]μων φα[

βρίσει νέας ἀιθέων μάλισ[τ   ] . χοων δ[

5 ἢ πόλεμόνδε κορυσσομε[ν   ]ωμενοι[

θεσπεσίας δ᾽ ἀπὸ κνίσας μ[   ]ομενο[

κ[. . . . .] πολλάκις Πυθοῖ π[

ἁ μὲν ταῦτ᾽ ἀίοισα γνάμψε[

ἐσσομ[έ]νου δ᾽ ὑέος οὐ μέλλε . [

10 [ἰὲ] παιᾶσ[ι]ν · συν αλιοι τριτα[

[ἰὲ] παιᾶσιν αὐχεν . . ουλα . [

[. .]ος · αὐτίκα δὲ σκοπιᾶς οἱ[

[. .]ντο μεταχρόνιαι . [

[. .]νοντι   γᾶν ἐρατὰν [

15 [ἰὲ] παίαν δ᾽ ἄρα νύκτα κ[

ANONYMOUS FRAGMENTS

921 Strasbourg papyrus[1] (2nd c. A.D.)

(a) ... good fortune ... (b) (ii) ... immortal ...
(song of praise?) ... Timo-[2] ... sprinter[3] ... ancient
... (iii) ... (I see?) ... (iv) ... name ... you appeared
... soul ... race[4] ... (v) ... other ... spirit ... fear[5]
... down over us ... blameworthy ... Hier(o)[6] ...
(sleep?) ...

[1] Ascribed to Simonides' epinician poetry for runners by the first
editor, Snell, but see Lobel, *Ox. Pap.* xxv (1959) p. 45 n. 2.
[2] Heading of a new poem.   [3] First word of the poem.
[4] In line 3 of a new poem.   [5] In line 7 of a new poem.
[6] Heading of a poem.

922 Oxyrhynchus papyrus (c. 100 A.D.)

... without experience ... (he?) will be[1] ... ië
paean! ... (of) hostile men ... without share ... (of)
arrows and iron-(tipped?) spears ... (he?) will weigh
down the ships with young men ... most of all ... or
to battle armed ... and from wonderful burnt
sacrifice ... many times (at Pytho?)[2] ...
When she heard this she bent ..., and of the son
that was to be born she did not intend ... ië paeans!
together with ... (third?) ... ië paeans! ... neck ...;
and immediately (from) a peak ... (they)[3] high in
the air ... lovely earth ... ië paean! ... night ...

[1] Seemingly a prophecy to a mother about an unborn son.
[2] Or (might learn?).   [3] Fem. pl.

suppl. ed. pr. (Grenfell, Hunt)   frr. (a) (b) quo distent inter-
vallo incertum   7 vel πύθοιτ[8 γνάμψε[ι ed. pr.

[μα]ρτυράμεναι δ[.]κ[
[. .]ας· ἰὲ πα[ιηο]ν· . [
[. .]ω πρω[ ]έ[
[. .]ν στολ[
20 [. .] ονα[
[. .]βροτο[
[. .] χρύσ[
[. .]αοιδ[
[. .]ακυν[
25 [. .]ος· ἰὲ [παι-

923 P. Tebt. 691

] . αχνε . . ων μένει αὔρας ἐπηγλαϊσμένον
  [. .]σιδ . οις
  ]ιος τρέφει φιλάνθεμα ναπᾶν   ὡς δωματασ[
] . ερ εὔγματι κουφήρει θεὰ νυμφᾶν θαλάμους
  ἐπιπεπτ[
] . ν ἀλλοτρίαις δ' οὐ μίγνυται μοῦσαν ἀρούραις
  μας
5] . ας . . . . καὶ λήγετε μοῦσαν ἀκοαῖσι παρασχεῖν,
  Φήμιε
δύσ]τανε

1 ἐπιγλαεισμ- pap.   fin. fort.]σιανοις   2 fort.]νος
vel νάπαν   ὡς δωμ. fort. schol. pars   fort. θαλάμους ἔπι π.
4 ed. pr. (Hunt, Smyly): ἀλλοτρίοις pap.   5 vel φημι ε-
6 ci. Page

924 = Bacch. fr. 66 (dub.): v. vol. 4 p. 315.

(they)[3] having borne witness ... ië paean! ...
(equipment?) ... mortal ... gold ... (song?) ... ië
paean! ...

[3] Fem. pl.

923 Tebtunis papyrus (late 3rd c. B.C.)

... awaits[1] the breezes ... decked out ... tends
the flower-loving ... of the valleys[2] ... with vain
(boast?) the goddess (visits?) the chambers of the
nymphs ... but (he) does not admit (his) muse to
strange fields ... and cease to offer your muse to the
ears, (wretched Phemius?)[3]!

[1] Translation very uncertain; the relationship even of adjacent
words is often indeterminable. [2] The following words may
be from a scholion: 'as home'. [3] Text doubtful. Phemius was
the singer in Odysseus' palace; 'cease!' is a plural verb ('you and the
others'?)

924 = Bacchylides fr. 66 (dub.): see vol. 4 p. 315.

925 P. Hibeh 693 ((a)(b)) + P. Heidelb. 178 ((c)–(f)) (v.
G. A. Gerhard, *Gr. Pap.* . . . *Heidelberg*, 1938, p. 26ss.)

(a)   ]ειδμ[
    φ]αεσφόρ[ο]ν ἀελ[ίου] δρόμον εν[
      ἐ]πὶ νέρτερον αὐγὴν νυκτ[
        ]ερισμ᾽ ἀντεφαε[   ] ̣νεκ[
5   ] τέκνον ὦ τέκνον ε[̣] ̣ ̣[
        ]ἀλλὰ τας Δαρδανι[
         ]υγοτα τε δεα[

2 φαεσφ. suppl. Grenfell, Hunt, ἀελίου Milne   4 ἀντέφαε [κ]αὶ
νεκ[ci. Page   6 vel]ελλα

(b)   ]μ μέλεος δ[̣]ο ̣ ̣[
        ἔ]κφυγον ἀλκα[
         ]ατα μὲν σκοτεα[
         ]αις δὲ πότμο[
5   ]αρμενος ὤλε[
      κα]ταστορέσας β[
       κ]εδρινὸν π ̣[
         ]ἀποσφαλτ[
        ] ̣σι υπε ̣ ̣[

7 suppl. Grenfell, Hunt

(c) 2   ] ̣ορα ̣ ̣[̣] ̣[̣] ̣ ̣[̣ ̣] ̣ ̣[̣]ν
        ]μ προχέω λόγοις ἐμῶν
        ] ̣αμοις · οἶδα γὰρ ὡς πα[
5   ]υ κυαναυγέος εὖ ἄγε[ι]ν
       ]Κίρκας εν ̣[̣]μεε ̣[̣ ̣ ̣] ̣ ̣
      ]σεη δὲ τάφου στηρίγματι

ANONYMOUS FRAGMENTS

925 Hibeh papyrus (280–240 B.C.)[1]

(a) ... the light-bearing course of the sun ... to the netherworld rays of light ... shone against ... (corpse?) ... child, my child! ... (but) ... Dardanian ...

[1] Six fragments dealing with Odysseus and his meeting with his mother in the world of the dead (cf. *Od.* 11. 152 ff.). Gerhard, editor of the Heidelberg fragments, saw evidence also for the story of Elpenor, who fell to his death from Circe's roof (*Od.* 11. 51 ff.): see (c) especially. He assigned the fragments to the *Elpenor* of Timotheus (fr. 779), but Page, *Select Papyri* iii 397 ff., showed how frail the evidence is.

(b) ... (unhappy?) ... (I/they) escaped ... strength ... dark ... doom ... perished ... (he) having strewn ... cedarwood[1] ... (tripped?) ...

[1] Description of a burial.

(c) ... I pour forth ... with words ... of my ... ; for I know how ... (of) the dark-shining ... to bring safely ... (of) Circe ... the foundation of a tomb ...

```
          ] τέκνων ἱκέτας προχέων
         ]πω οἱ μὲν βαθύπορον α[
10           πολ]υδέγμονα παι[ . . ]ν
             ] . αστε[ . . ]χας παθέων[
             ] . ρασδ . . ιαιδ᾽ ἤγειρον[
                ]γη μυχὸν αιλο . [
                ]ηρ, αἰαῖ ἡ δὲ νέα
15                 ]θεοι
                   ]μένα ψυχὰ
                   ] . . ιδα
```

11 τε [τύχ]ας Diehl   13 ἅιδου[Diehl   14 vel γ]ηραιαί, ἠδὲ
15 vel]μεν ἅ ψ.,]μεν ἄψυχα

(d) πολυπλάνητα δ[
     ἀπάται δολιμήτας δ[
     κτονα πήματα δ[
     ὁ δ᾽ ἐμὲ λυγρὰ κώλυσεν αλ[
5   ὡς ἀνὰ κύματα πόντια[
     ροις ἀλαλημένος ἠλυ[θ
     οσ . . . νας ὑψιτύπου π[
     β[. . . .]ε κρατεραυγέσι γορ[γ
     [. . . .]ατόπνευστος αὖρα [
10   [. . .]ηδ᾽ ὑποερείφθη γυ[ῖα
     [. .] . ἔπνευσε νεκυοπο . . [
     [μ]ᾶτερ ἐμά, θάμα το[
     [ἀ]λλ᾽ ἄγε μοι τόδε τ[
     [. . .]νομοι ἔννεπεν δα[
15   [. . .]εασυσταθανατ[

2 vel ἀπατᾶι   δολο- vel δολιο- ?   10 suppl. Diggle
11 -πομπ[?   14 κεῖ]νό μοι Diehl

312

of children ... a suppliant pouring forth ... some ...
with its deep crossing, receiver of many men[1] ...
misfortunes ... (I/they) gathered ... the recess (of
Hades?) ... alas! and the young ... the gods ... soul
...

[1] With reference to the world of the dead and its river.

(d) ... much-wandering[1] ... by deceit the wily
schemer[1] ... woes ... and he prevented me ...
grievous ... as on the waves of the sea ... (I/he)
wandering came ... high ... strong-shining grim
... -blown breeze ... limbs collapsed ... breathed
... corpse- .... My mother, often .... But come, ...
me this ... spoke ... death ...

[1] Epithets suitable to Odysseus.

(e)
           ] νεοιτεατε δι' ἀμέτρου
           ]αδεπω . . αχιρι . τιαδ
           ]ροσηβαν . μ . . νει . δολιχ . [
      ]ηρ τις σοι . εφα . . να ἀμφέβαλεν
5   σ]ὺν ναΐ μελαίναι πλαγχθεὶς κατα
        ] . ναις ἀνέμοις μα . . . ταις τε ἑμοῖσιν
     ]και λίφ' ἑκὼν . ρ . . . . . τις σοι κα . . . . ὀφρων
      ] . ἔλιπον ὦ μᾶτερ . . . . . . ραννυν . ο .
    ]νας καὶ Εὐμενιδᾶν ε . ω . . . ὑπὸ ζοφου δ' ἀερο-
10 εντος   κό]σμον μύθων ὁρμαν . . . ε τάδε δὴ πολυαν'
                             Ὀ[δυσ]σεῦ
     ] . δώματα καὶ φθιμένων βασιλῆα πανδ[οκέα]
    ]μεν προφυγὼν θάνατον θρασυαίγιδα τ[. . . .]αν
] δι' ἀπείρονα κύ[μα]τα θε . [. . .] . ασογκαιε[. . .]υμα
] . . . [. . .]ουσασπ[. . .] . ωουτ[. . .]σλατα[.]σει οὔτε
15]ανδιελε . [. . Κύκ]λωπος σιμ . ιαιαι[.] ἐξαΐσσων
]μυχὸν ημ[. . . .] πείρασιν ἄντρου ἀραιεγ[
]ου λώβαν τα[. . . . .] οὐκ εἶδον οὐδ' ἐδόκευσα νόωι
]ες εὐεριστα[. . . . .]ει θαλεράν φρένα ἐδρέψατο
]δρυ . . [. . . . . .] . σων δι[ὰ σ]ώματος
20   ]οι . βαθυπόλωμ μελά-
θρων   ]τος συνθεὶς κλίμακα
                 ]αδωραε . . . [. . . .]ιν

3 ξνει ed. pr. (Gerhard)   7 καρτερόφρων Diehl
10 κό]σμον suppl. Diggle   13 ὁγ καί?   15 Κύκ]λωπος ci.
Diggle

(f) 5 ψυχα[6 εκπρο[post 7 coronis

ANONYMOUS FRAGMENTS

(e) ... through the measureless ... long ...
(someone?)[1] put round you ... sent wandering with
black ship over ... by winds ... and my ... I will-
ingly left ... you ... (stout-hearted?) ... I left ...,
mother! and (of) the Eumenides ... under the misty
darkness ... a fashioning of words ... (impulse?)
..., much-praised Odysseus, ... these dwellings
and the all-welcoming king of the dead ... having
escaped death ... of the bold aegis ... through the
boundless waves ... neither ... nor ... of the
Cyclops ... rushing out ... the recess ... the
furthest end of the cave ... outrage I never saw nor
imagined in my mind ... (easily-contesting?) ...
vigorous heart he plucked ... through the body ...
deep-vaulted halls ... having constructed a ladder
...

[1] Or (who?).

(f) ... soul ... forth[1] ...

[1] The poem ends in the next line.

926 P. Oxy. 2687 (= P. Oxy. 9+): v. L. Pearson, *Aristoxenus: Elementa Rhythmica* 36ss., 77ss.

(col. i) οἰκε]ιότατοι (col. ii) μὲν οὖν εἰσιν οἱ ῥυθμοὶ οὗτοι τῆς τοιαύτης λέξεως· χρήσαιτο δ᾽ ἂν αὐτῆι καὶ ὁ δάκτυλος ὁ κατὰ ἴαμβον ἀνάπαλι τῶν περιεχουσῶν ξυλλαβῶν τεθεισῶν εἰς τοὺς χρόνους ἢ ὡς ἐν τῶι κρητικῶι ἐτίθεντο· ἔσται δὲ τὸ σχῆμα τοῦ ποδὸς δι᾽ οὗ ἡ ῥυθμοποιία πορεύσεται τὸ εἰς ἴαμβον οἷον

(a) ἔνθα δὴ ποικίλων ἀνθέων ἄμβροτοι λ<ε>ίμακες
    βαθύσκιον παρ᾽ ἄλσος ἁβροπαρθένους
    εὐιώτας χοροὺς ἀγκάλαις δέχονται·

ἐν τούτωι γὰρ οἵ τε πρῶτοι πέντε πόδες οὕτω κέχρηνται τῆι λέξει καὶ πάλιν ὕστεροι τρεῖς· καὶ

(b) ὅστις εὐθυμίηι καὶ χοροῖς ἥδεται·

ἐπὶ πολὺ δὲ τῆι τοιαύτηι ῥυθμοποιίαι οὐ πάνυ χρῆται ὁ ῥυθμὸς οὗτος.

χρήσαιτο δ᾽ ἂν τῆι τοιαύτηι λέξ[ε]ι καὶ ὁ ἀπὸ τροχαίου βακχεῖος ἐν καταμείξει τιθεὶς τὴν ἐκ μονοχρόνου καὶ ἰάμβ[ο]υ ξυνζυγίαν ὥστε ξυνεχ[ῆ] μὲν οὐδὲ ταύτην δεῖ ζητεῖν τὴν ῥυθμοποιίαν· οὐ γὰρ παραγίνεται· [διε]σπαρμένηι δ᾽ [ἔ]στι περιπε[σ]εῖν οἷον ἐν τῶι

(c) ῥιπτείσθω ποδὸς ἱερὰ βάσις

κατὰ τὸ (καὶ τὸν tent. Winnington-Ingram)

---

1 The text published as P.Oxy. 9 contained five fragments of verse, (a)–(e) in *P.M.G.*; the longer text, P.Oxy. 2687, provided two new fragments, here labelled (c) and (d); the original (c) (d) and (e) are now (e) (f) and (g). The author may be Aristoxenus himself or one of his school. The fragments, which will belong to 5th or 4th c. B.C., seem to be dithyrambic with the exception of (g), which may be the opening of a partheneion. 2 The author is discussing the rhythmising of verses in which a long syllable was protracted in performance so as to have the time value of – ᴗ or ᴗ –. He has just dealt with rhythms such as the Aristoxenian cretic (– ᴗ ᴗ –) which admit a *lexis* ('word-group', lit. 'speech, spoken phrase') of

ANONYMOUS FRAGMENTS

926 Oxyrhynchus papyrus (*c.* 250 A.D.): Aristoxenus, *Rhythmics*(?)[1]

These rhythms, then, are the most suitable for this sort of word-group.[2] But the iambic type of dactyl ($\cup-\cup-$) may also use it (in the form $\llcorner\cup-$), the outside syllables being assigned to the feet in an order the reverse of that in which they were assigned in the cretic ($-\cup\lrcorner$). The pattern of the foot in which the rhythmical composition proceeds will end in an iambus ($\llcorner\cup-$), e.g.

(a) There immortal meadows of many-coloured flowers welcome in their embrace by the deep-shadowed grove the bacchant choirs of tender maidens.

In this passage the first five feet use the word-group in this way, as do three later feet also.[3] And again

(b) He who takes pleasure in cheerfulness and dancing choirs . . .[4]

But this rhythm never uses such rhythmical composition for long.

The bacchius that begins with a trochee ($-\cup\cup-$) may use this sort of word-group, mixing (with $-\cup\cup-$) the coupling made up of a single element ($\lrcorner$) and an iambus ($\cup-$): not that one need look for this rhythmical composition used continuously either—that does not occur—but one can find sporadic use of it, e.g. in

(c) Let the holy step of the foot be flung high,

as in

the pattern $-\cup-$ if the final syllable is protracted ($-\cup\lrcorner$). (Trisemes which correspond to $\cup-$ and $-\cup$ are denoted by $\llcorner$ and $\lrcorner$ respectively.)   [3] I.e. v. 1 and the first three words of v. 3; v. 2 is iambic (or 'the iambic type of dactyl').   [4] $\llcorner\cup-$ four times.

317

(d) Διόνυσον τὸν ἐκ πυρός

μία ξυνζυ[γ]ία. προελθόντι δὲ κατὰ μὲν τὴν λέξιν [ἔ]στι λαβεῖν
τ[ὸ] προκείμε- (col. iii) νον εἶδος, κατὰ δὲ τὰ τῆς ῥυθμοποιΐας
σχήματα παραλλάττει ἐν τῶι

(e) φίλ<ι>ον Ὥραισιν ἀγάπημα, θνατοῖσιν ἀνάπαυ-
        μα μόχθων.

ἔστι δέ που καὶ ξυνεχὴς (Winnington-Ingram: -εχεις pap.) ἐπὶ
τρεῖς·

(f) φέρτατον δαίμον' ἀγνᾶς τέκος
    ματέρος, ἃν Κάδμος ἐγέννασέ ποτ' ἐν
    ταῖς πολυολβίοις<ι> Θήβαις.

χρήσαιτο δ' ἂν καὶ ὁ ἴαμβος τῆι αὐτῆι ταύτηι λέξει, ἀφυέστερον
δὲ τοῦ βακχείου· τὸ γὰρ μονόχρονον οἰκειότερον τοῦ τροχαϊκοῦ ἢ
τοῦ ἰάμβου, οἷον ἐν τῶι

(g) βᾶτε βᾶτε κεῖθεν, αἱ δ'
        ἐς τὸ πρόσθεν ὀρόμεναι.
    τίς ποθ' ἁ νεᾶνις; ὡς
    εὐπρεπής νιν ἀμφέπει·

τρεῖς πόδας διαλείπουσιν αἱ ξυνζυγίαι ὥστε περιοδῶδές τι
γίγνεσθαι.

(c) ἱρὰ Dale   (e) em. Page   (f) 3 -ολβοισιν pap. ante corr.,
-ολβιοις post corr., em. Page   (g) 1 εις pap.   3 ποθε in
ποθα corr. pap.

927 P. Hamb. 128 = Theophrast. π. λέξ. i

    v. 49   χρυσὸς αἰγλήεις
    v. 55   βοτρυοκαρποτόκος
    v. 56   ἀστερομαρμαροφεγγής

ANONYMOUS FRAGMENTS

(d) Dionysus born from the fire,[5]

there is a single coupling.[6] If one goes on, one can find the form under discussion unchanged as far as the word-group goes, but with variation in the patterns of the rhythmic composition,[7] e.g. in

(e) Beloved darling[8] to the Seasons, respite from toils to mortals.

It can even occur in a sequence of three[9]:

(f) The excellent deity,[10] child of the pure mother whom Cadmus once begot in prosperous Thebes.

The iambus also may use this same word-group ($\smile\smile-$), but less naturally than does the bacchius ($-\smile\smile-$), for the single element ($\llcorner$ or $\lrcorner$) is more at home in the trochaic part (of the bacchius) than in the iambus; e.g. in

(g) Come from there, come, and you other girls, come rushing to the front! Whoever is that young girl? What a handsome . . . surrounds her!

the couplings occur every third foot[11] so as to produce a kind of periodic effect.

[5] In the lightning-flash in which Zeus visited Semele. [6] -ρὰ βάσις and -σον τὸν ἐκ. [7] $\llcorner\smile\smile\smile$ replaces $\llcorner\smile-$ twice.
[8] Wine. [9] In v. 1. [10] Dionysus, son of Semele.
[11] $\llcorner\smile-|\smile-|\smile-|\llcorner\smile-|\smile\llcorner\lrcorner|\smile-$ twice.

927 Hamburg papyrus (c. 250 B.C.): Theophrastus, *On Diction*

> gleaming gold
> grape-cluster-bearing
> star-flashing-bright[1]

[1] Three lexicon entries; the last two may be dithyrambic (Snell).

928 P. Hibeh 172: v. *T.G.F.* ii Adesp. 720

ἀλογενέτωρ
δαιτόποινος
ἐτυμόγλωσσος
ἐτυμόμαντις
ἐτυμόφανος (fort. leg. -φαμος L.S.J.)
ἐτυμοφάς (fort. leg. -φα<ντο>ς L.S.J.)
καμψίγουνος
καμψίχειρ
κυανοέθειραι
μιλτοπάραος
σιδηροπέρσης (vel -πέρθης)
φοινικοπάραος

929 P. Gr. Vindob. 19996ab (*Mitteil. aus der Papyrus-samml. Rainer* n.s. i (1932) 136ss., ed. Oellacher)

(a) a I col. 3. 2ss.

μέλος μαλα[κὸν ἡ]γεῖτο πολ[λ]αχοῦ μὲν ἀποφαίνε[σ]θαι,
μάλιστα δ᾽ ἐν τῶι

τίς ἄρα λύσσα νῶι τιν᾽ ὑφαι[

ὑφαι[ρεῖ Diehl, ὑφαί[νει Page (Index, *P.M.G.*)

(b) a II col. 2

ἀναβόασον αὐτῶι·
Διόνυσον ἀ[ύ]σομεν
ἱεραῖς ἐν ἁμέρα[ι]ς
δώδεκα μῆνας ἀπόντα·
5 πάρα δ᾽ ὥρα, πάντα δ᾽ ἄνθη

2 vel ἀ[εί]σομεν

928 Hibeh papyrus (*c.* 270–230 B.C.): items from a list of compound adjectives

> sea-begetting
> feast-avenging[1]
> true-tongued
> truth-prophesying
> truth-revealing(?)[2]
> truth-speaking(?)[3]
> knee-bending[4]
> arm-bending
> dark-haired (fem. pl.)
> scarlet-cheeked[5]
> iron-destructive[6]
> crimson-cheeked[7]

[1] With reference to the feast of Atreus?   [2] Or 'truth-reporting'.   [3] Perhaps 'truth-showing'.   [4] Of a runner? Cf. 'knee-bending (καμπεσίγουνος) Erinys' in Hsch. K 610, καμψίπους ('leg-bending') of the Erinys in Aes. *Sept.* 791.   [5] Of a ship, e.g. *Il.* 2. 637; Doric form.   [6] I.e. destroying with the sword.   [7] Also of a ship, e.g. *Od.* 11. 124; Doric form.

929 Rainer papyrus (1st c. B.C. or 1st c. A.D.)[1]

(a) He believed that effeminate song was often in evidence, but particularly in

What madness, pray, (robs?) us two of a[2] . . . ?

[1] Dithyrambic fragments (*c.* 400 B.C.) cited in a prose work (*c.* 200 B.C.) in which the names Melanippides, Philoxenus and possibly Telestes occur.   [2] Or '(weaves) a . . . for us two'.

(b) Shout aloud to him! We shall sing of Dionysus on these holy days: he has been absent for twelve months, but now the springtime is here, and all the flowers . . .

321

(c) a II col. 3

Ζ[ε]ὺς μὲν ἐπέβρεμε βάρβαρα βρονταῖ,
γᾶν δ' ἐτίναξε Ποσειδὰν
χρυσεόδοντι τριαίναι.

(d) a II col. 5

. .]φύετο . [.]α . [ ] καρπῶι
ἀγ[ν]ὰ δρῦς·
φ[ύ]ετο στάχυς ἄμμιγα κριθαῖς
πασπερμεί,
5 ἄνθει καὶ λευκοχίτων
ἄμ[[ε]]α ζειὰ κυανότρι[χ-

(e) b I col. 1

Ἄ]μμωνος α[.]εθλ[. .
ἐπ]έβα τηλωπὸν ἱδρυθεὶς
ἀ[νύδ]ρου Λιβύας
ἀσπάσιος ποσὶ λειμώ-
νων τέρεν' ἄν[θ]εα τείρας
5 σῶμ' ἀκαμάτου [

2 suppl. ed. pr.

(f) b I col. 2

]ου
νύμφαν φοινικοπ[τέρ]υγα·
†κράτει δ' ὑπὸ γᾶς† θέτο βριαρὸν
τέκνον μαστοῖς Ἄρεως πεφρι-
κὸς πα[ί]δευμ' Ἀτυχίας

322

ANONYMOUS FRAGMENTS

(c) Zeus roared savagely with his thunder, Poseidon shook the earth with his gold-toothed trident.[1]

[1] Cf. *Il.* 20. 56 f. (Page).

(d) ... there grew the sacred oak with ... fruit, there grew the corn-ear mixed with barley, all seeds together, there flowered also the white-coated wheat along with the dark-haired ...

(e) ... of Ammon ... establishing himself far away, he set foot in waterless Libya, gladly treading underfoot the soft flowers of the meadows, unwearied ...[1]

[1] Heracles?

(f) ... the crimson-winged nymph[1]; (with strength under the earth?)[2] she put to her breast the mighty child of Ares, trembling, nursling of Misfortune.[3]

[1] A Siren or Harpy? [2] Text corrupt? [3] The Amazon Penthesilea? *Penth-* denotes grief.

323

(g) b II col. 1

              ]ε μαλακόμματος ὕπ-
νος [γ]υῖα περὶ πάντα βαλών,
ὡσεὶ μάτηρ παῖδ᾽ ἀγαπα-
τ]ὸν χρόνιον ἰδοῦσα φίλωι
5 κ]όλπωι πτέρυγας ἀμφέβαλεν

1 ἦλθεν δ]ὲ suppl. Croenert

(h) b II col. 2

    ὄμματα κλήισας ἐν δι[
τ αις ἄρκυσιν ἤδη βιο[
δεσμοῖς ἐνέχηι.

930 P. Gr. Vindob. 29774 (*Mitteil. aus der Papyrussamml. Rainer* n.s. iii (1939) 26, ed. Oellacher)

    ἐμιανατοδωριον δ[
μ ατα παιδων μενοπ[ἀ-
θλίαν ἐκεῖνος ἐμω[
πων καὶ θρῆνος αυ[
5 τέκνων
τόδε μὲν Σκυθικῶν [
γάμων ειμεδωρ[
κλείω δόμον θ[
θ . . . . οσφρ[
10   ]τισιν[
     ]θορ[

1 ἐμίανα τὸ Δώριον vel ἐμιάνατο Δώριον

(g) Soft-eyed Sleep (came), embracing all his limbs, as a mother on seeing her dear son after a long absence folds him with her wings to her loving breast.

(h) ... closing[1] his eyes in ... hunting-nets now ... he holds him in fetters.

[1] Sleep.

930 Rainer papyrus (2nd or 3rd c. A.D.)

... I defiled[1] the Dorian ... (of) children ... he ... (me?), wretched woman ... and a dirge ... (for) children. This then ... (of) the Scythian marriage ... I celebrate[2] the house ...

[1] Or 'he/she defiled'.   [2] Or 'I close'.

931 P. Gr. Vindob. 29819 (*Mitteil. aus der Papyrussamml. Rainer* n.s. iii (1939) p. 26ss., ed. Oellacher)

(i)

2]ωραιο . καπα[φ]οβερασεδρα[

3]εμονακεχ . ων[ά]γγελον εὐν[

4] . . . ν ὄρεσι β[α]κχ[

5 . . κισχροον ενδι[   ]ν ἀφελη μον[

6]ο̅ς̅ B̅

7   ]δρόμημα κου[. .]ν 'Αρκαδ[

      ]νον κρατουμένην ἄλλη[

      ]ην χειμέριος φέρων ὀρν[

10   ]ομορον τύπον δρακαίνης γόνον

      ]ραν καταντία βοῒ λασίωι φοινίαν βαλλ[

      ]ν μανεῖσαν ἄλλην 'Ινὼ δυσω[

      ]Νυκτέως τὴν πανδάκρυτον [

      ]χ̅η̅σ̅τ̅ρ̅α̅

2 ὡραῖος Καπα[νεὺς (vel cas. obliqu.) suppl. ed. pr.   φ]οβερα(ς) tent. Page   3 vel μοναισεχ   5 πολ]λάκις χρόον ed. pr. ίόχροον vel -ιόχροον tent. Page   ἀφέληι ? Page   6 χορ-, ἐπωιδ-, ἀντιστροφ- ? ed. pr.   7 κοῦ[φο]ν Radermacher, κού[ρω]ν ed. pr.   11 δυσω[νυμ- ed. pr.   14 ὀρ]χῆστρα ed. pr., qui Κλυταιμ]νήστρα negat

(ii) 11 γι]γάντων ?   12 ταυρο[13 -γα κυκλω[

931A = S443   P. Oxy. 2620 fr. 1

    ]ωι πιφαύσκων [

      ]ντι[.]εινον ἔγνωτ . [

        ]‾ υ . ιδι πτύον[

        ]ον τεοῦ δενώμ[

5   ] ἁμαρτὼν ζοᾶ[ς

      ] . πένθος αὐτοκρα[τ-

931 Rainer papyrus (2nd or 3rd c. A.D.)

(i) ... youthful (Capaneus?) ... fearful ... messenger ... in the mountains bacch- ... -skinned ... takes away ...[1] (nimble?) running ... Arcadia(n) ... (her,) overpowered ... other ... wintry ... (he) carrying ... (birds?) ... death ... (her), the image of a she-dragon, child (of) ... opposite the shaggy ox (he?) struck the murderous ... (her,) maddened, another Ino, ill-named, ... (or?) the miserable (daughter)[2] of Nycteus.

(ii) ... (of) giants ... bull ... circle ...

[1] Verse 6 indicates a new section of the poem: a second chorus, or a second epode or antistrophe?   [2] Antiope.

931A = S443   Oxyrhynchus papyrus (1st c. B.C. or 1st c. A.D.)

... (he/I) declaring ... (he?) learned ... winnowing-shovel ... of your ... (I?) deprived of property ... grief ... ruling absolutely ... (in) the glens

3 πρ]ᾱυ- vel τ]ᾱυ- ed. pr. (Lobel), sed etiam]˙χ possis   σιδι
vel ειδι   πτύον in πτέον corr., ut vid.   5 suppl. Page
6, 7, 8 suppl. ed. pr.

327

πτ]υχα[ῖσι] Ταιναρίας, τὶν δεὶ[.]ι̯ν̯[
   ] . ου θαλάσσας ὦ χρυσοτρίαι̯[να
   ]πέποιθα τοιῶνδε κο . [
10   ]νίοισιν χαρέντα πολλ[οῖς
   ἵ]κεσθαι χώραν πο . [
   ] . τον Αἰγαῖον ἀρμ[εν-
   ]ε̯ν Ὄσσαθεν α[
   ] . [ ] . νη . [

9 κόσ[μ- ? Page   10, 11 suppl. Page   12 πό]ντον ? ed. pr.
suppl. ed. pr.

931B = S 445–446   P. Oxy. 2626

fr. 1 2]αλκονα . [3 Ὄ]λυμπος · α[4 ἀ]μφὶ
πάντο[5 ἔ]μπεδον θ[6 ν ἀπρόσοπ[τ-
7]ετε̯κενδ[

fr. 2 1]ναυχε . .   2]Νίκανδρον . [3]Τλημ-
πόλεμ[ο-   4]ο̯ς ἀρεταν ετ[5] . κῦδος ἐν [
6]οστον[7]ανιπ[

fr. 1 2]αλκομα leg. ed. pr. (Lobel), χ]άλκον tent. Page
3–6 suppl. ed. pr.   4 πάντο[θεν vel πάντο[λμ- Renehan

931C = S 449   P. Oxy. 2627

2 -ότ]ατον θεῶ[ν   3] . ελθὼν   6]ν τότ᾽ ἐν
δαιτὶ π[7 ε]ὐανθεῖ γάμωι [8]ερον εἴρετο
φ . [9]ν ἑκατόγχειρα [10] . ιε μελαίνας
φερτ[11]ἀπὸ δαι̯τὸ̯ς [

2 var. lect. θεό[ν   suppl. ed. pr. (Lobel), Page   7 suppl.
ed. pr.

of Taenaria; and in you, gold-tridented (ruler)[1] of the sea, I trust ... of such ... rejoicing in many ... that I reach a country ... Aegean (sea?) gladly ... from Ossa ...

[1] Poseidon, who had a temple at Cape Taenarum.

931B = S445–446   Oxyrhynchus papyrus (200–250 A.D.)

fr. 1 ... (bronze?) ... Olympus ... round (on all sides?)[1] ... firmly ... not to be looked at ... (bore?) ...

fr. 2 ... Nicander ... Tlepolemus[2] ... virtue(s) ... glory in ...

[1] Or (all-daring?).   [2] The founder of Rhodes? Snell suggests that since the name is not in Doric form (Tla-) the poem is an epinician for an Athenian or Ionian (*Gnomon* 40, 1968, 121).

931C = S449   Oxyrhynchus papyrus (2nd c. A.D.?)

... most ... of gods ... (he) having come ... then at the feast ... full-flowering marriage ... (he) asked ... hundred-handed ... black ... from the banquet ...[1]

[1] The vocabulary suggested Pindaric authorship to Lobel.

931D = S 450–451   P. Oxy. 2628

fr. 1 4]ων σεταν   5] βροτῶν   6 π]άτρας
ὑπερ[7]μις τοδεν . [8]αρσον

fr. 2 4] . τελευταις[

fr. 1 4 σὲ τὰν Page   6 suppl. ed. pr. (Lobel)   8]αρ σὸν
Page, τ]αρσόν tent. Führer   fr. 2 4 -ταῖς vel -ταῖς

931E = S 452   P. Oxy. 2629

2 Ὀρχομ]ενός[3 Π]οσιδᾶν[4 Μι]νύας
τελ[6 -κ]ώμιον[

2, 4 tent. ed. pr. (Lobel)   3 suppl. ed. pr.   6 vel -β]ώμιον
(ed. pr.)

931F = S 453   P. Oxy. 2630

2   π]αιήονα ἰὴ ἰή [
    ]α ναῦς ἐπ᾽ ἄκρον οἰ[δμα
    ]ιρονας νάσων ἀπὸ κλεεν[ν-
5   ]αιτε πατρὶ κα[ὶ] παιδὶ τεκτ[

omnia suppl. ed. pr. (Lobel)

931G = S 454   P. Oxy. 2631 col. ii

3 φωρακα[4 ῥέοντι δ᾽ ουπ[5 μακροτερο[
6 καὶ τὸν αιδ[7 πλοῦτον θα[8 λασε θνατῶν [
9 μηδεναιω[10 . .]μαλησα . [

330

ANONYMOUS FRAGMENTS

931D = S450–451   Oxyrhynchus papyrus (*c.* 100 A.D.)

fr. 1 ... (you?) ... (of) mortals ... for (your?) father-land ... your ...

fr. 2 ... you end[1] ...

[1] Or 'the ends'.

931E = S452   Oxyrhynchus papyrus (*c.* 200 A.D.)

... (Orchomenus?)[1] ... Poseidon ... (Minyan?) ... (praise?)[2] ...

[1] Ancient Boeotian city, Minyan centre (*Il.* 2. 511) with a cult of Poseidon.   [2] Or (altar?).

931F = S453   Oxyrhynchus papyrus (3rd c. A.D.)

... paean, ië ië! ... ship(s) over the surface of the sea-swell ... from the islands glorious ... (to) father and child ...

931G = S454   Oxyrhynchus papyrus (*c.* 150 A.D.)

... thief[1] ... flowing[2] ... longer ... and the ... wealth ... (of) mortals ... (nor?) ...

[1] Or 'theft'.   [2] First word of a new metrical unit.

931H = S 455   P. Oxy. 2632 fr. 1

1] . ον ἐρωτο[2]εν δ᾽ Αἴσονο[ς   4]ειαν
<ἄρμα> δ[ι]ώκειν α[5] . σίνος . [.]σελλα[
6]αρ ἔργων ξένα π[7]ν ἀθανάτοις αν[
8 ἀ]νάγκας   9]ήλυθε καὶ τότ[

2 interpr. Page   cetera suppl. ed. pr. (Lobel)

931I = S 457   P. Oxy. 2633

2 .]ν φρεν[4]υξαισα . [5 καὶ μὰν
τοῦ[6 οσσας ὕδατο[ς   11 . .]υς δι᾽
ἀστερ[12] . ον· περί οἱ νεφ[13]υ
κελαινω[14 .]ν χέε δεσμὸν α . [15 .] . τον
μὲν ἐθαψ[16 . .]σὺν κριτοῖσιν[17 κα]λλι-
κόμοιο δεπ[18 .]υν τε χθονιαν[

6 ὄσσας, nisi Ὄσσας Page (Index, *S.E.G.*)   17 suppl. ed. pr.
(Lobel)

931H = S455   Oxyrhynchus papyrus (1st c. A.D.)

... (of) love ... (of Aeson?)[1] ... to drive the chariot ... for of deeds the foreign (woman?) ... (to) the immortals ... necessity ... came then too ...

[1] Jason's father. Is the poem about Medea?

931I = S457   Oxyrhynchus papyrus (c. 150 A.D.)

... in (his?) heart ... (she) having ... And indeed ... water ... through the starry ... Over him ... black cloud ... (he/she) cast a chain ... (him?) (he/she) buried ... along with chosen ... (of) the lovely-haired ... underworld ...

931J = S 458   P. Oxy. 2879

col. i

```
           ] ̣ ε κυανέας [πο]λυόμματον
        ποί]κιλμα νυκτ[ός
     αἶψα δ'] ὁ δυσμογέων αἰηνὲς ὑπέρβιος
     ὦρθ' Ὑπερ]ιονίδας ̣ ̣[ ̣]ατωι τε καὶ ὀξυτάταις
  5  σὺν σπι]νθαρύγεσσ[ι ̣] ̣[ ]μελε . . . [ ]
           ]ατος ἀλιβάτο ̣ ̣ ̣
           ]ον ὄμβρον ἄπο νοτέει
           ]να παιπαλόεσσαν
        δ]ολιοπλανὲς ἐκχέεται πέλαγος
 10        ] βυθὸν ̣ ̣ ρια λειβό[με]νον
           ] ̣ ουσι ̣ [ ̣ ̣] ̣ ̣ τη ̣ [ ̣ ]ρω ̣ ̣
           ] ̣ ̣ [ ]ου λιβάδων ἄπ' ἀέξεαι
```

16]ἀτρεκέω[ς]   18 ὑψί]βατος πόλις

col. ii 1 σιγα[3 τανυ ̣ [10 θαμιζε[

1, 2 suppl. ed. pr. (Lobel)   3–5 tent. Page   6 κύμ]ατος ?
ed. pr.   9 suppl. Page   10, 16 suppl. ed. pr.   18
tent. ed. pr.

931K = S 459   P. Oxy. 2880

1 θέλων γὰρ[̣   2 ἀνδράσι π[3 πόρε δ'
ἄμμ[ι(ν)   4 τα βροτο[5 μακάρεσσι[6 οὔτε
σοὶ οὔτ[ω(ς)   7 νωμα ̣ ̣[8 μέγα τεῖχ[ος
9 ̣ ̣ ̣ δεδρ[10 τ ̣ πεδοιχ[11 μεστεπαυ[

3, 6 tent. Page   8 vel μεγατειχ[-

ANONYMOUS FRAGMENTS

931J = S458   Oxyrhynchus papyrus (*c.* 100 A.D.)

col. i ... the many-eyed embroidery of blue-black night, (and at once rose?) Hyperion's son,[1] hard-toiling eternally, almighty, with ... and bright sparks ... from the steep (wave?) drips a shower ... rugged ... the treacherously-deceiving sea pours out ... (into?) the flowing depths ... from streams you are fostered ... truly ... high-set city ...

col. ii ... silence ... long- ... goes[2] frequently ...

[1] The sun.   [2] Or 'went'.

931K = S459   Oxyrhynchus papyrus (1st c. A.D.)[1]

For (he), wishing ... (to) the men ..., and he gave us ... mortal ... (to) the blessed (gods) ... neither to you so ... great wall ...

[1] The beginnings of the last 11 lines of a poem.

931L = S 460–472   P. Oxy. 2625 frr. 1–13: v. R.
Führer, *Maia* 21 (1969) 79ss.

fr. 1 1a   ἴ]τω χορό[ς] . [

1   ]πλέον · ἆγε δ᾽ Ἑλλάδος στρατὸν ἀρι- [
στέος τιμα]όχου στολᾶι
          ]νως προτέραισι φάμας λ[εγο]ντο [
μεγαλ]ώνυμος ἀρετὰ κυανόσελ[μον
5   ποντο]πόρον δόρυ Ἀργὼ τῶν αἰμ[.] . [
Ἀπόλλω]νος ἀμφὶ ναὸν ἀγλαὸν ἔπει . [

ΔΗ]ΜΗΤΡΟΣ ΚΕΙΟΙΣ

          ἐ]ν κάποις ἀηδονὶς ὧδε λέλακε σ[
ἐκ π[   ] . Ὀρχομενοῦ δ᾽ ἰαχεῖ πεδίον κλε[εννοῦ
10 μήν[   ]ς
φ[πό]τνια Δάματερ Ἐλευσινία ῥοδόπαχυ μελ[
εὖ[δ] έ[ξ]ο στέφανον τ[   ]ει ταῖσδ᾽ ἐν ὥραις · [
ἴτω ἴτω χ]ορός ·
          Διὸς]αὐτοκασι[γνή]τα †δ᾽ αὖ† θυγά[τ]ηρ βασι-
                                    λῆος ὄλβιαι
15   ] . ἀμφότερ[αι μακ]άρεσσι φίλα[ι] θεοῖσιν · ἴτω ἴτω
                                    χορός ·
          ]π᾽ ἀπήμον[   ] . [   ]ε καλὸν ἵκ[ε]σθε πλού-
σιό]ν τε κα[   ]ἐρατᾶς ἀν[ύ]σαι · ἴτω ἴτω χορός · [

1a suppl. ed. pr. (Lobel)   1 fin. χρυ legere possis (Page)
2 schol. marg. τ[ο]ῦ Πελία   3 tent. ed. pr.   4 vel ἐρατ]   4 fin.,
5, 6, 7 suppl. ed. pr.   8 tent. Page   9 vel κλε[εννόν Page
10 μήν[ας tent. ed. pr.   11 suppl. ed. pr.   φ[ίλα πό]τνι᾽
Ἐλευσ. (Δαμ. secl.) Führer   12, 13 suppl. Führer
14, 15 suppl. ed. pr.   16 init.]παιτη μον[leg. ed. pr.
16, 17 suppl. ed. pr.   17 κα[ὶ , ἀν[ύ]σ<σ>αι Führer

ANONYMOUS FRAGMENTS

931L = S460–472 Oxyrhynchus papyrus (2nd c. A.D.)

fr. 1 Go, chorus![1] ... they were sailing; and
(Jason) was leader of the band of Greeks at the
sending of (the honour-holding chief?)[2] ... (they)
were said in earlier reports ... (great-)named
valour ... the dark-benched sea-faring ship Argo of
those ... tends Apollo's splendid temple.[3]

IN HONOUR OF DEMETER; FOR THE CEANS

... in the garden the nightingale sings thus from
...; and the plain of (glorious?) Orchomenus cries
out ... (months?) ... (dear?) lady Demeter, Eleu-
sinian, rose-armed! ... well ... (accept?) the garland
... at this season. Go, chorus, go![4] King Zeus' own
sister and also his daughter[5] (are) happy, both, and
dear to the blessed gods. Go, chorus, go! ...
unharmed[6] ... you came ... fair ... and wealth ...
and ... lovely ... to achieve.[7] Go, chorus, go! ...

---

[1] Written in small letters in the upper margin; literally, 'let the
chorus go!' See n. 4.   [2] Pelias, as the marginal scholiast says,
but the supplement is insecure.   [3] Apollo authorised the
expedition.   [4] See n. 1. The refrain is repeated two and four
lines later, in alternate lines thrice in fr. 2 (= S461), twice in fr. 6
(= S465), and perhaps in fr. 3 (= S462).   [5] Demeter and
Persephone.   [6] Or 'kindly'; reading uncertain.   [7] Per-
haps 'to achieve wealth'.

fr. 2.1]ς θυγα[τ-   fr. 3.2]προχέοις[
fr. 11.1]κος θείου πωτάιλα[3]πος βουλευ-
σαμε . [fr. 12.2] . βαρειας . [fr. 13.2]ναν
ταδικα . [

931M = S 473   P. Oxy. 2635 col. i

```
            ]ε νύκτερον εὔφρονα
         ]ων ἀμπνύουσιν ὄρφναν
        ]ἀστέρα γειομόρ[ο]ις
        ] ἀήτη δ' αἴθοπα νήδυμον
   5    ] . . . [ . ] .
            ] ὤπασαν
            ]
        ]λεται παρὰ παστάσιν
        ]ες ἁζόμενα[ι] μέλπουσι θε[
  10    ]να καὶ χρυσέω<ι> Τμώλω<ι>
        ] . . γος ἀγλαΐα σέβεται
        φ]οίνικος ταναοῦ[
        ]πτόρθους ἐλαίας
        ] ον
  15    Τά]ναϊν μέλπουσι[ ]
        ἀμ]πνύουσιν ὄρφναν
        ]ου Τυφῶνος ὁλκὸς
        ]νεας
        ]υσι θυ[η]πολ[ι]αν
  20        ]τεύουσιν αἰγλα[
```

1 vel εὐφρόνα   3, 9 suppl. ed. pr. (Lobel)   12]οινεικος
corr. et suppl. ed. pr.   vel ταναοὺ[ς   13 -πτόρθους ?
15, 16, 19 suppl. ed. pr.   19 -ίαν vel -ιᾶν

(fr. 2) ... daughter ... (fr. 3) ... you might pour forth ... (fr. 11) ... (of) divine ... took counsel ... (fr. 12) ... heavy ... (fr. 13) ... just ...

931M = S473 Oxyrhynchus papyrus (before 200 A.D.)

... nightly kindly ... (they) breathe out darkness ... star[1] to farmers, and the gale ... the gleaming sweet (wine) ... (they) gave ... by the porch ... they,[2] revering ..., sing ... and (on?) golden Tmolus ... the splendour is worshipped ... (of) the tall palm-tree ... branches of the olive-tree ... the Tanais they sing ... (they) breathe out darkness ... the coiling of Typhon ... sacrifice ... they ... radiant ...

[1] Venus, welcome to farmers?   [2] Feminine.

931N = S 474   P. Oxy. 2506 fr. 88(b)

2] . μελλε δαίμων[5] . . . ποιναῖς [

931O = S 475 = 992 *Suppl. Hell.*   P. Mich. 3499, ed.
R. Merkelbach, *Z.P.E.* 12 (1973) 138: v. 13 (1974) 209ss.
(H. Lloyd-Jones)

] . . . [. .]η . . γαν Ἰλιάδαις ἀκαλὰ κτυπήσῳ[
] . . . [. .] . . . . τὰς ἐνάλους ἀπέβα κελεύθους.
] . . . [. . .]ζ . . . ς ἐκ πολέμου παρὰ ναυσὶν εἶρπε
] . . . [. .] . . . ρος Ἡρακλέους, συνέθεντο δ᾽ οὗτος
5] . . . [. . .] . . . νο . . . . α . [.]απ . . αιδ . (.)ἔθηκε
] . . . . . υγας οὓς ἔλαβεν Διὸς ἒκ τύρανν[ος
] . . . . . θεος οἰνοχόου χάριν ἀντιδώσει

1]η μέγαν ed. pr.   3 ὁ δ᾽ Ἀ[μα]ζόνος ? Parsons, Lloyd-
Jones   4 σθένος εὔπατ]ρος Ἡρ. tent. Holford-Strevens
οὗτοι coni. ed. pr.   5 ἀδηλ᾽ ἔθηκε Page   6 Φρύγας ? Par-
sons, Lloyd-Jones   fin. suppl. Lloyd-Jones   vel ἐκ
τυράνν[ου   7 φιλογαθέος ?, ἀντιδώσει<ν> ? Lloyd-Jones

ANONYMOUS FRAGMENTS

931N = S474   Oxyrhynchus papyrus (1st or early 2nd c. A.D.: comment on lyric poems)

... god intended ... (with) requital ...

931O = S475 = 992 *Suppl. Hell.*   Michigan papyrus (3rd or 2nd c. B.C.)

'... (not?) quietly shall I[1] make (great?) ... resound for Ilus' line.' ... he went away along the sea-roads ... From the battle (against the Amazon?) by the ships came (the mighty figure?) of Heracles,[2] and he (and Laomedon) made an agreement: ... he (destroyed utterly?) ... he[3] would give him in return (the horses) which the ruler had got from Zeus as recompense for his cup-bearer ...[4]

[1] Poseidon is threatening the Trojans after Laomedon had cheated him and Apollo of their reward for building the walls of Troy.   [2] After his ninth labour (the acquisition of the girdle of the Amazon Hippolyta) Heracles put in at Troy. He agreed to destroy the sea-monster which was ravaging the country if Laomedon would give him the horses which his grandfather Tros received from Zeus in return for his son Ganymede.   [3] Laomedon; the syntax of the sentence is unclear.   [4] The papyrus has scraps of 4 more lines; the author may be Callimachus, who used the metre (archebulean, fr. 228) and dealt with the subject (frr. 537, 698) (Lloyd-Jones).

931P = S 477 P. Mich. 3498ᵛ: ed. pr. D. L. Page, *Z.P.E.* 13 (1974) 105ss.

col. i

]. . . α̣πεν̣ . ο̣τ̣ . [.] .
ἀλί]ρραντον ἀκτὰ̣ν
]πεμποντες . . [ ]
Φ]ρύγιο̣ς λιμὴ̣ν[ ]
]ν̣· Δαναΐδαι δα . . [ ]α̣ι
]δ̣ονης ἁλια . υ . . [ ] .
]κησιοι Λοκροὶ α[. .] . . . ς
]κοι Κρῆτες ἐπ[. . .]σι
]ω Τρο̣ίης ειτε . .
-ο]τρόφ̣' Ἴδα . ια . υ .
] . . . τ̣αλα π̣ιτυοκο̣μ̣[ ]

col. ii

2 πεύκα συν[
ὀξυθηκτ[
Ἄρεως βίαι κε[
κόπτε τ' Ἴδα[
πται . αστη̣ . . [
ῥ̣[ί]π̣τε δ' ὡς ὅ̣τ̣ε̣[
κεῖρέ θ' οἱ μ̣ὲν ἀσ̣[
ἐπὶ γᾶι τε δοχμο[
δ . μ̣ους πρῶνας[
σωμ̣ατους ῥιπτ[

col. i 10 μηλο]τρόφ' ?

ANONYMOUS FRAGMENTS

931P = S477   Michigan papyrus (c. 150 B.C.)

col. i ... sea-sprayed promontory ... (they) sending
... the Phrygian harbour ... Danaans ... Locrians
... Cretans ... (of) Troy ... (sheep?)-feeding Ida! ...
pine-(tressed?) ...

col. ii ... pine ... keen-sharpened ... (by) the
strength of Ares ... and (he) cut ... Ida ... and (he)
hurled (them) as (when?) ... and (he) sheared ...:
some ... and on the ground slanting ... headlands
... -bodied (he) hurl(ed?) ...

931Q P. Oxy. 3539

fr.1　2　　　　　　　　　　　　Εὐ]ρώπην [
　　　　　　　　　　　　　　　　]φίλε θήρ[
　　　　　　　　　　　　　　　　]ενίης ἀρετη[
　　　　5　　　　　　　　　　　]ος ἄλλω<ι> · [
　　　　　　　　　　　　　　οὐ]δὲ δυσώδης[

fr. 2　　　　] ˙ ἰδ' ἀπὸ σώματος ἀμβροσίο[ιο
　　εἰς] ὄργια δ' ἔρχεται θυμὸ[ν] ἔχων[
　　　　　]ο ˙ ˙ γῆς κόνιν ἐγίρων [
　　　　　]ηφιον ὄμμασι σαλεύιν [
　　5　 ἐ]πὶ πολὺ φίλτρον Ἐρώτων [

fr. 1 tent. ed. pr. (Haslam)　　　3 παρθ]ενίης, ξ]ενίης, π]ενίης al.
5 tent. ed. pr.　　　　fr. 2 1 vel ἰδ', i.e. εἰδ'　　fin. tent. ed. pr.
2 tent. ed. pr.　　　　4 vel]ηφην　　5 suppl. ed. pr.

931R P. Oxy. 3696

　2　ζ[
　　δεξιᾶι τω[

　　εἶπεν καλέ[
　5　'νῦν φαῖνε[
　　σῶμα δ' εὐειδ[ὲς　　　　　ἀσυ-
　　χαίοις μελέω[ν
　　ἄρθρο[ι]ς · ἐπὶ δ' [εὐξάμενος
　　εὐχὰν πόδας [κούφους νεῖμον.'
　10　ὤ]ιχετο καλλ[

(pap. vers.) 6]ε Κλειοῖ ·　　7]ν Πολυ[δ]εύκ[
8 βαρ]βαρικ[

344

ANONYMOUS FRAGMENTS

931Q Oxyrhynchus papyrus (3rd or 4th c. A.D.)

(fr. 1) ... (Europa?) ... (dear beast!) ... (of) (virginity?) excellence ... (other?) ... (and not) foul-smelling ... (fr. 2)[1] ... see![2] from the ambrosial body ... he comes to the rites with ... heart, raising dust from (the ground?) ... to roll the eyes[3] ... afar the charm of the Loves ...

[1] The gap between the frr. may be small.   [2] Or 'saw'.
[3] Or 'with the eyes, to toss (on the sea)'.

931R Oxyrhynchus papyrus (3rd–4th c. A.D.)

... (by) the right hand (of Zeus?) ... (he/she) spoke[1] (calling?)[2] ... 'Now reveal[3] ..., and handsome body ... (leisured?) joints of limbs; and (having made your) prayer (ply nimble) feet.' He had gone ... beauty ...[4]

(on the other side of the papyrus) ... Clio! ... Polydeuces ... barbaric ...

[1] Beginning of new triad.   [2] Or 'beautiful'.   [3] Or 'Now seems'.   [4] Perhaps by Stesichorus or Ibycus (Haslam).

4 vel καλο[5 vel φαίνε[ται   6 suppl. ed. pr. (Haslam)
6s. vel 'A-, ἀρ-   8, 9 tent. Parsons   10 suppl. ed. pr.

931S P. Oxy. 3697

1]υ βιο[2]ν γε γεννα[3]ἀρχαγέτα[ι
4]αν θεμίξ[εν-   5 ο]ὖ μέμαλεν[6 ΄]ϲοντ᾽
αμμ[7]ν οὐδ᾽ ὅϲ᾽ Ἡρα[κλ

1 vel Ταλθ]υβιο[2 κεῖνό]ν , τῶ]ν vel sim.   3, 4, 5 tent.
ed. pr. (Haslam)   5 vel μέμαλε ν[7 vel οὐδ᾽ ὅς, οὐδὸς

931T P. Haun. I 7 col. ii

. . . τοὶ Ἀ[σκληπι]άδαι . . . [νῆ]ας . . . Φηρᾶθε . . .

932 *S.E.G.* xix 222 (p. 84)   *Ath. Mitt.* 67 (1942)
159s., n. 333, ed. W. Peek

```
              ]ισε[
   . . . . . . . ]δωταт[
   . . . . . . . ]νεοχμὰν κα[
   . . . . . . σ]τείβοισα πόδ[εσσι
5  . . . . . . ]α Καλλιόπας ανε[
   . . . . . . ]δια μελέτα πεδ᾽ ἀειτρ[
   . ]οινον ἔχοισα πόνον κάμνε[ι
   ἦτ]ορ ὅμως·
   οὔ]τι γὰρ εὐπαλές ἐστι· Δᾶτίς τ᾽ ἀγασ[
10 οἴ]δε παθὼν
   καὶ χώρα Ἀχαιμενιδᾶν μεγαλαύχων.
```

4 suppl. ed. pr. (qui πόδε[σσι legit)   5 ὅπ]α Καλλ. ed. pr.
6 μοιρι]δία ? Page   7 init. *S.E.G.*,]μνον vel]ηνον ed. pr., τερ]πνὸν ?
Page   8–10 suppl. ed. pr.

ANONYMOUS FRAGMENTS

931S Oxyrhynchus papyrus (2nd c. A.D.)

... life ... origin[1] ... leader[2] ... just to strangers[3] ... does (not) concern ... (nor all that Heracles?) ...

[1] Or 'offspring'. [2] Or 'founder'. [3] Epithet of Aegina in Pindar (*Pae.* 6. 131).

931T Copenhagen papyrus (1st c. A.D.)

... (from Tricce) the sons of Asclepius (forty) ships ... from Pherae (Eumelus eleven) ...[1]

[1] Poetic forms in a catalogue of Thessalian ships at Troy, based on *Iliad* 2. 695 ff. 'Perhaps Stesichorus?' (M. L. Haslam, *Ox. Pap.* LIII p. 31 n. 3).

932 Inscription from Rhamnus[1] (1st c. B.C. or 1st c. A.D.)

... new ... (she) treading with her feet ... (of) Calliope ... (Fate's?) providence with ever- ... enduring ... toil is distressed in her heart nevertheless; for it is no easy matter; ... Datis[2] knows it, having suffered, as does the land of the vainglorious Achaemenids.[3]

[1] In Attica, north of Marathon; famous for its temple of Nemesis, who brought about the Persian defeat at Marathon (Paus. 1. 33. 2). [2] Joint Persian commander at Marathon. [3] The royal family to which Darius belonged. The text ends here.

933 Inscr. Erythraea (Wilamowitz, *Nordionische Steine* pp. 40–41)

ὅσοι δὲ ἐγκατακοιμηθέντες θυσίην ἀποδιδῶσι τῶι Ἀσκληπιῶι καὶ τῶι Ἀπόλλωνι ἢ εὐξάμενοι θυσίην ἀποδιδῶσιν, ὅταν τὴν ἱρὴν μοῖραν ἐπιθῆι, παιωνίζειν πρῶτον περὶ τὸμ βωμὸν τοῦ Ἀπόλλωνος τόνδε τὸμ παιῶνα ἐστρίς·

ἰὴ Παιών, ὤ, ἰὴ Παιών (ter)
[ὦ] ἄναξ Ἄπολλον φείδεο κούρων
  φείδ[εο

(v. 7) χοροὶ ἰὴ   (v. 8) μάκαιρα   (v. 9) [Πα]ιὰν Ἀπόλ-
λω[ν]   (v. 10) [χ]ρυσηλακα[τ   (v. 11)]ᾶι θεᾶι, ἰὴ ἰὴ [
(v. 12)]ος εὐκάρπου τε [(v. 13)]οι δέ σε Ὧραι τε   (v.
14)] αὐτίκα χερ[σὶν (?)   (v. 15) ἰὴ ἰὴ Παιὼν   (v. 16)
]τειλας Ἀπολ[λ-   (v. 17) Δ]ελφοῖς   (v. 18) ἰὲ Παιάν

934 Inscr. Erythraea (Wilamowitz, *Nordionische Steine* pp. 42ss.)

[Παιᾶνα κλυτό]μητιν ἀείσατε
κοῦροι Λατοΐδαν Ἕκ]ατον,
      ἰὲ Παιάν,
ὃς μέγα χάρ[μα βροτοῖσ]ιν ἐγείνατο
5 μιχθεὶς ἐμ φι[λότητι Κορ]ωνίδι
ἐν γᾶι τᾶι Φλεγυείαι,
[ἰὴ Παι]άν, Ἀσκληπιὸν
δαίμονα κλεινό[τατ]ον,
      ἰὲ Παιάν·

10 [το]ῦ δὲ καὶ ἐξεγένοντο Μαχάων
καὶ Πο[δα]λείριος ἠδ' Ἰασώ,
      ἰὲ Παιάν,
Αἴγλα [τ'] εὐῶπις Πανάκειά τε

ANONYMOUS FRAGMENTS

933 Inscription from Erythrae (380–360 B.C.)[1]

If anyone after sleeping in the temple or making a vow is offering due sacrifice to Asclepius and Apollo, when he puts on the altar the sacred portion he must first sing this paean three times around Apollo's altar:

Ië Paeon, oh, ië Paeon![2] Lord Apollo, spare the youths, spare ... choruses ... ië! ... blessed (goddess)... Paean Apollo ... gold-distaffed ... goddess, ië ië! ... fruitful ... the Seasons ... you ... at once with hands ... ië ië Paeon! ... Apollo ... Delphi ... ië Paean!

[1] The paean of Erythrae (*P.M.G.* 934 below) follows on the stone.   [2] The refrain is sung three times.

934 Inscription from Erythrae (continued)[1]

Sing, youths, of Paean, skill-famed, Leto's son, Far-shooter[2] — ië Paean! — who fathered a great joy for mortals when he mingled in love with Coronis in the land of the Phlegyae[3] — ië Paean! —, Asclepius, the most famous god — ië Paean!

By him were fathered Machaon and Podalirius and Iaso (Healer) — ië Paean! — and fair-eyed Aegle (Radiance) and Panacea (Cure-all), children of

[1] Inscribed copies of the paean with some textual variation are known from Ptolemais in Egypt (97 A.D.), Dium in Macedonia (2nd c. A.D.) and Athens (2nd or 3rd c. A.D.).   [2] Apollo, father of Asclepius.   [3] Thessalian race; the texts from Ptolemais and Dium read 'Coronis, daughter of Phlegyas'.

1–13 suppl. cetera exemplaria (Ptolem., Di., Athen.)   6 ἐν γᾶι om. Ptolem., Di.   τῆ Φλεγύαο Di.

349

Ἠπιόνας παῖδες σὺν ἀγακλυτῶι
15 εὐαγεῖ Ὑγιείαι·
ἰὴ Παιάν, Ἀσκληπιὸν
δαίμονα κλεινότατον,
ἰὲ Παιάν.

χαῖρέ μοι, ἵλαος δ' ἐπινίσεο
20 τὰν ἀμὰν πόλιν εὐρύχορον,
ἰὲ Παιάν,
δὸς δ' ἡμᾶς χαίροντας ὁρᾶν φάος
ἀελίου δοκίμους σὺν ἀγακλυτῶι
εὐαγεῖ Ὑγιείαι·
25 ἰὴ Παιάν, Ἀσκληπιὸν
δαίμονα κλεινότατον,
ἰὲ Παιάν.

13 Αγλαια Erythr.: corr. Ptolem., Di.   23 δόκιμον Erythr.:
corr. Ptolem., Di., Athen.

935 *I.G.* iv² 131: v. P. Maas, *Epidaurische Hymnen*
134ss., M. L. West, *C.Q.* 20 (1970) 212ss.

Πιμπληϊάδε]ς θεαί,
δεῦρ' ἔλθετ' ἀπ' ὠρανῶ
καί μοι συναείσατε
τὰν Ματέρα τῶν θεῶν,

5 ὡς ἦλθε πλανωμένα
κατ' ὤρεα καὶ νάπας,
σύρουσα ῥυτὰ[ν] κόμαν
φρένας <τ' ἀλύουσα>.

Epione, along with Hygieia (Health), all-glorious,
undefiled; ië Paean! Asclepius, the most famous
god[4]—ië Paean!

Greetings I give you: graciously visit our wide-
spaced city—ië Paean!—and grant that we look on
the sun's light in joy, approved with the help of
Hygieia, all-glorious, undefiled; ië Paean!—
Asclepius, the most famous god[4]—ië Paean!

[4] The words here form part of the refrain.

935 Inscription from the shrine of Asclepius at Epi-
daurus[1] (3rd or 4th c. A.D.)

(Pimplean?) goddesses,[2] come here from heaven
and sing with me of the Mother of the gods, how she
went wandering through the mountains and glens,
trailing her flowing hair and (distraught) in her

[1] The stonecutter worked from a text that was gravely corrupt,
especially at vv. 7 f. and 12–20: drastic emendation is called for,
and West's version is given here. The poem may belong to the 3rd
c. B.C.   [2] The Muses.

1 suppl. Peek   7 ρπα[̣]ται[̣]κομαν leg. edd., suppl. et
interpr. West (ῥυτὰν [[τὰν]] κόμαν)   8 West: κατωρημεναφρενας
lapis (κατ' ὤρη et μενα de vv. 6, 5)

ὁ Ζεὺς δ' ἐσιδὼν ἄναξ

10 τὰν Ματέρα τῶν θεῶν

11 κεραυνὸν ἔβαλλε καὶ

13   πέτρας διέρησσε·

13a καὶ <Κύπρις ἔπειθε, καὶ>

14(=12) τὰ τύμπαν' ἐλάμβανε·

15 'Μάτηρ ἄπιθ' εἰς θεούς,

15a   <πατήρ σε καλεῖ Ζεύς·>

καὶ μὴ κατ' ὄρη πλαν[ῶ]·

μὴ σοὶ χαροποὶ λέον-

18 τες ἢ πολιοὶ λύκοι

18a   <φίλοι γεγόνασιν ;>'

ἡ δ' 'οὐκ ἀπ<ελεύσομαι>,

20 ἂν μὴ τὰ μέρη λάβω,

τὸ μὲν ἥμισυ ὠρανῶ,

τὸ δ' ἥμισυ γαίας,

πόντω τε τρίτον μέρος·

χοὔτως ἀπελεύσομαι.'

25 χαῖρ' ὦ μεγάλα ἄνασ-

σα Μᾶτερ Ὀλύμπω.

11ss. suppl. et corr. West   13 διερρησσε lapis   15a
West   17 West: μη σε lapis   18a West   19 West:
καὶ οὐκ ἄπειμι εἰς θεούς lapis (de v. 15)   21 ουρανω lapis
23 Latte: τὸ τρίτον lapis   26 ολυμπου lapis

mind.[3] When lord Zeus saw the Mother of the gods, he threw a thunderbolt and smashed the rocks; and (Cypris urged her) and took the tambourines: 'Mother, go off to the gods: (father Zeus summons you); and do not keep on wandering over the mountains; have fierce lions or grey wolves (become your friends)?' She replied, 'I shall not go off unless I get my portions, half of the heaven and half of the earth and a third portion, half of the sea: only then shall I go off.' Greetings, great Mother, queen of Olympus!

[3] The Mother is identified with Demeter, who wandered in search of her daughter Persephone: see *Hom. Hymn to Demeter* 301 ff., Eur. *Helen* 1301 ff.

936 *I.G.* iv² 130: v. P. Maas, *Epidaurische Hymnen* 130ss.

ΠΑΝΙ

Πᾶνα τὸν νυμφαγέταν
Ναΐδων μέλημ᾿ ἀείδω,
χρυσέων χορῶν ἄγαλμα,
κωτίλας ἄνακτ[α μ]οίσα<ς>,
5   εὐθρόου σύριγγος εὖ[τ᾿ ἀν]
ἔνθεον σειρῆνα χεύηι,
ἐς μέλος δὲ κοῦφα βαίνων
εὐσκίων πηδᾶι κατ᾿ ἄντρων
παμφυὲς νωμῶν δέμας,
10 εὐχόρευτος εὐπρόσωπος
ἐμπρέπων ξανθῶι γενείωι.
ἐς δ᾿ Ὄλυμπον ἀστερωπὸν
ἔρχεται πανωιδὸς ἀχὼ
θεῶν Ὀλυμπίων ὅμιλον
15 ἀμβρόται ῥαίνοισα μοίσαι.
χθὼν δὲ πᾶσα καὶ θάλασσα
κίρναται τεὰν χάριν· σὺ
    γὰρ πέλεις ἔρεισμα πάντων,
ὦ ἰὴ Πὰν Πάν.

4 suppl. Hiller   5 εὖ[τ᾿ ἀν] tent. Page   6 χευη lapis
15 ραινοισαι lapis

ANONYMOUS FRAGMENTS

936 Inscription from the shrine of Asclepius at Epidaurus (3rd or 4th c. A.D.)

TO PAN[1]

I sing of Pan, Nymph-leader, darling of the Naiads, adornment of golden choruses, lord of winsome muse (when) he pours forth the god-inspired siren-song of the melodious syrinx, and stepping nimbly to the melody leaps down from shadowy caves, moving his all-shape[2] body, fine dancer, fine of face, conspicuous with blond beard. To star-eyed Olympus goes the all-tune sound, sprinkling the company of the Olympian gods with immortal muse. All the earth and sea are mixed[3] thanks to you, for you are the bulwark of all, oh ië Pan, Pan!

[1] Date uncertain, perhaps Hadrianic.   [2] The name Pan was often associated with *pas, pan*, 'all', four forms of which occur in the poem.   [3] I.e. created by the All-god? Translation insecure.

937 *I.G.* iv² 129: v. P. Maas, *Epidaurische Hymnen* 128ss.

π]υριμηλ[. . .]α
]ον Διὸς μεγίστου
]ινον Βρόμιόν τε χορευτάν
]εύιον
5 ἠδ᾽ Ἀσκλαπιὸν ὑψιτέχναν·
δισσ]ούς τε καλεῖτε Διοσκούρους
σεμνάς τε [Χάρ]ιτας εὐκλεεῖς τε Μοίσας
εὐμενεῖς τε Μοίρας
Ἥλιόν τ᾽ ἀκάμαντα Σελήνην τε πλήθουσαν,
10 ἐν δὲ τὰ τείρεα πάντα τά τ᾽ οὐρανὸς ἐστεφάνωται.
χαίρετε ἀθάνατοι πάντες θεοὶ αἰὲν ἐόντες
ἀθάναταί τε θεαὶ καὶ σώιζετε τόνδ᾽ Ἐπιδαύρου
ναὸν ἐν εὐνομίαι πολυάνορι Ἑλλάνων,
ἱεροκαλλίνικοι
15 εὐμενεῖ σὺν ὄλβωι.

6 suppl. Wilamowitz   7 suppl. Hiller

938 (a) Vas. Compiègne 1106: v. J. D. Beazley, *A.J.A.* 45 (1941) 593s.

κάλει μ᾽ ὅπως πίεσθε

(b) Vas. Boston 10. 193: v. J. D. Beazley, *A.J.A.* 31 (1927) 348s., 33 (1929) 364, P. Kretschmer, *Gr. Vaseninschr.* 64 (p. 90)

ὀρτὴν ἐ]ς πανιωνίην

suppl. Beazley

937 Inscription from the shrine of Asclepius at Epidaurus[1] (3rd or 4th c. A.D.)

... fire ... (of) greatest Zeus ... and Bromius the dancer, Euius[2] ... and high-skilled Asclepius; and summon the two Dioscuri and the august Graces and glorious Muses and kindly Fates and the unwearied Sun and the Moon at her full and all the signs with which heaven is crowned.[3] Greetings, all you immortal gods everlasting and immortal goddesses! Preserve this temple of Epidaurus in orderliness as it is thronged by the Greeks, you happy victors, bringing with you kindly prosperity.

[1] Date uncertain; Page suggested 3rd or 2nd B.C. Many lines, in which the major deities were listed, seem to be missing at the beginning of the fragment.   [2] Dionysus.   [3] The two lines are clumsily taken over from Homer's description of Achilles' shield (*Il.* 18. 484 f.).

938 *Vase inscriptions in lyric metre*

(a) On a red-figured cup[1] from the period of Anacreon

Call me that you may drink.

[1] The cup depicts a youth garlanded with ivy and carrying a wine-jar; Beazley refers to the ice-cream vendor's 'Stop me and buy one!' 'Call' is sing., 'you' pl.

(b) On a red-figured bowl[1] (*c.* 500 B.C.)

To the pan-Ionian (festival)

[1] The words come from the mouth of a bald lyre-player.

GREEK LYRIC

(c) Vas. Naucrat.: v. C. C. Edgar, *B.S.A.* 5 (1898/9) 64s., H. L. Lorimer, *J.H.S.* 25 (1905) 120

$$\sigma\tau\eta\sigma\acute{\iota}\chi o\rho o\nu\ \H{\upsilon}\mu\nu o\nu\ \H{\alpha}\gamma o\iota\sigma\alpha\iota$$

fort. -χόρων ὕμνων (Page)

(d) Vas. Nat. Mus. Athens 1260: v. J. D. Beazley, *Greek Vases in Poland* 8ss.

$$\mathring{\eta}\epsilon\rho\acute{\iota}\omega\nu\ \mathring{\epsilon}\pi\acute{\epsilon}\omega\nu\ \H{\alpha}\rho\chi o\mu\alpha\iota\ \alpha\tau\ .\ .\ \tau\ .\ \nu$$

---

[1] Illustrated in G. M. A. Richter, *Portraits of the Greeks* i fig. 262, E. G. Turner, *Athenian Books in the Fifth and Fourth Centuries* B.C., frontispiece. Sappho is shown reading from a roll which after the word θεοί, 'gods', has this text and in the margins πτεροετα (sic) and επεα, 'winged words'. J. M. Edmonds, *C.Q.* 16 (1922) 1–14, argued that the text was the opening of Sappho's introductory poem in her own collection of her works, 'Winged Words' being its title, but he convinced no one.   [2] Lofty? Early?

(e) Vas. Berlin, Staatliche Museen 2285: v. P. Kretschmer, *Gr. Vaseninschr.* 87 (p. 104s.)

$$\text{Μο}\hat{\iota}\sigma\acute{\alpha}\ \mu o\iota\ \mathring{\alpha}\mu\phi\grave{\iota}\ \Sigma\kappa\acute{\alpha}\mu\alpha\nu\delta\rho o\nu\ \mathring{\epsilon}\acute{\upsilon}\rho\rho o o\nu\ \H{\alpha}\rho\chi o\mu'\ \mathring{\alpha}\epsilon\acute{\iota}\delta\epsilon\iota\nu.$$

vas. μοισαμοι | αφισκαμανδρον | ευρωναρχομαι | αεινδεν

(f) Vas. *Mon. dell' Instituto* 2 tab. 44g

(i) $\hat{\omega}\ \text{Ζε}\hat{\upsilon}\ \pi\acute{\alpha}\tau\epsilon\rho,\ \alpha\H{\iota}\theta\epsilon\ \pi\lambda o\acute{\upsilon}\sigma\iota o\varsigma\ \gamma\epsilon\nu[o\acute{\iota}\mu\alpha\nu.$

(ii) $\H{\eta}\delta\eta\ \mu\grave{\epsilon}\nu\ \H{\eta}\delta\eta\ \pi\lambda\acute{\epsilon} o\nu,\ \pi\alpha\rho\alpha\beta\acute{\epsilon}\beta\alpha\kappa\epsilon\nu\ \H{\eta}\delta\eta$

(g) Vas. Hartwig, *Meisterschalen* 257 Anm.

$$\epsilon\H{\iota}\mu\iota\ \kappa\omega[\mu\acute{\alpha}]\zeta\omega\nu\ \mathring{\upsilon}\pi'\ \alpha\mathring{\upsilon}[\lambda\hat{\omega}\nu$$

ANONYMOUS FRAGMENTS

(c) On a red-figured kylix[1] (by Duris, i.e. *c.* 500–460 B.C.?)

> Bringing[2] a chorus-establishing hymn

[1] The cup shows a school scene in which a boy is copying the text; see *J.H.S.* 25 (1905) pl. VI 5.   [2] Fem.: addressed to the Muses or a female chorus.

(d) On a red-figured Attic hydria[1] (440–430 B.C.)

> Airy[2] words I begin . . .

(e) On a red-figured cup[1] by Duris (*c.* 480 B.C.)

> Muse, I begin to sing for myself of fine-flowing Scamander.

[1] A school scene in which a teacher holds open a roll for a pupil; illustrated in J. Boardman, *Athenian Red Figure Vases: The Archaic Period* no. 289, W. Schubart, *Das Buch bei den Griechen und Römern* 137.

(f) On a black-figured pelike (*c.* 510–500 B.C.)[1]

> (i) Oh father Zeus, if only I could become wealthy!

> (ii) More now, more now; it's gone beyond now!

[1] The vase-painting represents a man selling oil to another: on one side he prays for a successful deal (i), on the other he protests that he has given good measure and more (ii); see C. Robert, *Bild und Lied* 81 ff. (with drawings of the scenes).

(g) On a red-figured bowl (early 5th c. B.C.?)

> I shall go revelling to the accompaniment of the pipes.

939 Aelian. *N.A.* 12.45 (iii 70ss. Scholfield): v. M. L. West, *Z.P.E.* 45 (1982) 5ss.

τὸ τῶν δελφίνων φῦλον ὥς εἰσι φιλῳδοί τε καὶ φίλαυλοι τεκμηριῶσαι ἱκανὸς καὶ Ἀρίων ὁ Μηθυμναῖος ἔκ τε τοῦ ἀγάλματος τοῦ ἐπὶ Ταινάρῳ καὶ τοῦ ἐπ᾽ αὐτῷ γραφέντος ἐπιγράμματος (*F.G.E.* anon. CLXXVII, p. 499). ἔστι δὲ τὸ ἐπίγραμμα·

    ἀθανάτων πομπαῖσιν Ἀρίονα Κυκλέος υἱὸν
      ἐκ Σικελοῦ πελάγους σῶσεν ὄχημα τόδε.

ὕμνον δὲ χαριστήριον τῷ Ποσειδῶνι μάρτυρα τῆς τῶν δελφίνων φιλομουσίας οἱονεὶ καὶ τούτοις ζωάγρια ἐκτίνων ὁ Ἀρίων ἔγραψε. καὶ ἔστιν ὁ ὕμνος οὗτος·

    ὕψιστε θεῶν
    πόντιε χρυσοτρίαινε Πόσειδον
    γαιάοχ᾽ ἐγκύμον᾽ ἀν᾽ ἅλμαν·
    βραγχίοις δὲ περί σε πλωτοὶ
5 θῆρες χορεύουσι κύκλῳ
    κούφοισι ποδῶν ῥίμμασιν
    ἐλάφρ᾽ ἀναπαλλόμενοι, σιμοὶ
    φριξαύχενες ὠκύδρομοι σκύλακες, φιλόμουσοι
    δελφῖνες, ἔναλα θρέμματα
10 κουρᾶν Νηρεΐδων θεᾶν,
    οὓς ἐγείνατ᾽ Ἀμφιτρίτα·
    οἵ μ᾽ εἰς Πέλοπος γᾶν
    ἐπὶ Ταιναρίαν ἀκτὰν ἐπορεύσατε
    πλαζόμενον Σικελῷ ἐνὶ πόντῳ,

cf. schol. Tzetz. *Chil.* 1. 393 (p. 549s. Leone) (vv. 1–7 ἀναπ.)

2 -τρίαινα ci. Hermann   3 Bergk: γαιή- codd.   Hermann: ἐγκυμονάλμαν Ael. cod. a, ἔγκυμον ἄλμαν g, κυμόναρχα b, κυμοναλ Vat., ἐγκύμον (vel -ου) ἅλμας schol. Tzetz., ἐ<χων πολυ>κύμον᾽ ἅλμαν tent. West   4 Hermann: βράγχιοι, -ιε Ael., βράγχιοι,

ANONYMOUS FRAGMENTS

939 Aelian, *On the Nature of Animals*

Dolphins love song and pipe-music: adequate testimony is provided by Arion of Methymna both in the statue at Taenarum[1] and in the epigram inscribed on it, which runs as follows: 'At the sending of the immortals this mount[2] saved Arion, son of Cycleus, from the Sicilian sea.' A hymn of thanksgiving to Poseidon, which testifies to the dolphins' love of music, was composed by Arion,[3] payment to the creatures, as it were, for saving his life. This is the hymn:

Highest of gods, gold-tridented Poseidon of the sea, earth-shaker amid the teeming brine, with their fins[4] swimming beasts dance round you in a ring, bounding lightly with nimble flingings of their feet, snub-nosed bristle-necked swift-racing pups, the music-loving dolphins, sea nurslings of the young goddesses the Nereids, whom[5] Amphitrite bore: you brought me to the cape of Taenarum in Pelops' land when I drifted in the Sicilian sea, carry-

---

[1] See Hdt. 1. 24 = Arion test. 3 with n. 7.   [2] The statue represented a man on a dolphin.   [3] The poem is in the dithyrambic manner of *c.* 400 B.C.   [4] Text uncertain; the noun should mean 'gills'. West suggests 'bright-gilled'.   [5] I.e. the dolphins, not the Nereids: see West.

-ια schol. Tzetz., <λιπαρο>βράγχιοι tent. West   περὶ δέ σε codd., transp. Page   5 ἐν κύκλῳ Ael. codd. M a c   6 ῥιπάσμασιν, ῥιάσμμασιν schol. Tzetz. codd.   7 σιμοὶ Ael. codd. b Vat., σεισμοὶ rell.   10 νηρε- Ael. codd. ma, νηρη- rell.   11 West: ᾶς codd.   13 ἐπορεύσατο Ael. codd. b Vat., ἐπόρευσαν ci. Brunck   14 Σικ. ἐνὶ π. post Ἀμφιτρίτα transp. West

15 κυρτοῖσι νώτοις φορεῦντες,
    ἅλοκα Νηρεΐας πλακὸς
    τέμνοντες, ἀστιβῆ πόρον,
    φῶτες δόλιοί μ᾽ ὡς ἀφ᾽ ἁλιπλόου γλαφυρᾶς νεὼς
    εἰς οἶδμ᾽ ἁλιπόρφυρον λίμνας ἔριψαν.

15 φορ. Page, χορεύοντες codd., del. West   18 Page: ὥς με
codd.   19 Hermann: ῥίψαν codd.

[**940** = *T.G.F.* adesp. F 13a (ii 24)   Aelian. *N.A.* 14.
14 (iii 156 Scholfield)

   ἥ γε μὴν καλουμένη ⟦καὶ: secl. Reiske⟧ ὑπὸ τῶν ποιητῶν

                        κεμὰς

δραμεῖν μὲν

              ὠκίστη, θυέλλης δίκην,

ἰδεῖν δὲ ἄρα πυρρόθριξ καὶ λασιωτάτη . . .

μὲν om. codd. pars]

941 = Terpander 4   *Anal. Gramm.* (6. 6 Keil)

   σπονδεῖος δ᾽ ἐκλήθη ἀπὸ τοῦ ῥυθμοῦ τοῦ ἐν ταῖς σπονδαῖς ἐπαυ-
λουμένου τε καὶ ἐπᾳδομένου, οἷον

    σπένδωμεν ταῖς Μνάμας παισὶν Μούσαις
    καὶ τῷ Μουσάρχῳ ⟨τῷ⟩ Λατοῦς υἱεῖ.

1 Keil: μνάμας codd.   1, 2 Μωσ- Bergk   2 ⟨τῷ⟩ add. Page
Λατῶς Bergk

362

ing me on your humped backs, cleaving the furrows of Nereus' plain, a path untrodden, when treacherous men had thrown me from the sea-sailing hollow ship into the sea-purple swell of the ocean.[6]

[6] For the story see Hdt. loc. cit.

[940 Aelian, *On the Nature of Animals*

The animal called *kemas,*

pricket,

by the poets is a runner

most swift, like a hurricane[1];

in appearance it is red-haired and very shaggy . . .

[1] G. F. Brussich, *Q.U.C.C.* 22 (1976) 135 ff., argues convincingly that *kemas,* which is found in Homer and later epic, is the only poetic word in the passage, the rest being Aelian's prose.]

941 = Terpander 4   *Grammatical Extracts*

The spondee (– –) was named after the rhythm played on pipes and sung at σπονδαί, 'libations', e.g.

Let us pour libation to the Muses, the daughters of Memory, and to the leader of the Muses, Leto's son.[1]

[1] Apollo. Bergk ascribed the lines to Terpander; see A. Gostoli, *Terpander* 55, 148 ff.

942 *Epim. Hom.* (*Anecd. Oxon.* i 171s. Cramer) (cf. Hdn. ii 261, n. ad fr. 266 Lentz)

σεσημείωται τὸ Πολύμνια ἐπὶ τούτου, καὶ τὸ κύριον καὶ τὸ προσηγορικὸν ἐξέθλιψε τὸ υ·

Πολύμνια παντερπὴς κόρα,

Πολύμνιά τ᾽ Οὐρανίη τε (Hes. *Theog.* 78).

943 = 1028 *Suppl. Hell.*   *Epim. Hom.* (*Anecd. Oxon.* i 413 Cramer) (cf. Hdn. i 180 Lentz)

ἀπὸ δὲ τῶν εἰς ην οὐ γίνεται συγκριτικόν· ἔνθεν σημειοῦνται τὸ

ναρκίσσου τερενώτερον

καὶ λέγουσιν ὅτι ἀπὸ τῆς τέρενος εὐθεῖα γίνεται ὁ τέρενος· ἐκ τούτου τὸ τερενώτερος.

944 Ap. Dysc. *Pron.* 58a (i 46 Schneider)

καὶ ἔτι τὸ

μήτ᾽ ἐμωῦτᾶς
μήτε κασιγνήτων πόδας ὠκέας
τρύσῃς

διέσταλκεν δυσὶ περισπωμέναις· ἠδυνάτει γὰρ συντεθῆναι διὰ τὸ ἐπιφερόμενον ῥῆμα.

1 Page: μητεμ᾽ῶυτας cod.   2 π. ὠκ. <ἵππως> Bergk

ANONYMOUS FRAGMENTS

942 *Homeric Parsings*

The word Polymnia is noted as exceptional since both the proper name and the adjective drop the v,[1] as in

> Polymnia, all-delightful maiden,[2]

and 'both Polymnia and Urania' (Hes. *Theog.* 78).

[1] I.e. the Muse's name is shortened from Poly-(h)ymnia, 'she of the many hymns'.　　[2] Blass for no good reason ascribed the words to Alcman.

943 = 1028 *Suppl. Hell.*　　*Homeric Parsings*

Words ending in -ην have no comparative form. That is why they note τερενώτερος (from τέρην, 'soft') as exceptional,

> softer than the narcissus,

saying that from the genitive τέρενος is formed a nominative τέρενος, and that the comparative τερενώτερος comes from it.

944 Apollonius Dyscolus, *Pronouns*

Moreover the composer of the lines

> Do not weary the swift feet of myself[1] nor of my brothers

has shown that the words (ἐμῶ αὐτᾶς) are separate by means of two circumflex accents (ἐμωῦτᾶς), since they could not be made one word (as the reflexive ἐμαυτᾶς) because of what follows.

[1] Feminine. Bergk emended the text to read 'the swift-footed horses'.

GREEK LYRIC

945 Ap. Dysc. *Adv.* 563 (i 153 Schneider) (=*Anecd. Gr.* ii 563 Bekker)

βαρύνεται καὶ ὅσα ἐκ μεταλήψεώς ἐστι τῶν εἰς θεν, ὅπερ ἐστὶ παρ' Αἰολεῦσι καὶ Δωριεῦσι . . . · ὄπισθεν ὄπισθα,

> ὁ δ' ἐξύπισθα καστάθεις

Ahrens: ὁ . . . -σταθείς cod.

945A Ap. Dysc. *Conj.* (i 1. 251 Schneider)

ὁ περ ἐναντιωματικός ἐστι μετ' αὐξήσεως . . . ·

> σώφρων περ ὤν ·

τὸ γὰρ ἐναντίον τῷ

> τοῦτό γε μοι χάρισαι

ἀπειργάσατο.

v. Wilamowitz, *Hermes* 37 (1902) 324 = *Kl. Schr.* iv 160

946 Apollon. Tyan. *Ep.* 73 (p. 76ss. Penella)

τῷ αὐτῷ (viz. Ἑστιαίῳ). πατρίδος ἐσμὲν πορρωτέρω σὺν δαίμονι, ἤδη δὲ τὰ τῆς πόλεως πράγματα ἐν νῷ ἐβαλόμην ·

> ὁδεύει
> Μοῖρα πρὸς τέλος ἀνδρῶν
> οἵ <τε> τὰν πρώταν λελόγχασι τιμάν.

ἄρξει δὲ τὸ λοιπὸν παιδάρια . . .

3 suppl. Bergk

ANONYMOUS FRAGMENTS

945 Apollonius Dyscolus, *Adverbs*

The grave accent is found also in adverbs which are altered in dialect from adverbs in -θεν, as in Aeolic and Doric ..., e.g. ὄπισθα[1] for ὄπισθεν:

> and he, standing behind ...

[1] Not ὀπισθά. The dialect of the fragment is Aeolic.

945A Apollonius Dyscolus, *On conjunctions*

The particle περ ('though') marks opposition along with amplification ...:

> Although you are chaste, grant me this.[1]

'Although you are chaste' has created the opposition to 'grant me this.'

[1] Wilamowitz thought that the words, addressed to a boy, might be from an epode of Anacreon or Archilochus.

946 Apollonius of Tyana, *Letter* (to his brother Hestiaeus)

By god's will I am a long way from my native land, but just now I thought of the city's affairs:

> Fate travels towards the life's end of the men who have obtained the highest office.

In the future boys will govern ...

947 Ael. Aristid. *Or.* 28. 66s. (ii 163 Keil)

ὥστε ὥρα σοι σκώπτειν αὐτοὺς ὡς ἀδολέσχας τινάς νεκροὺς καὶ οὐκ εἰδότας ἡσυχίαν ἄγειν· κᾷτά σε ἀνήρ τις Σιμωνίδειος ἀμείψεται· ὤνθρωπε, κεῖσαι ζῶν ἔτι μᾶλλον τῶν ὑπὸ γῆς ἐκείνων. φέρε δὴ καὶ ταῦτα ἐξέτασον·

(a) ἁ Μοῦσα γὰρ οὐκ ἀπόρως γεύει τὸ παρὸν μόνον
ἀλλ᾽ ἐπέρχεται πάντα θεριζομένα.

ταῦτ᾽ οὐ δοκεῖ σοι σαφῶς ὁ ποιητὴς ἑαυτὸν ἐπαινῶν λέγειν ὡς γόνιμον καὶ πόριμον εἰς τὰ μέλη; τί δ᾽ ἐπειδὰν λέγῃ·

(b) μή μοι καταπαυέτ᾽ ἐπεί περ ἤρξατο
τερπνοτάτων μελέων ὁ καλλιβόας πολύχορδος
αὐλός;

948 : v. vol. iii p. 328s. (Cydias)

949 Aristot. *Eth. Nic.* 7. 7. 3, 1149b 15 (p. 141 Bywater)

ἡ δ᾽ ἐπιθυμία (sc. ἐπίβουλος) καθάπερ τὴν Ἀφροδίτην φασίν·

δολοπλόκου γὰρ Κυπρογενοῦς

-γενέος <πρόπολον> Bergk ex Hsch. K 4654

ANONYMOUS FRAGMENTS

947 Aelius Aristides, *Orations*

So this is the moment for you to jeer at them[1] as prating corpses who do not know how to keep quiet; and then some Simonidean fellow will respond: 'My good man, you may be alive, but you lie dead even more than those men under the earth.' Or take a close look at this:

(a) For the Muse does not helplessly taste only what is to hand but goes forward harvesting all things.[2]

Don't you think that the poet clearly says this in praise of himself as being productive and resourceful in his songs? Similarly when he adds

(b) Do not check it, I beg you, now that the fine-shouting many-stringed[3] pipe has begun its delightful songs.

[1] The 'speakers' in epitaphs, e.g. 'We lie dead . . .'. [2] Ascribed to Stesichorus or, with more probability, to Simonides. [3] I.e. with wide range.

948: see vol. iii p. 328 f. (Cydias)

949 Aristotle, *Nicomachean Ethics*

But desire is crafty, as they say of Aphrodite:

for (of) the wile-weaving Cyprus-born[1]

[1] Cf. Sapph. 1. 2, Theogn. 1386. Bergk used an entry in Hesychius to expand the fragment: 'for the servant of the wile-weaving Cyprus-born' (i.e. Persuasion); Wilamowitz regarded 964(a) as the beginning of the poem, which he ascribed to Sappho. See D. Page, *S. & A.* 6.

GREEK LYRIC

950 Aristot. *Rhet.* 3. 8, 1409a 12 (p. 194s. Römer, p. 158 Ross)

ἐστὶν δὲ παιᾶνος δύο εἴδη ἀντικείμενα ἀλλήλοις, ὧν τὸ μὲν ἓν ἀρχῇ ἁρμόττει, ὥσπερ καὶ χρῶνται· οὗτος δ᾽ ἐστὶν οὗ ἄρχει μὲν ἡ μακρά, τελευτῶσι δὲ τρεῖς βραχεῖαι·

(a) Δαλογενὲς εἴτε Λυκίαν

καὶ

(b) χρυσεοκόμα Ἕκατε παῖ Διός·

ἕτερος δ᾽ ἐξ ἐναντίας, οὗ βραχεῖαι ἄρχουσι τρεῖς, ἡ δὲ μακρὰ τελευταία·

(c) μετὰ δὲ γᾶν ὕδατά τ᾽ ὠκεανοῦ ἠφάνισε νύξ·

οὗτος δὲ τελευτὴν ποιεῖ, ἡ γὰρ βραχεῖα διὰ τὸ ἀτελὲς εἶναι ποιεῖ κολοβόν.

cf. schol. ad loc. (*Anecd. Par.* i 308 Cramer)

(a) ἦτε codd. ΘΔΕ, schol.   Λ. <ἔχεις> Bergk   (b) -κόμας
ci. Bergk   (c) Bergk: ὠκεανὸν codd.

951 Aristot. *Rhet.* 3. 11, 1412b 34 (p. 209 Roemer, p. 170 Ross)

εἰσὶν δὲ καὶ αἱ εἰκόνες, ὥσπερ εἴρηται καὶ ἐν τοῖς ἄνω, αἱ εὐδοκιμοῦσαι τρόπον τινὰ μεταφοραί· ἀεὶ γὰρ ἐκ δυοῖν λέγονται, ὥσπερ ἡ ἀνάλογον μεταφορά, οἷον ἡ ἀσπίς, φαμέν, ἐστὶ φιάλη Ἄρεως, καὶ τόξον

φόρμιγξ ἄχορδος

cf. Demetr. *Eloc.* 85 (p. 23 Radermacher)

ANONYMOUS FRAGMENTS

950 Aristotle, *Rhetoric*

There are two kinds of paeon, one the opposite of the other. The first is suitable for a beginning, and that is how they use it: it begins with the long syllable and ends with three short:

(a) Delos-born! whether (you dwell in?) Lycia . . .

and

(b) Gold-haired Far-Shooter, son of Zeus![1]

The second is the opposite: it begins with three shorts, and the long syllable comes last:

(c) and thereafter night made the land and the waters of the ocean invisible.

This one creates an ending; for the short syllable,[2] being incomplete, provides a curtailed effect.

[1] The opening words of hymns to Apollo.   [2] At the end of the first paeon.

951 Aristotle, *Rhetoric*

As I said above, the comparisons[1] that are highly regarded are also in a certain sense metaphors, since they are always expressed in two terms like the analogical metaphor; for example, we say that the shield is the cup of Ares,[2] and a bow is the

stringless lyre.[3]

[1] *eikones*, often 'similes'; see M. H. McCall, Jr., *Ancient Rhetorical Theories of Simile and Comparison*, esp. p. 42 ff., 145 f.   [2] Cf. Timotheus 797.   [3] Different nouns were used for bowstring (νευρά) and lyrestring (χορδή). Demetrius, *On Style* 85, says the risky metaphor is made safe by the addition of the adjective 'stringless', attributing the phrase to Theognis, presumably the tragic poet of that name (*T.Gr.F.* i 28 F1).

GREEK LYRIC

952 Athen. 11. 781c (iii 16 Kaibel)

αὐτός γε μὴν ὁ Ζεὺς τῆς Ἡρακλέους γενέσεως ἄξιον ἡγεῖται δῶρον Ἀλκμήνῃ δοθῆναι ποτήριον, ὅπερ Ἀμφιτρύωνι εἰκασθεὶς δίδωσιν·

ἁ δ' ὑποδεξαμένα θαήσατο χρύσεον αἶψα ποτήριον.

cf. 11. 474f (iii 43 K.) (καρχήσιον), Paus. 5. 18. 3

ποτήριον del. Kaibel

953 Athen. 13. 599cd (iii 321 Kaibel)

Χαμαιλέων δ' ἐν τῷ περὶ Σαπφοῦς (fr. 26 Wehrli) καὶ λέγειν τινάς φησιν εἰς αὐτὴν πεποιῆσθαι ὑπὸ Ἀνακρέοντος τάδε (fr. 358) . . . καὶ τὴν Σαπφὼ δὲ πρὸς αὐτὸν ταῦτά φησιν εἰπεῖν·

κεῖνον, ὦ χρυσόθρονε Μοῦσ', ἔνισπες
ὕμνον, ἐκ τᾶς καλλιγύναικος ἐσθλᾶς
Τήιος χώρας ὃν ἄειδε τερπνῶς
πρέσβυς ἀγαυός.

ὅτι δὲ οὐκ ἔστι Σαπφοῦς τοῦτο τὸ ᾆσμα παντί που δῆλον.

372

ANONYMOUS FRAGMENTS

952 Athenaeus, *Scholars at Dinner*

In fact Zeus himself regards a cup as a worthy gift to Alcmena for giving birth to Heracles; he presents it disguised as Amphitryon,

and when she received the gold cup she immediately gazed at it in wonder.

953 Athenaeus, *Scholars at Dinner*

Chamaeleon in his treatise *On Sappho* actually declares that some say it was to her that the following verses were addressed by Anacreon (fr. 358) ... and that Sappho directed the following lines to him:

You uttered that hymn, oh golden-throned Muse, which from the fine land of fair women the glorious old Teian man delightfully sang.

But that this is no song of Sappho's must be obvious to everyone.[1]

[1] See Sappho test. 8.

GREEK LYRIC

954 Athen. 14. 633a (iii 396 Kaibel)

ὅθεν καὶ Πρατίνας φησί (fr. 709)· Λάκων ὁ τέττιξ εὔτυκος εἰς χορόν. διὸ καὶ οἱ ποιηταὶ διετέλουν προσαγορεύοντες οὕτως τὰς ᾠδάς·

(a) γλυκυτάτων πρύτανιν ὕμνων

καὶ

(b) μέλεα μελιπτέρωτα Μουσᾶν

(a) Casaubon: ὑμῶν cod. A   (b) Casaubon: μοῦσαν cod. A, Μωσᾶν Bergk   (καὶ μέλη· in comment.) μέλεα πτ. dub. Dindorf

955 Athen. 14. 636cd (iii 404s. Kaibel)

περὶ ὧν (sc. τῶν κρεμβάλων) φησι Δικαίαρχος ἐν τοῖς περὶ τοῦ τῆς Ἑλλάδος Βίου (fr. 60 Wehrli) ἐπιχωριάσαι φάσκων ποτὲ καθ' ὑπερβολὴν εἰς τὸ προσορχεῖσθαί τε καὶ προσάδειν ταῖς γυναιξὶν ὄργανά τινα ποιά, ὧν ὅτε τις ἅπτοιτο τοῖς δακτύλοις ποιεῖν λιγυρὸν ψόφον. δηλοῦσθαι δὲ ἐν τῷ τῆς Ἀρτέμιδος ᾄσματι οὗ ἐστιν ἀρχή·

Ἄρτεμι, σοί μέ τι φρὴν <ἐφίησιν> ἐφίμερον
    ὕμνον ὑφαινέμεναι·
  α<ἶρε> δέ τις καλὰ χρυσοφάεννα
  κρέμβαλα χαλκοπάραα χερσίν

1 <ἐφίησιν> ci. Wilamowitz   2 Bergk: ὕμνον νεναιτε ὅθεν cod. A
3 Page: αδε τις ἀλλὰ cod. A   Bergk: -φανια cod. A
4 Schweighäuser: -παραα cod. A

956 Bacchius, *Isagoga* (p. 316 Jan)

δέκατος δὲ ἐνόπλιος ἐξ ἰάμβου καὶ ἡγεμόνος καὶ χορείου καὶ ἰάμβου, οἷον

ὁ τὸν πίτυος στέφανον

374

954 Athenaeus, *Scholars at Dinner* (on the Spartan devotion to music)

That is why Pratinas says (fr. 709) 'the Spartan, that cicada apt for the choral song'. And so the poets continually described their songs in these terms:

(a) the lord of sweetest hymns

and

(b) honey-winged songs of the Muses.[1]

[1] Bergk tentatively ascribed the quotations to Alcman; so C. Calame, *Alcman* 635.

955 Athenaeus, *Scholars at Dinner*

Dicaearchus speaks of castanets in his work *On Greek Culture*, saying that they were a kind of instrument once extremely fashionable for women to sing and dance to: when touched by the fingers they produced a sharp sound. This, he says, is shown in the song to Artemis which begins,

Artemis! my heart (bids me weave?) a delightful hymn for you; and someone (take in your) hands the (beautiful?) gold-shining bronze-cheeked castanets.[1]

[1] Text extremely corrupt: translation insecure.

956 Bacchius, *Introduction to Music*

The tenth enoplius is made up of an iamb, a hegemon ($\cup\cup$), a choree ($-\cup$) and an iamb, e.g.

he who . . . the garland of pine

GREEK LYRIC

957 Choerob. in Heph. *De Synecph.* 2 (p. 209 Consbruch)

ὁ δ' Ἡλιόδωρός φησιν ἐν τῇ Εἰσαγωγῇ ὅτι καὶ τρεῖς εἰς μίαν συνεκφωνοῦνται συλλαβαί, ὡς τὸ διπενθημιμμερὲς τοῦτο [[οἱονεὶ]] τὸ δοκοῦν εἶναι ἐλεγεῖον·

Ἀστερίς, οὔτε σ' ἐγὼ φιλέω οὔτ' Ἀπελλῆς.

οὐ γάρ ἐστιν ἐλεγεῖον, ἀλλὰ τὸ πρῶτον αὐτοῦ μέρος ἐστὶ δακτυλικόν, τὸ δὲ δεύτερον ἰαμβικόν· δύο γὰρ ἰαμβικοὺς ἔχει πόδας καὶ συλλαβήν. τὸ οὖν φιλέω οὐ ἀπὸ βραχείας καὶ μιᾶς μακρᾶς.

958 Chrysipp. π. ἀποφατ. 24 (*S.V.F.* ii 58 Arnim)

εἰ ποιητής τις οὕτως ἀπεφαίνετο·

οὐκ εἶδον ἀνεμώκεα κόραν . . .

959 = Bacchyl. fr. 55 (dub.) (vol. iv p. 300)

960 Clem. Alex. *Strom.* 5. 4. 27. 5 (ii 343 Stählin-Früchtel)

ναὶ τὰν Ὄλυμπον καταδερκομέναν σκηπτοῦχον Ἥραν
ἐστί μοι πιστὸν ταμιεῖον ἐπὶ γλώσσας,

ἡ ποιητικὴ φησιν. ὅ τε Αἰσχύλος (fr. 316 Radt).

ANONYMOUS FRAGMENTS

957 Choeroboscus on Hephaestion, *On Synecphonesis*

Heliodorus says in his *Introduction* that as many as three syllables may be combined into one, as in this dipenthemimer[1] which looks like an elegiac:

Asteris, I do not love you, nor does Apelles either.[2]

It is no elegiac: the first part is dactylic, the second iambic, having two iambic feet plus one syllable; so φιλέω οὐ is made up of a short syllable (φι) and a single long syllable (λέω οὐ).

[1] A line consisting of two penthemimers, i.e. two units of two-and-a-half feet (here dactylic + iambic). [2] Plausibly ascribed to Anacreon by Bergk on metrical grounds (fr. 188 dub. Gentili); for the metre see Anacr. 391, 392, 393, 416, Alc. 383. The names Apelles and Asteris are tentatively identified in a commentary on Anacreon (P. Oxy. 3722: see frr. 6. 2, 28. 8, 82. 2; 30. 6).

958 Chrysippus, *Negatives*

If some poet declared[1]

I did not see the wind-swift maiden[2] . . .

[1] Part of a Stoic exercise in logic. [2] Iris? Atalanta? See G. F. Brussich, *Q.U.C.C.* 22 (1976) 139 ff.

959 = Bacchylides fr. 55 (dub.) (vol. iv p. 301)

960 Clement of Alexandria, *Miscellanies*

By sceptre-bearing Hera, who looks down upon Olympus, I have a secure treasure-house on my tongue,

as the poet puts it; and Aeschylus says (fr. 316 Radt).

961 Clem. Alex. *Strom.* 6. 14. 112. 2 (ii 488 Stählin-Früchtel)

. . . αἰχμάλωτοι γενέσθαι ἡδονῆς αἰσχυνόμενοι·

οὐ μή ποτε τὰν ἀρέταν ἀλλάξομαι ἀντ᾽ ἀδίκου κέρδους.

Bergk: μήν ποτ᾽ ἂν cod.   Sylburg: ἀλλάξωμαι cod.

961A Clem. Alex. *Paedag.* 2. 1. 3. 2 (i 155 Stählin) = *T.G.F.* adesp. 107b

ὅσα τε χθών
πόντου τε βένθη κἀέρος
ἀμέτρητον εὖρος ἐκτρέφει

962 Demetr. *Eloc.* 91 (p. 24 Radermacher)

ληπτέον δὲ καὶ σύνθετα ὀνόματα, οὐ τὰ διθυραμβικῶς συγκείμενα, οἷον

　(a) θεοτεράτους πλάνας

οὐδὲ

　(b) ἄστρων δορίπυρον στρατὸν

ἀλλ᾽ ἐοικότα τοῖς ὑπὸ τῆς συνηθείας συγκειμένοις.

(b) Lloyd-Jones: δορύ- cod.

963 Demetr. *Eloc.* 143 (p. 33 Radermacher)

γίγνονται δὲ καὶ ἀπὸ λέξεως χάριτες ἢ ἐκ μεταφορᾶς, ὡς ἐπὶ τοῦ τέττιγος (Alc. 347b), ἢ ἐκ συνθέτου του ὀνόματος καὶ διθυραμβικοῦ·

δέσποτα Πλούτων μελανοπτερύγων·

τουτὶ δεινὸν †προπτερύγων αὐτὸ ποίησον†, ἃ μάλιστα δὴ κωμῳδικὰ παίγνιά ἐστι καὶ σατυρικά (Gale: σατύρια cod.).

ANONYMOUS FRAGMENTS

961 Clement of Alexandria, *Miscellanies*

They are ashamed to be prisoners of pleasure:

Never shall I exchange virtue for unjust gain.

961A Clement of Alexandria, *Tutor*

All that is nourished by the earth and the depths of the sea and the measureless breadth of the air.

962 Demetrius, *On Style*

We should also use compound words; not compounds in the dithyrambic manner like

(a) god-portented wanderings

or

(b) the fire-speared host of the stars,

but compounds like those in everyday use.

963 Demetrius, *On Style*

Literary grace may be due to the choice of words or to metaphor, as in the lines on the cicada (Alc. 347b), or to a compound word of dithyrambic type:

Pluto, master of the black-winged[1] . . . !

. . . these are for the most part the jokes of comedy or satyr-plays.

[1] Dreams? Ghosts? Text corrupt.

Bergk: πλοῦτον cod.   post μελ. <ὀνείρων> Bergk, <ψυχῶν>
Page

964   (a) = Sapph. 168C (Voigt) (v. vol. i p. 172)
       (b) = Hom. *Od.* 19. 518

965 Dio Chrys. *Or.* 33. 59 (i 314 Arnim, i 400 de Budé)

καὶ μὴν οὐχ οὕτω δεινόν ἐστιν εἰ ἄνθρωποι μεταξὺ προβάτων
φωνὴν λάβοιεν οὐδ᾽ εἰ βοῶν οὐδ᾽ ἂν χρεματίζωσιν οὐδ᾽ ἂν ὑλακτῶ-
σιν, ὥσπερ τὴν Ἑκάβην οἱ ποιηταὶ λέγουσιν ἐπὶ πᾶσι τοῖς δεινοῖς
τελευταῖον ποιῆσαι τὰς Ἐρινύας

     χαροπὰν κύνα· χάλκεον δέ οἱ
  γνάθων ἐκ πολιᾶν
  φθεγγομένας ὑπάκουε μὲν Ἴ-
     δα Τένεδός τε περίρρυτα
5 Θρηίκιοί τε φιλήνεμοι πέτραι.

2 Geel: γναθμῶν codd.   3 Geel: ὑπακούεμεν codd.
5 Jacobs: φιλίην ἔμοιγε codd.

966 Diogen. 7. 82 (i 301 Leutsch-Schneidewin)

     πῦρ ἐπὶ δαλὸν ἐλθόν·

ἐπὶ τῶν ταχέως γινομένων· ἀπὸ τοῦ Κύκλωπος ἡ μεταφορά.

967 D. H. *Comp.* 25 (vi 130 Usener-Radermacher)

ὁρῶ δὴ τούτω μετὰ τὴν προσαγόρευσιν τῶν Ἀθηναίων εὐθέως
τὸν κρητικὸν ῥυθμόν, εἴτε ἄρα παιᾶνά τις αὐτὸν βούλεται καλεῖν,
διοίσει γὰρ οὐδέν, τὸν ἐκ πέντε συγκείμενον χρόνων οὐκ
αὐτοσχεδίως μὰ Δία ἀλλ᾽ ὡς οἷόν τε μάλιστα ἐπιτετηδευμένως δι᾽
ὅλου τοῦ κώλου πλεκόμενον τούτου· τοῖς θεοῖς εὔχομαι πᾶσι καὶ
πάσαις (Dem. *de Cor.* 1)· οὐ τοιοῦτος μέντοι κἀκεῖνός ἐστιν ὁ
ῥυθμός,

     Κρησίοις ἐν ῥυθμοῖς παῖδα μέλιψωμεν;

ἐμοὶ γοῦν δοκεῖ· ἔξω γὰρ τοῦ τελευταίου ποδὸς τά γε ἄλλα πανπά-
πασιν ἴσα.

380

964 (a) = Sappho 168C (Voigt) (vol. i p. 173)
(b) = Homer, *Od.* 19. 518

965 Dio Chrysostom, *Orations*

And indeed it is not such a terrible thing that men should for a while take on the voice of sheep or cattle or should neigh or bark: why, the poets say of Hecuba that to crown all her misfortunes the Furies made her

a flashing-eyed bitch; and from her grey jaws came a brazen cry that was heard by Ida and sea-girt Tenedos and the wind-loving Thracian rocks.

966 Diogenian, *Proverbs*

fire came to the fire-brand;

used of things that happen quickly. The metaphor is from the *Cyclops.*[1]

[1] Perhaps the *Cyclops* of Philoxenus: see *P.M.G.* 815 ff.

967 Dionysius of Halicarnassus, *On Literary Composition*

In this speech[1] too I notice that immediately after the address to the Athenians the cretic rhythm, or paeon if you wish to give it that name (it will make no difference), the rhythm consisting of five time-units, is interwoven not haphazardly but with the greatest possible care throughout the whole phrase: 'I pray to all the gods and all the goddesses.' The rhythm of the words[2] is the same, in my view at least, as in the following:

in Cretan rhythms let us sing of the child[3];

everything except the last foot[4] is exactly the same.

[1] Demosthenes, *On the Crown*; D. quotes from the opening sentence. [2] $- \cup - \mid - \cup - \mid - \cup - \mid - - .$ [3] Presumably the child Zeus, born on Crete. [4] $- \cup$ in the lyric fragment.

968 *Et. Gen.* (p. 20 Calame) + *Et. Mag.* 199.52 (cf. Hdn. ii 428. 32 Lentz)

βλείς· . . . ἢ ἀπὸ τοῦ βλῆμι· ὁ δεύτερος ἀόριστος ἔβλην, οἷον

πόθεν

δ' ἕλκος εὐπετὲς ἔβλης;

Ahrens· δὲ ὥλκος cod. A, δ' ἐωλκως B

969 *Et. Gen.* p. 21 Calame = *Et. Mag.* 230.58

ἐστὶ δὲ πρώτης καὶ δευτέρας συζυγίας τὸ γηρᾶς, ὥσπερ τὸ πιμπλᾶς, οἷον πιμπλῶ πιμπλᾶς καὶ πιμπλεῖς, οἷον

†τὰς Ῥαδάμανθυς πιμπλεῖν βίαν.†

τᾶς Ῥαδαμάνθυος ci. Edmonds

970 *Et. Gen.* p. 28 Calame (cf. *Et. Mag.* 417.15)

ἠβαιόν· . . . ἐξ οὗ καὶ τὸ βαιός κατὰ ἀποβολὴν τοῦ η· . . . οἱ δ' ἐλθόντες οὐδ' ἠβαιόν, καὶ

βαιῷ δ' ἐν αἰῶνι βροτῶν,

καὶ βαιὸν ἐπὶ ποταμοῦ.

971 = 1042 *Suppl. Hell.*

972 *Et. Gen.* p. 37 Calame = *Et. Mag.* 579.18

Μενέλας· οἷον

Μενέλας τε καὶ Ἀγαμέμνων.

ἀπὸ τοῦ Μενέλαος . . .

τε κ' Ἀγ. Bergk

ANONYMOUS FRAGMENTS

968 *Etymologicum Genuinum*

βλείς: (from βληθείς) or from βλῆμι, 'strike', 2nd aorist ἔβλην, as in

and whence were you struck with the fortunate wound[1]?

[1] Text and translation very insecure.

969 *Etymologicum Genuinum*

The verb γηρῶ (2nd sing. γηρᾷς), 'grow old', belongs to both the first and the second conjugation, like πιμπλῶ, 'fill', which has both πιμπλᾷς and πιμπλεῖς, as in

from which to fill the mighty Rhadamanthys.[1]

[1] Text and translation very uncertain.

970 *Etymologicum Genuinum*

ἠβαιόν, 'small': ... from it comes βαιός with the η dropped; ... cf. 'and they, coming not even a small distance'[1] and

within the small space of mortals' life

and 'a small way over the River'.[2]

[1] Cf. *Od.* 9. 462 'and they, coming a small distance'.   [2] Cf. Aratus 358.

971 = 1042 *Suppl. Hell.*

972 *Etymologicum Genuinum*

Menelas, as in

Menelas and Agamemnon;

from Menelaos ...

973 = 25B Inc. Auct. (Voigt): v. vol. i p. 452

974 Heph. *Ench.* 4. 4 (p. 14 Consbruch)

ὑπερκατάληκτα δὲ ὅσα πρὸς τῷ τελείῳ προσέλαβε μέρος ποδός, οἷον ἐπὶ ἰαμβικοῦ·

εἶμ' ὦτ' ἀπ' ὑσσάκω λυθεῖσα,

τοῦτο μὲν οὖν συλλαβῇ [[πλέονι]] περιττεύει.

cf. schol. A (p. 114 C.)

Bentley: ὦ ταπυσσάκω cod. A, ἆτ' ἀπυσσάλω I, ὦστ' ἀπισσάλω D, ὦστ' ἀπὸ πυσσάλω H   λυθεῖσα A, λυεῖσα cett.

975 Heph. *Ench.* 9. 1 (p. 29 Consbruch)

περαιοῦται μὲν γὰρ (sc. τὸ χοριαμβικὸν ὅτε καταληκτικόν ἐστιν) καὶ εἰς τὴν ἰδίαν (sc. κατάκλειδα), τὸν δάκτυλον ἢ κρητικόν, οἷον δίμετρον μὲν τὸ

(a) ἱστοπόνοι μείρακες

τρίμετρα δὲ

(b) οὐδὲ λεόντων σθένος οὐδὲ τροφαί

τετράμετρα δὲ

(c) αἲ Κυθερήας ἐπιπνεῖτ' ὄργια λευκωλένου

cf. schol. ad loc. (p. 137s. C.), epitom. Heph. (p. 360 C.), Mar. Plot. Sacerd. (vi 534 Keil), Rhet. Gr. vii 988 Walz

(c) αἱ A, ἐκ Rhet. Gr.   κυθερήας C, -ῆας AP, -είας DI Rhet. Gr. fort. ἐπίπνειτ', -ωλένω scribendum

976 = Sapph. 168B (Voigt): v. vol. i p. 170ss.

ANONYMOUS FRAGMENTS

973 = 25B (Voigt) ('Sappho or Alcaeus'): see vol. i p. 453

974 Hephaestion, *Handbook on Metres*[1]

Hypercatalectic lines are those which have added part of a foot to the complete metron, e.g. in iambic:

I shall go as if freed from the peg.[2]

This has an extra syllable.

[1] The passage follows Alcman 174.   [2] Like an untied animal? The speaker is female. Bergk attributed the words to Alcman (cf. Calame, *Alcman* p. 199).

975 Hephaestion, *Handbook on Metres*

The catalectic choriamb ends also in its own peculiar close with dactyl or cretic,[1] e.g. the dimeter

(a) loom-toiling maidens,

trimeters such as

(b) neither the strength nor the living of lions,

tetrameters such as

(c) you[2] who look on the rites of white-armed Cytherea.[3]

[1] (a) shows dactylic close, (b) and (c) cretic.   [2] Fem. pl.   [3] Aphrodite.

976 = Sappho 168B (Voigt): see vol. i p. 171 ff.

977 Hdn. π. παθ. fr. 341 (ii 281 Lentz) = Choerob. i 243 Hilgard

τὸ πός οἷον

ὡς πὸς ἔχει μαινομένοισι

ἀπὸ τοῦ πούς γέγονε κατὰ ἀποβολὴν τοῦ υ.

cf. Choerob. i 192 H., *Et. Mag.* 635. 22

πὸς χειμαιν- Choerob. i 192, *Et. Mag.*

978 Hdn. π. κλισ. ὀνομ. fr. 23 (ii 642 Lentz) = *Anecd. Oxon.* (iii 237 Cramer)

ἰστέον ὅτι τοῦ Ζήν Ζηνός ἐφύλαξαν οἱ παλαιοὶ Ἴωνες τὴν κλίσιν, οἷον

(a)   ἐπὶ δ' ἴαχε
Ζηνὸς ὑψερεφὴς δόμος
ζαχρειές·

μεταγενέστεροι Αἰολεῖς ἔτρεψαν Ζανός καὶ Ζάν· καὶ ἔτι μεταγενέστεροι οἱ Ἴωνες διὰ τοῦ α Ζάν ὁμοίως τῷ Λυκᾶνι·

(b) κλῦθί μοι Ζανός τε κούρη

(c) Ζανί τ' ἐλευθερίῳ

(a) 1 Bergk: ἐπεὶ δ' ἴσχε cod.   2s. Bergk: δόμοις ζάρης cod.
(b), (c) Bergk: Ζανός τε κουρηξαν τε λευθεριω cod.

979 = 1001 *Suppl. Hell.*

ANONYMOUS FRAGMENTS

977 Herodian, *On the Modification of Words*

The form πός, 'foot', as in

> like the foot of madmen,

comes from πούς with the υ dropped.

978 Herodian, *On the Declension of Nouns*

Note that the ancient Ionians[1] kept the declension Ζήν, gen. Ζηνός, as in

(a) and the high-roofed house of Zeus resounded violently.[2]

Later Aeolic writers changed it to Ζάν, Ζανός, and later still the Ionians used the form with α as in Λυκᾶν, 'Lycaon':

(b) Hear me, daughter of Zeus and . . .

and

(c) to Zeus, giver of freedom.

[1] Attributed to Anacreon by Crusius (fr. 186 dub. Gentili).
[2] With thunder? Text and translation uncertain.

979 = 1001 *Suppl. Hell.*

980 Hdn. π. τῶν εἰς μι fr. 7 (ii 833 Lentz) = Choerob. ii 334 Hilgard, *Anecd. Oxon.* iv 356 Cramer

καὶ πάλιν ὁ εἷς τοῦ ἔντος τῷ ἔντι τὸν ἔντα ἀντὶ τοῦ ὑπάρχοντα, ὡς καὶ ἡ χρῆσις δηλοῖ οὕτως ἔχουσα·

παῖδα ἔντα

ἀντὶ τοῦ παῖδα ὑπάρχοντα.

fort. παῖδ᾽ ἔντα scribendum

981 Hsch. E 7178 (ii 236 Latte)

εὐσέλανον δῖον οἶκον·

ἤτοι παρὰ τὸ σέλας ἢ παρὰ τὴν σελήνην.

Meineke: εὐσελανόνδιον cod., εὐσέλαον Διὸς ci. Salmasius

982 Hsch. Π 1079 (iii 291 Schmidt)

πασσύριον· ἀντὶ τοῦ πασσαδίην. Αἰολεῖς·

†τὸ πασσύριον ἡμῶν ἁπάντων γένος†.

983 Hsch. T 1615 + 1616 (iv 184 Schmidt)

τυιδε (τύδαι cod.)· ἐνταῦθα. Αἰολεῖς.

τυῖδ᾽ ὂν κολώναν Τυνδαρίδαν.

Bergk, Hoffmann: τυδᾶν κολωνᾶν· Τυνδαριδᾶν κολωνᾶν cod.

984 Himer. *Or.* 38. 1 (p. 154 Colonna)

ἔκατι δὲ σοῦ,

ἔφη τις ἤδη τῶν πρὸς λύραν ᾀσάντων . . .

980 Herodian, *On Verbs in* -μι

Or take (the participle of εἰμί), εἷς ἔντος ἔντι ἔντα, used in the sense of 'being', as is made clear by the passage that runs

> being a boy.

981 Hesychius, *Lexicon*

> moonlit divine home,[1]

the first adjective derived either from σέλας, 'brightness', or from σελήνη, 'moon'.

[1] Text uncertain: with Salmasius' emendation, 'bright home of Zeus'.

982 Hesychius, *Lexicon*

πασσύριον : for πασσυδίην, 'altogether', an Aeolic form:

> our whole race (perished?) altogether.[1]

[1] Text quite uncertain.

983 Hesychius, *Lexicon*

τυῖδε : 'hither', an Aeolic form[1]:

> hither to the hill of the Tyndaridae.[2]

[1] E.g. at Sappho 1. 5.   [2] Text garbled; the reference may be to Therapne where the Dioscuri were worshipped: cf. Alcman 2, 7, 14(b).

984 Himerius, *Orations*

> but for your sake,

as one of the lyre-singers has put it . . .

984 A = S 318   Himer. *Or.* 46. 47 (p. 187 Colonna)

ἢ οἷον τὸν

Βακχειώτην,

οὕτω γὰρ αὐτὸν ἡ λύρα καλεῖ, τὸν Διόνυσον λέγουσα, ἦρος ἄρτι τὸ
πρῶτον ἐκλάμψαντος, ἄνθεσί τ᾿ ἠρινοῖσι καὶ κισσοῦ κορύμβοις Μού-
σαις κάτοχοι ποιηταὶ στέψαντες, νῦν μὲν ἐπ᾿ ἄκρας κορυφὰς Καυ-
κάσου καὶ Λυδίας τέμπη, νῦν δ᾿ ἐπὶ Παρνασσοῦ σκοπέλους καὶ
Δελφίδα (-ῖνα cod.) πέτραν ἄγουσι πηδῶντά τε αὐτὸν καὶ ταῖς
Βάκχαις ἐνδιδόντα τὸν εὔιον.

Βακχιώταν ? Renehan

985 Hippol. *Haer.* 5. 7 (p. 79 Wendland, p. 143s. Marco-
vich)

ἐπεὶ γὰρ ὑπόθεσις αὐτοῖς ὁ ἄνθρωπός ἐστιν Ἀδάμας, καὶ
λέγουσι γεγράφθαι περὶ αὐτοῦ 'τὴν γενεὰν αὐτοῦ τίς διηγήσεται;'
(Isaiah 53. 8) μάθετε πῶς κατὰ μέρος παρὰ τῶν ἐθνῶν τὴν
ἀνεξεύρητον καὶ ἀδιάφθορον (Wendland: ἀδιάφορον codd.) τοῦ
ἀνθρώπου γενεὰν λαβόντες ἐπιπλάσσουσι τῷ Χριστῷ. γῇ δέ, φασὶν
οἱ Ἕλληνες, ἄνθρωπον ἀνέδωκε πρώτη καλὸν ἐνεγκαμένη γέρας,
μὴ φυτῶν ἀναισθήτων μηδὲ θηρίων ἀλόγων ἀλλὰ ἡμέρου ζώου καὶ
θεοφιλοῦς ἐθέλουσα μήτηρ γενέσθαι. χαλεπὸν δέ, φησίν, ἐξευρεῖν
εἴτε Βοιωτοῖς Ἀλαλκομενεὺς ὑπὲρ λίμνης Κηφισίδος ἀνέσχε
πρῶτος ἀνθρώπων, εἴτε Κουρῆτες ἦσαν Ἰδαῖοι, θεῖον γένος, ἢ Φρύ-
γιοι Κορύβαντες, οὓς πρώτους ἥλιος ἐπεῖδε δενδροφυεῖς ἀναβλα-
στάνοντας, εἴτε προσεληναῖον Ἀρκαδία Πελασγόν, ἢ Ῥαρίας οἰκή-
τορα Δυσαύλην (Wilamowitz: δίαυλον cod.) Ἐλευσίν, ἢ Λήμνος
καλλίπαιδα Κάβιρον ἀρρήτῳ ἐτέκνωσεν ὀργιασμῷ, εἴτε Πελλήνη
Φλεγραῖον Ἀλκυονέα πρεσβύτατον Γιγάντων. Λίβυες δὲ Ἰάρ-
βαντά φασι πρωτόγονον αὐχμηρῶν ἀναδύντα πεδίων γλυκείας

ANONYMOUS FRAGMENTS

984A = S318   Himerius, *Orations*

... or as

Bacchiotes[1]

— for so the lyre calls him, meaning Dionysus — when
spring has newly shone forth is garlanded with spring
flowers and ivy clusters by poets in the Muses' grip and
brought now to the topmost peaks of Caucasus and the
vales of Lydia, now to the crags of Parnassus and the
Delphic rock, leaping himself and to his Bacchants grant-
ing the cry Euius.

[1] The Reveller: Soph. *O.C.* 678. Part of what follows seems to be
based on hexameter poetry.

985 Hippolytus, *Refutation of all the Heresies*

For since the man Adamas is the foundation of their
theory[1] and they claim that the words 'Who will set forth
his lineage?' were written of him, note how they have in
part taken from the Gentiles the unsearchable, indestruc-
tible lineage of the man and mould it on to Christ.

Earth, say the Greeks, was the first to produce man,
having won that fine privilege, wishing to be mother not of
senseless plants nor of unreasoning beasts but of a civil-
ised, god-loving creature. But it is hard to discover, he[2]
says, whether Boeotian Alalcomeneus on the shore of the
Cephissian lake was the first of men to appear, or if it was
the Idaean Curetes, divine race, or the Phrygian Cory-
bants that the sun first saw shooting up tree-like; or
Arcadia gave birth to the pre-moon Pelasgian, or Eleusis to
Dysaules, dweller in Raria, or Lemnos to Cabeirus, fair
offspring, in secret rites, or Pellene to Phlegraean
Alcyoneus, eldest of Giants. Libyans say that Iarbas was
the first-born, rising from the dry plains to offer first-fruits

[1] See 862 n. 1.   [2] The unidentified poet adapted by Hippol.

GREEK LYRIC

ἀπάρξασθαι Διὸς βαλάνου. Αἰγυπτίαν δὲ Νεῖλος ἰλὺν ἐπιλιπαίνων
<καὶ> μέχρι σήμερον ζωογονῶν, φησίν, ὑγρᾷ σαρκούμενα θερμό-
τητι ζῷα [[καὶ σῶμα]] ἀναδιδῶσιν. Ἀσσύριοι δὲ Ὠάννην ἰχθυο-
φάγον γενέσθαι παρ' αὐτοῖς, Χαλδαῖοι δὲ τὸν Ἀδάμ.

inde Page, Bergkium secutus:

   (a) ... καλὸν ἐνεγκαμένη γέρας ...
   (b) εἴτε Βοιωτοῖσιν Ἀλαλκομενεὺς λίμ-
          νας ὑπὲρ Καφισίδος
      πρῶτος ἀνθρώπων ἀνέσχεν·
      εἴτε <που> Κουρῆτες ἦσαν, θεῖον Ἰδαῖοι γένος·
   5 ἢ Φρύγιοι Κορύβαντες
      τοὺς ἅλιος πρώτους ἐπεῖδε
      δενδροφυεῖς ἀναβλαστάνοντας· εἴτ' <ἄρ'>
      Ἀρκαδία προσεληναῖον Πελασγόν·
      ἢ Ῥαρίας δύσαυλον οἰκητὴρ' Ἐλευσίν·
  10 ἢ καλλίπαις δι' ὀργιασμῶν
      Λῆμνος ἀρρήτων ἐτέκνωσε Κάβειρον·
      εἴτε Πελλάνα Φλεγραῖον
      Ἀλκυονῆα, γιγάντων
      πρεσβύτατον· Λίβυες δέ
  15 φασιν αὐχμηρῶν πεδίων ἀναδύντα
      πρωτόγονον <τὸν> Ἰάρ-
      βαν βαλάνου Διὸς ἄρξασθαι γλυκείας.

985A Philod. *Rhet.* (i 179 Sudhaus)

  [ἢ οἷον

     σπιν]θῆρες Ἀφαίστου σταλαγμοί.

of the sweet nut of Zeus. The Nile, he says, enriching the
Egyptian mud and to this day generating living things,
produces creatures made flesh by moist warmth. Assyri-
ans say Oannes the fish-eater was born in their land, Chal-
daeans Adam in theirs.

985A Philodemus, *Rhetoric* (on metaphor)

Or, for example,

sparks, Hephaestus' drops.

GREEK LYRIC

986 Plat. *Meno* 77b

δοκεῖ τοίνυν μοι, ὦ Σώκρατες, ἀρετὴ εἶναι καθάπερ ὁ ποιητὴς λέγει,

χαίρειν τε καλοῖσι καὶ δύνασθαι,

καὶ ἐγὼ τοῦτο λέγω ἀρετήν, ἐπιθυμοῦντα τῶν καλῶν δυνατὸν εἶναι πορίζεσθαι.

987 Plat. *Resp.* 10. 607bc

ταῦτα δή, ἔφην, ἀπολελογήσθω ἡμῖν ἀναμνησθεῖσιν περὶ ποιή-
σεως, ὅτι εἰκότως ἄρα τότε αὐτὴν ἐκ τῆς πόλεως ἀπεστέλλομεν
τοιαύτην οὖσαν· ὁ γὰρ λόγος ἡμᾶς ᾕρει. προσείπωμεν δὲ αὐτῇ, μὴ
καί τινα σκληρότητα ἡμῶν καὶ ἀγροικίαν καταγνῷ, ὅτι παλαιὰ μέν
τις διαφορὰ φιλοσοφίᾳ τε καὶ ποιητικῇ· καὶ γὰρ ἡ

(a) λακέρυζα πρὸς δεσπόταν κύων

ἐκείνη κραυγάζουσα καὶ

(b) μέγας ἐν ἀφρόνων κενεαγορίαισι

καὶ ὁ

(c) διασόφων ὄχλος κρατῶν

καὶ οἱ

(d) λεπτῶς μεριμνῶντες

ὅτι ἄρα

πένονται,

καὶ ἄλλα μυρία σημεῖα παλαιᾶς ἐναντιώσεως τούτων.

(c) διασοφῶν, δία σοφῶν, διὰ σοφῶν codd.

ANONYMOUS FRAGMENTS

986 Plato, *Meno*

Well, Socrates, I consider that virtue is, as the poet puts it,

> to rejoice in what is fine and to be able for it,[1]

and this, I say, is virtue, when one desires fine things and is able to procure them.

[1] By Simonides? Cf. Aristot. *Pol.* 8. 1339b 1, 1340b 38 (Bergk).

987 Plato, *Republic*

Let this, then, I said, conclude our defence in our renewed consideration of Poetry: we were quite right, it seems, to favour her banishment from our city then,[1] since that is her character. The argument was too strong for us. And let us say also to her, in case she charge us with some harshness and boorishness, that there is an ancient quarrel between philosophy and poetry. Look at these passages[2]:

> (a) that bitch yelping at her master

as she barks, and

> (b) he, great in the empty talk of fools,

and

> (c) the mob of all-wise that holds sway,[3]

and

> (d) those who subtly meditate starve

after all, and thousands of other indications of an ancient opposition between them.

[1] In book 3.   [2] Poetic references to philosophers; (c) and (d) may be from comedy.   [3] Text uncertain.

988 [Plat.] *Epist.* 1, 310a (p. 2 Moore-Blunt)

κἀκεῖνο δὲ τὸ ποίημα τοῖς νοῦν ἔχουσιν οὐ κακῶς ἔχειν δοκεῖ·

οὐ χρυσὸς ἀγλαὸς σπανιώτατος ἐν θνα-
τῶν δυσελπίστῳ βίῳ, οὐδ' ἀδάμας,
οὐδ' ἀργύρου κλῖναι πρὸς ἄνθρω-
πον δοκιμαζόμεν' ἀστράπτει πρὸς ὄψεις,
5 οὐδὲ γαίας εὐρυπέδου γόνιμοι βρί-
θοντες αὐτάρκεις γύαι,
ὡς ἀγαθῶν ἀνδρῶν ὁμοφράδμων νόησις.

1 αἰγλάεις ci. Bergk   2 -ώπου ci. Richards   3 γύαι codd.

989 Mar. Plot. Sacerd. *Art. gramm.* 3. 3 (vi 510 Keil)

de pentametro integro acatalectico monoschematisto:
est metrum integrum pentametrum dactylicum quod
semper quinque dactylis constat, quale est exemplum
graecum illud:

Ἴλιον ἀμφ' Ἑλένῃ πεπυρωμένον ὤλετο

Bergk: ΔΕΙΜΟΝΑΜΦΕΑΗΝΕΝΗΠΥΩΜΕΝΟΝΩΑΗΤΟ cod. A, ΔΕΙ-
ΜΟΝΑΛΑΦΕΛΕΝΕΙΠΥΩΜΕΝΩΛΕΣΟ post corr. cod. B

990 = 1131 *Suppl. Hell.*

991 Mar. Plot. Sacerd. *Art. gramm.* 3. 4 (vi 524 Keil)

tetrametrum (sc. iambicum) brachycatalectum colurum
fit hoc modo, cum novissimus pes debens habere syllabas
quattuor duas habeat, ut est

ὁ Πύθιος μὲν ὀμφαλοῦ θεὸς παρ' ἐσχάραις

ΟΡΙΘΙΟΣΜΕΝΟΜΦΑΛΟΥΟΕΣΠΑΡΕΣΧΔΑΡΑΙΣ cod. A, ΟΡΙΟΙ-
ΟΣΜΕΝΩΜΦΑΛΩΥΘΕΣΠΑΡΕΣΧΑΑΡΑΙΣ cod. B

988 'Plato', Letter to Dionysius

This poem too is highly regarded by sensible men:

Neither splendid gold, most rare in mortals' hope-cheating life, nor diamonds nor couches of silver flash so brilliantly in the eyes in a man's assessment, nor fertile, laden, self-sufficient acres of the spacious earth, as the unanimous thinking of good men.

989 Marius Plotius Sacerdos, *Grammar*

On the complete acatalectic monoschematist pentameter: the complete measure is the dactylic pentameter, which always consists of five dactyls, as in the Greek example:

For Helen Troy was set ablaze and perished.

990 = 1131 *Suppl. Hell.*

991 Marius Plotius Sacerdos, *Grammar*

The brachycatalectic docked (iambic) tetrameter is formed when the last foot, which should have four syllables, has only two, e.g.

the Pythian god at the hearth of the navel[1]

[1] I.e. Apollo at Delphi, 'navel' of the earth.

992 Mar. Plot. Sacerd. *Art. gramm.* 3. 9 (vi 540 Keil)

> ἑλικόπεταλε . . .
> καλλικέλαδε . . .
> φιλοχορευτά

Bergk: ΕΛΙΚΟΣΤΙΗΤΑΛΗ cod. A, ΕΛΥΚΟΣΠΗΤΛΑΗ cod. B
Keil: ΚΑΑΑΤΚΕΑΛΗ cod. A, < >ΛΛΔΕ cod. B   Putsch:
ΦΙΛΟΚΧΟΡΕΙΤΑ cod. A, ΦΙΑΟΚΟΛΟΡΕΙΤΑ cod. B

993 Mar. Plot. Sacerd. *Art. gramm.* 3. 9 (vi 542 Keil)

minus ionicum dimetrum catalecticum fit ionico minore et anapaesto:

> ἴθι, μᾶτερ μεγάλα

Bergk: ΙΘΜΑΤΗΡΜΕΤΑΑΝ cod. A, ΙΕΜΗΤΙΡΜΕΓΑΛΗ cod. B

994 Plut. *consol. ad Apoll.* 28 (i 240 Paton-Wegehaupt-Gärtner)

εἰ γοῦν ἡ Νιόβη κατὰ τοὺς μύθους πρόχειρον εἶχε τὴν ὑπόληψιν ταύτην ὅτι καὶ ἡ

> θαλέθοντι βίῳ
> βλάσταις τε τέκνων βριθομένα γλυκερὸν
> φάος ὁρῶσα

τελευτήσει, οὐκ ἂν οὕτως ἐδυσχέραινεν ὡς καὶ τὸ ζῆν ἐθέλειν ἐκλιπεῖν.

995 Plut. *de amic. mult.* 5 (i 191 Paton-Wegehaupt-Gärtner)

τὰ γὰρ εὔχρηστα τῆς φιλίας δύσχρηστα γίγνεται διὰ τὴν πολυφιλίαν·

> ἄλλον τρόπον ἄλλον ἐγείρει
> φροντὶς ἀνθρώπων.

ANONYMOUS FRAGMENTS

992 Marius Plotius Sacerdos, *Grammar* (on the ionic *a maiore* and related metres)

> leaf-twined!
> fine-shouting!
> dance-loving![1]

[1] All may be addressed to Dionysus, as is 'dance-loving!' in Ar. *Frogs* 403 ff.; the words may be consecutive.

993 Marius Plotius Sacerdos, *Grammar*

The catalectic ionic *a minore* dimeter is formed from an ionic *a minore* and an anapaest:

> Come, great Mother!

994 Plutarch, *Letter of consolation to Apollonius*

At any rate if Niobe in the stories had kept this belief to hand, that even the woman must die who

> laden with vigorous life and the blossoming of children looks on the sweet daylight,

she would not have been so distressed as to wish to leave life behind.

995 Plutarch, *On having many friends*

For the conveniences of friendship become inconveniences when there are many friends:

> men's thinking rouses one in this way, another in that.

---

1 τρόπον LCΔn: τρόπος rell.   γὰρ post τρόπον add. Δn

996 Plut. *de E apud Delph.* 21 (iii 23 Pohlenz-Sieveking)

λέγεται γὰρ ὁ μὲν ᾽Απόλλων ὁ δὲ Πλούτων, καὶ ὁ μὲν Δήλιος ὁ δ᾽ ᾽Αϊδωνεύς, καὶ ὁ μὲν Φοῖβος ὁ δὲ Σκότιος, καὶ παρ᾽ ᾧ μὲν αἱ Μοῦσαι καὶ ἡ Μνημοσύνη, παρ᾽ ᾧ δ᾽ ἡ Λήθη καὶ ἡ Σιωπή· καὶ ὁ μὲν Θεώριος καὶ Φαναῖος, ὁ δὲ

> νυκτὸς ἀϊδνᾶς ἀεργηλοῖό θ᾽ ὕπνου κοίρανος.

cf. *de lat. viv.* 6 (vi 2. 221 Pohlenz)

ἀϊδνᾶς *de lat. viv.*: αἰδοίας (-ης cod. x) *de E*

997 Plut. *de Pyth. orac.* 29 (iii 58 Pohlenz-Sieveking)

οἱ μὲν οὖν περὶ τὸ Γαλάξιον τῆς Βοιωτίας κατοικοῦντες ᾔσθοντο τοῦ θεοῦ τὴν ἐπιφάνειαν ἀφθονίᾳ καὶ περιουσίᾳ γάλακτος·

> προβάτων γὰρ
> ἐκ πάντων κελάρυξεν, ὡς
> κρανᾶν φέρτατον ὕδωρ,
> θηλέον γάλα· τοὶ δὲ
> 5 πίμπλων ἐσσύμενοι πίθους·
> ἀσκὸς δ᾽ οὔτε τις ἀμφορεὺς
> ἐλίνυε δόμοισιν·
> πέλλαι γὰρ ξύλιναι <καὶ>
> πίθοι πλῆσθεν ἅπαντες.

1 Leonicus: πρὸ πάντων codd.   3 Bergk: ἀπὸ κρηνάων codd.
4s. Page: δ᾽ ἐπίμπλων codd.   7 Page: ἐλίννυε δόμοις codd.
8 Wilamowitz: ξύλινοι codd.   καὶ add. Bergk

ANONYMOUS FRAGMENTS

996 Plutarch, *On the E at Delphi*

For the one is called Apollo ('not many'), the other Pluto ('wealthy'), the one Delian ('clear'), the other Aïdoneus ('unseen'), the one Phoebus ('bright'), the other Scotius ('dark'); with the one are the Muses and Memory, with the other Forgetting and Silence; the one is Theorius ('watching') and Phanaeus ('illuminating'), the other is

lord of obscure night and idle sleep.

997 Plutarch, *The Oracles at Delphi*

Now those who lived near Galaxium[1] in Boeotia sensed the god's epiphany thanks to the copious and abundant supply of milk:

for from all the flocks, as finest water from springs, gurgled milk in plenty, and they speedily filled their jars; and neither wine-skin nor amphora lingered idle in their houses: wooden buckets and jars were all filled.[2]

[1] Apparently the site of a sanctuary of Apollo: see A. Schachter, *Cults of Boeotia* i 48 f. The name suggests milk (*gala*).
[2] Unconvincingly ascribed to Pindar by Schneidewin; fr. 104b Snell.

998 Plut. *de defect. orac.* 30 (iii 95 Pohlenz-Sieveking)

ὥσπερ οἱ Τυνδαρίδαι τοῖς χειμαζομένοις βοηθοῦσιν

σπερχόμενόν τε μαλάσσοντες βίαιον
πόντον ὠκείας τ' ἀνέμων ῥιπάς.

cf. *non posse suaviter* . . . 23 (vi 2. 163 Pohlenz)

1 Diggle: ἐπερχόμενόν *non posse,* ἐπερχόμενοί *de defect.* μαλά
ξοντας *non posse* βία τὸν *de defect.*, unde βιατὰν ci. Bergk

999 Plut. *de tranqu. anim.* 17 (iii 215 Pohlenz-Sieveking)

κυβερνήτῃ γὰρ οὔτε κῦμα πραῦναι τραχὺ καὶ πνεῦμα δυνατόν
ἐστιν, οὔθ' ὅποι βούλεται δεομένῳ λιμένος τυχεῖν, οὔτε θαρραλέως
καὶ ἀτρόμως ὑπομεῖναι τὸ συμβαῖνον· ἀλλ' ἕως οὐκ ἀπέγνωκε τῇ
τέχνῃ χρώμενος

φεύγει μέγα λαῖφος ὑποστολίσας ἐς ἐνέρτερον ἱστὸν
ἐρεβώδεος ἐκ θαλάσσας,

<ἐπειδὰν δὲ τὸ πέλαγος (suppl. Pohlenz)> ὑπέρσχῃ, τρέμων
κάθηται καὶ παλλόμενος.

cf. *de superstit.* 8 (i Paton-Wegehaupt-Gärtner)

1 μάλα *tranqu.* ΠΘ, *superstit.* Θn ἐς ἐν., ἔστεν., ἔστ' ἐν., εἰς ἐν.,
ἔως εἰς ἐν., ἔως ἐν. codd. 2 -ας, -ης codd.

1000 Plut. *de garrul.* 2 (iii 281 Pohlenz-Sieveking)

ὅταν εἰς συμπόσιον ἢ συνέδριον γνωρίμων λάλος εἰσέλθῃ,
πάντες ἀποσιωπῶσι μὴ βουλόμενοι λαβὴν παρασχεῖν· ἂν δ' αὐτὸς
ἄρξηται διαίρειν τὸ στόμα,

πρὸ χείματος ὥστ' ἀνὰ ποντί-
αν ἄκραν βορρᾶ ζάεντος

ὑφορώμενοι σάλον καὶ ναυτίαν ἐξανέστησαν.

cf. *de tuend. sanit.* 13 (i 266 P.-W.-G.), *de cohib. ira* 4 (iii 162 P.-S.)

ANONYMOUS FRAGMENTS

998 Plutarch, *On the obsolescence of oracles*

... just as the Tyndaridae[1] come to the aid of storm-tossed men,

soothing the raging violent sea and the winds' swift blasts.[2]

[1] Castor and Polydeuces; cf. Alc. 34.   [2] Bergk suggested Pindaric authorship; fr. 104c Snell.

999 Plutarch, *On tranquillity of mind*

For a pilot cannot soothe a savage wave or wind, nor find a harbour wherever he wants in his need, nor await the outcome without fear and trembling: as long as he has not despaired he uses his skill and

furling the great sail to the foot of the mast he flees from the hell-dark sea;

but when the water rises above him, he sits trembling and shaking.

1000 Plutarch, *On garrulity*

When a chatterbox comes into a drinking-party or a gathering of acquaintances, everyone falls silent, unwilling to give him a handle; and if he begins to open his mouth,

as when Boreas blows over an ocean headland before a storm,

they see a tossing and seasickness ahead and get up and go.

βορρᾶ *sanit.*, garrul. G[1]: βορέου garrul. rell.   Crusius: πνέον-
τος, ζεπνέοντος, ζέοντος codd.

1001 Plut. *de garrul.* 5 (iii 285 Pohlenz-Sieveking)

σκόπει τὴν Λυσίου πειθὼ καὶ χάριν· κεῖνον γὰρ ἐγὼ

φαμὶ ἰοπλοκάμων Μοισᾶν εὖ λαχεῖν.

κεῖνον, ἐκεῖνον, κἀκεῖνον codd.

1002 Plut. *Quaest. Conviv.* 1 proem. (iv 1 Hubert)

τὸ

μισέω μνάμονα συμπόταν,

ὦ Σόσσιε Σενεκίων, ἔνιοι πρὸς τοὺς ἐπιστάθμους εἰρῆσθαι λέγουσιν, φορτικοὺς ἐπιεικῶς καὶ ἀναγώγους ἐν τῷ πίνειν ὄντας· οἱ γὰρ ἐν Σικελίᾳ Δωριεῖς ὡς ἔοικε τὸν ἐπίσταθμον μνάμονα προσηγόρευον· ἔνιοι δὲ τὴν παροιμίαν οἴονται τοῖς παρὰ πότον λεγομένοις καὶ πραττομένοις ἀμνηστίαν ἐπάγειν.

cf. Martial. 1. 27. 7, Lucian. *Symp.* 3 (i 145 Macleod), Stob. 3. 18. 27 (iii 520 Hense), Apostol. 11. 71c, *Mantiss.* 2. 22 (ii 533, 761 Leutsch-Schneidewin)

1003 Plut. *Quaest. Conviv.* 4. 6. 1 (iv 146 Hubert)

ὁ Σύμμαχος, ἆρ᾽, ἔφη, σὺ τὸν πατριώτην θεόν, ὦ Λαμπρία,

εὔιον ὀρσιγύναικα
μαινομέναις Διόνυσον
ἀνθέοντα τιμαῖς

ἐγγράφεις καὶ ὑποποιεῖς τοῖς Ἑβραίων ἀπορρήτοις;

cf. *de E apud Delph.* 9 (iii 12 Pohlenz-Sieveking), *de exilio* 17 (iii 531 P.-S.)

2s. Διόν. μαιν. θύοντα τιμ. *exil.* (excepto cod. v), μαιν. ἀνθ. τιμαῖσι Διόν. *Quaest.*, μαιν. Διόν. ἀνθ. τιμ. *de E*, *exil.* cod. v

ANONYMOUS FRAGMENTS

1001 Plutarch, *On garrulity*

Consider the persuasiveness and charm of Lysias! Of him

I say that he obtained a fine share of the violet-haired Muses.

1002 Plutarch, *Table-talk*

The saying,

I hate a fellow-drinker with a good memory,

Sosius Senecio, is explained by some with reference to masters of ceremonies, who were rather tiresome and lacking in good taste as the drinking went on, since it seems that the Sicilian Dorians used to call the master of ceremonies 'the remembrancer'. Others think the proverb recommends forgetfulness of what is said and done during the drinking.

1003 Plutarch, *Table-talk*

Symmachus said, 'Lamprias, are you enrolling and enlisting your national god,[1]

Euius, rouser of women, Dionysus, flourishing in crazed honours,

among the mysteries of the Hebrews?'

[1] Dionysus, as son of Theban Semele, and Lamprias, Plutarch's brother, were both Boeotian.

GREEK LYRIC

1004 Plut. *an seni ger. resp.* 12 (v 1. 39 Hubert)

ἢ πλοίων μὲν ἄρχοντας οὐ ποιεῖ γράμματα κυβερνητικά, μὴ
πολλάκις γενομένους ἐν πρύμνῃ θεατὰς τῶν πρὸς κῦμα καὶ πνεῦμα
καὶ νύκτα χειμερίων ἀγώνων,

ὅτε Τυνδαριδᾶν ἀδελφῶν ἅλιον ναύταν πόθος βάλλει.

ναύταν, ναύτην codd.

1005 Plut. *praec. ger. reip.* 2 (v 1. 59s. Hubert)

πολλοὶ δ᾽ ἀπὸ τύχης ἁψάμενοι τῶν κοινῶν καὶ ἀναπλησθέντες
οὐκέτι ῥᾳδίως ἀπελθεῖν δύνανται, ταὐτὸ τοῖς ἐμβᾶσιν εἰς πλοῖον
αἰώρας χάριν εἶτ᾽ ἀποσπασθεῖσιν εἰς πέλαγος πεπονθότες· ἔξω
βλέπουσι ναυτιῶντες καὶ ταραττόμενοι, μένειν δὲ καὶ χρῆσθαι τοῖς
παροῦσιν ἀνάγκην ἔχοντες·

λευκᾶς καθύπερθε γαλάνας
εὐπρόσωποι σφᾶς †παρ(ι)ῆσαν† ἔρωτες ναΐας
κληῖδος χαραξιπόντου δαιμονίαν ἐς ὕβριν.

2 παρῆσαν, παρίησαν, παρήσαν codd., παράιξαν Bergk, <ἐ>π᾽ ἄρ᾽ ἦσαν
Page   3 de Meziriac: χαράζει, χαράξει, χαλάξει π. codd.

1006 Plut. *de primo frigido* 17 (v 3. 107 Hubert)

ὁ γὰρ ἥλιος ἀνίσχων, ὥς τις εἶπε τῶν διθυραμβοποιῶν,

εὐθὺς ἀνέπλησεν ἀεροβατᾶν μέγαν οἶκον ἀνέμων.

Emperius: -βάταν codd.

406

ANONYMOUS FRAGMENTS

1004 Plutarch, *Should old men govern?*

Navigation manuals do not make ships' captains of men who have not watched many times from the stern the stormy struggles against wind and wave and night,

when longing strikes the sailor at sea for the Tyndarid brothers.[1]

[1] See 998.

1005 Plutarch, *Political Precepts*

Many who have become politically involved by mere chance and have had their fill find it no longer easy to withdraw; they are in the same condition as men who have boarded a ship to enjoy rocking motion and then have been carried off to the open sea: they look out seasick and distressed, but they must stay put and endure their plight:

fair-faced desires for the sea-furrowing oar-bench of the ship have snatched[1] them over the white calm to a god-sent violence.[2]

[1] Text uncertain.   [2] Ascribed to Simonides by Schneidewin.

1006 Plutarch, *On cold as an element*

For the rising sun, as one of the dithyrambic poets said,

immediately filled the great house of the air-walking winds.

1007 Plut. *de commun. notit.* 19 (vi 2. 80s. Pohlenz)

δέκα φαύλους ἢ χιλίους ἢ μυρίους ἔδει γενέσθαι, καὶ μὴ κακίας
μὲν φορὰν τοσαύτην τὸ πλῆθος —

οὐ ψάμμος ἢ κόνις ἢ πτερὰ ποικιλοτρίχων οἰωνῶν
τόσσον ἂν χεύαιτ' ἀριθμόν —

ἀρετῆς δὲ μηδ' ἐνύπνιον.

cf. *de amore prolis* 4 (iii 265 Pohlenz-Sieveking)

1 Basiliensis: οὖ *commun.* codd.   -τρίχων *commun.* codd.:
-θρόων *prol.* codd.

1007A Plut. *non posse suaviter* . . . 13 (vi 2. 145 Pohlenz)

εἰ δὲ Πτολεμαῖος ὁ πρῶτος συναγαγὼν τὸ μουσεῖον τούτοις ἐνέ-
τυχε τοῖς καλοῖς καὶ βασιλικοῖς παραγγέλμασιν, ἆρ' οὐκ ἂν εἶπε

τοῖς Σαμίοις, ὦ Μοῦσα, τίς ὁ φθόνος ;

1008 Plut. *non posse suaviter* . . . 13 (vi 2. 146 Pohlenz)

ποῖος γὰρ ἂν αὐλὸς ἢ κιθάρα διηρμοσμένη πρὸς ᾠδὴν ἢ τίς
χορὸς

εὐρύοπα κέλαδον ἀκροσόφων
ἀγνύμενον διὰ στομάτων

φθεγγόμενος οὕτως εὔφρανεν Ἐπίκουρον καὶ Μητρόδωρον ὡς Ἀρι-
στοτέλη καὶ Θεόφραστον καὶ Δικαίαρχον καὶ Ἱερώνυμον οἱ περὶ
χορῶν λόγοι καὶ διδασκαλιῶν καὶ τὰ αὐλῶν προβλήματα καὶ
ῥυθμῶν καὶ ἁρμονιῶν ;

ANONYMOUS FRAGMENTS

1007 Plutarch, *On common conceptions against the Stoics*

There should have been ten base men or a thousand or ten thousand, not such an enormous crop of evil —

neither sand nor dust nor the plumage of dapple-feathered birds could be heaped in such number —

and not even a phantom of virtue.

1007A Plutarch, *That Epicurus actually makes a pleasant life impossible*

If Ptolemy, the first to assemble the Museum, had come across these fine royal precepts,[1] he would surely have said,

Why, Muse, do the Samians[2] bear you a grudge?

[1] The Epicurean rejection of music and poetry.   [2] Epicurus was born on Samos.

1008 Plutarch, *That Epicurus actually makes a pleasant life impossible*

For what pipe or lyre tuned for song, what chorus uttering

the wide-voiced shout bursting from high-skilled mouths[1]

could have given as much pleasure to Epicurus and Metrodorus as discussion of choruses and the productions of plays and questions about pipes and rhythms and tunings gave to Aristotle and Theophrastus and Dicaearchus and Hieronymus?

[1] Ascribed to Pindar by Boeckh.

1009 Plut. *non posse suaviter* . . . 26 (vi 2. 166 Pohlenz)

ἀλλ᾽ ἐκεῖνο τοῦ θανάτου τὸ πρόσωπον ὡς φοβερὸν καὶ σκυθρω-
πὸν καὶ σκοτεινὸν ἅπαντες ὑποδειμαίνουσι, τὸ τῆς ἀναισθησίας καὶ
λήθης καὶ ἀγνοίας· καὶ πρὸς τὸ ἀπόλωλε καὶ τὸ ἀνῄρηται καὶ τὸ
οὐκ ἔστι ταράσσονται καὶ δυσανασχετοῦσι τούτων λεγομένων <ὡς>
τὸ

> ἔπειτα κείσεται βαθυδένδρῳ
> ἐν χθονὶ συμποσίων τε καὶ λυρᾶν ἄμοιρος
> ἰαχᾶς τε παντερπέος αὐλῶν.

1 Dübner: ἐπιτακήσεται codd.

1010 Plut. *non posse suaviter* . . . 27 (vi 2. 168 Pohlenz)

οὐδὲ ῥᾳδίως οὐδ᾽ ἀλύπως ἀκούομεν

> ὡς ἄρ᾽ εἰπόντα μιν τηλαυγὲς ἀμβρόσιον
> ἐλασίππου πρόσωπον ἀπέλιπεν ἁμέρας.

ἀμβρ. τηλ. ci. Bergk   Wyttenbach: πρὸς τόπον codd.

1011 Prisc. *inst.* i 20 (ii 15 Keil)

pro Aeolico digamma ϝ, u ponitur. quod sicut illi
solebant accipere digamma modo pro <u, modo pro : *add.
Edmonds>* consonante simplici teste Astyage, qui diversis
hoc ostendit usibus, ut in hoc versu:

(a) ὀψόμενος ϝελέναν ἑλικώπιδα,

sic nos quoque pro simplici habemus plerumque con-
sonante u loco ϝ digamma positum, ut 'at Venus haud
animo nequiquam exterrita mater'; est tamen quando
idem Aeolis inveniuntur pro duplici quoque consonante
digamma posuisse, ut

(b) Νέστορι δὲ ϝῶ παιδός

(a) ΟϮΟΜΕΝΟΣ, sscr. 'aspiciens', in litura l: ΟΥΟ- RA, ΟΦΟ-
rGD   (b) Νέστορι, Νέστορα codd.

1009 Plutarch, *That Epicurus actually makes a pleasant life impossible*

But the aspect of death that everyone fears as terrifying and gloomy and dismal is the aspect of insensibility and forgetting and ignorance. Confronted by expressions like 'he is lost' and 'he is destroyed' and 'he is no more' they are distressed, and they are much vexed when words such as these are spoken:

then he will lie in the deep-wooded earth with no share in drinking-parties and lyres and the all-delightful cry of the pipes.

1010 Plutarch, *That Epicurus actually makes a pleasant life impossible*

And it is with distress and pain that we hear the words

So he spoke, and the far-shining ambrosial face of horse-driving Day abandoned him.

1011 Priscian, *Grammar*

The letter u is put in place of Aeolic digamma[1]; and as they took digamma sometimes as u, sometimes as a single consonant — see Astyages, who makes the point by means of various examples, as in the verse

(a) (he) about to see glancing-eyed Helen,

— so we too most often have u for digamma as a single consonant, as in *āt Venus*[2]; but sometimes those Aeolic writers are found using digamma as a double consonant;

(b) but (to) Nestor . . . of his son[3]

---

[1] E.g. Alc. 70. 12 ἀνάταν.   [2] The V (or U) of Venus helps to lengthen the preceding vowel, like the digamma in (a).   [3] The digamma as a double consonant lengthens the preceding vowel.

GREEK LYRIC

1012 Schol. Ap. Rhod. 1. 146 (p. 20 Wendel)

Φερεκύδης δὲ ἐν τῇ β′ (*F.Gr.H.* 3 F9) ἐκ Λαοφόνης (Wilamowitz: -φόντης codd.) τῆς Πλευρῶνος Λήδαν καὶ Ἀλθαίαν Θεστίῳ γενέσθαι φησίν. ὅτι δὲ Γλαύκου ἐστὶ θυγάτηρ καὶ Ἀλκμὰν (Bergk: Ἀλθαίας codd., Ἀλκαῖος Wendel) αἰνίττεται λέγων·

> τὼς τέκεν θυγάτηρ Γλαύκω μάκαιρα.

Bergk: τοὺς codd.   Hiller: τέκε codd.   Bergk: Γλαύκωι codd.
τοῖς τέκε Γλαύκω θ. μ. Page

[**1013** 'Elias' *In Aristot. Categ. comment.* p. 124 Busse (*Comm. in Aristot. Graeca* 18. 1)

ἐν μὲν τοῖς διαλογικοῖς, τοῖς καὶ ἐξωτερικοῖς, σαφής (sc. ὁ Ἀριστοτέλης), ὡς πρὸς τοὺς ἔξω φιλοσοφίας διαλεγόμενος, ὡς δὲ ἐν διαλεκτικοῖς, ποικίλος ταῖς μιμήσεσιν, Ἀφροδίτης [[ὄνομα]] γέμων καὶ Χαρίτων ἀνάμεστος.

ὄνομα ('quod primitus supra ἀφροδ. additum fuisse videtur') secl. Busse   γέμων HKP, τέμνων Brandis ex cod. R   ἄλοκα τέμνων ci. Bergk]

1014 Schol. A Hom. *Il.* 16. 57c (iv 173 Erbse)

ὅσοις κυρίοις εἰς ης λήγουσι βαρυτόνοις συνθέτοις παράκειται ἐπιθετικὰ ὀξυνόμενα, Διογένης, αὐτὰρ ὁ διογενής (*Il.* 21. 17, *Od.* 23. 306), Πολυνείκης,

> ἀλλ᾽ ἁ πολυνεικὴς δῖ᾽ Ἑλένα

Hermann: ἀλλὰ cod.   Schneidewin: -νίκης cod.   Hermann: διελένα cod.

412

ANONYMOUS FRAGMENTS

1012 Scholiast on Apollonius of Rhodes ('Aetolian Leda' sent her sons Castor and Polydeuces to join the Argonauts)

Pherecydes says in Book 2 that Leda and Althaea were daughters of Thestius[1] by Laophone, daughter of Pleuron; but that Leda is daughter of Glaucus[2] is implied by (Alcman?)[3] too:

the sons whom the blessed daughter of Glaucus bore.

[1] King of Aetolia; see Ibycus 304. Pleuron is an Aetolian city.   [2] Son of Sisyphus; this version is given by Hellanicus (*F.Gr.H.* 4 F119).   [3] Text corrupt; Bergk proposed 'Alcman' (fr. 230 dub. Calame), Wendel 'Alcaeus' (so Page).

[1013 'Elias', *Commentary on Aristotle's Categories*[1]

In his dialogic writings, also called the exoteric writings, Aristotle's manner is clear, since he is addressing himself to non-philosophers; and as is fitting in dialectical works he is varied in his representations of character, laden with Aphrodite and full of the Graces.[2]

[1] Now attributed to the Christian philosopher David (*fl. c.* 550).   [2] Bergk thought that the last phrase was verse, emending the text to give 'cutting the furrow of Aphrodite'; but this is quite unlikely.]

1014 Scholiast on Homer, *Iliad* 16. 57

Alongside compound proper names in -ης with acute accent on the penultimate syllable we find epithets with acute accent on the final syllable: Διογένης, 'Diogenes', but διογενής, 'Zeus-born'; Πολυνείκης, 'Polyneices', but πολυνεικής, 'much fought over':

But godlike Helen, much fought over, . . .

1015 Schol. Pind. *Nem.* 6. 85b (iii 112 Drachmann)

δίκρουν γάρ (sc. τὸ δόρυ τοῦ Ἀχιλλέως), ὥστε δύο ἀκμὰς ἔχειν καὶ μιᾷ βολῇ ⟦ὥστε⟧ δισσὰ τὰ τραύματα ἀπεργάζεσθαι. καὶ Αἰσχύλος ἐν Νηρεῖσι (fr. 152 Radt) καὶ Σοφοκλῆς ἐν Ἀχιλλέως Ἐρασταῖς (fr. 152 Radt)· ἢ δορὸς διχόστομον πλᾶκτρον·

δίπτυχοι γὰρ ὀδύναι μιν ἤρικον Ἀχιλληίου δόρατος.

ἤρεικον ci. L. Dindorf   Ἀχιλλείου ci. Bergk

1016 Stob. 1. 1. 31b (i 39 Wachsmuth-Hense) (ὅτι θεὸς δημιουργὸς τῶν ὄντων κτλ.)

ὑμνέωμες μάκαρας, Μοῦσαι Διὸς ἔκγονοι,
ἀφθίτοις ἀοιδαῖς.

1017 Stob. 1.5.19 (i 81 Wachsmuth-Hense) (περὶ εἱμαρμένης καὶ τῆς τῶν γινομένων εὐταξίας)

Πλουτάρχου ἐκ τοῦ Εἰ ἡ τῶν μελλόντων πρόγνωσις ὠφέλιμος· τὸ γὰρ εἱμαρμένον ἄτρεπτον καὶ ἀπαράβατον,

χᾦπερ μόνον ὀφρύσι νεύσῃ,
καρτερὰ τούτῳ κέκλωστ᾽ ἀνάγκα

καὶ πεπρωμένη.

1 Gaisford: χῶπερ, χῶπερ codd.   Meineke: νεύσει, νεῦσι codd.
2 Meineke: κέκλωτ᾽ codd.

ANONYMOUS FRAGMENTS

1015 Scholiast on Pindar, *Nemean* 6. 53 (Achilles' 'furious spear')

It was forked, so that it had two points and with one throw inflicted two wounds. So Aeschylus in his *Nereids* (fr. 152 Radt), Sophocles in his *Lovers of Achilles* (fr. 152 Radt), 'or the double-biting point of the spear';

for two-fold pains from Achilles' spear tore him.[1]

[1] This may be part of the Sophoclean fragment; see Pearson and Radt *ad loc.* Bergk regarded it as lyric, perhaps Pindaric.

1016 Stobaeus, *Anthology* (that god is the creator of the world . . .)

Muses, daughters of Zeus, let us hymn the blessed ones with immortal songs.[1]

[1] In the mss. the line follows nine dactylic hexameters, but it seems to be the beginning of a new poem; the sequel may be missing from the mss.

1017 Stobaeus, *Anthology* (on fate and the orderliness of events)

From Plutarch, *Is foreknowledge of the future useful?*: For what is fated may not be turned aside nor passed by,

and if he[1] merely nods his brows at a man, strong necessity is at once spun for him,

and fated for him.

[1] Zeus? Or 'she . . . her brows' of one of the Fates?

1018 Stob. 1. 5. 10–12 (i 76s. Wachsmuth-Hense) (περὶ εἱμαρμένης καὶ τῆς τῶν γινομένων εὐταξίας)

(a) κλῦτε, Μοῖραι, Διὸς αἴ τε πα-
ρὰ θρόνον ἀγχοτάτω θεῶν
ἑζόμεναι περιώσι᾽ ἄφυκτά τε
μήδεα παντοδαπᾶν βου-
λᾶν ἀδαμαντίναισιν ὑφαίνετε κερκίσιν.

(b) Αἶσα <καὶ> Κλωθὼ Λάχεσίς τ᾽, εὐώλενοι
κοῦραι Νυκτός,
εὐχομένων ἐπακούσατ᾽,
οὐράνιαι χθόνιαί τε
δαίμονες ὦ πανδείματοι·
5 πέμπετ᾽ ἄμμιν <τὰν> ῥοδόκολπον
Εὐνομίαν λιπαροθρόνους τ᾽ ἀδελφὰς
Δίκαν καὶ στεφανηφόρον Εἰράναν,
πόλιν τε τάνδε βαρυφρόνων
λελάθοιτε συντυχιᾶν.

(a) 2 Grotius: περιώσια· φυκτά FP   3 Grotius: -πὰν βουλὰν FP
Wilamowitz: -αις ὑφαίνεται FP
(b) 1 suppl. Bergk   2 Νυκτὸς κόραι ci. Wilamowitz
3 -σατε F, -σαται P   4 Wachsmuth: -δείμαντοι FP   5 suppl.
Wilamowitz   9 Grotius: -ίαν FP

ANONYMOUS FRAGMENTS

1018 Stobaeus, *Anthology* (on fate and the orderliness of events)[1]

(a) Listen, Fates, who sit nearest of the gods to the throne of Zeus and weave on adamantine shuttles countless and inescapable devices of counsels of all kinds.

(b) Aisa,[2] Clotho and Lachesis, fair-armed daughters of Night, hear our prayers, you all-terrible deities of heaven and the lower world: send us rose-bosomed Eunomia[3] and her bright-throned sisters Justice and garland-wearing Peace, and make this city forget its heavy-hearted misfortunes.

---

[1] The mss. give three passages, numbered 10 (κλῦτε–ἐζόμεναι), 11 (περιώσια–κερκίσιν) and 12 (Αἶσα–συντυχιᾶν) by editors; 10 is ascribed to Eur. *Peleus*, 11 and 12 to Soph. *Phaedra*, but the ascriptions may refer to the preceding extracts (adesp. F 503, F 504 Kannicht-Snell) and to the following extract (Soph. F 686 Radt). 10 and 11 should certainly be joined to give (a). Nauck joined all three; so Diehl, Bowra (see esp. *G.L.P.*[2] 404 ff.); but it is not certain that the metre of (a) is dactylo-epitrite as in (b), and (b) seems to begin a new poem. Meineke ascribed 12 to Simonides or Bacchylides, Wilamowitz 11–12 to Sim., Bowra 10–12 to Sim. [2] Dispensation or Destiny; in Hesiod, *Theog.* 905 the Fates are Clotho, Lachesis and Atropos. [3] Good Order in civic government; in Hesiod, *Theog.* 901 ff. the sisters are the three Seasons (Horai).

GREEK LYRIC

1019 Stob. 1. 6. 13 (i 86 Wachsmuth-Hense) (περὶ τύχης ἢ ταὐτομάτου)

Τύχα, μερόπων ἀρχὰ
καὶ τέρμα, τὺ καὶ Σοφίας θακεῖς ἕδρας
καὶ τιμὰν βροτέοις ἐπέθηκας ἔργοις·
καὶ τὸ καλὸν πλέον ἢ κακὸν ἐκ σέθεν,
5 ἅ τε χάρις λάμπει περὶ σὰν πτέρυγα χρυσέαν,
καὶ τὸ τεᾷ πλάστιγγι δοθὲν μακαριστότατον
τελέθει·
τὺ δ' ἀμαχανίας πόρον εἶδες ἐν ἄλγεσι
καὶ λάμπρον φάος ἄγαγες ἐν σκότεϊ, προφερε-
στάτα θεῶν.

2 Grotius: τέρματι FP   Jacobs: ἄκος δρᾷς F, lacun. P
4 κακὸν P²: καλὸν FP¹   7 Grotius: σὺ FP   Grotius:
ἄλγεσιν FP   8 Page: σκότῳ FP

1020 Str. 1. 2. 14 (i 25 Aly)

ἢ καὶ Ἡσιόδῳ μὲν ἔπρεπε μὴ φλυαρεῖν ἀλλὰ ταῖς κατεχούσαις
δόξαις ἀκολουθεῖν, Ὁμήρῳ δὲ

πᾶν ὅττι κεν ἐπ' ἀκαιρίμαν
γλῶσσαν ἴῃ κελαδεῖν;

cf. D. H. *Comp.* 1 (vi 5 Radermacher), Lucian. *Rhet. Praec.* 18 (ii 326 Macleod), *Hist. Conscr.* 32 (iii 307 M.), Athen. 5. 217c (i 481 Kaibel)

1 ὅττι κεν, ὅτι κεν, ὅτι ἂν codd.   ἀκαιρ. varie corruptum in Str. et Lucian. codd.   2 γλῶτταν codd. plerique   γλ. ἔπος ἔλθῃ λέγειν D. H., γλ. ἔλθῃ Lucian., Athen.

418

1019 Stobaeus, *Anthology* (on fortune or accident)

Fortune, beginning and end for mankind, you sit in Wisdom's seat and give honour to mortal deeds; from you comes more good than evil, grace shines about your gold wing, and what the scale of your balance gives is the happiest; you see a way out of the impasse in troubles, and you bring bright light in darkness, you most excellent of gods.

1020 Strabo, *Geography*

Surely it was not fitting for Hesiod to refrain from talking nonsense and follow accepted opinions, but fitting for Homer

to sing of everything that comes to an ill-timed tongue.

1021 Theodorus Metochita, *misc. philos. et hist.* (p. 515 Müller-Kiessling)

καὶ ποιηταὶ δέ φασιν·

> ὦ γλυκεῖ᾽ Εἰράνα,
> πλουτοδότειρα βροτοῖς.

1 εἰρήνη codd.

1022 Theodorus Metochita, *misc. philos. et hist.* (p. 562 Müller-Kiessling)

καὶ λαμβάνειν ἐξὸν καὶ χρηματίζεσθαι ῥᾷστα, κἂν εἰ πλάττωνται παρολιγωρεῖν καὶ παρορᾶν ἀνεπιστρόφως καὶ παρατρέχειν,

> νύσσει γ᾽ ὅμως σφᾶς θέλγητρ᾽ ἁδονᾶς

φησὶν ἡ ποίησις.

νύττει, ἡδονὰς codd.

1023 = *T.G.F.* adesp. F 692   P. Schubart 17 = P. Berol. inv. 13428

col. i 1]μα πέτρηι ξ[υ]ν   2]ν ἔβρεμεν μ[ν]ᾳ
3]γλυκὺν ἐκ τ[ῶ]ν

coll. i–ii

```
                              ]ι συνω-
12        ρί | ζουσαι νυχίαν κέλ[ευθ]ον
          αἱ τᾶν ['Εσ] | περίδων χ[ο]ραγ[ο]ί̣
          π[οτὶ νε]ότροφον [τρο] | πάν,
14        ἵνα τε Νὺξ δ[ιαμε]ίβεται
```

vv. 11–19 cola distinx. Kannicht-Snell, Merkelbach secuti; cetera ut in pap.

omnia suppl. ed. pr. (Schubart), exceptis quae sequuntur:
12 κέλ[ευθον]⟦ον⟧ ed. pr.   13 χ[ο]ραγ[έ]τ̣[ι Maas (voc. an dat. ?)
14 K.-S.: [ἀπαμε]ίβεται ed. pr.

ANONYMOUS FRAGMENTS

1021 Theodorus the Metochite, *Miscellany*

And poets say,

O sweet Peace, wealth-giver to mortals![1]

[1] Bergk suggested Pindaric authorship.

1022 Theodorus the Metochite, *Miscellany*

When they can easily acquire it and make money, even if they pretend to disregard it and overlook it in indifference and pass it by,

yet the beguilements of pleasure sting them,[1]

as the poet has it.

[1] Bergk again suggested Pindar's authorship; fr. 223. 3 Snell. Perhaps only the words 'the beguilements of pleasure' belong to the quotation.

It is uncertain whether frr. 1023–1028 belong to lyric or tragedy.

1023 = *T.G.F.* adesp. F 692   Berlin papyrus (3rd–2nd c. B.C.)

col. i ... rock ... roared ... sweet ...[1]

col. ii ... the choir-leaders of the Hesperides[2] driving their two-horse chariot along the path of night to the new turning-point, where Night passes

[1] These words may belong to a different poem.   [2] Cf. Mimnermus 12, where a gold bed carries the sleeping Sun over the sea from the Hesperides to the Ethiopians (i.e. from west to east), where his chariot and horses await Dawn's coming. For the singing of the Hesperides see Hesiod, *Theog.* 275 with West's note, Prop. 3. 22. 10 *Hesperidumque choros.*

τὰ[ν φαεσ] | φόρον αἴγλαν
ἑῶιον [ἀ]ν] αἰθέρα,

16   φέρε[ι δ᾽ ἀ] | μέριον φάος
διὰ κύματος ἀερίου πτ[αμέ] | να
ναύταισ<ι> ποδαγ[ὸ]ς ὤν

18   περας θυ[   ] | τερ γαν λ[.]τες[
ὦ] χρυσόθρον᾽ Εὐ[φρό] | να
(να) κήρυξιν[. . . .]ιαν δι᾽ α[ἱ]γλάε[

20   ηταμεναι[. .]ελ . . . . . τωλ[.]γκα[
λοφ[ο]ρον λοχ[.] αντι παρθεν[
πρὶν ἐπικ[.]λλατα[.] αι τλατα . [

15 Page: φωσ] ed. pr.   Snell: εοιον pap.   16 suppl. Page:
φέρο[ισα ed. pr.   κυβατος ut vid. pap.   17 <ι> Merkelbach
πέρας vel περᾶς?   17s. θύ[γα]τερ vel θύ[ον]τες ed. pr.
19 κηρύξ<ε>ιν Merkelbach

1024 = *T.G.F.* adesp. F 681   Ox. Pap. 2436

col. ii

. .]ιον μεσο[   ]ηποη· ψαύω δὲ λ[
.]ν· ὁ δεμο[.] . [. .] . . . . [.]αις Ἄρεως Ὑμησ[σ
μου μᾶλλον ηὐτέκνησ᾽ ἐγώ· σπευσο[
ἀπαλλα[γὴν ἐμ]ῶν κακῶν· χορεύσατε . [
5 καὶ μὴ π[.]ε[. .]μάθητε μνημονεύσατ[ε
εἴ τις κατὰ στέγας θύρσος ἔτι λείπεται πυρὶ παι[
λάσσεται· ἤν, π[α]ῖδες αἰπόλων καὶ . . . . σο[
πης ποι[μένε]ς βουκόλοι μαινάδες [[δὸ]]

through the light-bringing radiance in the eastern
air; and she brings the day's light, flying over the
misty wave, a guide for sailors ... Gold-flowered
Night! ... heralds ... through the radiant ...
maiden(s) ... before ...³

³ Much of text and translation uncertain.

1024 *T.G.F.* adesp. F 681   Oxyrhynchus papyrus (early
2nd c. A.D.)¹

... I touch² ... (child?)³ of Ares ... Hymettus⁴ ...
I was more happy in my children (than Priam?);
hasten- ... release from my ills; dance! ... and do
not go unnoticed ...⁵; remember! ... if any thyrsus⁶
still remains in the house ... fire ...; see! sons of
goatherds and ..., shepherds, herdsmen, Bacchants
...⁷

¹ Text with musical notation, the music dated to 2nd c. B.C.–2nd c.
A.D., probably much later than the text.   ² Perhaps 'I touch
(the spring)': see n. 4.   ³ Eros? Cf. Simon. 575.   ⁴ E. K.
Borthwick, *A.J.Ph.* 84 (1963) 225 ff. suggests that the reference is
to Aphrodite's shrine at Kyllupera on Mt. Hymettus with its
spring, where childless women went to be cured. 'Hymen' is a less
probable reading.   ⁵ Or 'and do not learn ...'.   ⁶ Or
'torch'.   ⁷ The song perhaps ends here. It may be a monody
from a satyr-play; note the call to dance and the rustic setting.

1 λ[ουτρῶν Borthwick   2 ὁ δ᾽ ἐμὸ[ς vel ὁ δὲ μο[[π]αῖς
dubit. ed. pr. (E. G. Turner)   Ὑμήσ[σ pot. quam Ὑμην[
2s. Πριά] | μου ed. pr.   3 -τέκνησα ἐγώ, σαε disyll. musico
σπευσό[μεθα, -σο[μεν, al. ed. pr.   4 ἐμ]ῶν Gentili
5 vel λάθητε   6 σπγας pap.   πυρσὸς ed. pr.
6s. φυ] | λάσσεται ?   7 καινσος in και κισσος corr.?
8 μαινάδες fort. fin. cantici

1025 'Hdn.' π. κλίσ. ῥημ.: *Anecd. Oxon.* (iii 261 Cramer)

Μάγνης, Μάγνησσα·

Πελίου τε Μάγνησσαν κόραν

1026 = *T.G.F.* adesp. F 85   Aristot. *Poet.* 21. 1457b
29 (p. 35 Lucas)

ἐνίοις δ' οὐκ ἔστιν ὄνομα κείμενον τῶν ἀνάλογον, ἀλλ' οὐδὲν
ἧττον ὁμοίως λεχθήσεται· οἷον τὸ τὸν καρπὸν μὲν ἀφιέναι σπείρειν,
τὸ δὲ τὴν φλόγα ἀπὸ τοῦ ἡλίου ἀνώνυμον· ἀλλ' ὁμοίως ἔχει τοῦτο
πρὸς τὸν ἥλιον καὶ τὸ σπείρειν πρὸς τὸν καρπόν, διὸ εἴρηται

σπείρων θεοκτίσταν φλόγα.

1027 D. H. *Comp.* 17 (vi 68ss. Usener-Radermacher)

ὁ μὲν οὖν βραχυσύλλαβος ἡγεμών τε καὶ πυρρίχιος καλεῖται,
καὶ οὔτε μεγαλοπρεπής ἐστιν οὔτε σεμνός· σχῆμα δ' αὐτοῦ
τοιόνδε·

(a) λέγε δὲ σὺ κατὰ πόδα νεόχυτα μέλεα.

... ὁ μὲν γὰρ ἐξ ἁπασῶν βραχειῶν συνεστώς, καλούμενος δὲ ὑπό
τινων χορεῖος [[τρίβραχυς πούς]], οὗ παράδειγμα τοιόνδε·

(b) Βρόμιε δορατοφόρ' ἐνυάλιε πολεμοκέλαδε,

ταπεινός τε καὶ ἄσεμνός ἐστι καὶ ἀγεννής ...

(c) = Terp. 5 (vol. ii p. 317)

ὁ δ' ἐκ μακρᾶς καὶ δυεῖν βραχειῶν μέσην μὲν λαβὼν τὴν μακρὰν

cf. Epitom. (p. 171s. U.-R.); *Anal. Gramm.* 8. 11 Keil, ubi Βρόμιε –
Ἄρη (b), Macrob. *Sat.* 1. 19. 1 (i 108 Willis) Bacchus ἐνυάλιος cog-
nominatur

(a) νεόχυτα F Epitom., νεόλυτα PMV   (b) πολέμοιο κέλαδε F Epi-
tom., πολεμόκλονε *Anal. Gramm.*   πάτερ Ἄρη post πολ. *Anal.*
Gramm.

424

ANONYMOUS FRAGMENTS

1025 'Herodian', *On the inflexion of verbs*

Μάγνης, masculine, Μάγνησσα feminine:

> and the Magnesian daughter[1] of Pelias

[1] Alcestis? See *Il.* 2. 715, Eur. *Alc.* 37, 82. Iolcus, the home of Pelias and Jason, was in Thessalian Magnesia.

1026 = *T.G.F.* adesp. F 85   Aristotle, *Poetics*

Sometimes there is no established word for one term of the analogy, but it can be expressed all the same: for example, to scatter seed is 'to sow', but there is no word for the sun scattering its flame; yet this has the same relationship to the sun as sowing to the seed, and so we find the expression

> (the Sun) sowing the god-created flame.

1027 Dionysius of Halicarnassus, *On Literary Composition* (on rhythms)

The rhythm which has two short syllables is called the *hegemon* ('leader') or *pyrrhich*, and it is neither impressive nor solemn; its pattern is as follows:

(a) Pick up the newly-scattered limbs[1] at your foot.

... The trisyllable which consists entirely of shorts, sometimes called the *choree*, for example,

(b) Bromius, spear-bearer, warrior, battle-shouter[2]!

is mean and lacks solemnity and nobility ...

(c) = Terpander 5 (vol. ii p. 317)

The one which has a long and two shorts with the long in

[1] Of Pentheus?   [2] *Analecta Grammatica* adds 'father Ares'.

ἀμφίβραχυς ὠνόμασται, καὶ οὐ σφόδρα τῶν εὐσχημόνων ἐστὶ ῥυθμῶν ἀλλὰ διακέκλασταί τε καὶ πολὺ τὸ θῆλυ καὶ ἀηδὲς ἔχει, οἷά ἐστι ταυτί·

(d) Ἴακχε θρίαμβε, θρίαμβε, σὺ τῶνδε χοραγέ.

... ἕτερός ἐστιν ... ὃς ἀπὸ τῶν βραχειῶν ἀρξάμενος ἐπὶ τὴν ἄλογον τελευτᾷ· τοῦτον χωρίσαντες ἀπὸ τῶν ἀναπαίστων κυκλικὸν καλοῦσι παράδειγμα αὐτοῦ φέροντες τοιόνδε·

(e) κέχυται πόλις ὑψίπυλος κατὰ γᾶν.

... ἓν ἔτι λείπεται τρισυλλάβων ῥυθμῶν γένος, ὃ συνέστηκεν ἐκ δύο μακρῶν καὶ βραχείας, τρία δὲ ποιεῖ σχήματα· μέσης μὲν γὰρ γινομένης τῆς βραχείας, ἄκρων δὲ τῶν μακρῶν, κρητικός τε λέγεται καὶ ἔστιν οὐκ ἀγεννής· ὑπόδειγμα δὲ αὐτοῦ τοιοῦτον·

(f) οἱ δ' ἐπείγοντο πλωταῖς ἀπήναισι χαλκεμβόλοις.

ἂν δὲ τὴν ἀρχὴν αἱ δύο μακραὶ κατάσχωσιν, τὴν δὲ τελευτὴν ἡ βραχεῖα, οἷά ἐστι ταυτί·

(g) σοί, Φοῖβε, Μοῦσαί τε σύμβωμοι,

ἀνδρῶδες πάνυ ἐστὶ τὸ σχῆμα καὶ εἰς σεμνολογίαν ἐπιτήδειον. τὸ δ' αὐτὸ συμβήσεται κἂν ἡ βραχεῖα προτεθῇ τῶν μακρῶν· καὶ γὰρ οὗτος ὁ ῥυθμὸς ἀξίωμα ἔχει καὶ μέγεθος· παράδειγμα δὲ αὐτοῦ τόδε·

(h) τίν' ἀκτάν, τίν' ὕλαν δράμω; ποῖ πορευθῶ;

τούτοις ἀμφοτέροις ὀνόματα κεῖται τοῖς ποσὶν ὑπὸ τῶν μετρικῶν βακχεῖος μὲν τῷ προτέρῳ, θατέρῳ δὲ ὑποβακχεῖος.

(d) L. Dindorf: διθύραμβε codd.   (e) -πυλον PMV
(f) ἀπήναισι, -εσι, -εσσι codd., -ῃσι Stephanus   -βόλοισιν PMV
(g) σὺ F

---

[3] A syllable less long than the 'long'.   [4] Troy? G. F. Brussich,

the middle is called the *amphibrach*; it is not one of the elegant rhythms but is enervated and notably effeminate and unpleasant, like the following:

(d) Iacchus, thriambic, leader of this chorus!

There is another ... which begins with two shorts and ends with the irrational syllable [3]; they distinguish it from the anapaest and call it *cyclic*, citing the following line by way of example:

(e) the high-gated city[4] is scattered on the earth.

One kind of trisyllabic rhythm remains, that composed of two longs and a short. It has three patterns: when the short is in the middle and the longs on the outside, it is called the *cretic*, and it does not lack nobility; for example,

(f) and they hastened onwards in their bronze-beaked floating wagons.[5]

If the two longs come first and the short last, as in the following,

(g) To you, Phoebus and the Muses who share your altar,

the effect is very manly and appropriate for solemn language. The same will happen if the short is put before the two longs, for this rhythm too has dignity and grandeur; for example,

(h) To what shore, to what wood shall I run? Where shall I go?

The names given by the metricians to these two feet are *bacchius* and *hypobacchius*.

Q.U.C.C. 22 (1976) 144 ff., suggests Stesichorean authorship.
[5] From Timotheus, *Persians*, of the Greeks at Salamis? So Usener, Diehl, Wilamowitz, Edmonds.

1028 Hsch. O 781 (ii 759 Latte)

ὁμόπαιδα κάσιν Κασάνδρας·

ὁμοῦ παιδευθέντα (Musurus: -θέντες cod.) ἢ ὁμοῦ τεκνωθέντα·
ἐπειδὴ δίδυμοί εἰσιν.

Musurus: κάσι cod.

1029 Heph. *Ench*. 10. 2 (p. 32 Consbruch) (περὶ ἀντισπα-
στικοῦ)

δίμετρον δὲ ἀκατάληκτον τὸ καλούμενον Γλυκώνειον, αὐτοῦ
Γλύκωνος εὑρόντος αὐτό·

κάπρος ἡνίχ᾽ ὁ μαινόλης
ὀδόντι σκυλακοκτόνῳ
Κύπριδος θάλος ὤλεσεν.

cf. Epitom. Heph. (p. 360C.), Mar. Plot. Sacerd. 8. 2 (vi 537 Keil) (v.
1), schol. rec. Ar. *Nub*. 563 (p. 109 Dübner) (τὰ Γλύκωνος, vv. 1, 3)

1030 Heph. *Ench*. 12. 3 (p. 38s. Consbruch) (περὶ τοῦ ἀπ᾽
ἐλάσσονος ἰωνικοῦ)

τοῦτο μέντοι (sc. τὸ τετράμετρον καταληκτικόν) καὶ γαλλιαμ-
βικὸν καὶ μητρῳακὸν [[καὶ ἀνακλώμενον]] καλεῖται — ὕστερον δὲ
<καὶ> ἀνακλώμενον ἐκλήθη — διὰ τὸ πολλὰ τοὺς νεωτέρους εἰς
τὴν μητέρα τῶν θεῶν γράψαι τούτῳ τῷ μέτρῳ (ἐν οἷς καὶ τὰ τοὺς
τρίτους παιῶνας ἔχοντα καὶ παλιμβάκχειον καὶ τὰς τροχαϊκὰς
ἀδιαφόρως παραλαμβάνουσι πρὸς τὰ καθαρά), ὡς καὶ τὰ πολυθρύ-
λητα ταῦτα παραδείγματα δηλοῖ·

---

[1] Names derived from the Gallae, self-castrated worshippers of the
Great Mother, and from the Mother herself. For the worship see
Catullus 63, which is composed in a form of galliambic.

1028 Hesychius, *Lexicon*

twin brother[1] of Cassandra:

ὁμόπαιδα ('twin', literally 'fellow-child') is used for 'brought up together' or 'born together', since they are twins.

[1] Identity unknown: Paris? Helenus? Priam had fifty sons (*Il.* 24. 495).

Frr. 1029–1037 may belong to the Alexandrian period.

1029 Hephaestion, *Handbook on Metres*

The acatalectic 'antispastic' dimeter, the so-called glyconic, invented by Glycon[1] himself (× × – ∪ ∪ – ∪ –):

When the frenzied boar with dog-killing tooth destroyed the shoot[2] of Cypris.

[1] Unknown poet. Glyconics were used by Alcman and Sappho.
[2] A plant? More probably metaphorically of Aphrodite's beloved Adonis.

1030 Hephaestion, *Handbook on Metres* (on the ionic *a minore*)

This (sc. the catalectic tetrameter) is known as both the *galliambic* and the *metroac*[1] — later it was also called the broken rhythm — because the new school of poets often addressed the Mother of the Gods in this metre (admitting third paeans and the palimbaccheus and trochaic metra indifferently into their pure ionics),[2] as these much-repeated examples show:

[2] Since the two lines quoted do not show these variations (for which see M. L. West, *Greek Metre* 145), this phrase must be treated as a parenthesis, unless it is assumed that further examples of the galliambic have fallen out of the text.

GREEK LYRIC

Γάλλαι μητρὸς ὀρείης φιλόθυρσοι δρομάδες
αἷς ἔντεα παταγεῖται καὶ χάλκεα κρόταλα.

cf. Choerob. ad loc. (p. 245s. C.) ᾧ καὶ Καλλίμαχος κέχρηται.

1031 Heph. *Ench.* 13. 4 (p. 42 Consbruch)

συντιθέασι δέ τινες καὶ ἑτέρῳ τρόπῳ τὸ τετράμετρον ὥστε τρεῖς
εἶναι τοὺς καλουμένους τετάρτους παιῶνας, εἶτα τελευταῖον τὸν
κρητικόν·

θυμελικὰν ἴθι μάκαρ φιλοφρόνως εἰς ἔριν.

cf. Choerob. ad loc. (p. 249 C.) ἐκ τῶν καλουμένων Δελφικῶν ἐστιν ἡ
προκειμένη χρῆσις, μὴ ἐχόντων τὸ ὄνομα τοῦ ποιητοῦ.

1032 = Sotadea fr. 20 Powell (*Coll. Alex.* p. 244)
Schol. B Heph. 3 (p. 261 Consbruch)

τίθημι μέτρον ἰωνικὸν ἀπὸ μείζονος·

βλαστεῖ δ' ἐπὶ γῆς δένδρεα παντοῖα βρύοντα.

τοῦτο ἀπὸ μείζονος ἰωνικὸν τετράμετρον βραχυκατάληκτον.

cf. *Epim. Hom.* = *Anecd. Oxon.* i 96. 3 Cramer βλαστεῖ–βρύοντα.

Nauck ex *Anecd. Oxon.*: φύοντα schol. Heph.

ANONYMOUS FRAGMENTS

Gallae of the mountain Mother, thyrsus-loving, racing, by whom instruments and bronze cymbals are clashed, . . .[3]

[3] Choeroboscus in his commentary on the passage said Callimachus often used the metre, so the lines may be his: fr. 761 *incert. auct.* Pfeiffer.

1031 Hephaestion, *Handbook on Metres* (on paeons)

Some compose the tetrameter differently again, with three of the so-called fourth paeons ($\cup\cup\cup-$) and the cretic ($-\cup-$) at the end:

Come graciously, blessed one, to the altar contest.[1]

[1] Since the word is used particularly of the altar of Dionysus in the theatre, the words will be addressed to him and the contest will be poetic or dramatic. Choeroboscus says the line comes from the so-called *Delphic Works*.

1032 = Sotadea fr. 20 Powell   Scholiast on Hephaestion

I give an ionic *a maiore* rhythm:

and on earth grow swelling trees of all kinds.

This is ionic *a maiore* tetrameter brachycatalectic.[1]

[1] A form of sotadean, for which see M. L. West, *Greek Metre* 144 f.

1033 Schol. B Heph. (p. 299 Consbruch)

κατὰ διποδίαν δὲ συντιθέμενος (sc. ὁ πυρρίχιος) καὶ τὸν προ-
κελευσματικὸν ποιῶν τὰ καλούμενα προκελευσματικὰ ἢ πυρρι-
χιακὰ μέτρα ποιεῖ, ὧν παραδείγματα·

ἴθι μόλε ταχύποδος ἐπὶ δέμας ἐλάφου
πτεροφόρον ἀνὰ χερὶ δόνακα τιθεμένα.

cf. *Anal. Gramm.* 4. 17 Keil

1 ἐπὶ δέμας *Anal.* (cod. Ambros.): ἐπίδεσμα rell.   2 πτ. ἀνὰ
Bergk: πτεροφόραν, -ον codd.   Bergk: πτ. χελιδόνα καθημένην
Anal. cod. Ambros., χαιρηδόνα καθε^{μν} cod. Chisian.   χέρσον
καθημένα schol. codd. Y, χερσο' καθομαγ' cod. S

1034 = Sotad. fr. 4(c) Powell (*Coll. Alex.* p. 239)
Stob. 1. 1. 9 (i 24 Wachsmuth-Hense) (ὅτι θεὸς δημιουργὸς
τῶν ὄντων κτλ.)

Ζεὺς ὁ καὶ ζωῆς καὶ θανάτου πείρατα νωμῶν

1035 P. Oxy. 675

col. i

παιᾶνι φιλοστεφά[νωι]
μέλπ[ον]τες ω[. . . . .]
ἱερὰν κ[α]τέχων [. . . . .]
Ἀλεξάν[δρ]ειαν   [. . . . .]
5 πολιν [. . .] καὶ βα[. . . . . .]
ὁμοῦ π[. .]ωμεν[. . . . .]
ταισδε [
σπονδα[
δοις ὑμν[
10 σεβια[

col. ii

κε[. . .]μελψο[
κελάδου παιᾶν[
μέλεσι στειψα[
εὐιέρων πελά[νων
θῦμα δεδώκατ[ε
σταις ἐν ὠδα[ῖ]σ[
πολυώνυμοι ιλ[
[. . . . . .]σανδεφ[
[. . . . . .]ουτον[

omnia suppl. ed. pr. (Grenfell-Hunt)

ANONYMOUS FRAGMENTS

1033 Scholiast on Hephaestion

The pyrrhich (◡ ◡) used in a dipody to form the proceleusmatic (◡◡◡◡) creates the so-called proceleusmatic or pyrrhich metres, for example,

Come! Go swift-footed against the deer's body,
placing a feather-bearing reed[1] in your hand.[2]

[1] I.e. an arrow-shaft.   [2] Addressed to a female, probably
Artemis the deer-shooter.

1034 = Sotad. fr. 4(c) Powell   Stobaeus, *Anthology*
(that god is the creator of the world)

Zeus, who handles the ropes[1] of life and death[2]

[1] Or 'controls the limits'.   [2] Hense attributed the line to the
3rd c. poet Sotades; the metre is sotadean.

1035 Oxyrhynchus papyrus (*c.* 50 A.D.)

col. i ... to garland-loving Paean ... (we?) singing
... (he, possessing?) holy Alexandria ... city ... and
... together let us ... these ... libation ... (hymn?)
...

col. ii ... shall sing ... (of) the shout ... Paean ...
crowning with songs ... of sacrificial oils ... you
have given a victim ... in songs ... many-named
(gods) ...

GREEK LYRIC

1036 *Études de Papyrologie* 4 (1938) 121 s.

> προσίπταν[το
> θηρεύειν ἀκοὴν δι[
> ἀνά<ρ>θροις μινυρίσμ[ασιν
> μελιχρῶς ἐδίδαξα[ν
>
> 5   καὶ γὰρ κόσσυφος αγ[
> λάβρως εὐκέλαδον [μέλος
> φθόγγοις οὖλον ὑπ[
> ἦλθε μουσικὸς ὄρν[ις
>
>   ]λον ψιθυρο[

1, 3, 8 suppl. ed. pr. (Waddell)   2 δι[vel δρ[4 suppl.
Page   6 suppl. Goossens   7 ὑπ[οκρέκων Keydell

1037 *Inscriptions Grecques du Musée du Louvre : les textes inédits* (Paris 1933) n. 60 (p. 66ss.)

> ὠ]δῖσιν οὐδὲ Τριτογένευς λωβά[σεται ἄστυ χόλος . . .
> πηκτὰν τιθεὶς ἅλα· τάδε μὲν γὰρ ον[
> -ρων κείναις ἀνάγκαν τεῶν ἡσυχα[
> -φες, αὐτὰρ ἁμετέρας φροντίδος ὕμνο[ς
> 5 -φης ἱκέτας βλαστὸς μερίμνας πραΰ[ν-
> γάρ σε δᾶμος ὃν κτίσεν Ἐνδυμίων [ἀ-
> κοιμάτου σφετέρας ἀνίας ἀνέχε[ιν   λέκ-
> τρωι τῆνον ἐς τὸν ἀεικοίματον ὕ[πνον
> προύθηκεν ἄντροις, τὰν μὲν ἐκ το[ῦ

omnia suppl. ed. pr. (Dain) exceptis quae sequuntur: 1 fin. ci.
Page   4 fin. Page?   7 fin. Wilamowitz

ANONYMOUS FRAGMENTS

1036 Oxyrhynchus papyrus (2nd or 3rd c. A.D.)

. . . (they) flew towards . . . to hunt the sound . . . with inarticulate warblings they sweetly (taught?) . . . ; for the blackbird came, boisterously . . . its tuneful rapid song (with) notes, that musical bird[1] . . . twitterings . . .[2]

[1] For the blackbird's song cf. Theocr. *Epigr.* 4. 9 f.   [2] 'Perhaps late Hellenistic' (West).

1037 Louvre inscription[1]

. . . (neither Artemis with fruitless) childbirth nor (the anger) of Tritogenes[2] will maltreat (the city) by making the brine freeze solid; since these things . . . those . . . necessity . . . of your[3] . . . quiet . . . but the hymn of our anxiety, suppliant, offshoot of worry, . . . soothe . . . ; for the city which Endymion founded . . . you . . . (to) emerge from its/his unresting distress . . . (she?) put him in a bed into his ever-resting (sleep) . . . in the cave, the one[4] from the . . . (the city?) honours with libations . . . , the other[5] (we

[1] Various themes are combined in what seems to be a hymn (v. 4); an end of divine anger towards Endymion's city (the Carian Heraclea at the foot of Mt. Latmus), Endymion's cave and his eternal sleep, the treatment of two females (perhaps the Moon, lover of Endymion, and some other), public mockery of a female and civic rejoicing, and finally marriage. Translation often insecure.
[2] Athena.   [3] Singular, as elsewhere in the poem.   [4] The Moon?   [5] A second female.

435

10 -νοις λοιβαῖς γεραίρει, τὰν δ᾽ ἐς ἄστυ[ἔνθα πόσει
     σὺν βιαιολεχεῖ καὶ τέκνοις ἔστακε σ[μόχθων
     λαζυμένα πέρας· γέγαθε νῦν ἅπας μ[ἐν ὄχλος   βλέ-
     πων ἀπ᾽ ἄκρων ἐκ πολυθρίγκων τερά[μνων
     αὐχμὸν ἔς θ᾽ ἅλα ῥίψασαν ὑπ᾽ ἀμφιπολ[χαρί-
15 εν θῆκαν βιοτᾶς, ἅπασά θ᾽ ἥβα κῶμο[ν ἄγει   ὅ-
     δοις κέρτομον χέοισ᾽ ἰαχάν, οὐδέ τις[ἀ-
     πὸ στομάτων ἀχαλίνων ἡνία γλωσσ[ἀ-
     νάγκα τὰν ἀπὸ σώματος· ἀμφὶ γὰρ οις[θηλυτέ-
     ρων ἀπερύκουσα θιγεῖν. κόνις δ᾽ ἐς ἄπει[ρον αἰθέρα κα-
20 τ᾽ ἄστυ, παντοφώνοις δ᾽ ὀργάνοις θελ[γ
     ἄλλος παρ᾽ ἄλλον σὺν γέλωι γῆρυν προ[ἀνά-
     παυσιν, λύπα δὲ χαρὰν πλῆστυ[
     θαλίας, δμώων δ᾽ ὁ μέν τις ὦμον[πευκᾶν αἶ-
     θος πυριθηγὲς ἀσιν<έ>ας δόμους[
25 ζεύγλαι δ᾽ ὑπ᾽ ἄλλος ταυροτενεῖσ[περι-
     γλαγέας παντοῖον ὡρίων φερον[
     -τεροις, σιγᾶι δὲ κέρκις ἁ λεχέων φυλ[άκεσσι συνήθης
     ...] οἰκουρός, ἑπταύχενος δὲ δεσποιν[
     ... κ]οἰτόνδε ἐς οὖδας ὁμολεχὴς πιπτ[
30 .....]α δ᾽ ἐν ἄγγεσιν παρέστακεν[
     ....]ς τελετας· ὦ τὰν ἀείμναστο[ν
     ....] λέκτρων [ἄ]πειρος ἐφ᾽ ἇι σε οπ[
     ....]ας ἐπεὶ γάμων ἀκμᾶι δέμας [

10 fin., 11 fin. ci. Page   12 med. Wilamowitz   fin. Haus-
soullier   14 fin. Wilamowitz   15 med. ci. Page   18 fin.,
21 fin. Wilamowitz   23 fin. ci. Page   24 Page: πυρὶ θῆγ᾽
ἐς ed. pr.   25 Wilamowitz: ἀπ᾽ inscrn.   25 fin. Wilamowitz
27 ci. Page

have brought back?) to the town ... (where) she stands with her violent-bedding (husband) and her children, grasping the end (of her toils); now all the (crowd) rejoices ... (looking) from the heights from many-corniced chambers ... and (the city?) having thrown her filth into the sea ... by her attendants ... (they) made (graceful?) ... of life, and all the youth holds revel ... in the streets, uttering cries of mockery, and no rein ... from unbridled mouths ... tongue ..., but necessity checks bodily insult, for around ... restraining them from touching (a female). And dust (went up) to the limitless (heaven) ... (throughout) the town, and with all-voiced instruments enchant- ... one beside another with laughter (gave) utterance ... ceasing, and grief ... joy ... (of) festivity; and one of the slaves ... fire-sharpened (blaze of pines?) ... the unharmed houses ...; and another under the yoke-loop ... bull-stretched ... milky ... of every kind ... (of) seasonable (fruits?) ... brought ..., and the shuttle is silent, (the customary instrument of the) guardians of the beds ... home-watching, and (of) the seven-necked[6] ... the mistress ... to bed ... the bedfellow falls to the ground ...; and among the vessels stands ... rite; oh the ever-remembered ... with no experience of the bed, (upon?) whom ... you ... since at the fit time for marriage ... your body ...

[6] A seven-branched candlestick?

1038 (I) ostracon (Ashm. Mus. G. 141. 1), ed. D. G. Howarth, *J.H.S.* 25 (1905) 118, denuo D. L. Page, *J.H.S.* 67 (1947) 134s.

$$]ς \ εὗρε \ θνητ[$$
$$φ]ρενοβλαβές \ πα[$$
$$-κ]όρυμβε \ χαρ[$$

3 vel κ]ορυμβ᾽ ἐχαρ[

(II) Ostracon Skeat 13, ed. H. C. Youtie, *T.A.P.A.* 81 (1950) 111ss.

$$]σηις \ οὖσα$$
$$] \ . \ ω \ παύσασθε$$
$$] \ ἐμῆι \ κενώσω \ τελετῆι$$
$$] \ . \ ιου \ Ληναῖαι \ ὠκυ-$$
5 $$] \ . \ . \ μὴ \ φίσησθ \ ἔτι \ γ᾽ \ ὢ \ γυ-$$
ναῖκες $$]θροεῖτε \ τὸν \ Πᾶνα$$
$$]ν^η \ συρίζων$$
$$]μοις \ ἰάσκων$$
$$] \ . \ βω \ δὲ \ παρὼν$$
10 $$]ον \ πρ[όστ]αξον$$
$$] \ . \ οσι$$

2 fort. = παύσασθαι   3 fort. = καινώσω   5 φίσ- = φείσ-
vel -οισθε   6 suppl. ed. pr.   Pearl:]θιοειτε ostr.
10 suppl. ed. pr.

1039 = 1043 *Suppl. Hell.*   *Et. Gen.* AB (contul. A Lloyd-Jones, Parsons, B Alpers) (cf. *Et. Mag.* 702. 39)

εὕρηται ἡ σφιν ἀντωνυμία παρὰ τῷ ποιητῇ σὺν τῷ ν. Συρακό-
σιοι δὲ τὸ ψιν λέγουσι, Λάκωνες φιν.

πὰρ δέ φιν κόραι Λευκίππιδες

West: παρὰ δέ σφιν A, παραδέσφιν B   λευκυπιδες B

438

ANONYMOUS FRAGMENTS

1038 *Two ostraca*

(I) from Naucratis (*c.* 100 B.C.)

... (he) found ... mortal ... mind-damaged ... ivy-clustered ...

(II) from Egypt (Thebes?) (*c.* 100 A.D.)

... (she) being ... cease[1]! ... I shall make new with my rite[2] ... Lenaean women swift- ... do not spare any longer, women, ... cry 'Pan', (who) playing his pipes ... (leading?) ... being present ... (command!)...

[1] Plural imperative; or perhaps 'to cease'.　　　[2] Dionysus addresses his Bacchants ('Lenaeans'); perhaps 'I shall empty (the city)'.

1039–1045 may come from hexameter poetry.

1039 = 1043 *Suppl. Hell.*　　　*Etymologicum Genuinum*

The pronoun σφιν, 'them' (dative), is found in Homer with the ν (*Il.* 1. 73, *Od.* 1. 339); Syracusans say ψιν, Laconians φιν:

and beside them the young daughters of Leucippus[1]

[1] Ascribed to Alcman hesitantly by Bergk, confidently by West, *C.R.* 23 (1973) 100: fr. dub. 266 Calame. For the Leucippides see Alcm. 5 fr. 1(a), 7 n. 2, 8.

1040 = 1030 *Suppl. Hell.*   *Et. Gen.* B (contul. Jacques) (cf. *Et. Mag.* 48. 39 = Hdn. π. παθ. 5, ii 167 Lentz)

ἀκινάγματα· τὰ τινάγματα τῶν ποδῶν μετὰ ῥυθμοῦ, οἷον

χειρῶν ἠδὲ ποδῶν ἀκινάγματα·

κινήματα, καὶ πλεονασμῷ τοῦ α καὶ τροπῇ τοῦ η εἰς α καὶ πλεονασμῷ τοῦ γ ἀκινάγματα.

cf. Hsch. A 2404 (i 86 Latte)

χειρῶν ἠδὲ ποδῶν *Et. Mag.*: χεῖρ ἠδὲ ποδ' *Et. Gen.*

1041 = 1034–1035 *Suppl. Hell.*   *Et. Gen.* AB (contul. A Lloyd-Jones, Parsons, B Jacques) (cf. *Et. Mag.* 417. 12)

οἱ δὲ Δωριεῖς διὰ τοῦ α λέγουσιν ἆχι (ἄχι A, ἆχι B), οἷον

(a) ἆχι Λίχα μέγα σᾶμα,

τουτέστιν ὅπου τοῦ Λίχα τὸ μέγα μνημεῖον, καὶ

(b)
                 ἆχι ὁ κλεινὸς
Ἀμφιτρυωνιάδας.

cf. Hdn. π. καθ. προσ. 19 (i 505 Lentz)

(a) ἄχι A, ἆχι B, *Et. Mag.*   (b) 1 ἄχι AB, ἆχι *Et. Mag.*
2 Sylburg: -ίδας AB, *Et. Mag.* (sed -ίδης DM)

1042 *Et. Mag.* 420. 40

ἥδω· παρὰ τὸ ἅδω, τὸ ἀρέσκω·

ἅδον φίλον ὅς κεν ἅδησι·

τὰ γὰρ ἀρέσκοντα ἡδέα.

Sylburg: ὥς κεν codd., ὥκεν *Et. Gen.* A, sec. West (*C.R.* 23, 1973, 100)

1040 = 1030 *Suppl. Hell.*   *Etymologicum Genuinum*

ἀκινάγματα: the rhythmical shaking of the feet, as in

shakings of the hands and feet:

κινήματα ('movements'), altered to ἀκινάγματα by addition of
(initial) α, change of η to α and addition of γ.

1041 = 1034–1035 *Suppl. Hell.*   *Etymologicum Genui-
num*

For ἦχι, 'where', the Dorians say ᾶχι with α:

(a) where the great tomb of Lichas[1] is

and

(b) where famous Amphitryoniades[2] is.

[1] Herald of Heracles, thrown by him on to an islet near Cape
Cenaeum in N.W. Euboea; Strabo 9. 4. 4 speaks of the three
Lichades islands; cf. Soph. *Trach.* 756 ff., Aes. fr. 25e. 13 f. Radt.
[2] Heracles, son of Amphitryon.

1042 *Etymologicum Magnum*

ἥδω ('I delight'), from ἅδω, 'I please':

I delighted any friend who pleased me.[1]

For things that please are sweet (ἡδέα).

[1] Text and translation uncertain.

1043 Heph. *Ench*. 1. 3 (p. 2 Consbruch)

γίνεται δὲ τοῦτο κατὰ πέντε τρόπους · ἤτοι γὰρ λήξει εἰς δύο σύμφωνα, οἷον

Τίρυνς οὐδέ τι τεῖχος ἐπήρκεσε

1044 = 1055–1056 *Suppl. Hell.*   Hdn. π. καθ. προσ. 20 (i 523 Lentz) = π. διχρόνων (ii 7 Lentz)

τὸ δὲ

(a) στάδα λίμνην

ἤ

(b) κλάδα χρυσεόκαρπον

οὐχ ἕξει τινὰ εὐθεῖαν στάς ἢ κλάς · μεταπλασμοὶ γάρ εἰσι.

(a) cf. Choerob. in Theodos. iv 1. 392 Hilgard ἀπὸ γὰρ τοῦ 'εὐστάδα λίμνην' ἔχομεν ἁπλοῦν τὸ 'στάδα λίμνην'.
(b) cf. Hsch. K 2838 (ii 483 Latte)

1045 Prisc. *inst.* i 22 (ii 16 Keil)

digamma Aeolis est quando in metris pro nihilo accipiebant, ut

ἀμὲς δὲ Ϝειρήναν · τόδε γὰρ θέτο Μῶσα λίγεια,

est enim hexametrum heroicum.

codd. miris modis corrupt.

ANONYMOUS FRAGMENTS

1043 Hephaestion, *Handbook on Metres*

This (sc. the lengthening of syllables 'by position') occurs in five different ways: either the syllable will end in two consonants, as in 'Ti-ryns':

> nor did the walled city of Tiryns ward off . . .[1]

[1] Continued at Alcm. 15. Ascribed to Callimachus by Diehl: incert. auct. 760 Pfeiffer. Perhaps '. . . Tiryns; nor did its wall ward off . . .'

1044 = 1055–1056 *Suppl. Hell.*   Herodian, *Universal Prosody*

In the expressions

(a) standing pool

and

(b) gold-fruited branch

στάδα 'standing' and κλάδα 'branch' will have no nominative forms στάς and κλάς, since they are metaplasms.[1]

[1] Derived from stems σταδ(ι)- and κλαδ-.

1045 Priscian, *Grammar*

Aeolic poets sometimes neglected digamma, as in

But we (love?) peace; for this was established by the clear-voiced Muse.

For it is a heroic hexameter.

COMPARATIVE NUMERATION

CARMINA POPULARIA

Loeb/*P.M.G.* (margin)	*P.M.G.* (*Carm.Pop.*)	Bergk	Diehl
847	1	13	27
848	2	41	32
849	3	1	29
850	4	24	37
851(a)	5(a)	7	47
(b)	(b)	8	48
852	6	19	36
853	7	27	43
854	8	p.684	—
855	9	—	28
856	10	Tyrt.15	18
857	11	Tyrt.16	19
858	12	—	—
859	13	26	42
860	14	12	52
861	15	22B	41
862	16	10	51
863	17	14	20
864	18	17	22
865	19	16	23
866	20	15	21
867	21	45	II vi p.103
868	22	23	53
869	23	43	30
870	24	18	17
871	25	6	46

COMPARATIVE NUMERATION

Loeb/*P.M.G.* (margin)	*P.M.G.* (*Carm.Pop.*)	Bergk	Diehl
872	26	4	Alcm.66
873	27	44	44
874	28	39	16
875	29	—	33
876(a)	30(a)	20	34
(b)	(b)	22A	40
(c)	(c)	21	35
877	31	9	50
878	32	—	45
879(1)	33(1)	5	24
(2)	(2)	11	25
(3)	(3)	11	25
880	34	2	—
881	35	25	31
882	36	42	38
883	37	—	26

* * * * * * * * * * * * *

Bergk	Loeb/*P.M.G.* (margin)	Bergk	Loeb/*P.M.G.* (margin)
1	849	14	863
2	880	15	866
3	955 (adesp.)	16	865
4	872	17	864
5	879(1)	18	870
6	871	19	852
7	851(a)	20	876(a)
8	851(b)	21	876(c)
9	877	22A	876(b)
10	862	22B	861
11	879(2)(3)	23	868
12	860	24	850
13	847	25	881
446			

CARMINA POPULARIA REVERSE

Bergk	Loeb/*P.M.G.* (margin)
26	859
27	853
28	(ad. el. 17 West)
29–33	—
34	(Panarces (a) West)
35–38	—
39	874
40	(ad. el. 7 West)
41	848
42	882
43	869
44	873
45	867
46	(Hermocles, p.173 Powell)
47	(Macedonius, p.138 Powell)

* * * * * * * * * * * * * *

Diehl	Loeb/*P.M.G.* (margin)	Diehl	Loeb/*P.M.G.* (margin)
1–2	—	25	879(2)(3)
3	(ad. el. 7 West)	26	883
4	(ad. el. 19 West)	27	847
5	(ad. el. 17 West)	28	855
6–15	—	29	849
16	874	30	869
17	870	31	881
18	856	32	848
19	857	33	875
20	863	34	876(a)
21	866	35	876(c)
22	864	36	852
23	865	37	850
24	879(1)	38	882

COMPARATIVE NUMERATION

Diehl	Loeb/*P.M.G.* (margin)	Diehl	Loeb/*P.M.G.* (margin)
39	—	46	871
40	876(b)	47	851(a)
41	861	48	851(b)
42	859	49	941 (adesp.)
43	853	50	877
44	873	51	862
45	878	52	860
		53	868

SCOLIA

Loeb/*P.M.G.* (margin)	*P.M.G.* (Carm.Conviv.)	Bergk	Diehl
884	1	2	1
885	2	3	2
886	3	4	3
887	4	5	4
888	5	6	5
889	6	7	6
890	7	8	7
891	8	15	8
892	9	16	9
893	10	9	10
894	11	10	11
895	12	11	12
896	13	12	13
897	14	21	14
898	15	17	15
899	16	18	16
900	17	19	17
901	18	20	18
902	19	22	19
903	20	23	20
904	21	24	21

SCOLIA

Loeb/*P.M.G.* (margin)	*P.M.G.* (Carm.Conviv.)	Bergk	Diehl
905	22	25	22
906	23	27	23
907	24	14	24
908	25	26	25
909	26	28	Hybr. 1
910	27	1	Pytherm. 1
911	28	13	27
912	29	29	28
913	30	30	29
914	31	p.653 adnot.	—
915	32	—	—
916	33	—	—
917	34	—	30

FRAGMENTA ADESPOTA

Loeb/*P.M.G.* (margin)	*P.M.G.* (Frr. Adesp.)	Bergk	Diehl
918	1	—	—
919	1A	—	—
920	2	—	—
921	3	—	—
922	4	—	—
923	5	—	—
924	6	—	—
925	7	—	Timoth. 3
926	8	—	chor. adesp. 36–40
927	9	—	—
928	10	—	—
929	11	—	chor. adesp. 41–48
930	12	—	chor. adesp. 50
931	13	—	chor. adesp. 49
932	14	—	—
933	15	—	II vi p.108s.

Loeb/*P.M.G.* (margin)	*P.M.G.* (Frr. Adesp.)	Bergk	Diehl
934	16	—	II vi p.109ss.
935	17	—	Telesilla 2D
936	18	—	II v p.145
937	19	—	II v p.165
938(a)–(d),(f)	20(a)–(d),(f)	—	—
938(e)	20(e)	30A	—
939	21	Arion 1	Arion 1
940	22	134	—
941	23	Terp. 3	carm. pop. 49
942	24	105	Alcm. 69
943	25	76	mon. adesp. 4
944	26	41	mon. adesp. 16
945	27	67	—
946	28	142	chor. adesp. 18
947	29	Simon. 60+46	Stes. 25
948	30	102	Cydias 2
949	31	129	Sappho 156
950	32	Simon. 26B	II vi p.171
951	33	127	—
952	34	40	Alex. adesp. 8
953	35	Sappho 26	mon. adesp. 1
954	36	80–81	Alcm. 70+41
955	37	carm. pop. 3	Alcm. 60
956	38	103	chor. adesp. 21
957	39	Anacr. 72B	Anacr. 64
958	40	106	chor. adesp. 10
959	41	86B	—
960	42	87	Alex. adesp. 13
961	43	104B	chor. adesp. 11
962	44	128	—
963	45	126	—
964	46	104A	Sappho 156+22
965	47	101	chor. adesp. 31
966	48	p.610	—
967	49	118	mon. adesp. 25

Loeb/*P.M.G.* (margin)	*P.M.G.* (Frr. Adesp.)	Bergk	Diehl
968	50	75	mon. adesp. 21
969	51	83B	—
970	52	83A	chor. adesp. 7
971	53	73	mon. adesp. 20
972	54	38	Alcm. 86
973	55	123	mon. adesp. 13
974	56	46A	Alcm. 117
975	57	69–71	mon. adesp. 22–24
976	58	Sappho 52	94
977	59	72	chor. adesp. 3
978(a)	60(a)	78	Anacr. 7
978(b)	60(b)	82A	mon. adesp. 14
978(c)	60(c)	82B	mon. adesp. 15
979	61	62	Alex. adesp. 2
980	62	47A	—
981	63	79C	mon. adesp. 17
982	64	64	—
983	65	74	Alcm. 8
984	66	137	—
985	67	84	
986	68	130	
987	69	135	—
988	70	138	chor. adesp. 8
989	71	119	chor. adesp. 35
990	72	114	—
991	73	120	chor. adesp. 34
992	74	115B	Alex. adesp. 4
993	75	115A	Alex. adesp. 10
994	76	98	chor. adesp. 28
995	77	99	chor. adesp. 9
996	78	92	chor. adesp. 13
997	79	90	—
998	80	133	—
999	81	132	—
1000	82	100	chor. adesp. 20

Loeb/*P.M.G.* (margin)	*P.M.G.* (Frr. Adesp.)	Bergk	Diehl
1001	83	53	chor. adesp. 17
1002	84	141	chor. adesp. 6
1003	85	131	—
1004	86	91	mon. adesp. 11
1005	87	Simon. 23	[42]
1006	88	125	Delphic. 2
1007	89	94	chor. adesp. 15
1008	90	93	chor. adesp. 14
1009	91	96	chor. adesp. 16
1010	92	97	chor. adesp. 29
1011(a)	93(a)	31	Alcm. 75
1011(b)	93(b)	32	mon. adesp. 12
1012	94	Alcm. 8	Alcm. 6
1013	95	88	—
1014	96	44	Stes. 10A
1015	97	95	chor. adesp. 30
1016	98	p.681s.	Alcm. 68
1017	99	143	chor. adesp. 19
1018	100	140	chor. adesp. 5
1019	101	139	chor. adesp. 4
1020	102	86A	chor. adesp. 12
1021	103	89	—
1022	104	89 adnot.	
1023	105	—	—
1024	106	—	—
1025	107	p.741s.	—
1026	108	p.742	—
1027(a)	109(a)	112	Alex. adesp. 5
1027(b)	109(b)	108	chor. adesp. 22
1027(c)	109(c)	Terp. 4	chor. adesp. 23
1027(d)	109(d)	109	chor. adesp. 24
1027(e)	109(e)	111	chor. adesp. 26
1027(f)	109(f)	117	Timoth. 6d
1027(g)	109(g)	110	chor. adesp. 25
1027(h)	109(h)	116	chor. adesp. 27

FRAGMENTA ADESPOTA

Loeb/*P.M.G.* (margin)	*P.M.G.* (Frr. Adesp.)	Bergk	Diehl
1028	110	79B	chor. adesp. 32
1029	111	79A	Alex. adesp. 14
1030	112	121	Alex. adesp. 9
1031	113	107	Delphic. 1
1032	114	—	Alex. adesp. 7
1033	115	113	Alex. adesp. 6
1034	116	—	Sotades 8
1035	117	—	—
1036	118	—	—
1037	119	—	—
1038	120	—	—
1039	121	68	—
1040	122	30B	Alex. adesp. 12
1041(a)	123(a)	48	—
1041(b)	123(b)	49	—
1042	124	47B	—
1043	125	—	mon. adesp. 19
1044(a)	126(a)	—	—
1044(b)	126(b)	122	chor. adesp. 33
1045	127	33A	chor. adesp. 2

* * * * * * * * * * * * * *

Bergk	Loeb/*P.M.G.* (margin)	Bergk	Loeb/*P.M.G.* (margin)
30A	938(e)	40	952
30B	1040	41	944
31	1011(a)	42	Alcm.(?) 169
32	1011(b)	43A	Alcm.(?) 168
33A	1045	43B	Alcm.(?) 172
33B	(1002 *Suppl. Hell.*)	44	1014
34–37B	Alcm. 87	45	Alcm.(?) 174
38	972	46A	974
39	(*Coll. Alex.* p.71 n.1)	46B	Alcm.(?) 170

COMPARATIVE NUMERATION

Bergk	Loeb/*P.M.G.* (margin)	Bergk	Loeb/*P.M.G.* (margin)
47A	980	81	954(b)
47B	1042	82A	978(b)
48	1041(a)	82B	978(c)
49	1041(b)	83A	. 970
50	(1038 *Suppl. Hell.*)	83B	969
51	Sapph. vel Alc. 21	84	985
52	Sapph. vel Alc. 17	85	(Pind. fr. 333a dub.
53	1001	86A	1020
54	—	86B	959
55	—	87	960
56	Sappho 3–4	88	1013
57	Sapph. vel Alc. 19	89	1021
58	Sapph. vel Alc. 3	90	997
59	Sappho 2.6	91	1004
60	Sapph. vel Alc. 14	92	996
61	Sapph. vel Alc. 4	93	1008
62	979	94	1007
63	Sapph. vel Alc. 12	95	1015
64	982	96	1009
65	Sapph. vel Alc. 25A	97	1010
66	Sapph. vel Alc. 2	98	994
67	945	99	995
68	1039	100	1000
69–71	975	101	965
72	977	102	948
73	971	103	956
74	983	104A	964
75	968	104B	961
76	943	105	942
77	Alc. 349(d)	106	958
78	978(a)	107	1031
79A	1029	108	1027(b)
79B	1028	109	1027(d)
79C	981	110	1027(g)
80	954(a)	111	1027(e)

	Diehl	Loeb/*P.M.G.* (margin)
	13	973
	14	978(b)
	15	978(c)
	16	944
	17	981
	18	(adesp. F 456 *T.G.F.*)
	19	1043
	20	971
	21	968
	22–24	975
	25	967
	26a	(*Coll. Alex.* p.193 n.27)
	26b	(*Coll. Alex.* p.194 n.28)
chor. adesp.	1	(*Coll. Alex.* p.186 n.9)
	2	1045
	3	977
	4	1019
	5	1018
	6	1002
	7	970
	8	788
	9	995
	10	958
	11	961
	12	1020
	13	996
	14	1008
	15	1007
	16	1009
	17	1001
	18	946
	19	1017
	20	1000
	21	956

FRAGMENTA ADESPOTA REVERSE

Diehl	Loeb/*P.M.G.* (margin)
22	1027(b)
23	1027(c)
24	1027(d)
25	1027(g)
26	1027(e)
27	1027(h)
28	994
29	1010
30	1015
31	965
32	1028
33	1044(b)
34	991
35	989
36–40	926
41–48	929
49	931
50	930

* * * * * * * * * * * * * *

Alex. adesp.		
	1	(*Coll. Alex.* p.60 n.11)
	2	979
	3	(737 *Suppl. Hell.*)
	4	992
	5	1027(a)
	6	1033
	7	1032
	8	952
	9	1030
	10	993
	11	(1002 *Suppl. Hell.*)

COMPARATIVE NUMERATION

Diehl	Loeb/*P.M.G.* (margin)
12	1040
13	960
14	1029

N.B. Papyrus fragments published in *S.L.G.* have been numbered as follows:

S 318	= 984A	S 457	= 931I
S 443	= 931A	S 458	= 931J
S 445	= 931B	S 459	= 931K
S 449	= 931C	S 460–472	= 931L
S 450–451	= 931D	S 473	= 931M
S 452	= 931E	S 474	= 931N
S 453	= 931F	S 475	= 931O
S 454	= 931G	S 477	= 931P
S 455	= 931H		

Material not in Page's editions will be found under the numbers 768A, 931Q, 931R, 931S, 931T, 938(g), 945A, 961A, 985A, 1007A.

INDEX OF AUTHORS AND SOURCES

459

INDEX OF AUTHORS AND SOURCES

INDEX OF AUTHORS AND SOURCES

INDEX OF AUTHORS AND SOURCES

INDEX OF AUTHORS AND SOURCES

INDEX OF AUTHORS AND SOURCES

INDEX OF AUTHORS AND SOURCES

INDEX OF AUTHORS AND SOURCES

GENERAL INDEX

GENERAL INDEX

GENERAL INDEX

Calliope, Clio, Polymnia, Urania

Museum, centre of scholarship in Alexandria: 409

Music, personified: 1, 5, 19, 40, 63, 71, 145

Myrmex ('Ant'), name given to Philoxenus of Cythera: 139

Myrtilus, Thessalian, fellow-diner of Athenaeus: 283

Mysia, district of N.W. Asia Minor: 103, 167

Mytilene, chief city of Lesbos: 5, 65, 67, 253

Naiads, nymphs of rivers and springs: 355

Nanis, daughter of Croesus: 37

Naucratis, Greek emporium on Nile delta: 439

Nauplius, Argonaut, father of Palamedes: 89

Neaechmus, archon in 320/19 B.C.: 85

Nemea, sanctuary of Zeus N. of Argos, site of Games: 7, 91

Nemesis (Retribution): 347

Neomusus, said to be father of Timotheus: 73

Nereids, daughters of Nereus: 361

Nereus, sea-god, father of Galatea: 157, 363

Nestor, king of Pylos: 117, 411

Nicander, unknown: 329

Nicomachus, father of Aristotle: 213

Nicomachus, painter, *fl. c.* 350 B.C.: 125

Night (Nux): 417, 421, 423

Nile, the river of Egypt: 393

Niobe, daughter of Tantalus; boasted to Leto of the number of her children, whom Apollo and Artemis killed; turned into a stone: 91, 151, 399

Nycteus, king of Boeotia, father of Antiope: 327

Nymphs, nature-spirits of mountains, water, etc.: 3, 87, 103, 169, 281, 309, 355

Oannes, early inhabitant of Assyria: 393

Odysseus, king of Ithaca: 85, 87, 89, 113, 157, 159, 163, 165, 303, 309, 311, 313, 315

Oeagrus, father of Orpheus: 55

Oeneus, mythical king of Calydon; gave his name to wine (*oinos*): 27

Olympia, sanctuary of Zeus, site of Games: 175

Olympus, Mt., home of gods: 41, 281, 329, 353, 355, 377

Opis, name of Artemis, or a companion of Artemis: 83, 85

Orchomenus, city of Boeotia: 331, 337

Orestes, son of Agamemnon: 203

Orpheus, legendary Thracian musician: 111

Ortygia, island off Syracuse: 155

Ossa, mountain of N.E. Thessaly: 329

Paean, Apollo, god of healing: 109, 119, 245, 251, 307, 309, 331, 349, 351, 433

Paeonia, region of Macedonia: 191

Pallas, title of Athena: 1, 279

481